Morality, prudence, and nuclear weapons

With the passing of the Cold War, a chapter in the history of nuclear deterrence has come to an end. Nuclear weapons remain, however, and nuclear deterrence will again be practiced. Rather than simply assume that the policy of deterrence has worked, we need to learn the proper lessons from history in order to insure that its mistakes are not repeated. Professor Lee furnishes us with the kind of analysis that will enable us to learn those lessons.

This book is the first post-Cold War assessment of nuclear deterrence. It provides a comprehensive normative understanding of nuclear deterrence policy, examining both its ethical and strategic dimensions. The book poses the question: What kind of nuclear policy, if any, deserves both moral and prudential endorsement?

Professor Lee distinguishes what is essential to the nuclear deterrence relationship, and thus what we can expect to encounter again, from what is accidental, and thus merely a function of the particular political relationship between the United States and the former Soviet Union. It is only by grasping this distinction that we can hope to manage the nuclear menace in the future.

The book is principally a work of philosophy, but it is written to appeal to scholars and advanced students in political science, international relations, security studies, and peace studies.

D1517517

Cambridge Studies in Philosophy and Public Policy

GENERAL EDITOR: Douglas MacLean

The purpose of this series is to publish the most innovative and up-to-date research into the values and concepts that underlie major aspects of public policy. Hitherto most research in this field has been empirical. This series is primarily conceptual and normative; that is, it investigates the structure of arguments and the nature of values relevant to the formation, justification, and criticism of public policy. At the same time it is informed by empirical considerations, addressing specific issues, general policy concerns, and the methods of policy analysis and their applications.

The books in the series are inherently interdisciplinary and include anthologies as well as monographs. They are of particular interest to philosophers, political and social scientists, economists, policy analysts, and those involved in public administration and environmental policy.

Mark Sagoff: *The Economy of the Earth*
Henry Shue (ed.): *Nuclear Deterrence and Moral Restraint*
Judith Lichtenberg (ed.): *Democracy and the Mass Media*
William Galston: *Liberal Purposes*
Elaine Draper: *Risky Business*
R.G. Frey and Christopher W. Morris: *Violence, Terrorism, and Justice*
Douglas Husak: *Drugs and Rights*
Ferdinand Schoeman: *Privacy and Social Freedom*
Dan Brock: *Life and Death*
Paul B. Thompson: *The Ethics of Trade and Aid*

Morality, prudence, and nuclear weapons

STEVEN P. LEE

HOBART AND WILLIAM SMITH COLLEGES

CAMBRIDGE
UNIVERSITY PRESS

PUBLISHED BY THE PRESS SYNDICATE OF THE UNIVERSITY OF CAMBRIDGE
The Pitt Building, Trumpington Street, Cambridge CB2 1RP

CAMBRIDGE UNIVERSITY PRESS
The Edinburgh Building, Cambridge CB2 2RU, United Kingdom
40 West 20th Street, New York, NY 10011-4211, USA
10 Stamford Road, Oakleigh, Melbourne 3166, Australia

© Cambridge University Press 1996

First published 1993
First paperback edition 1996

Printed in the United States of America

Library of Congress Cataloging-in-Publication Data is available.

A catalog record for this book is available from the British Library.

ISBN   0-521-38272-6 hardback
ISBN   0-521-56772-6 paperback

for Cherry

Contents

vii

Preface and acknowledgments

Nuclear weapons have created the permanent possibility of a unique and peculiar military relationship, often referred to as the state of *mutual assured destruction* or *mutual vulnerability*. This is the form that deterrence with nuclear weapons has taken. Its coming into being was largely an unintended consequence of actions taken by individual nations in an attempt to promote their national security, and its defense has had the character of an effort to make a virtue out of necessity. I seek to examine this defense, in both its prudential and moral dimensions. Given our notions of military prudence and morality, nuclear weapons, because of their immense and terrible destructive capability, pose a challenge to the coherence of our normative understanding. I attempt to explain this challenge and to move toward a solution to the problems it raises.

The prudential and moral debates over nuclear weapons have taken place largely independently of each other. On the prudential side, nuclear strategists have argued over which form of nuclear deterrence best promotes national security, with little or no reference to the question of whether nuclear threats are morally justifiable. On the moral side, those engaged in the debate over the moral justifiability of nuclear deterrence have given little attention to strategic matters and the consequences of different strategic options. The one-sided character of the debates has made them partial and incomplete, for the prudential and moral issues are intimately related. A proper understanding of the problems nuclear weapons pose must be based on an appreciation of their normative implications taken together, not their prudential or their moral implications treated separately. Indeed, the novel challenge of nuclear weapons lies in the way they have disrupted the traditional relation between prudence and morality. This challenge can be met only by taking up the problem from both sides. This book is a philosophical examination of the public debate over nuclear weapons policy under the assumption that the two parts of this debate, which have been largely kept separate, must be joined.

My concern is the difference nuclear weapons make in our normative understanding of military matters. In order to pursue this question, I make two assumptions. First, I take as a given the world of international politics as we know it, because that is the world in which our normative understanding of military matters has developed. I assume a world composed of sovereign nations, each of which may be a military opponent of any of the others, and that war between military opponents is always a possibility. I am not sure that such a world is inevitable, but it *is* our world, and if we are to understand the difference nuclear weapons have made, that world should be held as a constant. Obviously, this assumption precludes radical political diagnoses and solutions, such as the claim that the nuclear problem arises from national sovereignty and can be solved only by a surrender of that sovereignty to a world authority. But I believe that a proper understanding of the difference nuclear weapons have made is a necessary preliminary for assessing the adequacy or the necessity of that solution. In any case, even if a world government were to be established, the potential for large-scale intergroup violence would continue to be a part of human affairs. And now there are nuclear weapons.

The second assumption I make is that a rough distinction may be drawn, for the sake of analysis, between the political and military dimensions of the relations between nations. On the political side, nations may or may not be strong adversaries. On the military side, nations may or may not possess nuclear weapons. If two nuclear nations are strong adversaries, a relationship of nuclear deterrence exists between them. Nations that are not strong adversaries at one point may later become so, and vice-versa. For example, the United States and Great Britain were once strong adversaries and then were not, so that though both nations are nuclear powers, they are not in a relationship of nuclear deterrence. The general point is that there is a logic to the military relationship of nuclear deterrence that may be considered in abstraction from the logic of political relationships. Nuclear weapons are dangerous, but the danger is activated by the existence between nuclear powers of a strongly adversarial political relationship. If the danger that exists in the relations between two nuclear adversaries declines significantly, this may be due, in large measure, to a moderation in their political relationship, to their becoming less adversarial. If the moderation goes far enough, they will no longer be in a relationship of nuclear deterrence. The nuclear danger that had existed between them would then be over, but the danger from nuclear weapons remains potential, waiting to be reactivated in the future when two nuclear nations – those or others – enter into a strongly adversarial political relationship. I seek to understand this general, abstract nuclear danger, which is due to the destructive capability of nuclear weapons and to the logic of mutual vulnerability, and its potential in the relations between any nuclear or potentially nuclear powers.

Nuclear deterrence through mutual vulnerability is, in this sense, a general relationship. Any pair of nations that are strong political adversaries and have technological and industrial capabilities that are, by today's standards, fairly modest can become an instance of this relationship. So, in understanding nuclear deterrence, it is important not only to separate the political and military dimensions of the relations between nuclear powers, but also to separate the essential features of their military relationship from its accidental features. Both tasks are analytically difficult because we have come to know nuclear deterrence through one historical episode, the Cold War between the United States and the Soviet Union. Because that episode has dominated our historical experience, it is hard to distinguish the military from the political and the general from the particular. Although nuclear deterrence is a relationship that transcends the Cold War, in the sense that it is replicable or has other potential instances, it is difficult for us to think of nuclear deterrence in abstraction from the Cold War. It would be important to understand the general relationship of nuclear deterrence even were the Cold War continuing. As it is, with the Cold War's having ended, the need for an abstract understanding is even greater. We need to know what we can bring from our historical experience to future instances of nuclear deterrence. At the same time, the end of the Cold War should make this task easier – some of the dust may have settled. This study is not a historical examination of the nuclear relationship between the United States and the Soviet Union, nor of the evolution of our moral and strategic understanding of nuclear deterrence as it has developed in that relationship. Rather, I seek to extract from that historical episode the general features of the relationship of mutual vulnerability – in particular, its moral and prudential logic.

xi

The five-year period of this book's gestation has seen an extraordinary series of political developments that have ended not only the Cold War, but the Soviet Union. The United States is not now in a strongly adversarial political relationship with the nuclear successor states of the Soviet Union. This has put an end to the nuclear threat as we have known it, but it has not put an end to *the* nuclear threat. To say this is not to prejudge future political developments, but simply to point out that mutual vulnerability is a permanent possibility. Though the Cold War brought mutual vulnerability into being, the passing of the Cold War will not put it to rest. Mutual vulnerability is a possibility that transcends its origins and will continue to exist as its originating episode recedes into the past. The argument that the end of the Cold War has put an end to the nuclear problem is a version of the genetic fallacy. As one should not argue that a claim is false because of the questionable nature of its source, one should not argue that a problem ends when the historical episode in which it had its birth passes from the scene. The world is now safer not because nuclear weapons have become inherently less dangerous, but because what was an adversarial relationship between the two main nuclear powers has greatly moderated. Because of this moderation, some of the debates analyzed in this book may seem dated. They may seem to be period pieces from another era. But they must be understood, because their time will again come. There will be other adversarial relationships involving nuclear weapons. We must be ready.

The concern of this study is nuclear deterrence through mutual vulnerability. Nuclear deterrence can take other forms as well – in particular, as it exists between adversaries who do not have assured-destruction capabilities. The concern over nuclear proliferation is primarily a concern with this form of nuclear deterrence, because it takes some time after a nation has acquired nuclear weapons before it can develop the capacity for assured destruction. I will not say anything about this form of the nuclear relationship. As dangerous as it may be, it does not raise the unique normative problems and puzzles that a relationship based on assured destruction does. One other feature of the argument should be noted. For the sake of simplicity, I consider nuclear relations between pairs of adversarial nations (or, by implication, alliance blocs), even though mutual vulnerability can exist simultaneously among more than two nations (or alliance blocs). When nuclear deterrence is more than bilateral, this complicates matters, but not, I believe, in a way that alters the normative logic of nuclear deterrence, which I am concerned to understand.

I have accumulated many debts in the writing of this book. It was begun in 1987 during a year I spent at the Institute for Philosophy and Public Policy at the University of Maryland as a Rockefeller Resident Fellow. Members of the Institute gave me comments on early drafts and provided a stimulating and collegial atmosphere, an atmosphere in which I could not but thrive. Special help and encouragement were provided by Henry Shue, Doug MacLean, and Bob Fullinwider. Two years later, I was fortunate to receive support from the MacArthur Foundation, through a grant from its program in Research and Writing in International Peace and Security, which allowed me to take nine months off from teaching to advance the manuscript to the next stage. Another source of help was a 1988 NEH Summer Seminar on consequentialism, directed by Jonathan Bennett, in which I had the opportunity to try out some of my ideas on the members and to receive helpful comments, in particular, from the director and from Jonathan Schonsheck. My thanks to all the individuals involved and to the supporting institutions.

My institution, Hobart and William Smith Colleges, provides an environment that encourages, in teaching and research, the kind of interdisciplinarity represented by this book in philosophy and public policy. I first became interested in the ethics of nuclear deterrence through a course in the morality of war I taught in my first year on campus. I have had several occasions since to teach multidisciplinary courses on nuclear weapons policy with faculty from other departments. Out of one of those courses grew a collaboration that led to the writing of an introductory text on nuclear weapons, a process that greatly contributed to my thinking about nuclear issues. Thanks are due to my partners in this venture, Peter Beckman, Larry Campbell, Paul Crumlish, and Michael Dobkowski, and to other colleagues and students at the Colleges with whom I have discussed nuclear issues, as well as to the Colleges itself, not only for the environment it provides, but also for sabbatical support.

Over the years in which the ideas in this book were forming, I have had the opportunity formally to share them and have them subjected to critical scrutiny by colleagues at a number of institutions, including Albright College, City University of New York,

Colgate University, Cornell University, Georgetown University, George Washington University, Hamilton College, Polytechnic University of New York, Rochester Institute of Technology, University of Delaware, and University of Maryland. I thank all those who contributed to my thinking at these sessions.

Many others have read portions of the manuscript and provided me with helpful comments. Thanks are due to Greg Kavka, Jeff McMahan, Sterling Harwood, and an anonymous reviewer, all of whom generously provided me with extensive written comments on drafts of the first half of the manuscript. I would like to thank my friend Avner Cohen for stimulating my thinking on the issues with which this book is concerned. In the early 1980s we worked intensively together editing an anthology of essays on philosophical issues raised by nuclear weapons, and I first worked out some of the basic features of the argument of this book in an essay we jointly wrote for that volume. Members of Concerned Philosophers for Peace heard and provided helpful comments on early versions of two of the chapters. Others who have read and commented on portions of the developing manuscript include Andy Altman, Scott Brophy, Jan Cover, Earl Conee, Derek Linton, Alastair Norcross, George Quester, and Rosalind Simson. To all of them, and to many others unnamed who have contributed to my thinking about these issues, I express my appreciation. Let me also thank my editor, Terence Moore, my manuscript editor, Ronald Cohen, my indexers, Gary Thompson and Kim Kopatz, and, for support for the indexing, the Ruth and Elizabeth Young Fund.

Finally, for their tolerance and support, I would like to express my loving gratitude to Cherry, Amanda, Charlotte, and Lilah.

Chapter 1

The difference nuclear weapons make

Nuclear weapons have so changed our world that much of the truth does not make sense.

Robert Jervis[1]

Nuclear weapons have increased fantastically the amount of destructive force available for human use. The first atomic bombs were one thousand times more powerful than the largest conventional explosives, and the first thermonuclear bombs were one thousand times again more powerful.[2] The weapons in the nuclear arsenals of the United States and the Soviet Union* in the 1980s represented a destructive force of roughly 15 billion tons of conventional explosive.[3] This increase of several orders of magnitude in destructive force may well have fundamental implications for the traditional ways in which military force has been applied in human affairs and for the institutions for which and through which such force has been called into being.[4] The employment of destructive force – both its use and its threatened use – plays a major role in the relations among nations. How suitable are nuclear weapons for this role? Do nuclear weapons make a difference in the justifiability of the employment of military force?

Nuclear weapons have been developed and deployed in pursuit of the traditional military goal of national security. Military activity

*Because the Soviet Union, along with the Cold War, has ceased to exist, nuclear deterrence between the United States and the Soviet Union has become an episode of the past. Although this book is about the nuclear deterrence relationship in general, whatever nations are involved, rather than the particular instance of the relationship represented by the Cold War, there is much of general relevance to learn from that historical episode. The military relationship between the United States and the Soviet Union through the 1980s will be a frequent example for us.

in pursuit of national security is subject to appraisal in terms of norms or evaluative standards, both prudential and moral, that are internal to the institutional framework through which this activity is carried out. Some military activity is justifiable in terms of these institutional norms and some is not. When the question arises whether certain military activity is justifiable, it is to these norms that appeal should first be made.

The moral norms are restrictions or conditions on what a nation can do with its military power. They are not primarily concerned with the most effective military means whereby a nation may achieve its ends, but rather with whether those means, or the ends, are acceptable in themselves. These norms are embodied in the just-war tradition. The prudential norms are rules concerning what military actions or postures are or are not effective in pursuit of national security.[5] They may be referred to as prudential by analogy with norms of individual prudence, though the "self" whose interest they concern is, of course, the nation, not the individual who is bound by the norms through his or her role in the relevant institution.[6] These norms promote the national interest, insofar as national security is an important component of the national interest. National security can be taken to have the same fundamental role in the achievement of the national interest as personal security has in the achievement of an individual's self-interest. The analogy between national security and personal security is implicit in many characterizations of the former. National security, according to Harold Brown, "is the ability to preserve the nation's physical integrity and territory; to maintain its economic relations with the rest of the world on reasonable terms; to protect its nature, institutions, and governance from disruption from outside; and to control its borders."[7]

The proper scope of national security is, of course, a controversial matter, and the moral justifiability of its pursuit depends on the scope it is understood to have.[8] Indeed, the prudential justifiability of its pursuit depends on its scope as well, for action undertaken in the name of national security can, despite appearances to the contrary, be harmful overall to national interests. A minimum notion of national security requires a military capacity for paradigmatically defensive measures, such as repelling foreign invasion. National security may also seem to require military measures that would be regarded as instances of aggression, such as the use of a foreign expeditionary force to protect a nation's morally questionable overseas economic interests. To avoid moral complications that are not to my purpose, I will restrict my attention to those military activities in pursuit of national security that are paradigmatically defensive – that is, those that defend a nation's legitimate sovereignty against aggression.[9] (For simplicity, I will henceforth refer to paradigmatically defensive measures merely as defensive.)

The moral and prudential norms provide clear-cut support for military activity that is defensive. As a means of protecting a society from aggression, the use of military force is generally regarded as permissible from the just-war tradition. But such moral approbation is largely limited to military activity that is defensive. Defensive activity also receives strong prudential support, because its successful pursuit is a minimum condition for achieving other national interests. The prudential norms may not as strongly condemn aggression as the moral norms, because aggression can serve national interests. In prudential terms, however, it is generally easier to justify defense than aggression. Not only do the prudential costs of aggression tend to be high, but because the national interests served through defense are more basic than those served through aggression, the gains from defense can more easily outweigh the costs of the military activity itself than can the gains from aggression.

One may conclude that defensive military activity is generally morally and prudentially justifiable. This conclusion is fundamental to our understanding of the use of military force, for if the defensive use of military force cannot be justified, no use of military force can.[10] I will proceed under these two assumptions: first, that the defensive use of military force is generally morally justifiable and, second, that the defensive use of military force is generally prudentially justifiable. One way to discover whether or not nuclear weapons make an important difference in the role of military force is to ask whether these two assumptions hold when the defensive use of military force involves nuclear weapons. Have nuclear weapons falsified these assumptions? The question becomes: Is the defensive use of nuclear force, like the defensive use of military force in general, morally and prudentially justifiable?[11]

Putting the question in terms of the defensive use of military force leaves to one side the moral or prudential criticism that could be made of its aggressive use. This restriction is based not on the assumption that nations are unlikely to use military force for aggressive purposes, but on the concern to determine what, if any, difference nuclear weapons make. Such a difference should be more obvious in the case of defensive force, precisely because such force is assumed to be generally justifiable. For similar reasons, I will also ignore the pacifist's moral questions about the justifiability of any military force and the political theorist's concern about the legitimacy of the regime that is being defended. Raising these concerns would not be helpful in determining whether nuclear weapons make a difference.

Also to be set aside are moral and prudential concerns about the use of military force arising from the fact that military force is not all there is to the pursuit of the national interest, or even of national security. Overall judgments of national interest or national security might provide a prudential and moral basis for criticism of military force even in cases where the use of that force is in accord with the prudential and moral norms.[12] Military strength is not the only kind of strength a nation needs. One could, for example, criticize a large military establishment on prudential grounds that it is undermining the economy to such an extent that the overall effect was a loss for national security. Similarly, in moral terms, the value of military force could be set against the value of other governmental concerns. Resources must be distributed among institutions within a society, and when the military gets more, other institutions get less. Some of these others have a moral claim on adequate resources in light of the human needs they serve, resources that may be denied them due to an excessive concern with the pursuit of military strength. But attention to these criticisms, like the others, would lead away from the question of the difference nuclear weapons make.

MUTUAL VULNERABILITY

Whether nuclear weapons have falsified the assumptions that defensive military force is generally prudentially and morally justifiable depends on the nature of the military changes that nuclear weapons have wrought. Possession of large nuclear arsenals brings about basic changes in the relationship between military opponents. What has made these changes possible is not merely the invention of the nuclear explosives themselves, but also a host of other technological innovations. One set of innovations is the development of processes for making the weapons compact and relatively inexpensive, making economically feasible the deployment

4

of large nuclear arsenals. Another is the development of reliable and swift means of delivering the weapons over intercontinental distances, insuring that a nation could quickly bring its opponent under direct nuclear attack. A third set is the development of ways of making the delivery systems, especially missiles, less vulnerable to attack, which has guaranteed that a nation can deploy a capacity to retaliate that would survive a surprise attack.

The historical driving force behind these technological developments has been, in large part, the adversarial relation between the United States and the Soviet Union. Thus the nuclear situation had its origins in the great-power military rivalry that developed in Central Europe following the Second World War. But the nuclear situation is at once more peculiar and more general than its political origins suggest. It is more peculiar because though it developed out of one in a long historical series of great-power rivalries, it is in crucial respects a unique state of affairs. The nuclear situation is more general because now that it has come into being, it is not bound to the particular great-power rivalry that gave it birth. The problems nuclear weapons pose survive the U.S.-Soviet rivalry. The uniqueness of the nuclear situation must now be considered. What rival nuclear powers threaten each other with is not primarily territorial gain or political domination, which is the traditional form that military threats took. What is unique is that nuclear powers mutually threaten each other's very existence.

Referred to as the condition of mutual assured destruction (MAD), the situation is one in which each rival nuclear power is assured of its ability to destroy the other, no matter what the other does – that is, even if the other were to launch a massive surprise attack. This condition came into being in the 1960s, by which time both the United States and the Soviet Union had acquired nuclear arsenals sufficiently large and invulnerable. What is unique about this condition is not only the threat of destruction, but its mutuality. Never before was it possible that two nations could engage in a military conflict that would result in both being destroyed. This is how nuclear weapons differ fundamentally from conventional weapons. Conventional weapons are not powerful enough to make it possible for two military opponents mutually to bring about each other's destruction.

This novel military relation may also be characterized as a condition of *mutual vulnerability*, because each side's capacity for assured destruction entails the vulnerability of the other side to destruction.[13] What is vulnerable is the society of each side, which is why each can be said to threaten the other's existence. But for mutual vulnerability to exist, each side's nuclear weapons must be largely *in*vulnerable, because this is required for each side to have a capacity for assured destruction. Mutual vulnerability has been a historical achievement of sorts, but, as far as we can see, it is now, in potential, a permanent fixture, "a matter of physical fact."[14] According to Robert McNamara: "It is not a policy which we can choose to follow or not to follow, but a fact of life."[15] Given the existence of military rivalries among nuclear powers, short of a nation surrendering its capacity for assured destruction, mutual vulnerability would cease to exist only if nuclear nations were able to deprive their nuclear opponents of a capacity for assured destruction. This possibility is not on our technological horizon. According to Spurgeon Keeny and Wolfgang Panofsky:

> We are fated to live in a MAD world. This is inherent in the tremendous power of nuclear weapons, the size of nuclear stockpiles, the collateral damage associated with the use of nuclear weapons against military targets, the technical limitations on strategic area defense, and the uncertainties involved in efforts to control the escalation of nuclear war. There is no reason to believe that this situation will change for the foreseeable future since the problem is far too profound and the pace of technical military development far too slow to overcome the fundamental technical considerations that underlie the mutual hostage relationship of the superpowers.[16]

My concern in this book is the implications of the condition of mutual vulnerability. Not all military relations between opponents possessing nuclear weapons are conditions of mutual vulnerability, because one or both nations may lack a capacity for assured destruction. But nuclear weapons create the possibility of mutual vulnerability, and indeed an assured destruction capability is now readily achievable in technological terms. When I speak henceforth of nuclear war and deterrence, this should be understood to mean nuclear war and deterrence between nations in a condition of mutual vulnerability, nations that may appropriately be referred to as nuclear superpowers.

Mutual vulnerability is a condition in which each side threatens the other not merely with a high level of damage, but with societal destruction – that is, with the elimination of its social order. Robert McNamara asserts that "deterrence of nuclear aggression means . . . the certainty of suicide to the aggressor, not merely to his military forces, but to his society as a whole."[17] Walter Slocombe claims: "Massive exchanges will quite literally destroy the United States and the Soviet Union as organized societies."[18] A large-scale nuclear war, Harold Brown claims, "would be a catastrophe not only indescribable, but unimaginable." He continues: "Those societies would almost certainly cease to function, and the target nations cease to exist as physical entities. It would be unlike anything that has taken place on this planet since human life began."[19] The claim is that the tremendous destruction in a large-scale nuclear war would not only kill a substantial portion of the population of each of the belligerents, but would destroy so much of the complex social infrastructure on which modern society depends as to render that social order inoperative. As long as there were groups of survivors, there would, of course, be social order of some sort at the local level, but the claim is that there would be no social order at the national level.

Some writers on nuclear matters claim that nuclear war is survivable.[20] But either those who claim this are not contradicting the claim in the last paragraph, or there is good reason to think that they are mistaken. Often what those who claim that nuclear war is survivable mean is that a nuclear war might remain sufficiently limited that the nation's social order would remain intact. This does not contradict what is claimed in the previous paragraph, which is only that a large-scale nuclear war – that is, one involving a substantial portion of the belligerents' nuclear arsenals – would lead to the destruction of a nation's social order.[21] In a condition of mutual vulnerability, each side threatens the societal destruction of the other, even though a nuclear war might stop short of such destruction, just as a mugger with a gun threatens death, even though he might miss or only wound his intended victim.

On the other hand, if those claiming that nuclear war is survivable mean that large-scale nuclear war is survivable, they are either using a peculiar and misleading sense of "survivable" or they are almost certainly mistaken. As an example of the erroneous reasoning for such a claim, consider an argument for the survivability of large-scale nuclear war based on analogies with past human catastrophes that did not bring about the destruction of the social order. James Child, referring to such events as the Black Death, claims that "the consequences of any practically possible nuclear war are indeed commensurable with past human catastrophes."[22]

But the crucial difference between such past catastrophes and a large-scale nuclear war is that the destruction in a nuclear war would occur in a very brief period of time. A social order can survive a much higher level of destruction if it has time to absorb the shock. As Harold Brown points out, in cases like the Black Death, "social structures could continue in recognizable form," because "those events took place over many months or years."[23]

If what is at stake is the destruction of society, it is not straying too far into the metaphorical to claim that what each nation threatens is the death of its opponent. Gregory Kavka discusses two meanings that might be given to the claim that a nation has died: first, that its governmental institutions are fundamentally altered from the outside and, second, that all its citizens are annihilated.[24] Destruction of society represents an intermediate condition between these two. Although a large-scale nuclear war would probably not end human life in the nations involved, it would do more than put an end to the governing regimes. It would put an end to government. To say that a nation had died simply because there had been a change in regime would be an exaggeration. To say that all of a nation's citizens had died would be to say more than that the nation had died. But it is not inappropriate to draw a close analogy between the destruction of a nation's social order and the death of an individual.

The point of this analogy is to emphasize a quantity/quality distinction at work in the shift from conventional to nuclear war, similar to the one involved in the contrast between the injury and death of an individual. A human body can take just so much injury, and then the person dies. The injury that finally causes death represents more than simply an increase in the overall quantity of injury. It is the bringing about of the fundamental qualitative change from life to death. A nation can take just so much injury in war, and then it dies. It is the quantitative increase in destruction threatened by large-scale nuclear war that represents the new possibility of a mutual crossing of that qualitative threshold.

Improvements in military technology over the centuries have made war increasingly terrible, and each major advance in weapons design may have seemed to those alive at the time to represent the apogee of destruction, the threatened end of the world. But in the case of nuclear weapons, this "end of the world" impression is more than just a matter of relative perception. Societies have survived the use of all of the weapons technologies developed prior to the nuclear age, but they would not survive the large-scale utilization of nuclear technology. Societies have an objective breaking point, and the large-scale use of nuclear weapons would push them past this point. When fire became a weapon of war, this may have seemed as terrible to our ancestors as nuclear weapons seem to us, but this does not mean that our belief that the latest weapons technology could destroy society is not more accurate than theirs.

The contrast is sometimes drawn between fights between wild animals of the same species, where death seldom results, and fights between individual humans, where death often results. There is an analogous contrast between conventional wars, where societies involved in the conflict usually do not cease to exist as a result of the fighting (though regimes often do), and large-scale nuclear wars, where societies would cease to exist. Human violence at the international level has now become like human violence at the individual level, in that societies can now destroy each other as readily as human individuals have always been able to do. Of course, nations have occasionally died as a consequence of conventional war, but this has occurred not in war but subsequent to military defeat. Moreover, it was never possible for the infliction of societal destruction to be mutual.[25]

Unacceptable damage

What is threatened under a condition of mutual vulnerability is often labeled "unacceptable damage." This concept is, according to Bernard Brodie, "much overused and underanalyzed."[26] How does it distinguish between nuclear war and conventional war? A nation is likely to go to war only if it perceives an overall prudential advantage (or the avoidance of a greater prudential disadvantage) from doing so – that is, only if it perceives that its expected gains would outweigh its expected losses (or its expected losses would be less than its expected losses were it not to go to war). This is, of course, a difficult determination to make, not only because it requires comparing very different values, such as lives, territory, and economic prosperity, but because it depends crucially on which side would win the war. The magnitude of a nation's gains and losses has been highly dependent on whether or not it wins. Nuclear war changes this. A nation's losses in a large-scale nuclear war would be not only very high, but would be largely independent of which side "won." The losses or damage for both sides in such a war would be unacceptable, in comparison with what might be gained, meaning that neither side could achieve a prudential advantage or be better off than if there had not been a war. This is the point behind the cliche that a nuclear war would have no winner.

The expected prudential advantage (or disadvantage) from a war can, however, be calculated not only absolutely, but also relatively. The nation can calculate advantage not only by comparing the condition it expected to be in after the war (counting both its gains and its losses) with the condition it would be in without the war, but also by comparing its expected condition after the war with the expected condition of the opponent after the war.[27] A nation can determine prudential advantage by judging whether it would be better off in its own terms or in comparison with its opponent. Both kinds of (dis)advantage are suggested in the claim that the Soviet Union "would suffer unacceptable losses in a nuclear war, and . . . under no circumstances would such a war leave [it] better off in terms of achieving [its] geopolitical objectives than [it] otherwise would have been."[28] A nation's ability to achieve its geopolitical objectives is presumably a function of both its absolute and its relative conditions, its condition in itself and in comparison with its opponent. But the damage from a large-scale nuclear war is unacceptable whether advantage is measured in absolute or relative terms. Neither side could achieve advantage.

Consider first the case where advantage is judged in relative terms.[29] How could one society be better off than the other when both had ceased to exist? Consider the analogy of two gunfighters, both of whom die in a gunfight. One may have fewer bullet wounds than the other, but both are dead. The only sense it would make to say that one was better off than the other is if, as a consequence of the gunfight, one's values triumphed over those of the other. But this aspect of the example does not apply in the case of the death of a society, because values can only be realized in society, so that the possibility of realization dies with the society.

Likewise, the damage of a large-scale nuclear war should always be judged unacceptable when measured in absolute terms. Societal destruction – the death of the nation – is such a loss that no gains could make the nation better off after the war than it was before. There is a sense in which an individual can, speaking absolutely, be better off dead – that is, when his or her continued existence could only be one of intense misery. But this does not apply to societies, which are not subjects of pleasure or pain. Some might claim that there are, for a nation as well as an individual, some things worth dying for. Sidney Hook argues: "Survival at all costs is not among the values of the West. It was Aristotle who said that it is not life as such, or under any conditions, that is of value, but the good life. The free man is one who in certain situations refuses to accept life if it means spiritual degradation."[30] If the argument is that a nation itself is better off dead than unfree, because the same thing might be said of an individual, then the argument commits the fallacy of composition. If the argument is to be plausible, it must be taken to mean that the citizens are overall better off individually for the war's having taken place. In the context of the Cold War rivalry, the argument was that the citizens of the United States would be better dead than Red.

To focus on that argument as a instance of the general case, one should say two things about the claim that Soviet domination would be worse for an individual than either death in a nuclear war or survival in the post-holocaust world (which, if the survivors envy the dead, may be worse). First, it is highly implausible, for it requires denial of the claim that, in the words of Anthony Kenny, "the differences which at present exist between, say, the USA and the USSR would be insignificant in comparison with the differences between the USA as it is now and the USA as it would be after absorbing a full-scale nuclear attack."[31] The vast majority of those who lived under Soviet domination presumably would have preferred their actual lives to death or to life such as it would be for survivors of a large-scale nuclear war. Second, a preference for the consequences of nuclear war over the consequences of political domination by the nation's opponent is not a preference, in the absence of an overwhelming consensus, that a nation has a right to impose on its citizens. As a result, from the point of view of national policy, the destruction from a large-scale nuclear war must be regarded, in absolute terms, as unacceptable damage.

The notion of unacceptable damage distinguishes a large-scale nuclear war from a conventional war because the damage from such a nuclear war is *always* unacceptable – that is, always sufficient to deny prudential advantage to either side. The acceptability of the damage from a conventional war, on the other hand, is largely a function of whether a nation would win or lose the war. Nevertheless, the phrase "unacceptable damage" as applied to nuclear war is partly misleading, because the fact that it could be applied to conventional wars as well suggests a continuity where there is a break.[32] The difference this phrase is meant to mark can be brought out by distinguishing between damage that is *contingently unacceptable* and damage that is *necessarily unacceptable*. When the expected damage from a conventional war is unacceptable, it is contingently unacceptable, in that it might not be unacceptable were the nation to win the war. But in the case of a large-scale nuclear war, winning or losing makes no difference (or there is no winning or losing to make a difference), so that the damage is necessarily rather than contingently unacceptable.[33]

The condition of mutual vulnerability implies that the damage from a large-scale nuclear war is necessarily unacceptable. This is the difference that nuclear weapons make. But does this difference show that the assumptions of the general prudential and moral justifiability of defensive military force are falsified when the issue is the use of nuclear force? This question must be answered in two parts, corresponding to the two different ways in which military force can be employed. We will look first at nuclear war and then at nuclear deterrence.

NUCLEAR WAR

One indication of how the assumptions fare in the face of the condition of mutual vulnerability is the way in which some key military terms are now highly misleading when applied in the traditional way. For example, as many have noted, it is inappropriate to refer to a nuclear conflict as a war. As Michael Mandelbaum puts it: "In the sense that the term 'war' connotes some proportion between damage done and political goals sought, an all-out nuclear conflict would not be a war at all."[34] In prudential terms, war is a purposeful activity, a continuation of policy by other means, as Clausewitz observes. But, as Hans Morganthau points out: "The immensity of the military force which the nuclear age has generated goes hand in hand with the devaluation of its practical use. The more endowed a nation is with military force, the less is it able to use that force."[35] War is something nations engage in in the belief that they thereby can gain something that is worth the sacrifice in blood and treasure. Because a large-scale nuclear war could not be purposeful in this sense, the phrase "nuclear war" is misleading. Given the nature of nuclear weapons, it is just as inappropriate from a moral perspective as from a prudential perspective to refer to a nuclear conflict as a war.

Limited nuclear war

The claim that the damage in a large-scale nuclear war is necessarily unacceptable implies that such a war is not prudentially justifiable. What cannot be prudentially advantageous can have no prudential justification. Such a war, I will say, is *prudentially impossible*, meaning that it is impossible for an adequate prudential justification to be given for it, impossible that such a war could be acceptable in prudential terms.

But a large-scale nuclear war is not the only kind of nuclear war in which nations in a condition of mutual vulnerability might engage. Nuclear war might be limited.[36] A limited nuclear war might not lead to societal destruction, in which case the damage it would do might not be unacceptable. If the damage were unacceptable, it would be contingently rather than necessarily unacceptable. Such a nuclear war might be prudentially justifiable. But one does not know on entering a nuclear war whether or not it will be limited, because this is not simply a matter of what the belligerents intend. (Who would intend a large-scale nuclear war?) So, the question of the prudential justifiability of nuclear war, being a matter of the expected value of the gains and losses, must involve the question of the likelihood that a nuclear war would be limited. Beyond that, there is the question of the likelihood that a limited nuclear war would be limited enough to be prudentially justifiable. This suggests that there are two senses in which a nuclear war could be said to be limited.

A nuclear war between nations in a condition of mutual vulnerability might be limited in either a relative or an absolute sense. A nuclear war could be limited by virtue of either the number of nuclear weapons used or the amount of damage done. When less than a large portion of the belligerents' nuclear arsenals are used, the war is limited in a relative sense, and when the amount of damage done stops short of societal destruction, the war is limited in an absolute sense. All nuclear wars that are limited in an absolute sense are also limited in a relative sense, but not conversely. When a nuclear war is limited only in a relative sense, it involves societal destruction and so is no more prudentially justifiable than is a large-scale nuclear war. Given that a nuclear war could not be absolutely limited unless it were relatively limited, one must ask both what is the likelihood that a nuclear war would remain relatively limited, and what is the likelihood that a relatively limited nuclear war would be absolutely limited? The likelihood of a nuclear war's being relatively limited is a function of some factors characteristic of all nuclear wars. These factors create the general problem of nuclear-war limitation.

The amount of destruction in a war is limited by two kinds of factors: first, limitations in a nation's capacity to damage the other (what I will call capacity limitations) and, second, a nation's exercise of restraint in the use of its capacity to damage the other (restraint limitations). A war is usually called limited not because of the belligerents' capacity limitations, but because of their restraint limitations.[37] But restraint limitations have not in the past been necessary, as a rule, to insure the practical possibility that a war would be prudentially justifiable, because the capacity limitations of earlier military technologies were usually great enough to guarantee that the level of damage in the war could be low enough that the war would be prudentially advantageous for the winner. The capacity of the loser to do damage to the winner was not sufficient to deny the winner overall prudential advantage. The winner did not have to rely on the loser's restraint. In this sense, wars in the past were self-limiting.[38] But nuclear weapons change all this. The condition of mutual vulnerability is, in effect, the removal of capacity limitations. The amount of damage one side can do to the other is, in its practical effects, without limit. Thus, in a condition of mutual vulnerability, a nation can engage in nuclear war to prudential advantage only if the other side exercises restraint. "Now protection is possible only with the other's cooperation."[39]

But nuclear weapons mean not only the practical end of capacity limitations. They also make restraint limitations much more difficult to exercise, even though both sides would strongly desire a limited war. This is due to the inherently confusing character of military activity in war, what Clausewitz called "friction," which makes it difficult for military leaders to utilize their forces as they desire.[40] Nuclear weapons make restraint limitations more difficult to apply because they exacerbate this inherent confusion and amplify its impact. The confusing character of war creates problems for military leaders in communicating with their subordinates and acquiring adequate battlefield intelligence, making it difficult for them to exercise intelligent command over their forces.[41] In the pre-nuclear era, these factors helped to keep the war limited by strengthening capacity limitations, because, very often, the less well forces could be directed and coordinated, the less damage they could do. But in the nuclear era, these factors help to keep war from being limited by interfering with the desired imposition of restraint limitations. Nuclear weapons are so powerful that lack of control leads to more damage being done, not less. Richard Bauckham notes: "The irony of the nuclear situation is that our vast control over the forces of nature, which would have been unimaginable in the past, actually puts us *more* at the mercy of *un*controllable factors, including those which influence our own decisions, than the human race has ever been in the past."[42]

If restraint were to be exercised, it would almost certainly have to be exercised mutually. The primary motive each side would have for restraint would be to induce reciprocal restraint from the other side. Side A would restrain its nuclear attacks, limiting them, say, to certain kinds of military targets, in order to signal side B that if B wanted A's restraint to continue, B should restrain its own attacks, and A would expect a sign of restraint from B as a positive response. Limited attacks would be an attempt to strike a bargain for mutual restraint. A nuclear war is likely to be limited only if there could be a successful exchange of such signals. But due to the confusion of war, made worse by nuclear weapons, it would be overwhelmingly difficult for leaders successfully to send and to receive such signals.[43] First, each side would have a problem in getting information about the nature of the other side's attack, because sources of information (such as reconnaissance satellites) and the communication links to them are all highly vulnerable to the effects of nuclear explosions and are likely to be disrupted, whether deliberately or accidentally, in the early stages of the war. Second, the leaders would have severe problems in correctly assessing whatever information they did receive, because they would probably not be sure how complete or timely it was. Nor could they always easily read the signal that the other side was intending to send, even if their information were accurate. For example, how could they know whether a nuclear warhead landing near a city and a military target was an indication of lack of restraint or a sign of restraint? Third, the leaders would have trouble maintaining sufficient control over their own forces to send signals of restraint to the opponent.

These general problems of nuclear-war limitation show that no one should expect a nuclear war between nations in a condition of mutual vulnerability to be limited. It might, of course, turn out that way, but one cannot count on it. Limited nuclear war is, in general, not a reasonable expectation. It cannot be reasonably foreseen. Because we have had no experience on which to base our expectation of how a nuclear war might go, whatever expectation we have must be based largely on a consideration of factors such as those discussed earlier, and this provides little basis for optimism about successful limitation. Engaging in a nuclear war with a nation with whom one is in a condition of mutual vulnerability would be like running a red light across a high-speed, heavily traveled, multilane highway under conditions of near-zero visibility. One might make it safely across, but one could not form a reasonable expectation that one would. It may even be that the objective probabilities of making it safely across the highway are good. But by the nature of the case, one would not have knowledge of these probabilities, and so could not form a reasonable expectation of a successful crossing. Starting a nuclear war with a nation with whom one is in a condition of mutual vulnerability would be like playing Russian roulette in a situation in which one is not sure how many of the chambers are loaded. Again, one would have little on which to base a reasonable expectation of survival. In the absence of a sufficient basis for determining the probabilities of a nuclear war's remaining limited, the judgment that limited nuclear war is not a reasonable expectation is the best that one can do. It is the most that one can say about the question of likelihoods.

The argument so far concerns only relatively limited nuclear war, because the question has been the likelihood that a nuclear war would stop short of the belligerents' exhausting a substantial portion of their arsenals. It is, in general, not reasonably foreseeable that this will happen. But the important question concerns the likelihood that a nuclear war would be absolutely limited. Is a relatively limited nuclear war likely to be absolutely limited? One major study of the effects of (relatively) limited nuclear wars has determined that limited "nuclear attacks – even if limited to military targets – could cause casualties that approach those from all-out attacks."[44] One reason is that the marginal destructiveness of nuclear weapons on a society declines rapidly as the number of detonations increases, so that cutting the number of weapons used by, say, half may not greatly decrease the overall social destruction.[45] This suggests that one should have serious doubts about whether a relatively limited nuclear war would be absolutely limited. It is probably significantly less likely that a nuclear war would be absolutely limited than that it would be relatively limited. So the judgment that there is a lack of reasonable foreseeability about limitations in nuclear war applies more strongly for absolutely limited nuclear war than it does for relatively limited nuclear war.

The prospects for a nuclear war's being limited depend not only on these general considerations, but also on the details of the particular situation in question. Given the details, the prospects for absolute limitation will be better in some cases than in others. The general factors that make a nuclear war unpredictable would play less of a role in some cases. In these cases, an absolutely limited nuclear war might be reasonably foreseeable, so that the risk of societal destruction would be low. Robert Jervis argues: "Just as in the past some objectives were worth a war because the damage from the conflict was less than the expected gains, so now some objectives are worth a risk – albeit a low one – of total destruction." As a result, "some of the proportionality between means and ends that nuclear weapons destroyed is restored."[46] But the depth of the general problem of nuclear war limitation suggests that cases where absolutely limited nuclear war would be reasonably foreseeable are rare, at best. One may conclude that in general, if not invariably, absolutely limited nuclear war is not reasonably foreseeable.

The question of the prudential justifiability of nuclear war is the question of whether nuclear war can be a rational instrument of policy. That an absolutely limited nuclear war is not, in general, reasonably foreseeable shows that a nuclear war cannot, in general, be a rational instrument of policy, and hence is not, in general, prudentially justifiable. The judgment of prudential justifiability must be understood in this context as prospective rather than as retrospective, in that it must take account of limitations on our ability to predict the future. Its vantage point is not a retrospective knowledge of what did happen, but a prospective expectation of what is likely to happen. Though a nuclear war, were one to occur, might be sufficiently limited to be judged in hindsight to have been prudentially advantageous for one side or the other, still, given that it could not have been reasonably expected to stay absolutely limited, it would not be prudentially justifiable. So, the claim that nuclear war is not prudentially justifiable is not limited to large-scale nuclear war, though when extended to cover all nuclear wars, it must be stated in a qualified form. Nuclear war is, in general, not prudentially justifiable. Although it is possible for a nuclear war to be absolutely limited, few nuclear wars would be reasonably expected to be so limited. Nuclear war is a virtual prudential impossibility.

This judgment is indifferent to the way in which a nation enters a nuclear war – whether through a first or second strike. It applies not only to nuclear wars of aggression that a nation initiates, but also to "defensive" nuclear wars begun by the nation's nuclear retaliation in response to a nuclear attack.[47] If a nation is attacked by a nuclear aggressor, it has, of course, already suffered a great loss, but, assuming that the attack was a limited one, the nation cannot reasonably expect that continuing the war through retaliation would bring overall prudential benefit.[48] Even if the nation were judging the benefit in relative terms, so that the damage the opponent suffered in the retaliation would count as a relative advantage for the nation, still the nation could not reasonably foresee that the result of its nuclear retaliation would not be its eventual societal destruction, eliminating the possibility of relative advantage. Of course, retaliation might lead the opponent not to attack further, but this would not be a reasonable expectation. Defensive nuclear war is not, in general, prudentially justifiable. So the assumption that the defensive use of military force is, in general, prudentially justifiable is, in the case of nuclear war, falsified.

Moral justifiability

What about the moral justifiability of nuclear war? The moral norms, in contrast with the prudential norms, focus largely on what a nation does to its opponent in war, not on what the war does to the nation itself. There are two features distinguishing nuclear war that are of special moral relevance. First, a large-scale nuclear war would cause an unprecedented amount of harm and destruction. Second, the effects of nuclear explosions, especially in large numbers, are not merely local, either spatially or temporally. Nuclear explosions have powerful short-term effects that affect a large area. But, more importantly, they have severe long-term effects, such as radioactive fallout and other forms of environmental degradation, which extend lethality over a wide area and into the future. The first feature is morally relevant as a result of the moral norm (the principle of proportionality in the just-war tradition) that a war

should do more good than harm.[49] The amount of harm a war
causes should be no more than proportional to the harm it avoids,
or the good the war achieves should at least counterbalance the
harm it causes. The level of damage from a large-scale nuclear war
is certain to put the war in violation of this norm. Indeed, such a
war would be even more clearly in violation of this norm than of
the prudential norms, because, from the moral point of view, all
the damage done in the war is relevant, not just the damage done
to the nation making the calculations. The moral norms use a
broader notion of damage than the prudential norms.

The moral relevance of the extensive nonlocal effects of nuclear
weapons is by virtue of the norm (the principle of discrimination
in the just-war tradition) that persons on the other side who are
not involved in the war effort should not be subject to attack. Such
persons are often referred to as "innocent," but, as Anthony Kenny
points out: "The innocence in question had nothing to do with
moral guiltlessness or lack of responsibility: the 'innocent' were
those who were not *nocentes* in the sense of engaged in harming
one's own forces."[50] I shall refer to such persons simply as civilians.[51] A large-scale nuclear war would spread its lethal effects over
such a wide area that a very great number of the opponent's civilians would suffer or die, even if the nuclear weapons were not
aimed at cities. Such an attack on civilians would put the war in
violation of this moral norm. In addition, the extended temporal
effects of nuclear explosions would also put the war in violation
of this norm, because the nuclear explosions would continue to do
harm after the war was over, when everyone would be a civilian.[52]

A large-scale nuclear war would thus be in violation of the fundamental institutional norms of moral justifiability, and so is not
morally justifiable. Large-scale nuclear war is, in this sense, morally
impossible. But, again, the question of limited nuclear war arises.
Can the claim that large-scale nuclear war is morally impossible be
extended to apply to all nuclear wars between nations in a condition
of mutual vulnerability? Some would argue that if a nuclear war
were limited in the right way – that is, if only a small number of
nuclear weapons were used, and all against military rather than
civilian targets – then the war could satisfy both of the moral norms.
The norm prohibiting attacks on civilians would be satisfied because the attack would have been directed against military targets,
not against the civilians, and the extent of the nonlocal effects
would be greatly reduced. In addition, the norm requiring pro-

portionality of harm done might be satisfied because some gain from the war might be sufficient to outweigh the relatively small amount of damage done by the small number of weapons used.

This line of argument has some plausibility, but it is quite restricted in scope. A nuclear war is unlikely to be limited on one side without being similarly limited on the other, because limitation is likely to result only if there is an agreement for mutual restraint. Thus, if a limited nuclear war is not, in general, reasonably foreseeable, neither is it reasonably foreseeable, in general, that the damage a nation will do to its opponent would be limited. The factors discussed earlier making nuclear-war escalation likely show that the escalation would not necessarily be under the nation's intentional control. It follows that it is not, in general, reasonably foreseeable that a nation's participation in a nuclear war would be in conformity with the moral norms. Once the judgment of moral justifiability, like that of prudential justifiability, is seen as prospective rather than retrospective, a claim corresponding to the claim regarding prudential status is seen to hold: Nuclear war is, in general, not morally justifiable.[53]

Nuclear war is a virtual moral impossibility. Considering the principle of proportionality, a nation could not, in general, reasonably foresee that the total harm it would do in a nuclear war would be limited enough to be proportional to the harm avoided. This alone shows that nuclear war is almost never morally justifiable, because moral justifiability requires satisfaction of both of the moral norms. But there is a problem with the principle of discrimination as well. If limited nuclear war would seldom be a reasonably expected outcome, then a nation's leaders should expect that should they fight a nuclear war, they are likely to be drawn into a situation, as the war escalates, in which they will be using their weapons on civilian targets, or at least generating extensive nonlocal effects. They should foresee that the process is likely to lead them to take morally unacceptable actions that they may not initially intend to take.[54]

The assumptions falsified

Here, then, is one difference nuclear weapons make: They falsify the assumptions that defensive war is generally prudentially and morally justifiable. In the nuclear case, war (including defensive war) would seldom be either prudentially or morally justifiable.

Conventional defensive war is a prudential and moral possibility, but nuclear war is, in both prudential and moral terms, a virtual impossibility. The institutional norms imply one thing for conventional war and another for nuclear war. One upshot of this is that the so-called domestic analogy, which is used morally to justify defensive military activity, fails in the case of nuclear weapons. One of the strongest arguments for the moral justifiability of defensive war has been that a nation's defending itself from attack is morally analogous to an individual's defending himself or herself from attack. Because individual self-defense seems so morally unproblematic, it is argued that national self-defense is as well. But, despite the force of the analogy, it is generally not morally permissible to use nuclear force in a defensive response to aggression.[55]

But two points should be made about this difference between nuclear and conventional war. The first is that the assumptions about the prudential and the moral justifiability of defensive war are, in the case of nuclear war, *both* false. Although defensive conventional war is generally both prudentially and morally justifiable, nuclear war is neither. That nuclear war falsifies both assumptions is important because this keeps prudence and morality in rough agreement, and, as a result, does not contravene what I will call the *principle of tolerable divergence*. This principle is a general relation that holds between the prescriptive contents of the institutional norms of prudence and morality, according to which what the moral norms prescribe does not greatly diverge from what the prudential norms prescribe. Although the norms do diverge in their prescriptive content, what divergence there is is tolerable. By tolerable, I mean tolerable to those concerned with promoting the prudential goals of the institution, and tolerable in the sense that they would not find the moral requirements so greatly at odds with the prudential requirements that they would feel it necessary systematically to ignore the former. When the principle of tolerable divergence holds, acting morally is not, in general, regarded as requiring an unacceptable sacrifice of prudential interest.

One example of this principle is that both prudence and morality find the defensive use of military force generally justifiable, and another is that they both find the use of nuclear force generally not justifiable. Other examples of the principle concern prescriptions for actions in war. For instance, it is morally prohibited to attack civilians, but attacking civilians does not normally yield much of prudential military value. So the moral prohibition against attacking civilians is not, in general, greatly at odds with a nation's pursuit of its prudential interests in war. Thomas Schelling points out: "The technology and geography of warfare, at least for a war between anything like equal powers during the century ending in World War II, kept coercive violence from being decisive before military victory was achieved."[56] Avoiding the coercive violence of attacks on civilians, as the moral norms require, would not keep military leaders from the prudential goal of victory. But, of course, institutional prudence and morality have not been in complete accord. Institutional morality has some critical resources and still provides a stance apart from that of prudential demands. Otherwise, there would be no work for morality to do. One example of divergence is that aggressive use of military force is sometimes prudentially justifiable but not morally justifiable. But usually, if some policy is morally unacceptable, it will turn out that, unrecognized by the policy's supporters, there are overriding prudential reasons against the policy as well.

It is not surprising that there is not a large divergence between institutional morality and prudence, for the norms themselves have developed along with the institution in the context of the pursuit of the institution's ends. The moral norms and the prudential norms have a close working relationship within the institution, so they are not likely to be sharply at odds. A developmental constraint on institutional moral norms would be that they do not interfere greatly with the ability of the institution to achieve its prudential ends.[57] Such a line of reasoning constitutes a functional argument for the truth of the principle of tolerable divergence. The point of referring to the divergence as tolerable is that any divergence that was great enough to be intolerable to those pursuing the institution's prudential goals would result in the moral norms being systematically disregarded, and so in time being revised or replaced. Robert Jervis notes: "Realists probably are correct when they argue that moral standards will not be obeyed (and perhaps not even be seen as moral) if they conflict too much with self-interest."[58] Moral norms are likely to survive as part of the institution only if adherence to them does not require too great a sacrifice in terms of the institution's prudential ends. An institution whose prudential and moral norms were sharply at odds would be in an intolerable state of crisis.

The second point to note is that the prudential and moral impossibility of nuclear war has not gone unnoticed. Almost everyone acknowledges that a nuclear war would be an unprecedented moral and prudential disaster. It is constantly, ritualisticly observed that a nuclear war can have no winners, and that the nations of the world have a common interest in avoiding nuclear war. Because everyone admits that nuclear war is both prudentially and morally unacceptable, it is unlikely that either side would deliberately start a nuclear war. But there is a way to employ nuclear weapons without going to war, and that is, of course, to threaten their use. It is nuclear deterrence that seems to imply a breach of the principle of tolerable divergence, and thus to generate an institutional crisis.

NUCLEAR DETERRENCE

Deterrence is what the debate over nuclear weapons is all about. The issue is not whether or when to fight a nuclear war, in the belief that nuclear war might be acceptable or advantageous, but rather how to avoid a nuclear war, in the conviction that it would be utterly unacceptable and disadvantageous. Everyone has by now acknowledged Bernard Brodie's prescient judgment, offered at the beginning of the nuclear era: "Thus far the chief purpose of our military establishment has been to win wars. From now on its chief purpose must be to avert them. It can have almost no other useful purpose."[59] Traditionally, military power has been employed both to fight wars and to avoid them. But because nuclear war is a virtual prudential impossibility, military power, in the case of nuclear weapons, can no longer have the former purpose.

The primary goal of national security is the maintenance of national sovereignty, and this is the main reason that defensive wars are fought. The avoidance of war has traditionally been a secondary goal, in the sense that it has been conditional on the maintenance of sovereignty. Each nation wants both peace and freedom from outside interference, but peace is sacrificed when freedom is threatened. If the choice is forced, nations will seldom choose the surrender of sovereignty over the waging of war. In addition, the avoidance of war was a secondary goal because fighting a war might promote national interests in ways beyond insuring sovereignty. But given the potential for mutual societal destruction, avoidance of war has now become the primary goal. According to Russell Hardin, it is probably true that "any program of deterrence before nuclear weapons was an afterthought, a derivative realization from the principal purpose of defense systems, which was to defend against actual attacks." But with nuclear weapons, "the after-thought has become forethought."[60] Of course, the maintenance of national sovereignty remains an important goal, and nuclear deterrence is often praised as a policy that both avoids war and maintains sovereignty. But any military policy, nuclear or conventional, may succeed in this. Nuclear deterrence is deserving of special praise only if it is more effective at achieving these twin goals than traditional forms of military policy. Indeed, there is some reason to think that it is. But the negative aspect of nuclear deterrence, to be explored in later chapters, is that in making the avoidance of war the primary goal, nuclear deterrence undermines its own effectiveness.

Nuclear threats are sometimes thought to be useful for promoting national interests in ways that go beyond the primary goals of maintaining national sovereignty and avoiding war. The type of nuclear weapons policy that limits itself to these two goals is referred to as *basic deterrence*. There are two types of nuclear weapons policy beyond basic deterrence that are thought to enhance the pursuit of additional goals. The first is *extended deterrence,* under which a nuclear superpower uses its nuclear threats not only to maintain its own sovereignty, but also to maintain the sovereignty of its allies when this is viewed as vital to its own interests.

The second type of policy beyond basic deterrence is one where nuclear threats take the form not of deterrence, but of *compellence.* Compellence is "the threat of force not to *prevent* at attack but to make a state *do* something or *undo* something already done."[61] The intuitive basis of this distinction is that deterrence seeks to induce the opponent's restraint, whereas compellence seeks to induce the opponent to take some action.[62] Deterrence seeks to maintain the status quo, whereas compellence seeks to change it. It is natural to suppose that whereas deterrence represents a defensive use of nuclear threats, compellence represents their aggressive use, but it is not that simple. For example, using nuclear threats to induce an aggressor to withdraw from a territory unjustly invaded would count as compellence but would be defensive rather than aggressive. Compellence would not be expected, in general, to be a prominent feature of relations between nuclear superpowers, because the paramount focus on war avoidance means that the more ambitious purposes for which military coercion has traditionally been used have to be eschewed. In any case, because most instances of compellence are likely to be aggressive, and because our concern is primarily with the defensive use of military force, we can at this point focus our attention on deterrence rather than compellence.[63]

The common view

Now the question: Do the assumptions of the prudential and moral justifiability of the defensive employment of military force hold in the case of the threat to use nuclear weapons? Or, does nuclear deterrence, like nuclear war, falsify these assumptions? Because there is a clear consensus on the view that nuclear war is not prudentially or morally justifiable, I will begin by asking whether there is likewise a consensus or common view on the question whether nuclear deterrence is prudentially and morally justifiable. Regarding its prudential status, there is a clear consensus that nuclear deterrence, in contrast with nuclear war, is justifiable. The common view is that nuclear deterrence works well, that it did, in the case of the United States and the Soviet Union, keep the peace. In the view of most, although nuclear war would be an unmitigated disaster, nuclear deterrence is a splendid success.

Is there is a consensus or common view about the moral justifiability of nuclear deterrence? This question is complicated by the fact that many people appear to have given little or no thought to the morality of nuclear deterrence. In most discussions of nuclear deterrence, moral issues are not explicitly raised. Appraisal of deterrence is often exclusively prudential: If it works, it's OK.[64] But among those for whom moral issues are a concern, there is a noticeable disquiet about nuclear deterrence, captured in the characterization of the policy as one that threatens mass slaughter or genocide. This disquiet is represented by two events of the early 1980s that grew out of and made important contributions to the public debate over nuclear weapons policy. One is the United States Catholic bishops 1983 pastoral letter, *The Challenge of Peace*. The bishops provide strong reasons for concluding that the policy of nuclear deterrence is not morally justifiable, despite their ultimate claim that it is morally acceptable on a strictly conditional basis.[65] The other is Ronald Reagan's 1983 speech proposing the development of an extensive system of ballistic missile defenses. This speech contained an implicit moral critique of nuclear deterrence. Reagan spoke of the preferability of saving lives through destroying missile warheads in flight to avenging lost lives through nuclear retaliation.[66]

There is abroad a significant level of moral concern about nuclear deterrence, and among those who have given consideration to the matter, the common view seems to be that nuclear deterrence has serious moral problems, perhaps to the point of not being morally justifiable.[67] In terms of the common view, then, nuclear deterrence creates a basic conflict between prudence and morality. Nuclear deterrence is regarded as prudentially justifiable, but there are serious doubts about its moral justifiability. This view is presented in the words of George Quester, who speaks of the conflict "between the policy of deterrence and traditional morality," asking rhetorically: "Isn't the very essence of deterrence ('mutual assured destruction') immoral, and isn't it inconsistent with the traditional standards of Western civilization ..?" The only thing to be said in favor of deterrence "is that it has worked."[68]

How, in the common view, is this conflict between prudence and morality to be resolved? Given that there are few calls for the unilateral abandonment of nuclear weapons, it seems that the conflict is resolved in favor of prudence. Prudential concerns are, apparently, treated as overriding moral concerns. This is consistent with the way in which both the Catholic bishops and Ronald Reagan resolve their version of the conflict, because neither calls for the unilateral abandonment of nuclear weapons. Before nuclear weapons are abandoned, they must be made unnecessary, by mutual nuclear disarmament (for the bishops) or by a defensive capability (for Reagan). Each sees moral concerns as sufficient to call for the replacement of nuclear deterrence, but not until the policy is no longer needed to keep the United States safe from nuclear attack. In other words, each could be interpreted as holding that although nuclear deterrence is morally problematic, it is also prudentially justifiable, and that prudence should be given precedence over morality. It should be noted, however, that though this seems a plausible interpretation of Reagan's position, it is a controversial interpretation of the bishops' position, because they are, in principle, strongly opposed to giving precedence to prudence over morality in this way.[69]

The position that moral concerns with nuclear deterrence must give way in the face of its perceived prudential value has some affinities with realism, which is the view that morality is, in one sense or another, irrelevant to policy decisions about the use of military force, and that a nation's national interests are (or should be) all that it considers in its interactions with other nations.[70] Like realism, this position holds that moral concerns cannot override prudential concerns on the question of whether nuclear deterrence should be maintained, though the position does not view morality as irrelevant. In any case, realism is not a very interesting doctrine unless there is a strong opposition between morality and prudence, because otherwise the doctrine would have little practical import. The principle of tolerable divergence suggests that such a strong opposition does not exist, at least concerning the institutional norms governing the use of military force. But if prudence and morality are in conflict over nuclear deterrence, this is one area where realism becomes interesting. In fact, we may refer to the position that the prudential value of nuclear deterrence should take precedence over concern with its morally questionable nature as *nuclear realism*.

Implications of mutual vulnerability

Do the institutional norms support the common view that nuclear deterrence is prudentially justifiable but morally problematic? An answer to this must come from an understanding of the nature of nuclear deterrence. The unique character of nuclear weapons, their creation of a condition of mutual vulnerability, has important implications about the nature of nuclear deterrence and how it differs from traditional military deterrence (that is, conventional deterrence). These implications must now be explored. Nuclear deterrence is a policy (or a set of possible policies) chosen in the light of the condition of mutual vulnerability. As mentioned earlier, this condition is not itself a policy, though it comes into being as a result of policies chosen by the nations in question. Neither party is free by itself to avoid this condition, short of unilateral nuclear disarmament, which would not, of course, eliminate its own vulnerability. Nuclear weapons policy is not a matter of a nation's choosing to sustain its own vulnerability, but rather of its choosing a policy in the knowledge that its vulnerability cannot be avoided.

Military deterrence is not new with nuclear weapons, but it is different. With the development of nuclear weapons, says Bernard Brodie, "the term has acquired not only a special emphasis but also a distinct connotation."[71] The difference lies in what is threatened under a condition of mutual vulnerability. Jervis argues: "The forces that inflict damage on the adversary no longer protect the state, as they did in the past. Coercion, not brute force, deterrence, not defense, are the function of our weapons."[72] Because of mutual vulnerability, defense through brute force, through physical interference with an attack, is no longer possible. War cannot protect the nation, only deterrence can. In the past, in the case of conventional deterrence, the deterrent capability derived from the capability to defend the nation in the event of war, which is why the goal of war avoidance was secondary. Jonathan Schell argues: "In pre-nuclear military strategy, the deterrent effect of force was a useful by-product of the ability and willingness to wage and win wars. Deterrence was the shadow cast by force, or, in Clausewitz's metaphor, the credit that flowed from the ability to make the cash payment of the favorable decision by arms." Schell goes on to ask: "Of what object is nuclear deterrence the shadow? Of what cash payment is it the credit?"[73] The answer is not the threat of successful defense or of military victory, but the threat of societal destruction. Deterrence, in the case of nuclear weapons, results from the capability to destroy the opponent.

Thus the difference between nuclear and conventional deterrence lies in the difference in what each threatens, societal destruction in contrast with military defense or victory. There are several other ways to emphasize this central point. One is through the distinction implied when the nuclear situation is labeled, in Churchill's phrase, a "balance of terror." The contrast is with the traditional notion of the balance of power. What is balanced under a balance-of-power regime is primarily the traditional capacity of military forces to take and defend territory by inflicting military defeat, whereas what is balanced under a balance-of-terror regime is the capacity to do massive damage to the opponent's society.[74] As Schelling says: "Deterrence rests today on the threat of pain and extinction, not just on the threat of military defeat."[75] A related way to make the point is through the distinction between *countervalue* damage (destruction of civilians and social infrastructure) and *counterforce* damage (destruction of military assets). Nuclear deterrence threatens primarily the former and conventional deterrence threatens primarily the latter. Not exclusively, because each kind of weapon can inflict either kind of damage. First, all that is required to inflict civilian damage in war is a way to bypass the opponent's military forces, which has been done conventionally for centuries with naval blockades and during this century with conventional aerial bombardment. But the ability of conventional forces to do damage to society through such means is limited. Second, nuclear weapons can inflict counterforce damage, whether on the battle-field or on the homefront. But only nuclear weapons can inflict sufficient countervalue damage in war to threaten societal destruction.

A final way to make the point is in terms of the distinction between denial and punishment.[76] Nuclear deterrence is primarily deterrence by threat of punishment, whereas traditional military deterrence is primarily deterrence by threat of denial. Denial is defense, the physical interference with the opponent's military efforts, whereas punishment is the doing of damage to the opponent's society.[77] A capacity for denial is an ability to keep the opponent from achieving its military goals, so it affects what the opponent will gain from a war, whereas a capacity of punishment affects the losses the opponent will suffer. This distinction, like the distinction between counterforce and countervalue, does not draw the line sharply between nuclear and conventional deterrence, for each threatens both denial and punishment. As George Quester points out: "To be made to suffer intense pain *may* weaken one's ability to fight; and to be disarmed *may* also cause substantial psychological pain."[78] In addition, imposing military costs on an opponent through denial may indirectly harm its society through destruction of its resources, and attacking an opponent's society through punishment may indirectly contribute to denial, if not by undermining its will to fight, then through destruction of its society, by making impossible its gaining anything.[79] The importance of viewing nuclear deterrence as the threat of punishment is that it emphasizes that the threat is of necessarily unacceptable damage. Nuclear deterrence, because it is based primarily on a capacity for punishment rather than denial, threatens losses that are certain to outweigh or destroy the possibility of any gains.

The common view vindicated

Given this understanding of the distinctiveness of nuclear deterrence, the justifiability claims of the common view regarding nuclear deterrence should be examined in the light of the institutional norms. Do the norms support the view that nuclear deterrence is prudentially justifiable but morally problematic?

Consider, first, prudence. In terms of traditional measures of prudential effectiveness, nuclear deterrence should be much more effective than conventional deterrence. The traditional emphasis on greater military might suggests that the effectiveness of deterrence has been seen primarily as a function of the amount of loss the nation could impose on its opponent, and the certainty of the nation's ability to impose the loss. If the decision to go to war is a matter of weighing expected gains and losses, the more losses the opponent is likely to suffer and the more certain it is to suffer those losses, the less the likelihood that it would choose to go to war or to risk war. A threat of punishment is much more effective in this respect than a threat of denial, because punishment, unlike denial, would significantly affect the opponent's expected losses, not merely its expected gains. In addition, the condition of mutual vulnerability guarantees the ability of the nation to impose the punishment. Under mutual vulnerability, in contrast with conventional deterrence, an opponent is unlikely to be tempted into war by the belief that victory is possible. The threat of necessarily unacceptable damage induces in the opponent a fear of unavoidable societal destruction, whereas the threat of denial induces only a fear of military defeat, which the opponent may be able to avoid through its military efforts and fortune. Whereas the infliction of punishment in war may have little military effectiveness, the threat of devastating punishment would seem to be highly effective as a deterrent. Thus, according to traditional military measures, nuclear deterrence seems more effective than conventional deterrence.[80] If one assumes that conventional deterrence is generally prudentially justifiable, the comparative judgment implies that nuclear deterrence is as well.

What about the moral status of nuclear deterrence in terms of the institutional norms? The norms of the just-war tradition imply the same judgment about nuclear deterrence as they do about nuclear war, because what they prohibit the intentional doing of, they also prohibit having the intention of doing.[81] Nuclear deterrence is based on threats of nuclear retaliation, and these threats are the expression of an intention to retaliate. This intention is conditional, in the sense that its being enacted depends on the opponent's doing those actions that the policy is seeking to avoid, but it is an intention nonetheless. Moreover, an effective policy of nuclear deterrence could not be based on bluff, because, given the institutional nature of the policy, the absence of a retaliatory intention could not rest in a single mind but would have to be reflected in the military organization supporting the threat, and thus might easily be discovered by the opponent.[82] Because the waging of large-scale nuclear war is not morally justifiable, neither is the intention to wage such war, so neither is the policy of nuclear deterrence. Thus, the institutional norms affirm the view that nuclear deterrence is morally problematic, indeed that it is not morally justifiable.

The possibility of a limited nuclear war does not alter this assessment. In a condition of mutual vulnerability, each side threatens the other with societal destruction through the waging of large-scale nuclear war, and thus conditionally intends to wage such war. Each side hopes that should war start, it would not come to that, that the war would stay limited. A nation might disarm itself of nuclear weapons to the point where it threatened only limited nuclear war, and base its deterrent on this threat alone. But such a possibility is irrelevant to the present case, which assumes the condition of mutual vulnerability.[83] In a condition of mutual vulnerability, the possibility that a nuclear war might be limited does not refute the claim that nuclear deterrence is not morally justifiable.

A dilemma

Nuclear deterrence is, then, prudentially justifiable but not morally justifiable. In the case of nuclear deterrence, the assumption that defensive military force is prudentially justifiable holds true, but the assumption that it is morally justifiable proves false. This conflict between institutional norms represents a failure of the principle of tolerable divergence. The moral norms do not allow a basic form of military policy that the prudential norms allow. The conflict is, in fact, sharper than this. Because the avoidance of nuclear war and the maintenance of national sovereignty are such basic prudential goals, and because nuclear deterrence appears to be the only way in which they can be reliably achieved, nuclear deterrence seems, in prudential terms, not merely justifiable (which implies only that it is permissible), but required. Nuclear deterrence is prudentially necessary, but morally impossible. Nuclear deterrence thus creates a sharp break between the institutional norms. Morality and prudence are thrown into radical opposition. National defense requires nuclear deterrence, so national defense is now morally impossible. In this way, nuclear weapons create a practical contradiction or dilemma in the pursuit of national security within the context of the traditional institutional norms. The institution seems to be in fundamental internal conflict.

This conflict has been handled by morality being disregarded. Prudence has been given precedence. Nuclear weapons force a choice between the immoral – the practice of nuclear deterrence – and the imprudent – its abandonment. Given such a choice, nations choose the immoral. It is nuclear weapons that raise this conflict to the point where the choice to abandon morality must be made. Nuclear deterrence has made morality, as represented by the institutional norms, politically irrelevant. Jonathan Schell speaks of "the fissure that nuclear weapons have created between our political selves and our moral selves," as a result of which "we are compelled to choose between a position that is politically sound but immoral and one that is morally sound but politically irrelevant."[84] In the practice of political decision making about nuclear weapons policy, morality has lost its power to guide action, because its prescriptions are so at odds with the perceived requirements of national defense. When the principle of tolerable divergence holds, prudentially responsible leaders have room to respect moral requirements. When it does not hold, they do not. The just-war requirements, as the embodiment of the institutional moral norms, have always played an important political role by conferring legitimacy on military force. Politically, the just-war tradition has played this role by holding a middle position between realism and pacifism. But nuclear deterrence forces the just-war tradition from the middle toward pacifism, making it no longer able to confer legitimacy upon military force, and so no longer politically relevant.

As a guide for nuclear weapons policy, morality seems to have become, what in other contexts it is often, though mistakenly, said to be: a luxury we can no longer afford. As an example of this attitude, George Quester speaks of morality as being a burden in our efforts to adopt an appropriate policy of nuclear deterrence, and claims that there is a necessary hypocrisy in our claims concerning what nuclear deterrence is morally about.[85] The task I undertake in this book is to come to a full understanding of this apparent split between morality and prudence and of its implications for the knowledge and practice of military policy in the nuclear age. The urgency is one imparted by the specter of a basic social institution sharply in conflict with itself in its very practice. The goal should be to reconcile morality and prudence. Morality must be reclaimed from its state of political irrelevance.

To reclaim morality from political irrelevance, one must show that the apparent conflict between morality and prudence is merely apparent. The reclamation strategy I will adopt is based on the hypothesis that the appearance of conflict results from the limited perspective afforded by the institutional norms. A fuller or more adequate moral and prudential understanding of nuclear deterrence may show either that it is morally justifiable or that it is not prudentially justifiable. Such an understanding would have to be sought outside of the institutional context. The first step in this strategy will be to take a more thorough look at the moral issues raised by nuclear deterrence by broadening our moral perspective beyond the just-war tradition. This may afford a basis for criticizing the moral argument against nuclear deterrence based on the institutional norms. We will find, however, that broadening our moral view, far from solving the conflict, only deepens it.

Chapter 2

The moral problem

Nuclear weapons create a fundamental problem for our moral understanding. The condition of mutual vulnerability calls into question some basic features of our moral view. The fantastic destructive power of nuclear weapons seems to place them beyond our moral world, whereas their presence in our hands makes them inescapably part of that world. One aspect of the moral problem is the conflict nuclear weapons create between institutional morality and prudence and the resulting political marginalization of morality. But the moral problem goes deeper. Nuclear weapons appear to create a sharp conflict not only between morality and prudence, but within morality itself. Beyond forcing a choice between morality and prudence, they seem to confound moral choice itself.

The sharp conflict between morality and prudence implied by the institutional norms might be shown not to hold if appeal is made to a moral perspective broader than that of the just-war tradition. The way in which we reason about moral matters in everyday life, outside the context of particular social institutions and their special moral norms, provides a broader perspective. I will refer to this perspective as *everyday moral reasoning*. Everyday moral reasoning is pluralistic, in the sense that it recognizes different, often conflicting, approaches to assessing the moral status of actions or policies. The just-war tradition is not pluralistic in the same way.

The pluralism of everyday moral reasoning is exhibited most clearly in its recognition of both consequentialist and deontological approaches to determining the moral status of actions.[1] (Actions are understood here to include the corporate actions of establishing, maintaining, or abolishing institutional policies) The consequentialist approach assesses an action exclusively in terms of the overall value or disvalue of its consequences as they affect all humans or all sentient creatures, the morally required action being the one productive of the most value or the least disvalue among the available alternatives.[2] The deontological approach classifies an action in terms of its kind, irrespective of its overall consequences, and assesses the action exclusively on the basis of whether an action of that kind is required, prohibited, or permitted. The two approaches are sometimes in agreement and sometimes in disagreement in their assessments of a particular action. When they disagree, the overall moral status of the action is determined by comparing the conflicting assessments in terms of some intuitive notion of weight. The overall moral status of the action will be determined by whether the consequentialist or deontological assessment of that action carries greater weight.[3] To take a simple example, we recognize that there is a deontological requirement to keep promises, and also that sometimes promise keeping is not morally preferable in terms of its consequences. When there is a conflict, one weighs the divergent assessments in order to decide what one ought, overall, morally to do.

The just-war tradition does not recognize the consequentialist approach. It does not recognize that there is an independent set of moral considerations involving consequences alone that weighs against deontological considerations in determining the overall moral status of some military action or policy.[4] The principle of discrimination, which is crucial for judging that nuclear war and nuclear deterrence are not morally justifiable, is a deontological principle. It implies a duty not to perform (or not to adopt an intention to perform) actions of a certain kind regardless of the value of their consequences. This principle is treated as a necessary condition for the moral justifiability of military action, so that an independent appeal to consequences is not allowed to take precedence. In this sense, the tradition adheres to the principle that evil may not be done that good may come. The just-war tradition does take some account of consequences through the principle of proportionality. But it does not treat them as an independent moral consideration, because it does not allow this principle to override the principle of discrimination.[5] Satisfaction of the principle of proportionality is treated as a necessary condition for the overall moral justifiability of a military action, but never as a sufficient condition – that is, never as a condition that could by itself determine an action to be permissible or required. Moreover, this principle prescribes not that the value of an action's consequences be maximized, but merely that the consequences not involve a net loss of value.

Thus, the institutional moral perspective represented by the just-war tradition does not recognize the moral relevance of consequences in the way that everyday moral reasoning does. This limitation suggests that everyday moral reasoning may provide a way to avoid the sharp conflict between morality and prudence. But something stronger can be said in favor of adopting the perspective of everyday moral reasoning. The just-war tradition's failure to give independent consideration to consequences is, concerning nuclear weapons policy, not just a limitation, but a serious inadequacy. Choices about nuclear weapons policy put a great deal at stake in terms of consequences, because these policy choices affect the likelihood of nuclear war and superpower aggression. So a moral perspective that does not treat consequences as an independent moral consideration is not an adequate position from which to examine nuclear weapons policy.[6]

THE CONSEQUENCES OF NUCLEAR DETERRENCE

In applying everyday moral reasoning to the question of nuclear deterrence, I will first take up the consequentialist approach. In terms of this approach, there is reason to think that morality and prudence do not conflict. The argument in Chapter 1 shows that nuclear deterrence is justifiable in terms of institutional prudence. Indeed, given the national security stakes, we found it reasonable to hold that nuclear deterrence is prudentially not merely permissible, but required. But this argument can be extended to show that nuclear deterrence is required in consequentialist terms. Both prudentialism and consequentialism are concerned with the value and disvalue of consequences, but they differ in what consequences they consider. Prudence considers only those consequences affecting some limited subset of humanity, such as one individual or the citizens of one nation, whereas consequentialism is concerned with the effects of an action on all of humanity.[7] Prudence takes the interests of only some into account, whereas the consequentialist approach considers the interests of all. So the consequences of an action may be of overall prudential value while being of overall moral disvalue, or vice-versa – and this is often the case.

But the condition of mutual vulnerability brings about a situation where, in general, what is prudentially required in the choice of nuclear weapons policy is also morally required in consequentialist terms. Nations in a condition of mutual vulnerability have, as is often said, a common interest in the avoidance of nuclear war, and, given the global effects of such a war, they share this interest with all of humanity. There is not always common interest between (nonnuclear) opponents in the avoidance of conventional war, because the side that is likely to win may see the damage it would expect to suffer as acceptable, viewing the expected consequences of war quite differently than does its opponent. But with mutual destruction assured and damage necessarily unacceptable, a nuclear war would yield harmful consequences for all and for each. The overall moral disaster of a nuclear war would factor into prudential disasters for each of the belligerents. Because the most important consequence of a nuclear weapons policy is its effect on the likelihood of nuclear war, the fact that nuclear war would yield overall harmful consequences for all and for each supports the claim that what is prudentially required is also morally required in consequentialist terms, and conversely. In support of this, Gregory Kavka argues that it is a mistake to see national interest as opposed to overall human interest in the area of nuclear weapons policy. Nuclear deterrence is not merely the selfish pursuit of national interest.[8] Nuclear weapons lead to a confluence between the prudential and moral assessment of the consequences of military policy.

In order to show that this confluence holds, one must show that the prudential argument sketched in Chapter 1 can be turned into an argument that nuclear deterrence is morally required by virtue of its consequences. The prudential argument is that nuclear deterrence is more effective than alternative policies in avoiding war and maintaining national sovereignty as a result of two special features of the condition of mutual vulnerability – the capacity for societal destruction that each side threatens, and the certainty of the ability of each side to impose that loss on the other. The moral argument from the consequentialist approach (the *consequentialist argument*, as I shall call it) must develop the implications of these features for humanity as a whole. The argument is, in broad outline, a familiar one, but it has usually been cast exclusively in terms of the advantages of the nuclear balance between the United States and the Soviet Union. The argument, however, is general, being applicable to any opponents in a condition of mutual vulnerability,

37

though the example of the United States and the Soviet Union can serve illustrative purposes. The soundness and relevance of the argument is not hostage to a continuing enmity between these nations or their successor states.

(P1) In a condition of mutual vulnerability, a nation's policy of nuclear deterrence threatens the opponent with necessarily unacceptable damage, and the nation's capacity to inflict that damage is undoubtable. These features make it very unlikely that the opponent will start a war or otherwise seriously infringe on the nation's sovereignty, because the opponent is unlikely to be under the illusion that there could be prudential advantage in doing so. This makes the relations between the two sides very stable, in the sense that war is very unlikely, and this is the basis of the prudential argument that nuclear deterrence is required. But the consequences of this stability are of great value for all humanity, not simply the nation itself. The whole world benefits when the likelihood of war between two great powers is low, especially given the planet-poisoning potential of nuclear war.

(P2) To see that this is the case, consider what would happen if a nation unilaterally abandoned its policy of nuclear deterrence and the stability it brings.[9] Consider what would have happened during the Cold War if the United States had abandoned nuclear deterrence but the Soviet Union had not. The Soviet Union would likely have taken advantage of the military preeminence thus ceded to it to further its interests at the expense of the United States and its alliance partners as well as nonaligned nations. Its efforts to use its military power for gain might have taken the form of outright military aggression, but, more likely, they would have taken the form of coercive efforts to secure political concessions from other nations through military intimidation or nuclear blackmail. Although it would have been infeasible for the Soviet Union to occupy the United States or other large Western nations, occupation would not have been necessary for it to impose its political will. The nuclear arsenals of other nations, such as Britain, France, and China, would have had some moderating influence on Soviet aggressive behavior, but these arsenals were not large enough to have neutralized the Soviet military preeminence. For example, it is unlikely that Great Britain and France could have extended their nuclear deterrent to protect the whole of Western Europe, as the United States did.

Moreover, the abandonment of nuclear deterrence by the United States would have led to instability in the international order, which, independent of Soviet aggressive designs, would have made major military conflict, even nuclear conflict, more probable. This is due to the likely behavior of third parties. Many nations felt protected from Soviet aggression or coercion by the United States policy of extended deterrence. In the absence of the American nuclear "umbrella," these nations and others would have felt vulnerable to Soviet military power. As a result, some of them might have made efforts to build nuclear arsenals or to increase their existing nuclear arsenals. Three likely candidates for such efforts would have been China, West Germany, and Japan. Because of its history of enmity with these nations, especially Germany, the Soviet Union might have taken military action to thwart these efforts. The resulting military conflicts might have become nuclear. Moreover, in the event of such conflicts, the United States might have come to see its abandonment of nuclear deterrence as a mistake, and have sought to rearm. The Soviet Union would have been strongly tempted to oppose this militarily, increasing further the likelihood of conventional or nuclear conflict.

These points are general. To claim that the Soviet Union would have used its military power to advance its interests at the expense of others is not to attribute to it uniquely malevolent intentions, but is rather to recognize how any great power is likely to behave in a position of such military preeminence. Any nation with a heavy investment in military power is likely to desire that its investment "pay-off" in terms of the advancement of its interests, and when this nation has no adequate military counterweight among other nations, it is likely to act on that desire. Moreover, other nations, recognizing this, are likely to act to protect their perceived interests in ways that would make war, even nuclear war, more likely. Whenever one of two nuclear superpowers abandons nuclear deterrence, the resulting instability could have negative consequences for the rest of the world, though the particular political configuration of the world at that time will affect the nature and extent of those negative consequences.

(P3) What would be the consequences if nuclear deterrence were abandoned mutually instead of unilaterally? Negative consequences, such as those outlined in (P2), would still follow. Nuclear deterrence deters not only nuclear war, but also conventional war between nuclear superpowers. Without nuclear deterrence, conventional war between superpower opponents would be more likely. Moreover, in one of the ironies of the nuclear age, the mutual abandonment of nuclear deterrence would actually make nuclear war more likely. For in the midst of any conventional war that occurred after this abandonment, the erstwhile nuclear powers are likely to race to rearm themselves with nuclear weapons, making it very possible that the conflict would become nuclear. In the midst of the conventional war, each side would be likely to try to rebuild its nuclear weapons, first, because it would believe that a few such weapons would provide it with a decisive advantage in the war and, second, because it would suspect that the other side, believing this as well, was already secretly rearming. Each side would rearm in the hopes of gaining an advantage in the war and out of the fear that the other side might be trying to achieve that very advantage. The potential for or the actualization of this dynamic could lead other nations to behave in the way suggested in (P2). Instability would infect international relations whether the abandonment of nuclear deterrence were unilateral or mutual.

(C) A consequentialist argument for some policy needs to show not only that that policy would have good (or not so bad) consequences, but that alternative policies would have consequences that are worse. (P1)-(P3) allows this comparative evaluation in the case of nuclear deterrence. On the positive side, mutual vulnerability and the stability it creates makes nuclear deterrence a reliable way of keeping the peace, with the beneficial consequences for all persons that this entails. On the negative side, the alternative to nuclear deterrence – its abandonment – whether unilateral or multilateral, would result in instability that would have consequences that are worse not only prudentially, but morally as well. Many nations would become less sure of their ability to avoid aggression or coercion on the part of other nations, and so would make moves that would increase the likelihood of war. Part of this dynamic would be that nations' fears of the potential for other nations to arm or rearm themselves with nuclear weapons would make their own nuclear armament or rearmament more likely. So the risk of nuclear war would also increase. The result would be a set of expected consequences of great disvalue for people all over the world. Thus, nuclear superpowers are morally required, in consequentialist terms, to maintain their policies of nuclear deterrence.

This argument is brief and sketchy, and though the briefness can be remedied, some would say that the sketchiness cannot, that arguments of this sort are unavoidably inconclusive. Given the feebleness of our predictive powers, not only must a consequentialist argument be discussed in terms of likely rather than certain outcomes, but the assessment of the likelihoods must be imprecise.[10] The argument must be cast in terms of the expected value of the possible outcomes – that is, the value of the possible outcomes multiplied by their likelihood. But our uncertainty about the likelihood of the outcomes means that this can be done only in the roughest of ways.[11] As a result, many are strongly suspicious of consequentialist arguments about nuclear deterrence, whatever their conclusion. In any case, the consequentialist argument will be taken up in more detail in later chapters in a way meant to allay some of the suspicions.

The consequentialist argument concludes that the maintenance of nuclear deterrence is required whether nuclear deterrence is understood as each nation's policy of nuclear threatening taken by itself or the situation of mutual nuclear threatening. In other words, neither the unilateral nor the mutual abandonment of nuclear deterrence is preferable to the maintenance of nuclear deterrence. Although nuclear deterrence in each of these two senses is shown to be preferable to its abandonment, this is not necessarily the case, because the alternative to nuclear deterrence in one sense is different than the alternative to nuclear deterrence in the other sense, amounting to unilateral nuclear disarmament in one and mutual nuclear disarmament in the other. So comparing one sense of nuclear deterrence with its alternative need not yield the same preference order as comparing the other sense with its alternative. Of course, it is not within a nation's power to do away with the situation of mutual nuclear threatening in the way that it is within its power to do away with its own nuclear threatening. There is no agent for whom mutual nuclear threatening is a policy.[12] But the abandonment of mutual nuclear threatening may be indirectly within the power of one of the nations, if it is able, through a negotiating process, to convince its opponent to join it in abandoning nuclear weapons. In any case, although we will find reason later to distinguish these two senses of nuclear deterrence, the fact that the consequentialist argument yields the same result in either case means that we need not do so for now.

The confluence between morality and prudence demonstrated

by the consequentialist argument means a joining of the discourses of realism and morality on nuclear deterrence, because the risk of nuclear war swamps any consideration of realist goals that might be opposed to the general interests of humanity. But it would be too quick to claim that this succeeds in avoiding the conflict between morality and prudence, for only half of everyday moral reasoning has been heard from. One cannot claim that nuclear deterrence is overall morally permissible or required without also taking into account the deontological approach. This approach we must now again assume.

NUCLEAR DETERRENCE AS HOSTAGE HOLDING

Nuclear deterrence is sometimes compared to hostage holding. The analogy is especially appropriate for those features of the policy that are the basis of its deontological assessment. Douglas Lackey suggests this, claiming that "the proper moral examples" to use in analyzing nuclear deterrence are "examples of hostage-taking."[13] Morally speaking, nuclear deterrence is hostage holding. Once we broaden our moral perspective beyond the confines of the institutional norms, we see not only that the consequentialist perspective must be given its due, but that an alternative deontological analysis of nuclear deterrence is required. Nuclear deterrence as hostage holding provides a way of formulating the deontological argument that avoids problems that arise from applying the norms of the just-war tradition.

The problems have to do with the just-war tradition's misrepresenting the nature of nuclear deterrence. By focusing on the conditional intention to retaliate, it does not consider the policy as a whole and in its own right, but considers the policy only in relation to another action – nuclear retaliation – in which it might eventuate. This point is developed by Russell Hardin, who argues that focusing on the conditional intention to retaliate misrepresents what is intended, for nuclear deterrence is a policy designed to influence the behavior of another party and the outcome of the policy is dependent on how that party responds.[14] The expected outcome is nonbelligerency and nonaggression, and to focus on the unanticipated outcome (retaliation should deterrence fail) as what is intended by the nation and as something for which the nation would alone be responsible, is to misunderstand the interactive character of the outcome. More generally, nuclear deterrence is different from the military policies that the just-war tradition was developed to evaluate, and the conditional intention to retaliate in nuclear deterrence is unlike the intentions the tradition was developed to assess. Just-war norms were developed to apply to wartime actions, and their application to deterrence is derivative from this. In the case of wartime actions, there is normally little to separate the intention from the action. But in the case of nuclear deterrence, the retaliatory intention, although it relates to a possible future wartime action, is a part of another action, one that is designed to avoid war. As Gregory Kavka argues, deterrent intentions have "autonomous effects that are independent of the intended act's actually being performed."[15]

Although Hardin's main concern is to argue for a consequentialist approach to nuclear deterrence, we may take his criticism as a challenge to find a deontological approach better suited to nuclear deterrence, one that treats the policy of nuclear deterrence in its own right.[16] The analysis of nuclear deterrence as hostage holding does the job. A policy of nuclear deterrence is a policy of making a certain kind of threat to achieve a certain kind of end. The policy involves the conditional intention to retaliate against civilians because it involves threats of that kind. But the analysis of nuclear deterrence as hostage holding treats this intention not in isolation or as the only relevant feature of the policy, but in terms of the role it plays in the overall policy. The focus is on the nature of the threat and what the threatener seeks to do with that threat, not on the conditional intention that it involves. To consider nuclear deterrence as hostage holding is to consider the nature of the policy's threats in relation to its ends. The policy is treated as a whole, with the conditional intention to retaliate being only one of its defining characteristics. What is evaluated is *that* sort of threat-making activity, not merely the conditional intention.

Making nuclear threats is creating a risk that a large number of civilians would suffer or die in one's nuclear retaliation. Nuclear deterrence creates this risk because it involves the conditional intention to attack those persons. But it is the creation of the risk rather than the intention to actualize the harm that should be the focus of attention in a deontological evaluation. Consider an analysis by Douglas Lackey, who contrasts the creation of risk with the "act risked," which is, in the case of nuclear deterrence, the retaliation that is the object of the conditional intention.

This shift of attention from an act risked to the creation of the risk simplifies the evaluation of the intentional characteristics of the act being assessed. For when we consider the act that is risked, we are considering a conditionally intended act, an act that someone intends to perform if, and only if, worst come to worst. But when we consider the act of risk creation, we consider a directly intended act, an act which is a means to a desired end. The moral assessment of risk creation is logically distinct from the moral assessment of risked outcomes or risked acts.[17]

As Lackey suggests, the deontological evaluation should focus on the creation of risk, not on the conditional intention or its object. A hostage-holding analysis does this. Focusing on the creation of risk allows a proper understanding of the means-end relations involved in nuclear deterrence, and thus a clearer insight into the moral status of that policy.

Someone else who treats risk as central to the deontological evaluation of nuclear deterrence is Jefferson McMahan. But the risk he focuses on is not the risk of harm to civilians, but the risk that the nation making the nuclear threats will later do what is morally wrong – harm the civilians through nuclear retaliation. McMahan proposes the deontological principle "that it is wrong, other things being equal, to risk doing that which it would be wrong to do."[18] But this analysis seems to miss what is morally problematic about nuclear deterrence. For, on McMahan's deontological principle, a nation could escape moral objections to nuclear deterrence by creating the legendary doomsday machine, a device that would make nuclear retaliation automatic. If a doomsday machine were set up, retaliation would occur without the intervention of a human agent. So, in setting up such a machine, a nation could avoid creating a risk of a future wrongdoing, because retaliation would involve no doing at all. But it seems that nuclear deterrence is just as morally problematic with a doomsday machine as without, so McMahan's principle cannot be the basis of the moral objections to this policy. The way to view nuclear deterrence is as a practice of creating or imposing a risk on many civilians that they will be harmed. The value of a hostage-holding analysis is that this is the kind of risk that hostage holders impose on their hostages, and it is their imposing this risk that makes what they do wrong.

What is hostage holding? Hostages are persons who are threatened with harm in order to control the behavior of another party, to get that party to do (or not to do) something the hostage holder wants that party to do (or not to do). The party threatened is thus a third party in the threat transaction. Hostage holding is based on what may be called third-party threats. Hostages are innocent parties in the threat transaction, in the sense that they are not the agents of the behavior the threatener seeks to control, and so are not responsible for that behavior. In the case of the more usual sort of threats, second-party threats – where the party threatened is the party whose behavior the threatener seeks to control – that party is not innocent in this sense, because that party would be responsible for (would, in fact, be the agent of) the behavior the threatener seeks to control.[19] Moreover, in the standard case of hostage holding, hostages do not consent to the threat being made against them. This is not always the case, because hostages are sometimes voluntary. Voluntary hostages, in offering themselves as hostages, consent to the threat being made against them, and, for this reason, holding them may, in some cases, be morally permissible. But the more typical case of involuntary hostages is the one we consider here.

The immorality of hostage holding

Hostage holding is morally wrong because (1) it imposes a risk of harm (2) upon innocent persons (3) without their consent. First, the threat, assuming that it is not a bluff, imposes a risk of harm. Because the threat is not guaranteed of success, it may be carried out. Because hostage holding is wrong even when the threat is not carried out, it must be the mere imposition of the risk of harm that is wrong, whether or not the harm is actually inflicted.[20] The success of the threat does not make hostage holding morally acceptable. Analogously, what is wrong with drunk driving is the mere imposition of the risk of harm on others, because it remains wrong even when no one is in fact harmed. But many of our actions impose risk of harm on others, and certainly this is often morally permissible. What makes the risk imposition wrong in the case of hostage holding is the second and third features. Because hostages are not responsible for the behavior the threat is meant to control and because they have not consented to the risk of harm the threat imposes on them, hostage holding does not respect the hostages' choices and is a paradigm example of treating persons not as ends but as mere means.[21]

Hostages are treated as mere means in the sense that their holders use them by imposing a risk of harm on them in pursuit of the holders' own ends. But what makes it invariably the case that hostages are treated as mere means is the fact that they are innocent and have not given consent. If those threatened were not innocent in the sense discussed – that is, if it were their behavior the threatener sought to control – the occurrence of the threatened harm would be contingent on their behavior. The persons threatened might then be treated as ends, at least insofar as it would be their choice that would determine whether or not the harm would be inflicted. In the case of third-party threats, however, the choices of those put at risk of harm do not determine whether or not the harm will be inflicted. Lack of consent is also a crucial feature. If those threatened consented to the imposition of the risk, the imposition would, at least to that extent, be in respect of their choices.[22]

Nuclear deterrence is hostage holding in the sense that it exhibits those features that make hostage holding morally wrong. In a condition of mutual vulnerability, each side threatens the other with societal destruction, which would involve the killing of a large number of its civilians. Most of these people are third parties in the threat transaction, because they are not the agents of the behavior the threatener is seeking to control. Nor have they consented to the imposition of the risk. The threat of their being killed creates a risk of harm to those persons. The threat cannot be a bluff, and there is no guarantee that the threat will succeed, so retaliation may occur.[23] The risk is compounded by the real possibility that a nuclear war will start accidentally, just as the risk to airline hostages is compounded by the possibility that the hijacker's bomb will accidentally go off. Given enough time, the possibility of deterrence failure or accident is not negligible, so the risk is real.[24] The creation of the risk, along with the innocent and nonconsenting status of the hostages, puts the policy at odds with the injunction not to treat persons as mere means.

The kind of behavior the hostage holder seeks from the second party may or may not be something the hostage holder is morally or legally entitled to demand, but hostage holding is wrong in any case. Hostage holders' demands are often illegitimate, but that is not what makes what they do wrong. For example, holding hostages in demand of money is wrong even if the money rightfully belongs to the hostage holder. The tax collector threatening your children with harm unless you pay the government what you legitimately owe it is as much a hostage holder as a mugger threatening your children with harm if you do not hand over your wallet, and the action of each is to that extent morally wrong. Thus, nuclear deterrence cannot be justified by the fact that the behavior the threatening nation seeks from its opponent – nonaggression – is something to which the nation is morally entitled.

This is different from the case of second-party threats, where the moral status of what the threatener demands is relevant to the justification of the threats.[25] This point is not always appreciated. In a discussion of the morality of nuclear deterrence, William Shaw argues that it is in some cases morally permissible to threaten to do something immoral in order to deter a party from behavior from which the threatener is morally entitled to deter it.[26] In light of this, he argues that both nuclear deterrence and threatening a child with a spanking if he or she does not run from a burning building may be morally permissible, despite the immorality of carrying out the threat, because in both cases the threatener is morally entitled to deter (or compel) the behavior it seeks to deter (or compel). But these two cases differ in that one involves a third-party threat and the other involves a second-party threat. This is why, contrary to Shaw's analysis, threatening the child may be morally permissible, but nuclear deterrence is not. In both cases, something immoral is threatened, but in one case it is because of who is threatened (the hostage) and in the other case it is because of what is threatened (the spanking). This difference spoils the analogy.

Some have argued that it is misleading or incorrect to analyze nuclear deterrence as hostage holding because those threatened are not deprived of their liberty, as is normally the case with hostages.[27] But the deprivation of liberty is not a necessary condition of hostage holding, so that a third-party threat without deprivation of liberty, like the threat of nuclear retaliation, would still count as hostage-holding. Although the deprivation of liberty is essential for kidnapping, for example, it is not for the holding of hostages. Imagine that a master criminal laced the food at a banquet with tiny capsules of deadly poison, which the banqueters would unknowingly ingest and which would release their chemical only on a radio signal from the criminal, and that the criminal then demanded a billion dollars on threat of sending the signal. The banqueters would not be deprived of liberty, but it seems entirely appropriate to call them hostages. Deprivation of liberty is contingently required in most cases of hostage holding, because this is the only effective way to put the hostages under threat. But nuclear weapons, because of their tremendous destructive power, make deprivation of liberty unnecessary for the imposition of risk.

On the other hand, the imposition of risk does seem to be a necessary condition of hostage holding. Imagine a group hijacking an airliner with an empty box for a "bomb". One is inclined to say that although the hijackers appear to be holding hostages, they are not really doing so. This would be explained by the fact that though the hijackers appear to be imposing risk on the passengers, there is in fact no risk. If hostages are not deprived of liberty, they may not think much about their status as hostages because there is no confinement constantly to call to their attention the risk imposed on them. Hostages at large may not even realize that they are hostages. But this does not affect their status as hostages, any more than an infant passenger's lack of knowledge of what is going on in a hijacked airliner affects his or her status as a hostage. Even when hostages are deprived of liberty, they may not know they are hostages because they may not realize, for various reasons, that they are deprived of liberty. One is a hostage whether one knows it or not, as one has been robbed whether one knows it or not.

But the semantic issue of whether or not to call nuclear deterrence hostage holding is really beside the point, for the argument survives the loss of the label.[28] The important question is whether nuclear deterrence shares in the general moral wrongness of hostage holding. Those who question the moral analysis of nuclear deterrence as hostage holding would argue that deprivation of liberty is a clear moral wrong that nuclear deterrence does not share with most cases of hostage holding. Thus, Michael Walzer argues: "[Nuclear deterrence] cannot be condemned for anything it does to its hostages. It is so far from killing them that it does not even injure or confine them; it involves no direct or physical violation of their rights."[29] But nuclear deterrence does do something to its hostages: It puts them under a risk of harm, and in so doing treats them as mere means.

In more typical cases of hostage holding, the hostages will also be deprived of liberty, and the psychological cost of terror may be imposed as well, and these are additional reasons for condemning what the hostage holders are doing. A hostage holding that deprives the hostages of liberty and terrorizes them is a greater moral wrong than one that does not, given a similar risk of harm in each case. But neither the deprivation of liberty nor the imposition of terror is the central moral defect in hostage holding, because normally neither is the direct means by which the hostage holder seeks to control the behavior of the second party. Rather, it is through the risk of the harm that would result from the execution of the threat that the hostage holder seeks to wield influence over the behavior of the second party. This is the central moral defect in all cases of hostage holding, and this is the moral defect of nuclear deterrence, whether or not it is labeled hostage holding. Thomas Schelling claims that a stable regime of nuclear deterrence causes no more terror to those held hostage than is caused to pedestrians waiting to cross a busy street in the face of onrushing traffic. Stable nuclear deterrence is more a "balance of prudence" than a "balance of terror."[30] But a lack of such psychic harm, like the lack of confinement, does not undermine the basic moral objection. Walzer is correct that there is no need for the moral critics of nuclear deterrence to postulate psychic harm to the hostages from their being held.[31] Nuclear deterrence is morally wrong whether or not it causes nightmares.

But there are other grounds for arguing that nuclear deterrence does not share in the moral wrongness of hostage holding. Recall the three features that make hostage holding morally wrong: (1) a risk of harm is imposed (2) upon innocent persons (3) without their consent. Nuclear deterrence seems to share all three features, but doubts can be raised.

The risk of harm to innocents

(1) Nuclear deterrence clearly imposes a risk of harm on those persons who might be killed or injured in nuclear retaliation. To deny the existence of this risk would be to deny that deterrence may fail or that nuclear war may occur by accident. No one denies this. But one could argue that though nuclear deterrence creates some risk for its hostages, it actually lowers their risk overall. William Shaw argues that nuclear deterrence lowers the overall risk of death to its hostages because it lowers the risk of their dying in a conventional war more than it increases the risk of their dying in a nuclear war.[32] The conclusion of the consequentialist argument is that a nation's policy of nuclear deterrence leads to better consequences for humanity than its unilateral abandonment. Perhaps this includes better consequences for the opponent's civilians. If

so, then even though deterrence creates a risk of their dying in a nuclear attack that would not otherwise exist, it would be of overall benefit for those thus put at risk. But this criticism does not work.

The moral objection to nuclear deterrence as hostage holding is not simply that risk is created, but that that risk is used in a morally unacceptable way, that those put at risk are used as mere means. This objection applies because nuclear deterrence is based on the threat of societal destruction. Conventional military deterrence is not based on such a threat, so the risk posed to civilians by conventional war is not the principal element on which conventional deterrence is based. Conventional deterrence is based primarily on the threat of denial, whereas nuclear deterrence is based primarily on the threat of punishment.[33] A threat of punishment treats civilians as a means because it uses the risk to them to achieve deterrence, whereas the threat of denial does not do this. So even if nuclear threats lower the overall level of risk to their hostages, this does not blunt the chief moral objection to the risk the threats create.

(2) The second feature necessary for the moral wrongness of hostage holding is that the persons upon whom the risk is imposed are innocent. Recall that innocence here means that these persons are third parties in the threat transaction. They are not the agents of the behavior the threats are meant to control, and hence they exercise no choice in whether or not the threatened harm will be inflicted. But some claim that the citizens of a nuclear power are not completely immune morally from the risk of harm from nuclear retaliation. Gregory Kavka argues that accepted notions of collective responsibility may serve to justify nuclear threats.[34] When a collectivity takes an action that is morally wrong, its members' actions, which contribute, at least in some small way, to that action, are, taken individually, often morally blameless. Despite this, he argues, it is appropriate to hold the members of the group liable, at least partially, for the collective action. This shows that the citizens of a superpower would not be completely innocent concerning the behavior of their leaders for which retaliation is threatened, and so imposing on them a risk of harm by threatening such retaliation may be morally acceptable.

But this argument does not seem to apply to nuclear hostages, for the vast majority of them would make no contribution to the behavior for which retaliation is threatened, such as the initiation of nuclear war. It cannot be said that their contribution to such behavior makes them liable to being threatened, despite their moral blamelessness, for they would make no contribution at all to such behavior.[35] The collectivity to which Kavka's analysis would apply is not the nation as a whole, but only a small part of its governmental apparatus, primarily its military and political leadership. The number of persons making a contribution to the launching of a nuclear attack, whether by making or by carrying out the decision, may be very small, perhaps no more than a few hundred. Nor is there anything most of the citizens of the threatened nation could do to intervene to stop the launching of the attack once the decision had been taken. James Child argues that citizens may share in the responsibility for their nation's behavior not only by contributing positively to it, but by omitting actions they could have taken to stop it.[36] But this does not apply when the behavior in question is a nuclear attack. There would be nothing most citizens could do to stop a nuclear attack, if their leaders decide to launch one. Even for nuclear powers that are democracies, the decision to launch a nuclear attack would be made undemocratically by a very small group, and, for obvious reasons, the utmost efforts would be made to keep the decision secret prior to its execution. To claim that all the citizens of a nation must be liable for the initiation of nuclear war because the nation itself is liable is to commit the fallacy of division.

Nuclear weapons narrow rather than expand the class of those persons who may legitimately be attacked, or put at risk of attack. Recent great-power conventional wars have tended to turn into extended contests of economic attrition, and so have required for their pursuit the active contribution or passive acquiescence of virtually the whole of the adult populations of the belligerents. Such wars have tended to be total wars, in the sense that they have required the mobilization of entire nations. Some commentators have used this fact to argue that those traditionally treated as non-combatants need no longer be so treated, because virtually all citizens contribute to the war effort. This move to abandon the distinction between combatants and noncombatants has been resisted, in theory if not in practice.[37] But nuclear weapons have dramatically reversed the trend toward greater citizen involvement in wars.[38] A nuclear war would involve few military personnel and would be fought exclusively with the armaments at hand, lasting too short a time for public pressure to play any role in its termination. A nuclear war would be a total war in the sense that whole societies could be targets for destruction, but it would not be total in the sense that is relevant for claims of an expanded circle of responsibility. There is little case for collective responsibility where the fighting of nuclear war is concerned.

But this discussion may interpret Kavka's argument too narrowly. For although it is true that very few of the opponent's citizens would be directly involved in its initiation of nuclear war (or other aggressive behavior), a very large number might be indirectly involved, in the sense that they would have contributed, through positive action or acquiescence, to the creation of the military capability that is the instrumental prerequisite for the initiation of nuclear war. But if this wider net is cast only over those involved in making the weapons and formulating the policy, it would still capture far too few people to justify threats of societal destruction. For the argument to work, the net must be cast over virtually the whole population. What if the indirect contribution is understood to include political involvement? Nuclear weapons policies and capabilities are brought into being through a political process, and there is a clear sense in which society as a whole is involved in this process, through action or acquiescence, especially in a democracy, but also perhaps in a nondemocratic state.[39] The net, however, is still not cast widely enough, because large numbers of citizens, especially children, are completely outside the political process. There seems no way in which they could be regarded as responsible.[40] For this reason, the argument fails. The fact of society-wide political involvement (including acquiescence) in the creation of nuclear weapons policy and capabilities cannot show that all, or even almost all, of those put at risk by the nuclear threat are noninnocent, and so cannot justify nuclear threats of societal destruction.[41]

But there is a more fundamental reason why the argument from political involvement cannot show that nuclear deterrence does not share the moral status of hostage holding. The kind of responsibility it attributes to the opponent's civilians is not the sort that could justify the threat against them. On most accounts, a person's use of violence in self-defense is justifiable because of the danger the attacker poses to the person, whether or not the attacker is responsible for the attack, in the sense of being blameworthy. When this idea is extended to the case of national self-defense, the implication is that the opponent's military personnel are liable to be the target of defensive violence simply because of the danger they pose to the nation, whether or not they are blameworthy for posing that danger (which they may not be, if, for example, they have been forced to fight). This leads to the familiar idea, mentioned in the last chapter, that innocence in war is not lack of blameworthiness for military action, but simply lack of involvement in the action.[42] On the other hand, the blameworthiness of civilians for the opponent's initiation of war does not justify their being the target of the nation's defensive violence if they are not involved in the attack.[43] So a person who is responsible for the initiation of war but is not involved in the war is innocent in the sense relevant to the question of justifying military violence or the threat of such against that person. Thus, even if all the opponent's citizens were indirectly responsible for the opponent's initiation of a war as a result of their political involvement or acquiescence, they would be morally immune from being put at risk by military threats. This returns us to the earlier idea that the nuclear threat could be justifiably made only against that small number of people who would be involved in the attack the threat is meant to deter.[44]

The lack of consent

(3) The final feature essential to the moral wrongness of hostage holding is the lack of consent on the part of those upon whom the risk of harm is imposed. Nuclear hostages are not voluntary hostages. But although there clearly is no expressed consent from the nuclear hostages themselves, there may be an indirect basis on which their consent could be established. Perhaps consent has been given not by them, but for them. Thomas Schelling claims that nuclear deterrence "is simply a massive and modern version of an ancient institution: the exchange of hostages."[45] The hostages have been not so much mutually taken as mutually traded. This suggests that nuclear deterrence may be viewed as a situation in which each superpower has given consent for its citizens to be held hostage by the other superpower, in exchange for the other superpower's giving consent for its own citizens to be held. The governments have given proxy consent for their citizens to be subject to the nuclear threat.

Douglas Lackey suggests a historical episode that might be taken as the act by which the United States and the Soviet Union granted such proxy consent: the signing in 1972 of the SALT I and ABM treaties.[46] One could take the view that by signing these treaties, which limit the number of nuclear-weapons launchers and restrict the deployment of antiballistic missiles, each side agreed to allow its population to remain vulnerable to destruction by the other – that is, each side agreed not to attempt to escape from the condition of mutual vulnerability. If this is a correct interpretation of the treaties, does it mean that proxy consent to the imposition of the risk from the nuclear threats was then given? The question seems to be not merely whether the governments were attempting to give, or thought they were giving, proxy consent, but, in addition, whether they were morally entitled to give proxy consent. For the claim that one has given proxy consent is not made true merely by one's claiming to have given it, but by the legitimacy of one's giving it. Given the seriousness of the risk imposed by the opponent's nuclear threat, it would be a difficult matter to show that the government was morally entitled to give proxy consent for the making of that threat.[47]

But perhaps the government would be entitled to give proxy consent if in doing so it would be acting in its citizens' own best interests. This sort of paternalistic justification assumes that if the citizens correctly appreciated the situation, they would see the wisdom of consenting to the nuclear risk, and would consent. In a similar vein, Gerald Dworkin poses the question whether it might be possible to offer to those on whom the risk is imposed an adequate justification for its imposition in terms of their own interests.[48] If proxy consent to the nuclear risk would hold only when such risks were in the citizens' best interests, the issue becomes one of hypothetical consent.[49] The question is whether the citizens would consent to the nuclear risk if they were rational and fully informed. If so, the citizens may be taken to have hypothetically consented to the risk, and this may count for moral purposes in lieu of actual consent. In matters of large-scale social policy, such as nuclear deterrence, where risk is invariably created for or redistributed among citizens, hypothetical consent must count morally as real consent, otherwise the utter impracticality of acquiring expressed consent would mean that little in the way of social policy would be justifiable.[50]

Consider a case where hypothetical consent may be said to exist – the risk posed to others by the drivers of automobiles.[51] Drivers of automobiles put others at a significant risk of injury or death, a risk to which those others have not expressly consented. But the driving of automobiles provides a great economic and personal benefit to nearly all persons in society, whether they drive or not. One could argue that they have hypothetically consented to the risk, insofar as the risk is well worth the benefits in terms of their own interests. Is the risk from the nuclear threat like the risk from automobile driving in this respect? There is one important difference. The population that is put at risk from automobile driving is the same as the one that benefits from the practice, which is why it is plausible to argue that there is hypothetical consent. But in the case of nuclear threats, the population that directly benefits is not the one that is put at risk. It is the citizens of the nation who primarily benefit from the risk their government imposes on the opponent's civilians.

But still, the consequentialist argument concludes that all of humanity, not simply the nation's own citizens, benefit overall from that nation's policy of nuclear deterrence. This suggests that the opponent's civilians may also benefit overall from this policy, in which case the hypothetical consent of those civilians to that policy is established, even if they are not the policy's primary beneficiaries.[52] But it does not follow from the fact that a nation's policy of nuclear deterrence is of overall benefit to humanity as a whole that it is at the same time of overall benefit to the opponent's civilians. There is some reason to think that it is not, given the way in which the abandonment of the policy would raise the level of risk for humanity as a whole.

According to (P2) of the consequentialist argument, a nation's unilateral abandonment of nuclear deterrence is of overall disbenefit to humanity because it would create instability in the international order, increasing the likelihood of war, even of nuclear war. But the negative consequences of this instability would fall disproportionately on those who are not the citizens of the remaining nuclear superpower. The citizens of the remaining nuclear superpower would to some extent be insulated from the increased possibility of military conflict by their nation's preponderant nuclear might. This claim is controversial, but what is important for our concern is its very controversiality. A hypothetical consent argument works only when the benefit of consent is clear, for only then can consent be shown to be rational. If benefit is not clear – if it is a controversial matter whether there is overall benefit – then rational people could disagree, and hypothetical consent cannot be shown. Because it cannot clearly be shown that the opponent's citizens benefit overall from the nation's policy of nuclear deterrence, the notion of hypothetical consent cannot successfully be used to blunt the charge that that policy is a morally unacceptable form of hostage holding.

Apart from the hostage-holding argument, there is an important deontological defense of nuclear deterrence – namely, that it is justifiable on defensive grounds. As claimed earlier, nuclear deterrence is a defensive use of nuclear force. In a situation of mutual vulnerability, each nation's nuclear threatening is in response to the opponent's nuclear threatening, and hence is an effort at defense. But such an argument seems doomed from the start, as the discussion from Chapter 1 suggests. Although defensive use of military force is, in general, morally justifiable, nuclear threats are not, because they necessarily involve the intention to attack civilians. The conclusion is the same in terms of the hostage-holding analysis, where the point is that the legitimacy of the hostage holder's demands cannot justify the hostage holding. Nuclear weapons are morally special because in a situation of mutual vulnerability, they are weapons whose use or threatened use, even for legitimate defensive purposes, cannot be justified.

But Greg Kavka believes that "there are deontological arguments, based on the right to defend oneself and innocent others, that do serve to counterbalance deontological objections to nuclear deterrence."[53] He grants that there are moral limits on what a nation may do in self-defense, but he claims that these limits are more permissive than the limits assumed in the hostage-holding analysis. He argues that it is at least sometimes permissible to put innocent people at risk to protect oneself, and that nuclear deterrence may be such a case. Kavka's argument (and the arguments of others' as well) that nuclear deterrence is justifiable on grounds of self-defense relies partly on the characterization of nuclear deterrence as a policy that redistributes risks from some innocents to other innocents – that is, from the citizens of the nation adopting the policy to the citizens of its opponent.[54] A nation whose citizens are put at risk by an opponent's nuclear threatening may be justified in lessening that risk by redistributing some of it onto the opponent's citizens through reciprocal nuclear threatening. Nuclear threatening results in risk redistribution because, as Douglas Lackey puts it: "By deploying strategic weapons the United States *decreases* the chance of a Soviet attack on the United States by *increasing* the chance of an American attack on the Soviet Union."[55]

Kavka introduces several examples that he claims provide intuitive support for the view that self-defense sometimes justifies imposing risks on the innocent. One is the practice of quarantine, which confines the victim of a contagious disease to avoid its spread to others. Another is a situation in which a teacher discovers a bomb about to go off in the classroom, and tosses it out the window, thereby putting at risk anyone who might be passing by.[56] Both quarantine and the bomb tossing are justifiable, he claims, and both are cases where risk of harm (from loss of liberty, illness, or bomb blast) is self-defensively redistributed from some innocents to other innocents. Risk is redistributed from those who might catch the disease to those who would be quarantined or from those who would be in the classroom when the bomb is found to those who might be then passing by. But there are examples that seem to go the other way. Imagine a bank robber holding hostages. Would it be permissible for the hostages to lure innocent passers-by from the street into the bank so that they too could become hostages, thereby lessening the chances that the original hostages would be harmed (say, the robber has threatened to shoot one hostage chosen at random if demands are not met by the end of the day)? The original hostages might attempt to justify this on the grounds that it is simply a self-defensive redistribution of risk from some innocents to other innocents. Here, one's inclination is to say that this redistribution would not be justified.

What distinguishes these cases? The answer is that a hypothetical consent argument can successfully be made in the quarantine and bomb-in-the-classroom cases, but not in the bank-hostages case. The argument works in the first two cases because a rule allowing the redistribution of risk in such cases lowers everyone's expected level of risk – that is, the total amount of harm is lowered in such a way that each person, as far as he or she can know, is more likely to be better off from the policy than worse off. The person quarantined suffers for the sake of lessening the risk to those who might be infected, but the overall level of harm is less and, so far as each person can foresee, he or she is less likely to be quarantined than to benefit from another's being quarantined. The passer-by put at risk by the bomb tossed out of the classroom suffers for the sake of those in the classroom, but not only is the bomb likely to cause less harm outside the classroom than inside, assuming that fewer people are likely to be in its vicinity, as far as any individual can know, he or she is more likely to be inside the classroom than just outside of it. Under these conditions, it is in the interest of each person to give consent to the rule. This analysis explains why the hypothetical consent argument does not apply to the bank-hostages case. Everyone's expected level of risk is not lowered because there is no reason to think that the redistribution of the risk lowers the overall level of harm, so that it is not the case that each person should believe himself or herself to be better off as a result of a rule allowing innocents to be lured into the bank.

If the notion of hypothetical consent is the way to distinguish cases in which self-defensive redistribution of risk from some innocents to others is justifiable from cases in which it is not, then nuclear deterrence is a redistribution of risk which is not justifiable. The situation in this case is different from that in the previous discussion of hypothetical consent, where the issue was whether or not the opponent's civilians could be said hypothetically to consent because the nation's policy of nuclear deterrence is of overall benefit to them. Assuming that the policy is not of overall benefit to them, the current argument concludes that the risk or disbenefit the nation's policy of nuclear deterrence creates for the opponent's civilians is justifiable because it is a redistribution of risk from some innocents to others. But the opponent's civilians could not be said to have hypothetically consented to a rule allowing the risk redistribution that nuclear deterrence brings about, because although it may be that nuclear deterrence lowers the overall level of risk, it cannot be shown that each person's expected level of risk is lower. For a person's expected level of risk to be lower, that person must be able to foresee that he or she is more likely to benefit than to suffer from the rule. This is the case with the quarantine rule, because, as far as one can know, one could end up either a person quarantined or a person benefitting from the quarantining of someone else, and because there are more of the latter than of the former, one is more likely to benefit than to suffer from the risk redistribution of the quarantine rule. But this is not the case for the risk redistribution of nuclear deterrence.

One of the opponent's civilians cannot expect to be more likely to benefit than to suffer from the nation's policy of nuclear deterrence, because, unlike the case with the quarantine rule, the future does not hold out for him or her the realistic prospect of being a beneficiary of the policy instead of one who suffers from it. The marginal factor of emigration aside, one knows what one's nationality will be in the future. Although there is a sense in which it is true that a citizen of one nation might just as well have been that of another nation, that sense is not adequate to establish hypothetical consent. For if hypothetical consent is plausibly to substitute for actual consent, and hence do the theoretical work it is supposed to do, it must remain as close to actual consent as possible. As a result, it must assume the extent of knowledge that actual people would have available to them. In terms of such knowledge, each person should believe that his or her expected level of harm would fall from the quarantine rule, because, as far as this person can know, he or she could end up either beneficiary or victim of the rule. But a person knows his or her own nationality, and hence knows in advance whether he or she would be beneficiary or victim of a rule allowing some nation to redistribute risks by maintaining a policy of nuclear threats. As a result, such a rule is not in everyone's expected best interest, so that not all persons hypothetically consent to it.[57]

Thus, the argument for nuclear deterrence on defensive grounds – that it is a justified redistribution of risk from some innocents to other innocents – fails. This argument is not a successful challenge to the criticism of nuclear deterrence as hostage holding, and the conclusion must be that in terms of the deontological approach, nuclear deterrence is morally prohibited.

THE NATURE OF THE MORAL DILEMMA

Nuclear deterrence presents a moral dilemma. The consequentialist argument shows nuclear deterrence to be morally required, whereas the deontological argument shows nuclear deterrence to be morally prohibited. There are very strong moral reasons both for continuing the policy and for abandoning it. Of course, the pluralism of everyday moral reasoning frequently generates moral conflicts between the consequentialist and deontological approaches. Given this pluralism, moral conflicts are genuine or real, in the sense that everyday moral reasoning does not always provide a   univocal answer to the question of what ought to be done.[58] But the moral dilemma of nuclear deterrence is, in degree and in kind, unlike other moral conflicts arising in personal and political relations. The moral problem posed by nuclear weapons is special. The magnitude of the moral stakes involved in this dilemma represents a serious challenge to the coherence of our everyday moral view.

Some speak of the moral problem raised by nuclear deterrence as a dilemma and others speak of it as a paradox. Although these terms are often used interchangeably, they can be used to draw an important distinction. Consider Gregory Kavka's discussion of the moral paradox of nuclear deterrence.[59] According to Kavka, the balance of terror (the condition of mutual vulnerability) may well be an example of a "special deterrent situation" (SDS), and in an SDS "it would be wrong for the defender to apply the sanction if the wrongdoer were to commit the offense, but it is right for the defender to form the (conditional) intention to apply the sanction if the wrongdoer commits the offense." In other words, assuming that nuclear deterrence is an example of an SDS (which I shall), sincerely threatening nuclear retaliation is right, even though actually retaliating would be wrong. This is paradoxical because it is inconsistent with a widely accepted moral principle – the "wrongful intentions principle" (WIP) – according to which it is wrong for one to intend to do what one knows would be wrong to do. The reason why conditionally intending nuclear retaliation may be right while carrying out that intention would be wrong, despite the WIP, is that in an SDS, such intending has "autonomous effects" – that is, effects independent of the action that is conditionally intended. The autonomous effects are the threat's deterrent effects. The "paradox arises because the autonomous effects of the relevant deterrent intention are dominant in the moral analysis of an SDS, but the extremely plausible WIP ignores such effects."

The autonomous effects of nuclear threats provide a strong moral argument in favor of nuclear deterrence. In Kavka's view, this argument is morally decisive. The autonomous effects dominate the moral analysis. For him, the moral problem of nuclear deterrence is not a problem for practice, because there is no doubt that it is morally permissible or required to practice nuclear deterrence. Rather, it is merely a problem for reflection. Although there is no practical doubt about the moral permissibility of nuclear deterrence, one is puzzled by this and is led to reflect on how this can be, in light of the resulting contravention of the wrongful intentions principle. The moral situation is like the alleged inconsistency between the flight of the bumblebee and the laws of aerodynamics: There is no doubt about whether the bee can fly; the question is, rather, how is this possible, given our understanding of the laws of nature? Similarly, Kavka is uncertain only about *why* nuclear deterrence is right, not about *whether* it is right. This distinction between whether and why is the one I wish to mark: A moral dilemma is a problem for practice, in the sense that whether or not some action is right is not clear, whereas a moral paradox is a problem merely for reflection, in the sense that the right course of action is clear but there is puzzlement about why this should be. It is an important feature of the moral problem of nuclear deterrence that it is a dilemma rather than a paradox.

Kavka sees the moral problem of nuclear deterrence as a paradox rather than a dilemma because he gives clear precedence in his analysis to the consequentialist approach over the deontological approach. The reason is that he adopts the normative assumption that "the act favored by utilitarian considerations should be performed whenever a very great deal of utility is at stake."[60] In other words, whenever a great deal is morally at stake in terms of consequences (or, more narrowly, he later suggests, whenever consequences of great harm can be avoided), the consequentialist perspective is morally decisive. Kavka's argument, on this understanding, is consistent with everyday moral reasoning, which also gives precedence to the consequences whenever they put a great deal morally at stake. But this implies that the kind of moral paradox he discusses is not unique to special deterrent situations. For the paradox lies ultimately in the applicability of his normative assumption, the possibility of consequentialist considerations being given precedence in situations where there is a strong deontological argument pulling in the other direction. This suggests that if the moral problem of nuclear deterrence is a paradox, as Kavka understands it, there is nothing special about it. Many other kinds of moral conflicts would be paradoxical in the same sense. But the question is whether the moral problem of nuclear deterrence is better characterized as a paradox or a dilemma.

The adoption of something like Kavka's normative assumption has proven attractive in moral discussions of nuclear deterrence. Michael Walzer adopts a similar assumption, embodied in his doctrine of "supreme emergency," which holds that when a nation can avoid a catastrophic amount of harm (specifically, its own imminent destruction) only by violating the "war convention" (a set of just-war type deontological norms), it is entitled to do so.[61] A concern for the avoidance of catastrophic consequences outweighs a concern for deontological constraints in war. Nuclear deterrence is morally justifiable, in Walzer's view, because a nation's vulnerability to destruction by its opponent creates for it a permanent condition of supreme emergency, a situation where catastrophe always looms, and so allows a nuclear counterthreat, presuming this to be the only effective response available, despite the fact that it violates the war convention. Moral absolutists, who claim that deontological norms should never be overridden, often argue that the kind of counterexamples to their position offered by critics, where "the heavens would fall" but for someone's violating deontological constraints, are unreal, in that agents never in fact confront such situations. But the choice of whether or not to practice nuclear deterrence may well be such a situation, as Walzer suggests. A large-scale nuclear war would have to count as the heavens' falling, if any event within human control could.[62]

If ever there is a case, then, when consequentialist considerations should override deontological ones, it seems that nuclear deterrence is that case. "In normal circumstances," Douglas Lackey asserts, "one may have one's doubts about utilitarianism, but if nuclear war is among the results of policies under consideration, the gravity of the consequences carries all else before."[63] The moral problem of nuclear deterrence thus appears to be a paradox, as Kavka maintains, rather than a dilemma. But this is too quick. Nuclear deterrence does indeed put a great deal morally at stake in terms of consequences. It does so not simply because the weapons are tremendously destructive, but because nuclear deterrence is a large social institution. Only a large institution could develop and maintain a vast nuclear arsenal, and so make possible the catastrophe that raises the consequentialist stakes to unprecedented heights. But the institutional character of nuclear deterrence also magnifies tremendously what is at stake in terms of deontological considerations. It does not necessarily follow from the fact that there are great consequentialist stakes involved in nuclear deterrence that the consequentialist approach is morally decisive. The deontological stakes have been raised to unprecedented heights as well.

Resolving moral conflicts

Some distinctions are needed. The pluralism of everyday moral reasoning leads to the occurrence of moral conflicts, situations where different moral approaches, in particular, the consequentialist and the deontological approaches, are at odds. Some moral conflicts are real and some are merely apparent.[64] In addition, most conflicts, whether real or apparent, can be resolved, but the method of resolution is different depending on whether the conflicts are real or apparent.[65] Apparent conflicts are resolved when it is shown that they are apparent – that is, when it is shown in the case of two conflicting seeming obligations that only one is real. If one of the seeming obligations is not real, neither is the conflict. Real moral conflicts are resolved when a reasoned decision can be made between the conflicting obligations in the recognition that both obligations are real and continue to hold despite the resolution. In other words, real moral conflicts are resolved when, despite the conflict, it is clear overall what morally should be done. It is because this is not always clear that some real moral conflicts are not re-solvable. Our interest at this point is in real moral conflict, because given the soundness of the consequentialist and deontological arguments, nuclear deterrence represents such a conflict.

There are two strategies for resolving real moral conflicts. First, they are resolved when it is clear in the particular situation that one of the approaches in conflict outweighs the other in moral importance and so should be given precedence over the other and treated as morally decisive. This comparative weighing of the obligations the moral approaches imply in the situation in question must be rough and intuitive, because there is no precise measure of moral importance. When it is unclear which of two conflicting prescribed actions should be performed because the moral advantage and disadvantage seem roughly balanced, the first resolution strategy fails and the second should be considered. The second resolution strategy seeks some alternative action or policy that effectively turns the conflict into one that is resolvable under the first strategy. Considering a conflict to be a case where one of the two conflicting prescribed actions (say, A) has both a moral advantage and a moral disadvantage by comparison with the other (B), res-olution of the conflict involves finding a third alternative action (C) that would secure all or most of the moral advantage of A, while avoiding all or most of its moral disadvantage. If such a C could be found, the conflicts between C and A and between C and B would be weaker than the conflict between A and B, so that the conflict could then be resolved by the first strategy. An alternative action that satisfies this condition I will call a *viable alternative*.

The first resolution strategy for real moral conflicts would apply to Plato's example about whether to return the arms left with one for safe-keeping when their owner comes for them in a deranged state of mind. This example may be construed as a case of conflict between a consequentialist approach, which would require that the arms not be returned, and a deontological approach, which would require the return of the arms on the basis of the obligation to return property to its owner that one assumes in agreeing to watch over it. It is clear that the consequentialist approach should take precedence, because it is in this case clearly of greater moral importance. On the other hand, if the example were constructed so that there would be only relatively minor consequential advantage in failing to fulfill the obligation to return the property – for example, the property could not be used to do harm to others but might be damaged by the owner in his deranged state – then the deontological approach would take precedence, and the resolution of the conflict would be in the return of the property.

The following case illustrates the second resolution strategy. Imagine that Jones is driving to a very important county council meeting, which she, as the chair, has a strong obligation to attend, when she is first upon the scene of a serious auto accident. It is clear to her that if she does not stop to provide assistance, the risk that the motorist will die of his injuries is somewhat greater than if she does stop to render assistance, but that if she does stop she will miss the meeting. This is an example where, given the right details, the moral conflict is not resolvable under the first strategy, because neither approach would clearly outweigh the other in that situation. But if Jones has a car phone, her calling for assistance might be a viable alternative, allowing for the conflict's resolution, because calling could reasonably be thought to secure most of the consequentialist advantage of lessening the risk of the motorist's death while involving the less serious deontological disadvantage of only being late for the meeting.[66]

A real moral conflict that is not resolvable is a moral dilemma. A moral dilemma may thus be defined as a real moral conflict for which the two resolution strategies fail. A moral dilemma is a real moral conflict that satisfies two conditions. The first is that an intuitive weighing of the conflicting prescriptions of the moral approaches in that situation does not yield a clear sense that either is decisive. In other words, neither seems clearly of greater moral importance than the other. Different moral approaches can be compared only intuitively and in a rough way because they are only weakly commensurable. For a large class of cases, the comparison will not yield clear results.[67] Comparing moral approaches is, it seems, like comparing a string quartet and a novel in terms of overall artistic quality. The comparisons have an apples-and-oranges character. In some cases it will be clear that the novel is better than the string quartet (when the novel is good literature and the string quartet is bad music, for example), or vice-versa, but in other cases this will not be clear. In cases where the first condition is satisfied, a moral conflict may be formalized in terms of a moral antinomy – that is, a pair of conflicting arguments about what ought to be done each of which is of roughly equal persuasiveness. When such pairs of arguments exist, practical reason, given the weak commensurability of the moral approaches, cannot choose between them. The second condition for a moral dilemma is that there is no viable alternative – that is, no alternative action that turns the conflict into a one resolvable under the first strategy. If Jones lacked a car phone in the above example, her moral conflict would be a moral dilemma.

Moral dilemmas show practical reason to be at odds with itself. They are instances where everyday moral reasoning fails us, where morality provides equivocal practical guidance. But not all moral dilemmas are matters of life and death. They may be distinguished by the importance of what is at issue. When the moral stakes are very high, a moral dilemma is tragic, and when they are not, it is nontragic.[68] A moral dilemma involving the telling of a "white lie," for example, would be nontragic, because the stakes would be small – a trivial untruth on one side and a minor harm from hurt feelings on the other. An example of a tragic moral dilemma would be the situation of Sartre's young Frenchman who during the second World War was torn between staying at home to care for his aged mother and going off to join the anti-Nazi resistance. "Torn" is the word here, because with high moral stakes on both sides, one is not merely pulled in opposite directions, but is pulled very strongly. High-stakes moral dilemmas are tragic because whatever the agent does, he or she will be acting against very strong moral reasons. Whatever the agent does requires sacrificing a great deal of moral value.

A final distinction is that between moral conflicts that occur at the personal, individual level, and those that occur at the institutional level. Moral conflicts occur at the institutional level when the choice is over social policy, especially when the choice concerns establishing or maintaining a large-scale institution. A moral conflict is at the personal or individual level when the choice concerns a relatively small number of persons. Choices of social policy generally affect a very large number of persons. If there are any moral dilemmas among the moral conflicts at the institutional level, they are likely to be tragic, because the widespread effects of an institution can easily raise the moral stakes very high.

Kavka and Walzer see nuclear deterrence as a real moral conflict, but as one that is resolvable. They recognize that in the case of nuclear deterrence there is a conflict between the deontological and the consequentialist approaches, but they see this conflict as settled by the recognition that the consequentialist approach takes precedence. This is why for Kavka the moral problem of nuclear deterrence is a paradox rather than a dilemma. For Kavka and Walzer, the conflict does not puzzle the will, as it would if it were a moral dilemma. The test of whether nuclear deterrence is a resolvable moral conflict, as they believe, or a moral dilemma, is whether the consequentialist argument for the policy and the deontological argument against it constitute a moral antinomy, and, if so, whether there is a viable alternative. I will argue that the policy choice concerning nuclear deterrence is a moral dilemma, and, indeed, a tragic moral dilemma. What must first be shown is that the consequentialist and deontological arguments regarding nuclear deterrence constitute a moral antinomy.

Moral conflicts and social institutions

Because large-scale social institutions strongly affect, for good or ill, a large number of people, they are morally very important. In terms of both the consequentialist and deontological approaches, when large-scale social institutions are involved, the moral stakes are often very high. The high consequentialist stakes result from the large number of important consequences, affecting many people, that such institutions bring about or of which they significantly affect the likelihood. Assuming that the beneficial and the harmful consequences do not largely cancel each other out, there will be strong consequentialist reasons for either having or not having the institution. The consequentialist argument shows that there are strong consequentialist reasons for having the institution of nuclear deterrence.

Large-scale social institutions sometimes generate high deontological stakes as well. Many institutions are designed to correct serious conditions of social injustice (usually brought about by other social institutions), and to the extent that they succeed in this, there will be strong deontological reasons in favor of them. On the other hand, institutions may create serious conditions of social injustice, whether or not by design, in which case there will be strong deontological arguments against them. No human institution is free of injustice, but if the injustice is accidental and infrequent, the deontological case against that institution based on its injustice will be relatively weak. Often, however, the injustice perpetrated by an institution is systematic rather than accidental. Injustice is often a characteristic result, built into the operation of the institution. For example, an institution of criminal "justice" that always punishes members of one racial group more harshly than members of another for commission of the same crimes, or that sets out to "punish" those known not to be guilty of the crimes for which they are punished, would be systematically unjust. Such an institution would have a deontological defect characteristic of its operation, and there would be a strong deontological argument against it. So an institution may raise the deontological stakes high either because it successfully corrects serious conditions of social injustice or because it systematically creates such conditions.

The holding of hostages is a deontological disadvantage characteristic of nuclear deterrence. In its holding of hostages, nuclear deterrence is systematically unjust. This moral defect is not occasional and accidental, but is necessary to the operation of the institution. It is the means by which the institution seeks to achieve its goals. Nuclear deterrence raises the deontological stakes high. How high? A rough measure of the deontological disadvantage of the policy may be made by considering both the number of its victims and the seriousness of the injustice that it perpetrates on each. Some moral theorists may reject the idea of measuring the deontological wrongness of nuclear deterrence by taking into account the number of people against whom the wrong is done.[69] Some might maintain that, for example, because it is absolutely wrong to kill an innocent person, killing one innocent person is no less wrong than killing one hundred. But such an understanding of deontological norms seems incorrect, given the pluralism of everyday moral reasoning. There must be a deontological difference between killing one innocent and killing one hundred, because some sets of consequences would presumably outweigh the wrong in the one case but not in the other. In terms of this rough measure, the deontological stakes in the case of nuclear deterrence are very high. The number of people the policy holds hostage is very large – in the hundreds of millions – and the injustice against each of these victims is significant, for they are put at a substantial risk of death or severe suffering, and the risk is not temporary, but continues over long periods of time.[70]

The consequentialist stakes are indeed high, unprecedentedly so, but the deontological stakes are as well. In the light of this, is one or the other approach decisive or do the arguments constitute an antinomy? It is not surprising that many judge that the consequentialist approach has precedence, given the magnitude of the consequences. But those who are quick to judge it so may be like the yahoo who, when asked to judge a grand opera competition, awards the prize to the second competitor upon hearing only the first on the grounds that the second could not be worse. The consequentialist stakes must be weighed against the deontological stakes, and they are very high in both cases. Given the weak commensurability of the approaches, it cannot be said that one clearly outweighs the other. When one appreciates the force of both the consequentialist and deontological arguments concerning nuclear deterrence, one cannot clearly see that one is morally decisive in comparison with the other. These two arguments constitute a moral antinomy. Everyday moral reasoning, with its rough, intuitive method of comparing the conflicting prescriptions of different approaches, cannot clearly designate one or the other as having precedence.[71] It is not simply that the stakes in each case are very high, but that given how high they are in each case, one cannot decide between them.[72]

But to show that the moral problem of nuclear deterrence is a dilemma, the second resolution strategy must be tried. One must determine whether or not there is a viable alternative policy. That there is none is implied by the consequentialist argument. Its conclusion is that continuing to practice nuclear deterrence has great consequential value in comparison with its abandonment. But the abandonment of nuclear deterrence is a generic action covering all policies alternative to maintaining nuclear deterrence. It follows that there is no policy alternative to nuclear deterrence that would achieve most of the consequentialist advantage of nuclear deterrence. There is, then, no alternative policy that would allow the conflict to be resolved under the first strategy. This is inherent in the condition of mutual vulnerability. When a nation is vulnerable to destruction by its opponent's nuclear weapons, it either maintains a policy that is systematically unjust or it brings about a loss of great consequential value. In a situation in which the opponent threatens to destroy one's society, national security and great overall consequential value cannot be effectively achieved without a policy that holds the opponent's citizens hostage. Because the moral conflict of nuclear deterrence satisfies the two conditions, the conclusion is that the moral problem of nuclear deterrence is a dilemma. Moreover, it is a dilemma of tragic proportions.

Great nations are now in the position that individual terrorists are in. Both are, morally speaking, hostage holders. Only morally unacceptable means are available to individual terrorists to achieve the benefits they believe would follow from a redress of their political grievances. Nuclear weapons have put the great powers in the same situation. As enamored of consequences as individual terrorists, the great powers also practice terrorism. Individual terrorists face their moral dilemma because they are militarily too weak to challenge their opponents in a traditional military manner, whereas the nuclear powers face their moral dilemma because they are militarily too strong to challenge their opponents in a traditional military manner.[73] The only nonhypocritical objection that those practicing nuclear deterrence can make of individual terrorists is that the latter, unlike the former, face a moral conflict that is apparent rather than real. A nuclear deterrer could claim that the moral conflict of individual terrorists is not real because their consequentialist argument is unsound. Taking planeloads of hostages is not an effective way to make the world a better place. There is, of course, a difference in scale, because individual terrorists do not hold their hostages through a large-scale institution. As Richard Falk says: "Nuclear weaponry and strategy represents terrorist logic on the grandest scale imaginable."[74] The individual terrorist may hold a planeload of people hostage for a few days, whereas nuclear deterrence holds whole societies hostage into the indefinite future.

The moral uniqueness of nuclear deterrence

The argument so far has considered the nature of the moral problem of nuclear deterrence, concluding that it is a tragic moral dilemma. Now I would like to examine how this moral problem is distinctive in relation to other moral problems. The moral problem of nuclear deterrence, I will argue, is unique. It is the only moral dilemma involving the choice of a large-scale institution. The argument for this will be in two stages: first, that moral dilemmas are unlikely to occur in the choice of large-scale institutions; and second, that there is, as a matter of fact, no moral dilemma involving a choice of a large-scale institution but for the choice of maintaining or abandoning nuclear deterrence. The implication is that nuclear weapons policy is the only area of large-scale social policy where everyday moral reasoning is unable to provide guidance. This inadequacy in our everyday moral view in a matter of such overriding importance is disturbing. The moral problem nuclear deterrence presents is both unique and profound.

Two notions need to be introduced. First, a *central social purpose* is a purpose that a social order must serve to survive. Examples of central social purposes are providing a sufficient amount of agricultural product, keeping violence among individuals at a low level, and providing national security. Second, a *central institution* is a large-scale institution or institutional framework that serves a necessary and important function in achieving a central social purpose.[75] For example, slavery in the antebellum South, collective farms in the former Soviet Union, individual entrepreneurial farming, and corporate farming are different central institutions serving the central social purpose of providing sufficient agricultural product. Nuclear deterrence is a central institution serving the central social purpose of providing national security.

Central institutions have two notable features. First, they usually have a variety of social purposes in addition to their central social purpose, some of which they may have had from their inception and others of which they may acquire later as vested interests develop from the way the institution restructures the social situation. For example, Southern slavery had the social purpose of maintaining a landed aristocracy, but this purpose, not being necessary for the existence of the society, as agricultural production is, is not a central social purpose. In addition to providing national security, nuclear deterrence has also acquired the social purpose of maintaining certain military and industrial bureaucracies, but only the former is a central social purpose. A central institution must have at least one purpose that is a central social purpose. The other social purposes a central institution serves often create militant constituencies, which fight to preserve the institution even when it no longer serves, or is no longer the best way to serve, its central social purpose. The second feature is that because central social purposes must be fulfilled for a society to continue, successful central institutions normally have consequences of great moral value. But the strength of the consequentialist argument for successful central institutions will depend on comparing their consequences with those of other central institutions, if any, that could serve the same central social purpose.

The claim I argue for can now be stated more precisely. Nuclear deterrence represents the only moral dilemma involving the choice of a central institution, and in that sense the moral problem of nuclear deterrence is unique. The first stage of the argument is to show that moral dilemmas are unlikely to arise in the choice of central institutions. The reason is that large-scale institutions restructure the moral situation in such a way that there tend to be fewer moral dilemmas at the institutional level than at the personal level. As a result, there is less likelihood of there being moral dilemmas that involve a choice of central institutions.

The existence of large-scale institutions restructures the moral situation in such a way that the achievement of morally valuable consequences partly depends on respect for deontological norms. A just institution is more likely to be successful at achieving its social purpose than an unjust one. At the institutional level, more than at the personal level, justice tends to produce beneficial consequences and injustice harmful consequences. A large-scale institution that is systematically unjust tends to be ineffective because of its injustice. The reason is that the success of an institution, and hence its achievement of good consequences, depends on an adequate level of compliance with its rules, and compliance is fostered by the perception that it is just and fairly administered and undermined by the perception that it is not.[76] So if the institution is systematically unjust, its good consequences are less likely to be achieved. People will, over the long run at least, be less responsive to the demands of the institution, leading more often to institutional inefficiency and failure.

This point is related to the basic insight of rule utilitarianism, which is that consequential value will generally be maximized when a society follows social rules that are coincident with or respectful of deontological norms. More generally, consequential value will tend to be maximized when a society's large-scale institutions (including its social rules) are in accord with deontological norms. Consider the familiar comparison between blame at the personal level and punishment at the institutional level. At the personal level, there may be strong consequentialist reasons, in terms of deterrent effects, for A to blame B for some wrongful act of which

A knows B not to be guilty, if other members of the social group believe that B is guilty. But if this sort of reasoning were applied in the choice of a large-scale institution, and it became social policy to punish the nonguilty, the fact that the nonguilty were being punished would likely become known, and the resulting confusion and perception of unfairness would greatly undermine the deterrent effect of the institution and lead to other consequences of disvalue.

The restructuring of the moral situation brought about by institutionalization means that at the institutional level, bad consequences tend to follow policies that are not in accord with deontological constraints. Consider what this implies for the choice of central institutions. Choosing a central institution involves selecting from a set of alternative possible central institutions that could serve the central social purpose in question. Choosing from among the members of this set may involve moral conflicts, in the sense that an alternative that is more effective than another may have deontological shortcomings in comparison with it. But if bad consequences tend to follow policies not in accord with deontological constraints, it is unlikely that any member of the set that is systematically unjust would also be the one that is most effective – that is, has the best consequences. Only if this were the case could the choice involve a moral dilemma. Even if one of the alternatives combined systematic injustice with the best consequences, it would be likely, because systematic injustice and effectiveness tend not to go together, that another alternative would be a viable alternative, in which case the conflict would not be a dilemma. For example, the moral conflict involved in Southern slavery was not a dilemma, because even if it were true that slavery had the best consequences considered as a mode of agricultural production, there were other alternatives, such as agricultural wage-labor, which would not have been systematically unjust, but would have been nearly as effective in achieving the needed agricultural product.

Despite this tendency for institutionalization to bring about common cause between consequentialist and deontological approaches, there remain many moral conflicts at the level of social policy. Some of these conflicts are not moral conflicts in the sense discussed here, because they involve a conflict within a single moral approach rather than between different moral approaches. For example, the conflict over whether government should adopt a policy to fight inflation or a policy to ease unemployment, assuming that these are conflicting aims, may be construed as simply a consequentialist matter, there being no significant deontological issue necessarily at stake.[77] But many moral conflicts occurring at the level of social policy – for example, those involving trade-offs between liberty and welfare – are real conflicts between the moral approaches. But where such conflicts are present at the level of large-scale social institutions, the tendency of institutionalization to bring about common cause between the consequentialist and deontological approaches means that it is likely that one or the other resolution strategy will be applicable to them, so that they would not be dilemmatic. One area where large-scale social institutions may seem to raise a serious moral conflict between liberty and welfare is in the choice of a nation's economy. But debates over economic systems usually center around issues within a deontological approach and implicitly deny that there is any serious moral conflict involved. Socialists, welfare-state advocates, and free marketeers generally argue not only that their positions are required by respect for the moral rights of persons, but that consequentialist advantage is on their side as well.

The tendency for institutionalization to bring about common cause between consequentialist and deontological approaches is not evident in the case of nuclear deterrence. The systematic injustice of nuclear hostage holding seems to have no negative impact on the effectiveness of nuclear deterrence. Instead, if the consequentialist argument is sound, it is the very source of the policy's effectiveness. In this case, there is a moral dilemma at the level of a central institution. One reason for the difference may be that nuclear deterrence is institutional in a different sense than other institutions. Other institutions are contained within a single society. This means that those upon whom the institution has a major impact are part of the society which has the institution. Such institutions may be referred to as domestic institutions, meaning that their effects are largely contained within the society whose institution they are. But nuclear deterrence is nondomestic, in the sense that a major impact of that institution – namely, the risks it creates – falls upon members of a different society. Moreover, in the case of many other institutions, those who must comply with the rules if the institution is to succeed, are, by and large, those upon whom the institution has its major impact. This is not so for nuclear deterrence, where citizens of the other society are put at risk in order to induce rule compliance on the part of their leaders. Under these conditions, it is not surprising that the systematic injustice would have little impact on the effectiveness of the policy.

But the fact that nuclear deterrence is a nondomestic institution cannot alone be the reason that it involves a moral dilemma. Any military institution designed to achieve the central social purpose of providing national security is also a nondomestic central institution. Conventional military deterrence is such an institution, and, prior to the nuclear age, choosing this institution to achieve national security did not involve a moral dilemma. The reason is that conventional deterrence is based primarily on the threat of denial rather than punishment. The effectiveness of conventional deterrence comes in its threats against military forces. Because conventional weapons cannot create a condition of mutual vulnerability, a threat of societal destruction is neither possible nor needed as a counterthreat against such a threat from one's opponent. But nuclear weapons spoil the possibility of a nondilemmatic choice of policy to provide national security. In a condition of mutual vulnerability, the choice of whether to maintain a policy of nuclear deterrence or to abandon it for a policy of exclusively conventional deterrence is a moral dilemma, because the lack of systematic injustice that conventional deterrence allows would be purchased at the price of a great loss of moral advantage in terms of consequences. Speaking of nuclear weapons, Robert Tucker suggests: "Technology may render irreconcilable moral demands men had previously been able somehow to reconcile."[78]

The second stage of the argument for the uniqueness of the moral problem of nuclear deterrence seeks to show that there are in fact no other moral dilemmas involving the choice of a central institution. If there are no others, the conclusion that institutionalization tends to make it less likely that moral dilemmas will occur at this level of social policy would explain why this is the case. The argument now makes use of the notion of a *roughly just society*, which is a social order in which none of the central institutions is systematically unjust.[79] I will assume that with the exception of their nuclear deterrence policies, if any, all societies either are roughly just or could be made so through changes in their central institutions. This is a widely shared assumption, because it is held by both defenders of the political status quo and their radical reformist or revolutionary critics. The assumption is that in terms of all central institutions with the exception of those concerning national security (in the case of nations having or facing an opponent with an as-sured-destruction capability), a roughly just society is possible. In other words, all central social purposes, again with the exception of national security where nuclear weapons are involved, can be successfully achieved by central institutions that are not system-atically unjust.

From this assumption, it follows that there are no moral dilem-mas involving the choice of such institutions. For the possibility of a society's being roughly just shows that any of that society's in-stitutions that is systematically unjust has an alternative that would achieve the same central social purpose, but that is not systemat-ically unjust. That alternative institution would avoid the moral disadvantage of the systematically unjust institution. At the same time, it would secure at least most of the consequentialist advantage of the systematically unjust institution. The reason is that the al-ternative institution, by hypothesis, succeeds in achieving its cen-tral social purpose, and because most of an institution's good consequences come from its achieving its central social purpose, the alternative would have at least most of the consequentialist advantage of the systematically unjust institution. This means that the alternative institution is a viable alternative, and the existence of a viable alternative precludes the choice of the systematically unjust institution constituting a moral dilemma. With the exception of institutions of national security for nations possessing or con-fronting an assured destruction capability, there are, then, no moral dilemmas in the choice of central institutions.

So the moral problem of nuclear deterrence – the problem of choosing a central institution for national security when nuclear weapons have made possible a condition of mutual vulnerability – is unique. It is the only moral dilemma concerning the choice of central institutions. There have been institutions that have raised deontological problems more serious than that raised by nuclear deterrence – for example, slavery and the Holocaust. But either these institutions were not central institutions, because, like the Holocaust, they served no central social purpose, or there was no moral dilemma over their choice, because, as with slavery, there were viable alternative institutions. Thus, the existence of such iniquitous institutions never challenged the possibility of a roughly just society. But nuclear weapons make this challenge. As long as the central social purpose of providing national security remains, nuclear weapons make a roughly just society impossible, in the sense that nations facing an opponent with an assured destruction capability must adopt or maintain a systematically unjust institution if they are to achieve the central social purpose of providing national security. The uniqueness of the moral problem of nuclear deterrence reveals the fundamental character of the change in our world brought about by the invention of nuclear weapons.[80]

Consider, as a thought experiment, a group of American abolitionists meeting in the mid-nineteenth century to discuss the morality of slavery. Most of them probably would have argued against the institution on deontological grounds, but others might have chosen consequentialist grounds, arguing, against those who claimed that slavery was socially necessary, that there are alternative institutions that could achieve a high level of agricultural production without bringing about the harm that slavery does to those enslaved. Imagine this group, their conversation taking a speculative turn, pondering how the human condition would have to change in order for someone to be able successfully to argue on the grounds of social necessity for a central institution that, like slavery, is systematically unjust. One participant might suggest that, should someone invent a potion that made those who drink it completely unconcerned about their own personal welfare, but left them still concerned about the welfare of their loved ones, the institution of criminal punishment might have to be adjusted out of social necessity so that sanctions were threatened against family members of the lawbreakers rather than against the lawbreakers themselves. Another might go on to suppose that should humans invent a way for one nation to destroy another without defeating its military forces – for example, by the development of long-range flying machines and compact explosives of fantastic power – the only way to deter war might be to establish an institution that threatened such destruction. At the time, these two suggestions would have seemed equally incredible. What is surprising, now that that second speculation has become reality, is how much we take that reality for granted. We seem not to comprehend how the world has changed, and, as a result, we do not recognize the moral gravity of our situation.

Our adoption of the perspective of everyday moral reasoning has not caused the problem discussed in Chapter 1 to disappear, but rather has simply shifted its locus. In the context of the institutional norms, nuclear deterrence gives rise to a practical dilemma, a sharp conflict between morality and prudence, whereas, in the context of everyday moral reasoning, it gives rise to a specifically moral dilemma, a sharp conflict within morality itself. The conflict between morality and prudence replicates itself within the broadened moral perspective in the form of the moral dilemma. Because the institutional moral norms of the just-war tradition represent primarily a deontological approach, the conflict there is between prudence and a deontological moral approach. But because of the confluence nuclear weapons bring about between the prescriptions of prudentialism and consequentialism, the conflict between morality and prudence implies a conflict between a deontological approach and a consequentialist approach within morality itself. Thus, the two conflicts are closely related.

In Chapter 1, the claim was that the sharp conflict between morality and prudence showed that morality in the form of the just-war tradition had become politically irrelevant. But now it is clear that morality is irrelevant in a more profound sense. Morality, in the context of everyday moral reasoning, is irrelevant because the moral dilemma of nuclear deterrence implies that morality is unable to guide practice in the choice of a policy of national security. In the first instance, morality is made politically irrelevant by prudence, or, more precisely, by our tendency to let prudential considerations dominate political decisions. But in the other instance, morality makes itself irrelevant by having nothing to say, or, rather, having too much to say, speaking with equal conviction in favor of inconsistent prescriptions. The result is, in David Hollenbach's expression, "a crisis in moral reasoning itself."[81] Nuclear weapons challenge the coherence of our everyday moral view.

SOLVING THE MORAL PROBLEM

The moral problem of nuclear deterrence is represented by both of the conflicts. Unless the problem can be solved, there is no hope that reason can guide action in this crucial area of policy. Living with the two conflicts is not tolerable. Our tasks are to reconcile the moral and prudential assessments of nuclear deterrence and to remove the moral dilemma. These are in fact a single task. For the moral assessment of nuclear deterrence in terms of the just-war norms yields the same prescription as that of the hostage-holding analysis, whereas the prudential assessment yields the same prescription as the consequentialist evaluation. As a result, any solution that reconciles morality and prudence should also remove the moral dilemma, and vice-versa.

Solving the moral problem requires resolving the two conflicts. But because the conflicts are dilemmas, they have no resolution, if they are understood as real conflicts. As a result, resolution of the conflicts requires that one show them to be apparent rather than real. As discussed earlier, a conflict is shown to be apparent, and is thereby resolved, by a demonstration that one of the obligations in conflict is not real. There are three approaches one could take to show that the conflicts are apparent rather than real.

The first approach is to attempt to show that the obligation to maintain nuclear deterrence believed to arise from the consequences of its abandonment does not exist. Showing this would establish that both conflicts are apparent rather than real. Concern for consequences would then not be out of accord with the deontological considerations that find nuclear deterrence morally unacceptable. This approach would require showing that the consequentialist and prudential arguments for nuclear deterrence are unsound. Given the widespread belief in the soundness of the prudential argument, a showing that this argument is unsound would lead to a radical revision in what we normally count as prudent in the area of military activity. As a result, the first approach may be referred to as *prudential revisionism*. If this approach does not work, a second is available.

The second approach seeks to show that the conflicts are apparent by showing that the obligation not to practice nuclear deterrence does not exist. This obligation is thought to arise from the deontological arguments, and, taking this approach, one seeks to show that these arguments – the hostage-holding argument and the just-war argument – are unsound. This approach would remove the dilemma and reconcile institutional morality and prudence from the other direction, as deontological considerations would then be no bar to accepting the prudential and consequentialist requirement that nuclear deterrence be practiced. Those strategists and moralists who take this approach do not argue that all forms of nuclear deterrence avoid the deontological objections, but that some forms do – specifically, forms based on counterforce targeting. The second approach, unlike the first, distinguishes among different forms of nuclear deterrence, different deterrent strategies, arguing that the conflicts are apparent because some strategies avoid the deontological objections that apply to other forms or strategies of nuclear deterrence. (The deontologically acceptable forms of deterrence would then be viable alternatives to unacceptable forms.) The result of accepting this approach would be not a revision in our sense of what counts as prudent, but a revision in how nuclear deterrence is practiced – that is, a revision in nuclear strategy. So this approach may be referred to as *strategic revisionism*.

Up to this point, we have been treating nuclear deterrence in an undifferentiated way, as a single kind of institution rather than as an institution which may take different forms. But differences in nuclear strategy may be morally and prudentially relevant, and much of the later argument in this book will turn on distinctions among different forms of nuclear deterrence.

If either of these two approaches succeeds, it will turn out that the fundamental challenge nuclear deterrence appears to raise to our moral view does not stand. The success of either approach would leave nuclear weapons, however revolutionary they may be in other respects, more-or-less secure within the parameters of everyday moral reasoning. They would not be seen to call into question the coherence of our moral view. But if these two approaches do not succeed, the effort to show the conflicts to be apparent must be pursued in a very different manner.

In order to show the conflicts to be apparent, one of the obligations in conflict must be seen not to exist. If the first two approaches fail, it follows that neither obligation can be shown not to exist, because the argument for it would not have been shown to be unsound. But if one cannot show one of the obligations nonexistent, perhaps one can *make* one of them nonexistent, thereby making the conflict involving that obligation apparent rather than real. This might be done by altering the principles on which the argument for that obligation is based, which would make that argument unsound by falsifying its assumptions. The basic moral principle of respect for innocent civilians is at odds with both prudentialism and consequentialism. If that principle were altered in an appropriate way, the obligation not to practice nuclear deterrence would not exist. Both conflicts would then have been made apparent. This is the third approach to resolution of the conflicts.[82] It is to see the need to change the fundamentals of our moral view.[83] This approach may appropriately be called *moral revisionism*. Suggesting this, George Quester proposes that in the light of the moral objections to nuclear deterrence, "perhaps we ought simply to adjust our morality."[84] The Catholic bishops of West Germany spoke of the need created by the nuclear confrontation to adopt an "emergency set of ethics."[85] Robert Nozick speaks of nuclear deterrence as creating "a rift in the (moral) universe," and as representing "an unprecedented situation [that] may call for the revision of accepted principles which in no way envisioned that situation."[86]

Moral revisionism is clearly a last resort, an approach not to be adopted if it is at all avoidable. One reason is that it is not clear that it is an intelligible option, because the idea of altering morality may not make sense. Another reason is that though it would solve the moral problem of nuclear deterrence in one sense, it would leave it unsolved in another. It would solve the problem in the sense that it would provide a resolution of the conflicts, a way of showing them to be apparent rather than real. But in a deeper sense, the problem would remain unsolved. The motivation for finding a solution to the moral problem is the concern that were the conflicts to stand, our moral view would be revealed to be incoherent, as a result of its being unable to guide practice in the choice of national security policy. Although the third approach, if intelligible, would nominally resolve the conflicts, it would do so at the expense of admitting the conclusion we had sought to avoid – namely, that our moral view is incoherent. For it is the very incoherence of our moral view that would make it necessary to change it in the fundamental way prescribed by the third approach.[87]

The first approach implies the most radical critique of existing practices, requiring the abandonment of nuclear deterrence. The second approach implies a milder critique of existing practices, requiring, at most, that we revise the way in which we practice nuclear deterrence by adopting a different nuclear strategy. The third approach provides no critique of existing practices at all. Because this approach would adjust morality in order to accommodate prudence, it would leave everything as it is. It is a token of the revolutionary nature of nuclear weapons that the third approach, which is the most radical conceptually, would have the least impact on practice.

Prudential revisionism will be considered first. The next two chapters are devoted to the vexing question of whether nuclear deterrence works – that is, whether or not it is prudentially preferable. The answer to this question separates prudential revisionism from the other two approaches. If nuclear deterrence does not work, then prudential revisionism is the correct approach and we should, on both prudential and moral grounds, abandon the policy. But if it does work, we should continue to practice nuclear deterrence and seek the solution to the moral problem of nuclear deterrence in the second approach. What the next two chapters do is to take up again the prudential argument, and thus implicitly also the consequentialist argument on which it is based. These arguments need more careful scrutiny, in part because, as presented earlier, they relied on the institutional norms. These norms may prove to be an inadequate representation of prudence in the face of the changes that nuclear weapons have wrought. What we will find, however, is that enlarging our prudential perspective beyond the institutional norms leads to a conflict within prudence, in the way that enlarging our moral perspective beyond the just-war norms leads to a conflict within morality, though the logical character of the two conflicts is different.

Chapter 3

The logic of deterrence

Is practicing nuclear deterrence prudentially preferable to not practicing it? Does prudence in the end counsel maintaining or abandoning nuclear deterrence? This is the central question in any examination of the fundamentals of nuclear weapons policy. The conclusion in Chapter 1 was that nuclear deterrence is, in prudential terms, justifiable, hence preferable, but there the discussion was restricted to the traditional approach to the evaluation of military policy. A broader prudential perspective must now be considered, as a broader moral perspective was considered in Chapter 2. The results of considering nuclear deterrence from a broader prudential perspective will have important implications for the moral appraisal of the policy, because of the confluence between the prudential and the consequentialist assessments. The consequentialist argument in Chapter 2 is based on the prudential argument in Chapter 1, so that if nuclear deterrence is shown, from the broader prudential perspective, to be preferable, then one may assume that the consequentialist argument from Chapter 2 stands and that the moral conflict remains unresolved. But if nuclear deterrence is shown not to be prudentially preferable, the implication is that the consequentialist argument from Chapter 2 is unsound and that the consequentialist assessment is not opposed to the deontological assessment. Each would prescribe or allow the abandonment of nuclear deterrence. The pursuit of national security would then be plagued neither by the sharp conflict between prudence and morality nor by the conflict represented by the moral dilemma. In this chapter, a theory of deterrence effectiveness will be developed that will help to answer (in the next chapter) the question whether or not nuclear deterrence is prudentially preferable.

DOES NUCLEAR DETERRENCE WORK?

The question is often put: Does nuclear deterrence work? When considering this form of the question, it is important to note that "deterrence" is normally a success term.[1] To say that a party practices deterrence is to imply not only that it attempts to deter but also that it succeeds in deterring. On this understanding, however, the claim that nuclear deterrence works would be trivially true. To be interesting, the question requires reformulation: Does the attempt to deter with nuclear threats work? But for the sake of simplicity, I will mean by "deterrence" what is more precisely referred to as "attempted deterrence." Deterrence will be taken not to imply success, so that the question whether it works is not trivial.

How should the question whether nuclear deterrence works be understood? First of all, it must be taken as comparative. To say that nuclear deterrence works, or has been successful, means not only that the policy has some effect of the sort it is supposed to have, but that it is more effective in this regard than alternative policies. The question, understood as comparative, may be taken in at least three different ways. These three different senses of the question are illustrated by three different ways of arguing for the claim that nuclear deterrence during the Cold War did *not* work. (1) Some would argue that nuclear deterrence did not work because in the historical situation of the Cold War there was no work for it to do. There has never a need for the United States or the Soviet Union to deter each other through military means, because there was no deep history of national enmity between them nor any outstanding disputes sufficient to lead one to aggress against the other or to attempt to coerce the other with military force. (2) Some would argue that nuclear deterrence did not work because whether or not there was a serious adversarial relation between the United States and the Soviet Union, military force is not, in general, the most effective way of dealing with an adversarial relationship.

The lines of argument represented by (1) and (2) are really addressed to the broad question whether there is a need for any form of military deterrence between nations, the first raising this question about the U.S.-Soviet relationship in particular, and the second raising it about international relations in general. In either case, if there is no need for military deterrence, there is no need for nuclear deterrence. In contrast with these is a third way of arguing. (3) Some would argue that nuclear deterrence did not work because though some military deterrence will, in general, be needed between adversaries, nuclear threats themselves are not the most effective form of military threat. This line of argument is general, like (2), but it differs from both (1) and (2) in that it does not concern the broad question whether military deterrence of any kind is needed, but rather it addresses the narrower question whether military deterrence between adversaries is enhanced by the reliance on nuclear threats.[2]

The broad question is about the *absolute deterrent value* of nuclear threats – that is, the effectiveness of such threats in comparison with a policy of no military threats at all, whether the basis for questioning their effectiveness is that they are not needed in some particular case, as in (1), or in general, as in (2). On the other hand, the narrow question is about the *marginal deterrent value* of such threats – that is, their effectiveness in comparison with conventional military threats.[3] The broad question is political, in the sense that it concerns either the nature of the political relations between two particular nations and whether that relationship is sufficiently adversarial to require some form of military deterrence, or the nature of adversarial political relations in general and whether such relations between nations are best handled in military terms. The narrow question is specifically military, in the sense that it assumes that adversarial political relations between nations may require some form of military deterrence, and focuses on which form of military deterrence would be more effective.

The narrow question is our question, because my concern is the limited one of seeking to understand the difference nuclear weapons make. In other words, I assume that there is need for military force in the world, and ask what difference nuclear weapons make, given this need. In contrast, the broad question, represented by arguments (1) and (2), calls into question the need for military deterrence of any kind. In addition, our question differs from the question addressed by (1) in that our question, like the question addressed by (2), is general. Our question assumes that military deterrence is sometimes needed between adversarial nations and asks how nuclear weapons affect military deterrence where it is needed. The end of the Cold War and the Soviet Union does not affect the general question about the comparison between nuclear and conventional deterrence. The question addressed by (2), which is the pacifist's question, is not our question because though the pacifist's question is properly general in that it does not concern a particular adversarial relationship, it is too broad in that it does not distinguish between nuclear and conventional deterrence.

Given that our question assumes the need for military deterrence, it is clear that it concerns the marginal, rather than the absolute, deterrent value of nuclear threats. On the assumption that military deterrence is needed, the question of absolute deterrent value is not helpful in making policy decisions. Assume that one knows that nuclear deterrence has absolute deterrent value, that it leads to there being less of the sort of aggressive behavior it is meant to deter than would be the case were there no threats at all. This is not what one needs to know in order to decide whether or not to practice nuclear deterrence, given the alternative of conventional deterrence, because conventional deterrence might do the job better. One wants to know whether nuclear deterrence works better than conventional deterrence, and this is the question of its marginal deterrent value. By analogy, when one wants to know whether capital punishment works as a deterrent, the question is not whether threatening death leads to fewer murders than threatening no punishment at all, but whether threatening death leads to fewer murders than threatening some lesser punishment, such as life imprisonment.[4]

The question, then, is whether nuclear deterrence has marginal deterrent value. This question is not identical with the question whether nuclear deterrence is prudentially preferable, understood in an unqualified sense, because our assumption of the need for military deterrence restricts the range of alternative policies that might be considered. Some alternative arrangement for national security, such as nonviolent civilian resistance, might be preferable to any form of military deterrence. But for our purposes the question of prudential preferability should be understood in a restricted sense. The question is whether nuclear deterrence is prudentially preferable, given that military deterrence is necessary in some cases of adversarial relations between nations. This is to ask whether nuclear deterrence has marginal deterrent value in those cases. This restricted sense of the question of prudential preferability was implicit in the argument that nuclear deterrence is prudentially justifiable in Chapter 1, because that argument was cast in terms of the traditional norms of evaluation for military policy. It was also implicit in the consequentialist argument in Chapter 2, because that argument was based on the same considerations as the argument concerning prudential justifiability. In both cases, the alternative to the abandonment of nuclear deterrence was assumed to be the replacement of nuclear deterrence by conventional deterrence.[5] Although I consider in this chapter and the next a prudential perspective broader than that of the institutional norms, the questions of prudential and consequentialist preferability will remain restricted by the assumption that military deterrence is necessary in some cases of adversarial relations between nations.[6] Broadening the inquiry beyond this restriction is outside the scope of this book.

One complication in that an answer to the question whether nuclear deterrence has marginal deterrent value depends on what counts as deterrence effectiveness or success, and this depends on the range of the opponent's behavior the threats are meant to influence. How well nuclear deterrence works depends on the work it is meant to do. People have different expectations for what nuclear threats can deter and different views about what they should be used to deter. Most agree that nuclear threats can and should be used to deter war, but there is disagreement about the extent to which they can and should be used to deter lesser aggressive behaviors. People's view on this tend to vary to some extent with the kind of nuclear strategy they champion, with those advocating counterforce strategies often believing that nuclear threats can deter a broader range of aggressive behaviors than those critical of such strategies. To be a fair comparison, the judgment of marginal deterrent value should be based on the effect of nuclear deterrence and conventional deterrence in influencing a similar range of behavior. The two forms of military deterrence will be compared in terms of their effectiveness in avoiding war.[7] A chief virtue of military deterrence is its ability to avoid war. But a nation's efforts to avoid war will be understood to include, as well, its avoiding major aggression by the opponent against its interests, because such aggression would normally lead to war.[8] Thus the goal of avoiding war encompasses also the goal of maintaining national sovereignty, because threats to sovereignty can lead to war.

A common argument

How should the question whether nuclear deterrence has marginal deterrent value be answered? A common argument is that the absence of war between the United States and the Soviet Union during the Cold War has shown that nuclear deterrence works.

Presumably this argument is meant to show that nuclear deterrence has marginal deterrent value, because it implies that there would have been a war if the two nations had had only conventional weapons. The problem with this argument is that it offers no evidence for the claim that there would have been a war if there were only conventional weapons, and so establishes no substantive link between the presence of nuclear weapons and the absence of war. It commits the *post hoc ergo propter hoc* fallacy, in that it demonstrates no connection beyond mere concurrence between nuclear deterrence and the absence of war. An argument is needed to show that nuclear deterrence is responsible for there having been no war. As John Mueller asserts: "The absence of war – successful deterrence – does not necessarily prove that a *policy* of deterrence has been successful."[9] The argument that nuclear deterrence works because there has been no war exhibits the error made by the superstitious urbanite who is sure that the amulet she wears to keep elephants away works, because there have been no elephants about since she began wearing it. Like Russell's man falling from atop a skyscraper, we should not conclude that things will continue to go well because they go well for some period. That forty-five stories or forty-five years go by without catastrophe does not show that catastrophe is not likely.[10]

What the argument needs, of course, is evidence supporting the counterfactual claim that but for nuclear deterrence there would have been a war between the United States and the Soviet Union. More precisely, what needs support is the claim that during the Cold War the likelihood of a superpower war was less than it would have been had there been only conventional deterrence. It is important to recognize that the issue is one of likelihoods. What can be said for nuclear deterrence is not that it guarantees no war, but that it reduces the likelihood of war, and what can be said against it is not that it insures war, but that it increases the likelihood of war, in each case, in relation to the likelihood of war if only conventional deterrence had been practiced. The claim that nuclear deterrence has marginal deterrent value is (in large part) the claim that it decreases the risk of war. The need for the argument to be formulated in terms of likelihoods puts the fact that the Cold War never became hot even further from providing sufficient support of the claim that nuclear deterrence has marginal deterrent value. There simply has not been enough experience with nuclear deterrence to provide adequate support for the counterfactual judgment.[11] The history of nuclear deterrence has been too short, especially in the light of the fact that nuclear deterrence in the relevant sense (that is, in a condition of mutual vulnerability) did not come into being until the 1960s.[12] A simple appeal to the absence of war between the United States and the Soviet Union is inconclusive in showing that nuclear deterrence has marginal deterrent value.

The insufficiency of this evidence notwithstanding, most people take it to be an obvious truth that nuclear deterrence works. What can account for this conviction? It may be due to a belief in the effectiveness of military deterrence in general. Because nuclear deterrence is a form of military deterrence, the belief that military deterrence is effective may be uncritically assumed to imply that nuclear deterrence is as well. This is a plausible interpretation, given the kinds of justifications frequently invoked for nuclear deterrence, such as "we must meet force with force" or "all our opponent understands is force." But such justifications do not distinguish between different kinds of military force. To assume that the effectiveness of nuclear deterrence follows from the effectiveness of military deterrence in general is to beg the question whether nuclear threats have marginal deterrent value. Such an assumption, in effect, substitutes the notion of absolute deterrent value for that of marginal deterrent value. The mistake is in thinking that if nuclear threats have absolute deterrent value, they must also have marginal deterrent value. This is like believing that capitcal punishment is effective because threats of death, like threats of any form of serious harm, will have some deterrent effect. The real question is whether threats of death are more of a deterrent than threats of other harm, such as extended imprisonment. Strongly felt convictions about the effectiveness of nuclear deterrence and capital punishment may in this way be systematically mistaken.

The objection that a simple appeal to the absence of superpower war cannot support the claim that nuclear deterrence works connects to a more general doubt about the possibility of establishing such a claim. Some philosophers who have considered consequentialist arguments about nuclear deterrence have voiced this doubt. They have claimed that one cannot determine the likelihoods of possible events such as nuclear war and aggression with sufficient accuracy to make judgments about the effectiveness of nuclear deterrence. Speaking of nuclear war and aggression, John Finnis, Joseph Boyle, and Germain Grisez claim: "The immense evils involved in either prospect plainly are incalculable; their occurrence, timing, gravity, and persistence are not accurately predictable."[13] Gregory Kavka argues that "reliable quantitative utility and probability estimates" concerning the choice between continuing and abandoning nuclear deterrence are not available.[14] Richard Werner argues, regarding this choice, that there is "a great deal of speculation concerning expected outcomes of the various alternatives, but little by way of warranted assertions." This is due to the fact that participants in the debate approach the debate over nuclear deterrence with ideological commitments "severely underdetermined by the facts."[15]

Deterrence theory

These objections to the possibility of an adequate consequentialist assessment of nuclear deterrence show that the problem of determining whether nuclear deterrence has marginal deterrent value runs deeper than objections to the superficial argument based on the absence of superpower war. The problem is more general, and the only way it can be addressed is through a higher level of generalization in the argument. The question whether nuclear deterrence has marginal deterrent value must be treated in a more theoretical manner. Theorizing about nuclear deterrence is, of course, nothing new. It is something that nuclear strategists do. But the problem with much of strategic theory is that it is, in an important sense, insufficiently theoretical. Much of it does not generalize enough. It often simply compares different forms of nuclear deterrence with each other, rather than comparing nuclear deterrence with a broader class of deterrent threats. It examines the marginal deterrent value of one form of nuclear deterrence by comparing it with another form – for example, by comparing counterforce nuclear threats with countervalue nuclear threats. Little or no attention is given to the question whether nuclear deterrence has marginal deterrent value in comparison with conventional deterrence. The theoretical question is taken to be, in effect, which form of nuclear deterrence works best. This is like approaching the question of capital punishment by asking whether the threat of hanging is more effective than the threat of a firing squad.

There is another way in which theorizing about nuclear deterrence has been insufficiently general. This is evident in the work of Thomas Schelling. In one sense, Schelling generalizes to a remarkable degree, avoiding the objection discussed in the last paragraph. Nuclear deterrence, he argues, is simply one species of bargaining behavior, one in which the parties involved, because of a mixture of conflict and common interest that characterizes their relationship, interact in such a way that though one party gains at the expense of the other, each comes out ahead in terms of its own values.[16] Such a result comes about through threats. When threats are successful, the threatener gains at the expense of the party threatened (if only because the former party does not lose to the aggression of the latter), but the party threatened comes out ahead relative to what would have been the case had the threat been carried out. For example, when blackmail is successful, the blackmailer gains at the expense of the blackmailed, but the party blackmailed is also better off than he or she would have been had the blackmailer publicly revealed the incriminating or embarrassing information. For such bargaining situations, Schelling develops a powerful theory, "the strategy of conflict," from which he draws important conclusions that have become part of our basic understanding of deterrence. But Schelling acknowledges that a limitation of his theory is that it assumes rational behavior. Both rational and nonrational factors may play a role in the effectiveness of deterrent threats, so a theory of deterrence that does not consider nonrational factors may not be adequate.

In recent years, some social scientists have developed an alternative approach to what they call rational deterrence theory.[17] One advocate of the alternative approach, Robert Jervis, asserts: "Deterrence posits a psychological relationship, so it is strange that most analyses of it have ignored decision makers' emotions, perceptions, and calculations and have instead relied on deductive logic based on the premise that people are highly rational."[18] The nature of the alternative approach is explained by Patrick Morgan:

> Deterrence can be studied by expanding our understanding of how governments attempt to practice deterrence, how they bring themselves to the point of initiating a war, and how they behave when confronted with threats of retaliation. What do governments actually do in deterrence situations, and what factors appear to determine what they do? If we knew, we could better develop, test, and refine deterrence theory and derive from it a more satisfactory body of advice to the policymaker.[19]

Proponents of this approach have developed detailed case studies of successes and failures of military deterrence in an attempt to come to a better understanding of its actual workings, especially in regard to the nonrational factors that are involved.[20]

But this approach does not address the question of the marginal deterrent value of nuclear deterrence.[21] The case studies have been of two kinds, some concerning conventional deterrence, some concerning nuclear deterrence. But neither can be of great help to us. Those concerning conventional deterrence have predominated, because potential case studies involving conventional deterrence are more common than those involving nuclear deterrence. But studies involving conventional deterrence are relevant to nuclear deterrence only if one assumes that conclusions about conventional deterrence apply to nuclear deterrence as well. Assuming such a continuity between conventional and nuclear deterrence does not take account of the distinctiveness of nuclear deterrence. James Blight argues: "The psychological incommensurability between the non-nuclear and nuclear cases poses grave doubts about [the goal of producing] a more empirical approach to the study of nuclear deterrence by means of a psychological analysis of non-nuclear cases . . ."[22] A related point is made by Gregory Kavka, who speaks of the "unique historical situation" represented by the choice whether to maintain or to abandon nuclear deterrence, and argues that nuclear deterrence has no "natural reference class" of past situations with which to compare it to determine its likely outcomes.[23] But even if Blight and Kavka are wrong in rejecting the assumption of continuity between conventional and nuclear deterrence, this assumption cannot help. Determining the marginal deterrent value of nuclear deterrence requires attention to the differences between the two kinds of deterrence, which the assumption of continuity ignores.

Case studies of nuclear deterrence examine how nuclear threats have affected the decision making of the leaders of the United States and the Soviet Union, especially at such times as the Cuban missile crisis.[24] Such studies, unlike those of conventional deterrence, do directly contribute to our understanding of nuclear deterrence, though they are limited to one historical instantiation of the condition of mutual vulnerability. But as much as they can inform us about the workings of nuclear deterrence, these studies cannot by themselves answer the question whether nuclear deterrence has marginal deterrent value, because they do not attempt to compare nuclear deterrence with conventional deterrence.

This discussion shows that there are at least three conditions that should be met by a theory that seeks to provide an adequate answer to the question whether nuclear deterrence has marginal deterrent value. First, it should avoid the defect of rational deterrence theory by seeking to account for nonrational factors in the operation of deterrence. Second, it should have a broader focus than nuclear deterrence, otherwise it would tell us nothing about the comparison between nuclear and conventional deterrence. Third, it should avoid adopting the continuity assumption, which would beg the question regarding the differences between the two forms of military deterrence. Most importantly, in order to meet these conditions, the theory must generalize beyond both conventional and nuclear deterrence – that is, beyond military deterrence – in order that it provide a standard against which these two forms of military deterrence can be compared. For this reason, both the prudential argument and the consequentialist argument presented in the first two chapters are inadequately theoretical, because they do not look beyond military deterrence to find a basis for their comparative claims.

Deterrence is a pervasive kind of relation among persons and institutions at all levels of social grouping, from the domestic sphere (in both senses) to the international order.[25] Considering deterrence in a nonmilitary context will help to provide a basis for comparing conventional and nuclear deterrence. In particular, if one chooses a form of nonmilitary deterrence that is paradigmatically effective and seeks to understand how that form of deterrence is effective, it should be possible to use that understanding as a background against which to determine the relative effectiveness of conventional and nuclear deterrence. Such an approach might also satisfy the first of the three conditions if the workings of the nonmilitary form of deterrence involve nonrational factors. This is the approach I shall adopt.

DETERRENCE AND DETERRENCE EFFECTIVENESS

Deterrence is a relation in which one party seeks through threats of force to induce another party to conform its behavior to certain standards.[26] In what follows, *standards of behavior* will refer to the kinds of behavior (such as nonaggression) that the threatener is seeking to bring about on the part of the party threatened, *conforming behavior* will refer to behavior on the part of the party threatened that conforms to these standards, and *nonconforming behavior* to behavior that does not. A deterrent threat is the expression of a conditional commitment to do harm through use of force. Putting these points together and elaborating yields this definition of deterrence:

> Deterrence is a relation between parties (individuals, institutions, or groups) where one party (explicitly or implicitly) indicates standards of behavior and expresses a commitment to use force to harm a second party (or some relevant third party) if the second party's behavior does not conform to those standards.

Both the standards of behavior and the commitment to use force may be communicated either explicitly, in straightforward verbal form, or implicitly. For example, a police officer's thumping of a nightstick against the palm of his hand in a certain context implicitly communicates both a standard of behavior ("stay back") and a threat of harm in the event the other's behavior is nonconforming. The party against whom the harm is threatened, though normally identical with the party from whom conforming behavior is sought, may be some third party (in which case the threats are third-party threats). This third party must be a relevant party, in the sense that the threatener must believe that the second party cares what happens to the third party. When the harm is threatened against a third party, this is referred to as *vicarious deterrence*, whereas the standard case where the harm is threatened against the same party from whom conforming behavior is sought is *nonvicarious deterrence.*[27] Examples of vicarious deterrence are a teacher's threatening to penalize the whole class if any student misbehaves, and the Gestapo's threatening to shoot one hundred randomly selected local citizens for an act of sabotage.

The standards of behavior with which the threatener seeks conformity normally require that the second party refrain from certain activity. If the standards require instead that the threatened party perform some activity, the threats would be a form of compellence rather than deterrence. Normally, the threatener seeks to induce the second party to refrain from some activity that would cause the threatener or others harm, usually some form of aggression. So there are two different potential harms characteristic of the

93

deterrence situation: the harm that is threatened for nonconforming behavior and the harm that conforming behavior would avoid. These two may be related in different ways. First, the harm that is threatened may be either proportionate or disproportionate to the harm the threat is meant to avoid. Second, the harm that is threatened may or may not be meant to nullify or undo the harm the threat is meant to avoid (and if it were so meant, it would usually be proportionate as well). In other words, assuming that the harm the threat is meant to avoid would be a gain or benefit for the threatened party, the threatener may seek to deter the causing of this harm by threatening to do what would amount to denying the threatened party the gain or benefit. This is deterrence by threat of denial. Deterrence by threat of punishment, on the other hand, involves threats of harm that are meant to deter principally through the loss they would impose, rather than through the denial of benefit or gain. Threats of punishment are usually disproportionately large in comparison with the harm they are meant to avoid.

Deterrence is often institutional, but it may be so in two different senses. First, the deterrence *relation* may be institutional, in the sense that the parties to the threat transaction are related within a single institutional framework. In that case, the deterrence relation between the parties is institutionally sanctioned, and the threatener generally stands in authority over the party threatened, usually providing at least a perception of legitimacy for the threat. Second, where the deterrent relation is not institutional, the deterrent *threats* may be, in the sense that the party threatening is an institution (or individuals in institutional roles) and the force backing up the threat is institutionally organized. This distinction is connected to the distinction between domestic and nondomestic institutions of deterrence discussed in Chapter 2. Domestic institutions of deterrence, such as the law, are institutional in both senses. In the case of the law, the government institutionally relates legal officials and citizens, with the officials having authority over the citizens exercised in their issuing of deterrent threats, and the threats are backed by institutionally organized force. Nondomestic institutions of deterrence, such as military deterrence, are institutional only in the second sense, because, though the force behind them is institutionally organized, there is no overarching institution that relates one nation to the other and in virtue of which the one stands in a relation of authority to the other.

Our interest is in deterrence that is institutional. When deterrence is institutional, the threats are typically standing threats, that is, they are ongoing rather than occasional or episodic. Legal threats, for example, are embodied in general rules rather than particular commands. In addition, institutional deterrence, whether domestic or nondomestic, involves systems of threats rather than isolated, individual threats, because there is an institutional interest in controlling a variety of different types of behavior on the part of the party threatened. When deterrence is institutional, we may speak of deterrence systems or threat systems. In the case of such systems, the threats should be considered not in isolation, but in their institutional context.

Determining whether deterrence works requires determining whether the deterrent threats lead the parties threatened to conform to the standards of behavior when they otherwise would not have.[28] But this is not the whole of it, because the threats might also, on other occasions, lead the threatened parties not to conform to the standards when they otherwise would have. The total impact of the threats on the behavior of the parties threatened may include some increase in conformity to the standards as well as some decrease. Legal threats, for example, may both deter the parties some of the time and at other times lead them to break the law for the thrill of trying to get away with it or as a way of challenging authority.[29] To consider only the increase in conformity with the standards when there is also a decrease would be to misrepresent the overall deterrent effect of the threats. In looking at the marginal deterrent value of threats, then, we want to be sure to consider their *net deterrent effect*, which is the resulting decrease in nonconforming behavior offset by any resulting increase in such behavior.[30]

The strategy for determining the marginal deterrent value of nuclear deterrence is this. The first step is to present the conditions for the effectiveness of deterrent threats in general. This is an analysis of deterrence effectiveness, which is a set of conditions for the absolute deterrent value of any deterrent threat. The next step is to show how deterrent threats in general can satisfy these conditions. This will be done by considering how these conditions are satisfied in the case of deterrent threats of paradigmatic effectiveness – namely, legal deterrent threats. The last step of the argument, taken in the next chapter, is to apply our understanding of how these conditions are satisfied to determine the marginal deterrent value of nuclear deterrence. This will involve investigating the factors in military deterrence in general that influence the satisfaction of these conditions, and then comparing nuclear deterrence and conventional deterrence to see which better satisfies them. It is in the comparison between nuclear deterrence and conventional deterrence against a scale of absolute deterrent value, as revealed by the examination of how legal deterrent threats satisfy the general conditions for deterrence effectiveness, that the marginal deterrent value of nuclear threats can be assessed.

Absolute deterrent value

If a deterrent threat is to be effective in some particular instance, first, the threat must create in the party threatened a certain belief, and second, that belief must bring about that party's conforming its behavior to the indicated standard of behavior. This is a claim about what it is for a threat to have absolute deterrent value in some particular situation. Elaborating on this yields the following analysis of deterrence effectiveness.

A threat has absolute deterrent value in some particular situation, if and only if:

> (1) the deterrent threat creates in the mind of the party whose behavior the threatener is seeking to influence the belief that should that party fail to conform its behavior to the indicated standard of behavior, the threat is likely to be carried out and the threatened harm imposed upon it (or a relevant other, in the case of vicarious deterrence), this belief being based on the threatened party's belief that it is likely that the threatener would have, when the time would come to carry out the threat, (1a) the capability to carry out the threat, and (1b) the willingness to carry out the threat; and (2) the threatened party's having these beliefs, along with the beliefs that (2a) it is likely that the threatened harm would not be imposed should that party's behavior conform to the standard, and (2b) it is likely that the severity of the harm or the onerousness of its imposition would be, given the circumstances, such as to constitute (when the perceived likelihood of its imposition is taken into account) an overriding disadvantage, brings about the threatened party's conforming its behavior to the indicated standard of behavior.

This analysis is meant to indicate, with the locution "bring about," that the threat must be causally responsible for the conformity rather than merely being coincident with it. Also, the analysis is meant to rule out cases where the threat causes conformity in anomalous ways. Deterrent threats may bring about conformity of behavior in different ways, but, according to the analysis, a deterrent threat succeeds if and only if such conformity results from the kind of beliefs referred to in (1) and (2). For example, the analysis would rule out, as it should, a case where a deterrent threat causes a third party to bribe the party the threatener meant to influence to conform its behavior to the indicated standard, such that its conformity is due to the bribe rather than to its acting out of the kind of beliefs referred to in the analysis. As Robert Holmes points out: "Simply refraining, even if because of the threat . . . is not enough. Only if you refrain *in order to avoid* the execution of the threat have you been deterred."[31] The beliefs referred to in (1) and (2) are meant to show that the party conforms in order to avoid the execution of the threat. The importance of beliefs in the analysis is, of course, due to the fact that deterrence works through the choices of the conforming parties.

Some comments on certain aspects of the analysis may be helpful. The first belief referred to in (1) is that it is likely that the threatener will carry out the threat, as based on the beliefs (1a) and (1b) that the threatener is likely to have, when the time comes, the capability and willingness to carry it out. The threatened party will not always be certain that nonconformity would lead to the execution of the threat, but the belief that the threatener is likely to carry out the threat may be sufficient to lead to conforming behavior. Regarding (1a), capability concerns the means by which the threat would be executed, which may involve both instrumentality and personnel. The mugger's threat is likely to work only if the victim believes that the gun is or may be loaded. The threatened party may wonder whether the threatener is psychologically capable of executing the threat, but psychological capability would fall under (1b) rather than (1a). It is important to note that the beliefs in (1a) and (1b) concern what would be the case when the time came for the threatener to carry out the threat, not what is the case at the time the threat is made, because the party threatened may have good reason to believe that the threatener's capability and will will have changed when the time comes for threat execution.

Belief (2a) is included as a condition because a threat successfully deters only if the threatened party acts in order to avoid the harm of threat execution, and this can be the case only if that party believes that conforming is likely to avoid the harm, or at least is more likely to avoid the harm than nonconformity.[32] Belief (2b) is included because the threatened party would conform to avoid the harm of threat execution only if it perceived the harm as something worth avoiding. Whether or not the threatened party would see the harm as an overriding disadvantage would, of course, depend on the details of the situation, and would generally be based on a comparison of the expected harm and expected benefits from nonconformity with the indicated standards.

The analysis offers conditions for individual cases of deterrence success. Each individual attempt at deterrence is either a success or a failure. It either has absolute deterrent value or it has none. But for our purposes, effectiveness must be understood more broadly. A deterrence system covers a large number of cases, because such a system involves multiple threats meant to influence the behavior of a large number of parties over an extended period of time. No deterrence system will be a perfect success or a perfect failure. In practice, the effectiveness of a deterrence system – its absolute deterrent value – is a matter of degree. The absolute deterrent value will be between one and zero. A comparison of different deterrence systems in terms of marginal deterrent value involves determining which has a better success rate, an absolute deterrent value closer to one. In addition, when the focus shifts from individual cases of deterrent threatening to a deterrence system, our understanding of the conditions of effectiveness must change. What explains success in an individual case is that the beliefs in (1) and (2) bring about conforming behavior. But for a variety of reasons, these beliefs may be held without their bringing about conforming behavior. Deterrence may fail despite the threatened party's holding these beliefs. Because effectiveness of a deterrence system is its rate of success over a large number of individual cases, this must be explained, in part, in terms of some factor that indicates the likelihood that the threatened party's holding the beliefs would bring about its conforming behavior. This factor, I will say, is the *strength* with which the beliefs are held.

In the case of a deterrence system, conformity often occurs without deliberation, yet our analysis seems to presuppose deliberation, because deliberation would normally be the means by which the beliefs in (1) and (2) would bring about conforming behavior. But the analysis can account for *nondeliberative conformity*. For one can distinguish between direct and indirect ways in which the holding of the beliefs may bring about conformity. In the case of *deliberative conformity*, the beliefs bring about conformity directly, serving as premises in a practical syllogism. But the analysis allows a way for the beliefs to bring about conformity indirectly, so that it can encompass nondeliberative conformity.

LEGAL DETERRENCE

The next step in the argument is to investigate how the conditions for deterrence effectiveness specified in the analysis are satisfied in the case of a deterrence system that can be regarded as paradigmatically effective – that is, one whose high level of effectiveness can be taken for granted. If there is such a deterrence system, it could serve as a benchmark against which a comparison of nuclear and conventional deterrence could be made. I will take legal deterrence to be a deterrence system of paradigmatic effectiveness. It is hard to know how one could go about trying to prove that legal deterrence has a high absolute deterrent value. I will not attempt to do so, but simply assume that it does.[33] Of course, the effectiveness of legal deterrence varies among different legal systems and, within the same legal system, among different of its individual laws. But for most legal systems, one may assume that they exhibit a high level of effectiveness, at least in regard to those of its threats meant to enforce its central criminal statutes. It is the level of effectiveness of legal threats in enforcing central criminal statutes that I have in mind when I claim that legal deterrence is paradigmatically effective.

The question how legal deterrence satisfies the conditions of the analysis of deterrence effectiveness is the question how the legal system succeeds in getting those whose behavior it seeks to influence not merely to hold the beliefs in (1) and (2), but to hold them in such a way that they bring about conformity. As suggested, the conformity is, in part, a matter of the strength with which the beliefs are held. Specifically, the beliefs in (1) and (2) all involve, in their content, a dimension of likelihood and, as I shall use the notion of strength, the beliefs are held strongly to the extent that that perceived likelihood is high.[34] In particular, in regard to the beliefs referred to in (1), legal deterrence can be highly effective only if the state induces the belief not only that it may execute its threats in the event of the citizens' nonconformity, but that it is likely to do so. The level of effectiveness of a deterrence system depends in large part on how likely the parties threatened believe the threatener is to execute its threats. Assuming legal deterrence to be highly effective, the presumption is then that the state succeeds in getting most of those it threatens to believe that it is quite likely to carry out its threats in the event of their nonconformity.

How does the state get those it seeks to deter to expect the execution of its legal threats in the event of their disobedience of the laws? As (1) indicates, there are two components to this belief – the belief that the state is capable of carrying out its threats and the belief that it is willing to do so. The capability of the state to carry out its threats, in general, is not in doubt, because of the preponderance of force in its hands. But there is some room for doubt about the capability of the state to impose the threatened harm for particular cases of nonconforming behavior, because of difficulties the state sometimes has in detecting who is responsible for some nonconforming behavior. In addition, the state often limits its own power to impose threatened harm by adhering to procedural constraints on the detection and prosecution of suspected violators in respect of individual rights.

What about the other relevant belief, that the state is willing to carry out its legal threats? Willingness is a dispositional trait, so the basis for such a belief is to be found where evidence for dispositions is generally found – that is, in past behavior. Mere declarations of intent to carry out a threat, in the absence of a history of threat executions, are not a sufficient basis to establish a strong belief that a threat would be carried out. The basis for the strength of the belief that the state is willing to carry out its legal threats is to be found in the state's past behavior of legal threat executions. To induce a strong belief that it is willing to carry out its legal threats, the state must have a history of having done so. When this history is extensive, the likelihood that the state would carry out its threats would, in general, be seen to be high. Because states generally have extensive histories of carrying out legal threats, they are able to induce a strong belief in their willingness to carry them out. When the strengths of the beliefs about the state's capability and willingness to carry out its threats are taken together, they provide a solid basis for a strong belief that the state will execute its legal threats.[35]

There are interesting implications of the fact that evidence for the state's willingness to carry out its legal threats lies in its history of legal threat executions. One is that, paradoxically, the success of legal deterrence is dependent on its failure. Legal deterrence is, as a matter of fact, *restrictive* rather than *total* – that is, it succeeds in eliminating only a portion (though, by our assumption, a very large portion) of potential instances of nonconforming behavior, not all of them.[36] But the implication is that legal deterrence is not contingently restrictive, but necessarily so. Because its success depends on the belief that the state is willing to carry out its threats, which depends on a history of threat executions, its success depends on its failure. The point is that a legal system does not merely tolerate failures, maintaining an overall high level of success in spite of them, but actually makes use of them, and even requires them, for its success.

A hypothesis

It appears, then, that a legal system could not, by itself, reduce the number of instances of nonconforming behavior to zero for any extended period of time. If a legal system succeeded at some point in time in doing this, there would be no threats carried out, and over time the perception that the state is willing to carry out its threats would fade. The threats would then eventually lose their effectiveness and instances of nonconforming behavior would again occur. In our present legal system, the number of instances of nonconforming behavior violative of central criminal statutes is certainly much higher than it might be, and much could be done to lower it – for example, by strengthening the other factors of the legal system that bear on the system's effectiveness. There are also many measures extrinsic to the legal system that could be taken to lower the number – for example, a greater concern with social and economic justice. There are even science-fiction possibilities, such as brain implants, for reducing the number of instances of nonconforming behavior to zero. But a policy of brain implants would eliminate choice, so would not be a form of deterrence at all.

This suggests the following hypothesis. For a given system of legal deterrent threats in a given social order (understanding a social order to include a given set of extra-legal social policies and conditions affecting the number of instances of nonconforming behavior), there is, when the system of deterrent threats is operating most effectively, some minimum number of instances of nonconforming behavior that can be achieved over some specific extended length of time. This ideal minimum number would be at a point of equilibrium. At that point, any additional success at deterring a potential instance of nonconforming behavior would mean one less threat execution, so that this success would be offset by a deterrence failure that would not have occurred had the perception of the state's willingness to carry out its threats been strengthened by that threat execution. At that equilibrium point, any additional deterrent successes would lead to additional deterrent failures, because additional successes would weaken the evidential basis for the belief that the state is willing to carry out its threats, thereby making the threats less effective. Pushing down the crime rate at one point would cause it to bulge up at another.

A main purpose – a central social purpose – of a legal system is to keep the social peace, to keep the social order stable and functioning smoothly. When legal threats are effective, the social order is, to that extent, stable, in the sense that there are relatively few instances of nonconforming behavior to disrupt the social peace. Thus the degree of effectiveness of a legal system can be correlated with the degree of stability that that system induces in the social order. The more effective the legal threats, the more stable the social order. The point at which the legal system has reduced the instances of nonconforming behavior to the hypothetical ideal minimum number may thus be referred to as *the point of maximum deterrence-induced stability.* Of course, the legal system and its deterrent threats is only one of the many factors contributing to the stability of a social order. Moreover, stability, in this sense, may or may not be morally valuable, depending on the legitimacy of the social order that the deterrent threats stabilize. In addition, maintaining social peace is not the only central social purpose of the legal system. Another is promoting justice.

Social orders sometimes become so unstable, suffering so high a degree of internal disorder, that they completely break down and cease to exist, the disorder being relieved only by the establishment of a new social order. When social relations pass some threshold point of chaos and unpredictability (call it the breakdown point), the social order that has to that point obtained ceases to function. Such a complete social breakdown, which goes beyond the lesser levels of chaos sometimes resulting from a change in government or ruling regime, occurs when the law, including some of its central criminal statutes, is ignored by a large portion of the population so that the number of instances of nonconforming behavior becomes very large. If a system of legal deterrence were so ineffective that it allowed the number of instances of nonconforming behavior to rise high enough that complete social breakdown occurred, that system would have failed completely or generally. The general failure of a legal system is thus to be distinguished from its particular failures, which are particular instances of nonconforming behavior. In fact, some particular failures are necessary for the legal system's general success. This dissolves the "paradox" that the success of a system of legal deterrence depends on its failure. General success depends, up to a point, on particular failures, and it is only when the number of particular failures became very high that general failure would follow.

The generally high level of effectiveness of legal systems is not the only reason social orders are unlikely to collapse through the general failure of such systems. The likelihood of the collapse of a social order is a function not only of the effectiveness of institutions designed to keep it going, but also of how prone the social order is to collapse, how resilient it is. As a measure of resilience, consider the scale of the number of instances of nonconforming behavior or particular legal deterrence failures. There are two salient points on such a scale. Concerning some particular social order, these are (a) the point of maximum deterrence-induced stability – the hypothetical lowest number of particular deterrence failures that that legal system could bring about – and (b) the breaking point for the social order – that is, the point at which the number of particular deterrence failures becomes so great that that social order completely breaks down. The gap between (a) and (b) I will refer to as the *level of instability tolerance* of the social order. Each instance of nonconforming behavior beyond the point of maximum deterrence-induced stability will introduce an added degree of social chaos. But social orders can normally tolerate considerable chaos – that is, the number of instances of nonconforming behavior can rise quite high before the social order completely breaks down. The gap between (a) and (b) is normally large, which means that social orders tend to possess a high level of instability tolerance. Social orders are usually quite resilient in the face of large numbers of particular failures of legal deterrence. A system of legal deterrence could be relatively ineffective, the number of instances of nonconforming behavior that it allows going quite far beyond the hypothetical minimum, without the social order breaking down and deterrence failing generally.

Motivation and nondeliberation

The explanation of the effectiveness of legal deterrence can now shift to condition (2). Given that the parties threatened believe that the state is likely to execute its threats, what is necessary for the threats to result in conforming behavior is that the parties also believe, as (2) indicates, that it is likely, first, that if they conform their behavior to the standards, the harm threatened for nonconformity would not be inflicted on them and, second, that the threatened harm would be serious enough to provide an expected overriding disadvantage from nonconformity. Lacking these beliefs, they would lack motivation to conform. It is clear that legal systems are generally able to cause these beliefs to be quite strongly held. First, states normally do not carry out their legal threats upon their citizens independently of whether or not the citizens are believed to have conformed their behavior to the legal standards. The purpose of judicial systems is to ensure that this does not happen, though judicial systems are sometimes perverted from pursuing this aim. Second, the harm that legal threats threaten is usually significant. States are not, in general, inclined to go soft on crime by setting the severity of the harms threatened at a point at which they would not clearly result in an expected overriding disadvantage from nonconformity. Thus, in the case of legal deterrence, the beliefs referred to in (2) will generally be strongly held by the threatened parties.[37]

But how does the holding of the appropriate beliefs bring about conforming behavior? Most obviously, this comes about in the way in which beliefs normally bring about behavior – namely, through the agent's deliberating about his or her behavior through the content of the beliefs becoming premises in a practical syllogism. But if this were the only way, our analysis could not explain nondeliberative conformity. Moreover, the analysis would then be guilty of providing a model of deterrence that assumes rationality, as rational deterrence theory does. But our analysis does provide a way of taking account of nonrational factors in the operations of deterrence. One way to see this is to consider a particular bit of conforming behavior in the context of the operations of the system as a whole. Even if one assumes that our analysis implies that deterrence can be successful only when those threatened deliberate, the acts of deliberation lead to decisions to conform to the standards only when there have been other instances where deterrence has failed, many or most of which would be cases where prudential rationality has not been exercised. For the belief that the threatener is willing to carry out the threat, which is a necessary premise in the practical reasoning involved in such deliberations, depends on there having been particular failures of deterrence. Because general success requires some particular failures, deliberation bringing about conformity to the standards itself requires that there be some cases where rationality has not been exercised.

But those who criticize the assumption of rationality might not be impressed by this point. They would focus on the particular bit of conforming behavior in itself, arguing that an analysis of deterrence effectiveness must recognize that people often (a) act emotionally, and (b) act without deliberating about their own best interests. Concerning the former, the dichotomy between actions based on emotion and actions based on reason is a false one, because some emotional actions are deliberate and perfectly rational. For example, it is often said that deterrence works through fear, or even terror, but many actions done out of fear or terror are prudentially rational. Fear of the harm of threat execution may be quite rational. On the other hand, some may be led to nonconforming behavior out of, say, bravado, but not all behavior out of bravado would be prudentially irrational, given the expected outcomes in question. Some emotional action, however, would fall under (b), and this category would be the main concern of the critics. But though our analysis is based on deliberation, it can explain conforming behavior that does not itself involve deliberation. Prudential rationality is necessary for deterrence success, as the analysis maintains, but it does not follow that rationality is necessary in each individual instance of deterrence success. To think otherwise is to commit the fallacy of division. Although it is necessary that some instances of successful deterrence be the result of deliberation, it is not necessary for all of them to be.

This is the point of the claim that the appropriate beliefs could bring about conforming behavior indirectly as well as directly.[38] In the direct case, conformity would be deliberative, and in the indirect case, nondeliberative. Although our account requires deliberation, it allows a distinction between instances where conformity is based directly on deliberation and instances where it is based indirectly on deliberation. This distinction is related to a distinction drawn in the literature on legal deterrence between "simple deterrence," which involves "comparing *this* crime with *this* penalty for one particular moment," and "less direct mechanisms through which the threat of punishment may induce compliance."[39] The latter is nondeliberative conformity, whereas the former is deliberative conformity. What needs to be shown is that our analysis can explain at least some instances of nondeliberative conformity.

Because people seldom deliberate about whether or not to obey the law, but obey it much of the time nonetheless, most instances of conforming behavior are instances of nondeliberative conformity. Although not all cases of conforming behavior are cases of deterrence success, because conforming behavior may have explanations other than the existence of the legal threats, we may assume that many are. Deterrence success is not limited to deliberative conformity, despite the common picture called forth to explain why legal deterrence is needed. According to this picture, at least as old as Plato's story of Gyges' Ring, there is an untutored tendency on the part of most people to do many of the things the law forbids, so that a strong countervailing motivation must be supplied in order to bring about their conformity with the law. So, when their behavior happens to conform to legal standards, which is most of the time, the implication is that this is normally to be explained by their being restrained by legal threats, which would apparently involve their deliberating in each case. But a more plausible picture holds that only a minority in society, so-called "bad men," are like this. Society is composed not only of "bad men," who will often obey the law only after they deliberatively determine that it would not be to their advantage to break it, but also of "good men," who tend to do what the law requires without reasoning it out. The conformity of the "good man" is largely nondeliberative. The legal system would probably fail completely unless most people were good in this sense, but our assumption is that the conformity of the good, as well as the bad, is often a deterrence success.

How can an analysis of deterrence effectiveness based on deliberation explain instances of deterrence success that do not involve deliberation? Nondeliberative conformity is often the result of habits of obedience.[40] Most non-bank robbers who have some desire for the bank's money, and hence need to some extent to be deterred from robbing banks, refrain from robbing banks because they are either in a habit of thought by virtue of which the idea of their robbing banks simply does not occur to them or in a habit of action by virtue of which were such an idea to occur, it would be immediately dismissed. The question, then, is whether our analysis can explain instances of successful deterrence that arise out of habits of obedience to the law. Can our analysis explain how such habits are the result of legal threats? Can the habits be shown to result from the kinds of beliefs referred to in (1) and (2)? They can, if attention is paid to how the habits originate and how they are sustained.

The question of how habits originate is a complex one, but in many cases at least, actions that are habitual for some individual were once deliberate for that individual. A habit of doing or not doing some kind of action is often acquired by repeated deliberate performances or nonperformances of that kind of action. In this sense, conformity that is nondeliberative sometimes depends on conformity that is deliberative. It is plausible to suppose that at least some acts of nondeliberative conformity are the result of habits that originated with acts of deliberative conformity, hence with the agent's holding the beliefs referred to in (1) and (2).[41] But the argument that our analysis can explain how the existence of habits results from the holding of these beliefs is greatly strengthened by considering how the habits leading to nondeliberative conformity, whatever their origins, are sustained. Habits sometimes weaken or disappear, and the tendency toward this would be especially great in cases where the habits are set against strong inclinations, which is often the case with habits of legal conformity. Such habits generally need to be sustained in order that they not weaken or disappear. Two factors play a strong role in sustaining habits of legal conformity: first, the perception that the legal threats are legitimate; and second, the perception that there is fairness in the execution of the threats.

Many considerations determine whether or not legal threats are perceived as legitimate, but perhaps the most important is whether or not the threats are part of a domestic institution of deterrence. If they are part of a domestic institution, the authority relation between threatener and threatened characteristic of such systems will make it likely that the threats will be perceived as legitimate, whereas if they are not part of a domestic institution, the lack of such an authority relation will make it less likely that the threats will be perceived as legitimate. But more important is the second factor, that of perceived fairness. The point about fairness is a familiar one. In a social situation in which there are standards of behavior, conformity with which is to the benefit of others but contrary to one's own inclinations, one's willingness to conform to those standards is often crucially dependent on one's belief about what happens to others who fail to conform. If I conform and others do not, I would likely perceive them as having an unfair advantage, an advantage that can be eliminated only if they are made to suffer for their transgression. The perception of fairness requires, if not conformity by everyone, at least that those who fail to conform are likely to suffer in some way for that failure. A well-working system of legal deterrence would achieve this perception of fairness by a consistent execution of its threats against those who engage in nonconforming behavior.[42] The perception of fairness created when legal threats are consistently applied contributes indirectly to successful legal deterrence by helping to sustain habits of legal conformity.

The relevance of this is that one's having this perception of fairness results from one's holding the kinds of beliefs referred to in the analysis. One's belief that those who fail to conform their behavior to the law will be punished, on which the perception of fairness is based, is a result of one's having the kinds of beliefs referred to in (1) and (2), generalized so as to apply to others as well as to oneself. In other words, to believe that the nonconforming behavior of others will be punished is to believe that the state is capable of and willing to execute its threats and impose significant harm not only on oneself, but on others who engage in nonconforming behavior. The only difference is that when the beliefs lead to deliberative conformity, they concern what the state would do to the person holding the beliefs, whereas, when they contribute to the perception of fairness, they concern what the state would do to others.

So, in the case of legal threats, one's holding the kinds of beliefs referred to in (1) and (2), in addition to bringing about one's deliberative conformity with the law, does two other things. First, it helps to create habits of obedience to the law to the extent that such habits are based on earlier acts of deliberative conformity. Second, it helps to sustain those habits by creating a perception of fairness in the execution of the threats. By virtue of these effects, the beliefs bring about conforming behavior indirectly, through habits of obedience. This shows how instances of nondeliberative conformity can be instances of deterrence success and how our analysis can account for such nondeliberative conformity.

The way in which our analysis takes account of nonrational factors in the operations of deterrence should now be clear. First, because deterrence can only succeed generally when it suffers some particular failures, successful deterrence requires that there be some nonrational choices to engage in nonconforming behavior. To the criticism that deterrence cannot work because people do not always act rationally, the response should be that deterrence can work only if people do not always act rationally. Second, instances of deterrence success that are not rational, in the sense that they are not based directly on deliberation, can yet be brought about indirectly by the kinds of beliefs referred to in (1) and (2). Conforming behavior can be based on habit that is developed, in part, through earlier deliberate acts of conformity and that is sustained, in part, by a belief in the fairness of the execution of the threats, both of which are based on the agent's holding the kinds of beliefs referred to in (1) and (2). Critics charge that a theory of deterrence that assumes rationality is inadequate because deterrence sometimes fails in ways contrary to the dictates of reason and sometimes succeeds without there being a deliberate exercise of reason. The analysis of deterrence effectiveness proposed here forms the basis for a theory of deterrence that meets this charge.

This completes the discussion of legal deterrence and the way in which it satisfies the conditions of our analysis of deterrence effectiveness, and it sets the stage for the discussion in the next chapter of (1) the features of military deterrence that influence its effectiveness, and (2) the comparison between conventional and nuclear deterrence, with the goal of determining the marginal deterrent value of the latter.

Chapter 4

The prudential problem

Nuclear weapons give rise to a prudential problem as they give rise to a moral problem. When nuclear deterrence is assessed in terms of the traditional norms, morality and prudence are thrown into conflict, but when one seeks to go beyond these norms, other conflicts arise. The moral problem is the conflict between different moral approaches, represented by the moral dilemma. The prudential problem is the conflict between two arguments, one that nuclear deterrence is prudentially preferable to conventional deterrence and the other that it is not. But there is an important logical difference between the moral problem and the prudential problem. The moral problem is a conflict between two different assessment approaches, whereas the prudential problem is a conflict within a single assessment approach, that of maximizing the expected value of the consequences in terms of the nation's military security. So there is not the kind of obstacle to the solution to the prudential problem that there is to the solution to the moral problem.[1] The prudential problem is solvable simply by determining whether the better consequences lie with nuclear deterrence or with conventional deterrence. There are practical difficulties in determining this, but no obstacles in principle. The nature of the prudential problem and the beginnings of a solution to it are developed in this chapter.

The prudential problem, like the moral problem, can arise when one attempts to avoid the conflict between prudence and morality discussed in Chapter 1. The argument in Chapter 2 was an attempt to avoid the conflict through a broadening of the moral perspective beyond the norms of the just-war tradition. The attempt now is through a broadening of the prudential perspective beyond the traditional norms of military prudence, norms assumed in both the

110

prudential and consequentialist arguments from the first two chapters.[2] The way to broaden the prudential perspective beyond traditional military terms is to consider a broader class of deterrent threats. My current strategy is to develop a theory of deterrence effectiveness through an analysis of what is required for a deterrent threat to be successful and a discussion of how the conditions of that analysis are satisfied in the case of legal deterrence. This has set the stage for determining whether or not nuclear deterrence is more effective than conventional deterrence. But prior to determining if nuclear deterrence has marginal deterrent value, we must consider the differences between legal deterrence and military deterrence in general and the relevance of these differences for the effectiveness of military forms of deterrence.

It would be helpful first, however, to make clear what my overall argument does or does not assume about the similarities between nuclear deterrence and legal deterrence. The argument is not an argument from analogy between nuclear and legal deterrence. If it were, faulty analogy would be an appropriate charge. (If it were an argument from analogy, the conclusion that nuclear deterrence is highly effective would follow straightway from the assumption that legal deterrence is paradigmatically effective.) The direct comparison the argument makes is not between legal and nuclear deterrence, but between conventional and nuclear deterrence. The discussion of legal deterrence merely sets the stage for this comparison. Indeed, the comparison between conventional and nuclear deterrence will largely focus not on those features of deterrence that are points of similarity between legal deterrence and military deterrence, but on those features of deterrence on which they differ. The only similarity between legal deterrence and military deterrence that is assumed is that the conditions presented in the analysis of deterrence effectiveness apply to each, which is to say only that they are both forms of deterrence.

MILITARY DETERRENCE

If we examine military deterrence in general, without at this point considering the special features of nuclear deterrence, some basic differences with legal deterrence become evident. The task is to determine what these differences are and how they are relevant to assessing the relative effectiveness of military forms of deterrence. This requires determining how these differences affect the strength of the beliefs referred to in (1) and (2) of the analysis of deterrence effectiveness, as these beliefs are held by the threatened nations (or, more precisely, by their leaders). There are three important differences between legal deterrence and military deterrence. First, military deterrence is for the most part mutual, in that the threats run in both directions. Each party in the threat relationship is threatening the other. Each is both threatener and threatened. In the case of legal deterrence, the threats go in one direction only. One important result of this mutuality is that most instances of nonconforming behavior and consequent threat execution initiate a war, which extends the violence far beyond that initial interaction. Second, military deterrence involves many fewer actors and, as a result, many fewer instances of deterrence failure, and many fewer threat executions. A government may issue legal threats to millions of its citizens, whereas a nation will issue military threats to a small handful of other nations. Third, legal deterrence is a domestic institution, whereas military deterrence is a nondomestic institution. Because there is no world government, the military threatener and the party threatened are not institutionally related in a way that would give authority to the issuing of the threats. Each of these differences must be considered in some detail.

Mutuality

(1) Mutuality is an important distinguishing characteristic of military deterrence. In distinction from the threat system of legal deterrence, military deterrence is, to use Kenneth Boulding's phrase, a "counterthreat system," a system "in which each party says to the other, 'If you do something nasty to me I will do something nasty to you.' "[3] The mutuality of military deterrence results from the fact that nations represent independent centers of power, and so can effectively threaten to harm each other. Citizens do not represent independent centers of power vis-à-vis the state, and so cannot issue substantial counterthreats to the state's legal threats, much as they might like to do so.[4] The relevance of mutuality to the effectiveness of military deterrence is that mutuality tends to lessen the strength with which the threatened party holds three of the beliefs required for successful deterrence – namely, the belief that the threatener is capable of carrying out its threats, the belief that conforming behavior leads to the threatened harm's not being imposed, and the belief that the threatened harm would, given the

circumstances, make nonconformity disadvantageous. Consider each in turn.

Mutuality tends to lessen the strength of the threatened party's belief that the threatener is capable of carrying out its threat, because, as an independent center of power, the threatened party may be able to use its own military forces to thwart the efforts of the threatener to carry out its threats. The threatened party need not necessarily believe that it would win a war in order to doubt that the threatener could carry out its threats, because all that would be required is that it be able to fight the threatener to a draw. If the military forces of opposing nations are roughly equal, there is a good chance that each could thwart the other's efforts to carry out its threats, in which case each (in its role as threatened party) would doubt that the other (in its role as threatener) would be capable of carrying out its threats. Moreover, the prospective uncertainty of outcome, to which military engagements are prone, could feed this doubt. There is one respect, however, in which military deterrence holds an advantage over legal deterrence concerning the strength of the belief in capability. The state is sometimes not capable of carrying out its legal threats because it cannot identify those who have engaged in nonconforming behavior. But nations seldom have trouble determining what other nation is responsible for some nonconforming behavior, such as an act of aggression.[5]

The second effect of the mutuality of military deterrence is its tendency to weaken the threatened party's belief that should it conform, the threatened harm would not be imposed. In a mutual deterrence relationship, each side may have reason to initiate a war because of the advantages it believes it could thereby gain. Because of this, moreover, each side may fear, especially in a crisis, that the other side is itself about to attack, which could lead the first side to attack in order to preempt the opponent's expected attack.[6] These tendencies could be exacerbated by the fact that the side that attacks first often has a major advantage in war. So there is a real possibility that either nation could be subject to a military first strike by its opponent. This would amount to the attacker's imposing the harm it had threatened against its opponent without the opponent's having engaged in nonconforming behavior. Thus, the mutuality of military deterrence tends to weaken the belief on the part of the threatened party that it could avoid the threatened harm through conforming behavior.

The third belief whose strength is lessened by the mutuality of military deterrence is the belief that the imposition of the threatened harm would constitute, in the circumstances, an overriding disadvantage. The point is that wars can be won, and in some cases the winner gains more than it loses. If a nation believes not only that it could win a war, but also profit from it, that nation's belief that nonconforming behavior would be overridingly disadvantageous for it would be quite weak. Moreover, the belief would be further weakened by the notorious tendency of states to engage in wishful thinking about their prospects in war, "home (with victory) before the first snowfall" being a frequent and frequently mistaken expectation. The effect of mutuality on this belief is related to its effect on the belief that the threatener has the capability to carry out its threat, for in winning the war, the threatened party could keep the threatener from fully carrying out its threat.

Willingness

(2) The second distinctive feature of military deterrence is that it involves many fewer actors than legal deterrence. Nations practicing military deterrence issue their threats to only the small number of nations that are its military opponents. For this reason, in part, there are relatively few cases of deterrence failure, and military threats are not frequently carried out. The histories of particular nations carrying out their military threats are, at best, short. Military threats do not get carried out very often because the threatened parties, given their small number, do not provide many opportunities for the threatener to carry out its threats. Another factor is the costliness of war. Nations cannot afford to engage in it very often, so that nonconforming behavior and threat executions will be infrequent. The relevance of this to deterrence effectiveness is that it tends to lessen the strength with which the threatened party holds another belief required for successful deterrence – namely, that the threatener would be willing to carry out its military threat. Because willingness is a dispositional notion, willingness to carry out threats is attributable on the basis of there being a history of threat executions. Without an extensive history of threat executions, the strength of the threatened party's belief that the threatener would carry out its threats will be less.

In addition, whatever history of threat executions there is may be ambiguous. Past threat executions by a nation may have been under a different regime, against a different state with different military capabilities and a different relation to the threatener, and in response to a different sort of military challenge. Classifying all past military responses simply as executions of military threats may not be fine-grained enough to reflect how they are seen by the opponent. They may not all be regarded by the opponent as evidence for attributing to the threatener a willingness to carry out its threats in response to some bit of nonconforming behavior the threatened party is contemplating. A similar problem does not arise as readily in the case of legal deterrence, because there is usually strong legal continuity across different regimes and in how the law views different kinds of citizens and crimes.

When a threatener's history of threat executions is inadequate to *demonstrate* its willingness to carry them out, a surrogate measure of willingness may shape the threatened party's belief about the likelihood that the threatener would be willing to carry out its threats. This measure is one of *presumption*. When willingness cannot be demonstrated by the historical record, it may, in some cases, be presumed. When the threatener perceives that carrying out a threat is in its self-interest, the likelihood that it would be willing to carry out the threat is high. As a result, if the threatened party believes that the execution of the threat would be in the threatener's perceived self-interest, the threatened party may presume that the threatener would carry out its threat. The threatener's willingness to carry out its threats, then, may either be demonstrated, when there is an adequate history of threat executions, or presumed, when there is not such a history, but the threatened party believes that execution would be in the threatener's perceived self-interest. If the history of threat executions is weak and ambiguous, as it often is in the case of military threats, the threatener's willingness to carry out its threats is not clearly demonstrable. As a result, the strength of the threatened party's belief in this willingness will generally depend on the strength of its belief that threat execution would be in the threatener's perceived self-interest. Demonstration normally takes precedence over presumption, so that when there is an adequate history of threat executions, the threatened party's belief that the threatener would be willing to carry out its threats is usually strong, whether or not threat execution would be in the threatener's perceived self-interest.[7]

This distinction between demonstrated and presumed willingness is somewhat like the distinction in law between subjective

and objective standards of liability. *Mens rea,* or "guilty mind" –
in most cases a necessary condition for legal liability – is normally
determined by investigating the actual state of mind of the defendant – that is, applying a subjective standard of liability. Evidence
for the defendant's actual state of mind is his or her behavior.
Thus, subjective liability is analogous to demonstrated willingness,
which is also concerned with the actual state of mind of the party
in question as determined by its behavior – in particular, by its
history of threat executions. In some cases when subjective liability
is difficult to determine, legal liability is determined by appeal to
the mental state that would be attributed to a "reasonable person"
in the defendant's position. This objective standard of liability is
analogous, in its appeal to rationality, to the presumption of a
threatener's willingness to carry out its threats. Subjective liability,
when it can be effectively determined, takes precedence over objective liability, because the more basic concern is whether a particular person is guilty, not whether a rational person in that
person's position would have been guilty. This is similar to the
way in which demonstrated willingness takes precedence over presumed willingness, because the threatened party is more interested
in knowing whether its threatener would carry out its military
threats, not whether a "rational nation" in that nation's position
would do so.

Given that presumption is a surrogate measure of willingness,
we need to know its basis. What are the factors that determine
whether or not the execution of a military threat is in the threatener's (perceived) self-interest? The prime reason a state has for
carrying out legal threats is the deterrence of future nonconforming
behavior. This may be a reason for carrying out military threats as
well. As Glenn Snyder observes: "Limited wars may be fought in
part with an eye to deterring future enemy attacks by convincing
the enemy of one's general willingness to fight."[8] But the deterrence of future nonconforming behavior does not often provide a
very strong reason for the execution of a military threat. Consider
the situation in terms of the distinction between special deterrence,
which is deterring future nonconforming behavior on the part of
the party against whom a threat is carried out, and general deterrence, which is deterring future nonconforming behavior on the
part of others.[9] Normally, little in the way of general deterrence
can be achieved by the execution of a military threat. Because a
nation has at most a handful of military opponents, there is only

a small audience to draw the deterrence lesson. The execution of a military threat can have a special deterrent effect, leading the nation upon whom the threat is executed to avoid nonconforming behavior in the future, as the quotation from Snyder suggests. But history suggests that military deterrence, like legal deterrence, has a high a rate of recidivism.[10]

The execution of a military threat, however, has two kinds of prudential advantage that normally play little or no role in justifying the execution of legal threats.[11] The main reason for carrying out a military threat is for the sake of denial – that is, nullifying or undoing the gain achieved by the opponent's nonconforming behavior, getting back what the opponent has gained by its aggression. Second, the threatener may be able to win the war that it would enter through carrying out its military threat, in which case it might gain more from carrying out the threat than it would lose. There is in these potential advantages, if not in the deterrent effect on future nonconforming behavior, a basis on which it would in some cases be prudentially rational for a nation to carry out its military threats. So a threatened party may have good reason to believe that it would be in the threatener's perceived self-interest to carry out its military threats. Hence the threatened party may sometimes have a basis to presume that the threatener would be willing to carry out its military threats.

Nondeliberative conformity

(3) The third relevant point of difference is that although legal deterrence is a domestic institution, military deterrence is a nondomestic institution. Arthur Waskow argues: "Deterrence as a military, international concept claims its roots in the notion of the internal police force as a deterrent against crime. But the basic assumption of the police force as deterrent does not exist in international relations."[12] This assumption is the existence of "agreed law," and its lack in the case of military deterrence is a consequence of there being no overarching institutional structure relating the parties in the threat relationship, so as to give the threatener authority to issue its threats. There is no world government, which is to say that military deterrence is a nondomestic institution.[13] The implications of this for deterrence effectiveness concern not the strength of the beliefs required for successful deterrence, but the role of these beliefs in indirectly bringing about conforming be-

havior – that is, their role in nondeliberative conformity. Nondeliberative conformity is often not recognized as a factor in military deterrence.[14] It is less important for military deterrence than it is for legal deterrence because legal threats must deter so many more parties than military threats. Detecting nonconforming behavior and determining who is responsible for it are much more problematic in the case of legal deterrence, because the police cannot be everywhere.[15] So legal deterrence must rely extensively on habits of conformity. Nonetheless, nondeliberative conformity does play some role in military deterrence. But the basis for it is much weaker in the case of military deterrence than it is in the case of legal deterrence.

The extent of nondeliberative conformity in the case of a deterrence system depends on the effectiveness of the factors that create and sustain habits of conformity. The basis of nondeliberative conformity is weaker in the case of military deterrence than in the case of legal deterrence because the factors sustaining habits of conformity are weaker. Military threats are less likely than legal threats to be perceived as legitimate or as fair in their application. Military threats are less likely to be perceived as legitimate because military deterrence, as a nondomestic institution, cannot provide a threatener with authority to issue its threats. Because military deterrence is a nondomestic institution, military threats are also less likely to be perceived to be fairly applied. Legal threats, under the rule of law, apply to all, including those who issue them, but military threats do not apply to those who issue them, or to their allies. Military powers often get away with doing the kind of aggressive actions that they use threats to deter others from doing. Legal deterrence is often perceived to be in the interest of all, or of society as a whole, but military deterrence is recognized to concern parochial rather than universal interests – in particular, the interests of the nation issuing the threats. As a result, military threats are less likely to be perceived as fair in their application, and habits of conformity are, to that extent, less likely to be sustained.

This comparison between legal and military deterrence in terms of effectiveness, though it seems much to the disadvantage of military deterrence, is not meant to be an indictment of it. A comparison between military deterrence and legal deterrence can tell us nothing about the marginal deterrent value of military deterrence, because these two forms of deterrence are not policy alternatives. They operate in different realms, one at the domestic level and the other at the international level. Even if one could draw the conclusion that legal deterrence in its realm is more effective than military deterrence in its realm, that would not show that there is any policy alternative that would be more effective than military deterrence in its realm. A true indictment of military deterrence would have to examine it in relation to some feasible alternative method of controlling aggressive behavior at the international level, perhaps a policy of nonviolent resistance, and seek to show that that alternative has marginal deterrent value in comparison with military deterrence. Points from the above discussion might be relevant to such a comparison, but my purpose is not to make this comparison. Instead, it is to determine the factors to be examined in a comparison between nuclear and conventional deterrence.

NUCLEAR DETERRENCE AND CONVENTIONAL DETERRENCE

Nuclear deterrence differs from conventional deterrence by virtue of the condition of mutual vulnerability that nuclear weapons create. Nuclear deterrence involves the mutual threat of societal destruction and conventional deterrence does not. Important implications concerning comparative effectiveness flow from this difference. These implications will now be explored in order to determine whether nuclear deterrence has marginal deterrent value in comparison with conventional deterrence. Despite the differences entailed by mutual vulnerability, however, nuclear deterrence shares with conventional deterrence the features that distinguish military deterrence from legal deterrence: both are mutual, involve few parties, and are nondomestic institutions. But nuclear and conventional deterrence differ in the way they exhibit these three features, and, as a result, differ in their comparative effectiveness. So the comparison will proceed by our considering how nuclear and conventional deterrence differ over the three features, and the implications concerning effectiveness that follow.

The crystal ball effect and reassurance

(1) Nuclear deterrence, like conventional deterrence, is mutual. But as the phrases "mutual vulnerability" and "mutual assured destruction" suggest, nuclear deterrence is mutual in a novel sense. The question is what impact this new kind of mutuality has on the

relative effectiveness of nuclear deterrence. The discussion of military deterrence has shown that mutuality tends to weaken three crucial beliefs of the threatened party: that the threatener has the capability to carry out its threats; that the threatened party's not engaging in nonconforming behavior would lead to the threatened harm's not being imposed; and that the imposed harm would represent an overriding disadvantage. But the mutuality of nuclear deterrence, in comparison with the mutuality of conventional deterrence, is more likely to strengthen rather than to weaken these beliefs. In this respect, nuclear deterrence has a clear advantage over conventional deterrence in effectiveness. Consider how this is so.

First, in the case of nuclear deterrence, the threatened party normally has no doubt that the threatener is capable of carrying out its threats. Mutual vulnerability exists only when each side's nuclear forces are sufficiently invulnerable to attack that no military actions of the other side could eliminate its capability to carry out its threat of societal destruction. In contrast, in the case of conventional deterrence, the military forces of the threatened party may be able to thwart the threatener in its attempt to carry out its threat. With nuclear deterrence, each nation (as threatened party) has a very strong belief that the other (as threatener) has the capability to carry out its threat of societal destruction. This is suggested by the metaphor of two scorpions in a bottle, which is often used to characterize the mutuality of nuclear deterrence.[16] The capability of each to sting the other to death cannot take away from the other its capability to sting its attacker to death in retaliation.

But, second, the scorpion image is misleading in one important respect, because it suggests that the nuclear situation is a tense one in which the two nuclear nations are likely to go at each other with nuclear weapons at any moment, despite the prospects for their mutual destruction. This might be the case, if each side feared that the other was likely to strike at any time, for then one or the other might well strike out of that fear – that is, the initiating strike would be an attempt by one side to preempt the other's anticipated attack. But the existence of such a fear would mean that each side's belief that it could avoid the threatened harm through its own conforming behavior would be weak, at best, for the threatener's attacking first, which it fears, would be an unprovoked imposition of that harm. This is why each side's believing that its own conforming behavior would likely avoid the threatened harm is an important element in deterrence success. This is made clear by Thomas Schelling: "The pain and suffering have to appear *contingent* on his behavior; it is not alone the threat that is effective – the threat of pain or loss if he fails to comply – but the corresponding assurance, possibly an implicit one, that he can avoid pain or loss if he does comply." Schelling says later: "Any coercive threat requires corresponding *assurances*; the object of a threat is to give somebody a choice."[17] Deterrence operates through the choice of the threatened party, the choice of conformity to avoid the threatened harm, but a party can choose conforming behavior in order to avoid the threatened harm only if it believes that such a choice would succeed in avoiding the harm.

Nuclear deterrence leads to a strong belief that conformity is likely to avoid the threatened harm. The reason is that nuclear deterrence is better able than conventional deterrence to reconcile this feature with other aspects of effective deterrence. Michael Mccgwire speaks of the need for nuclear deterrence to include "mutual reassurance." Speaking of the development of strategic theory, he claims that as "the 'stability' of the strategic balance" was understood, "the simple requirement for Soviet aggression to be *deterred* came to be qualified by the somewhat contradictory requirement for the Soviet Union to be *reassured* that the United States would not initiate a nuclear war, in case the Soviet Union should be driven to launch a pre-emptive attack."[18] More precisely, *reassurance* is not, as MccGwire suggests, a goal different from that of deterrence, but is rather an additional requirement of deterrence. The purpose of reassurance, as of deterrence more generally, is the avoidance of war.[19] But there is, as MccGwire also suggests, a tension between reassurance and other requirements of deterrence. This is a tension between the need for strong military forces and the need for nonprovocative military forces. This tension is the reason that conventional deterrence tends to weaken the belief that conforming behavior can avoid the imposition of the threatened harm. Stronger military forces make a better deterrent in one respect, but they also can provoke the threatened party by leading it, out of fear that the threatener is planning to start a war, to attack first, thereby weakening deterrence in another respect. This fear is fed by the belief that the side that attacks first gains a clear advantage in a war.

But mutual vulnerability, through its capacity to reassure, removes the tension between strength and nonprovocativeness, because it removes any advantage from attacking first. Under mutual vulnerability, the very strength of the military forces, their capacity for assured destruction, guarantees, when both sides have such a capacity, that they do not provoke. The opponent can destroy one's society even if one attacks first, so there is no reason to attack first, hence no reason to fear such an attack. Reassurance, like each side's capacity to carry out its threat no matter what the other side does, is inherent in the condition of mutual vulnerability. Each aspect strengthens one of the beliefs necessary for successful deterrence. Reassurance supports the effectiveness of nuclear deterrence because it leads "national leaders in a crisis to be complacent in the knowledge that nuclear war is so unlikely that initiating it is never prudent."[20] Reassurance is sometimes referred to as *self-deterrence,* because the factors in the condition of mutual vulnerability that provide reassurance are factors that make each side reluctant to use its military forces. A nation in a relationship of mutual vulnerability has a military policy that not only deters the opponent, but also deters itself, in the sense that the disincentives it provides for using military force apply to both parties. We will see later, however, that although reassurance removes one tension characteristic of military deterrence, it creates another.

The third belief that mutual vulnerability strengthens is that the harm threatened would constitute an overriding disadvantage. Societal destruction represents not merely an unprecedentedly high level of harm, but harm of a different order, harm that makes the metaphor of national death an appropriate one. The harm threatened is certain to seem a disadvantage that is overriding. No gain a nation might hope to make in a nuclear war would be seen as sufficient to outweigh the loss, given that the loss would be the death of that nation's society. Conventional deterrence, with its mutuality, tends to weaken the threatened party's belief that the threatened harm would represent an overriding disadvantage, because conventional war can be won. But nuclear deterrence, with a mutuality of assured destruction, strengthens this belief.[21]

The effect of mutual vulnerability on the threatened party's beliefs concerning the threatener's capability to carry out its threat and the overwhelming disadvantageousness of threat execution may be thought of together as creating what has been called the *crystal ball effect.*[22] Under mutual vulnerability, either nation, contemplating attacking the other, can foresee clearly, as if in a crystal ball, an outcome of total ruin. As Robert Tucker claims: "Given their speed and destructiveness, nuclear missile weapons enable men to see the future as they have never before been able to see it."[23] The strength of the two beliefs means that the prospects for ruination are clearly foreseen, not merely conjectural and not easily deniable. Of course, ruination is not a certainty, because a nuclear war might be limited. But because limited nuclear war is not reasonably foreseeable, its mere possibility does not undermine the claim that these beliefs are stronger in the case of nuclear deterrence. With conventional deterrence, things are not so clear, because a belief that victory in war is likely at an acceptable price is not hard to sustain, even when it is not true. Speaking of military deterrence prior to the nuclear age, Phil Williams argues: "There was considerable room for miscalculations and mistakes, and ample opportunity for rival states to initiate hostilities, each with a firm expectation of victory. Since the actual ratio of gains to costs could only be discovered through war itself, deterrence was fragile and subject to frequent breakdowns."[24] Now such things can be known in advance, in such a way as to strongly discourage war, or nonconforming behavior in general, on the part of both parties. The threat of nuclear war, like the threat of execution, concentrates the mind.

The crystal ball effect and reassurance are two features by virtue of which nuclear deterrence has a clear advantage over conventional deterrence in terms of effectiveness.[25] These features, it is argued, show that nuclear deterrence possesses great *stability*, meaning that it has a low likelihood of breaking down and leading to war. Nuclear threats did not always result in such stability. Prior to the advent of mutual vulnerability, each side's nuclear forces may have been vulnerable to destruction in a surprise attack by the other. Under such conditions, deterrence was, in the words of Albert Wohlstetter, "a delicate balance of terror."[26] The motivations for preemption may then have been high. If so, mutuality would then have had the same negative impact on the effectiveness of nuclear deterrence as it has on the effectiveness of conventional deterrence, if not more. But with mutual vulnerability has come stability. Nuclear deterrence has come to include the element of reassurance, and so has become, not delicate, but robust or rugged. Nuclear deterrence has, it seems, solved the traditional tension in military deterrence between strength and nonprovocativeness, making it a much more effective form of deterrence.

This claim concerning the great stability of nuclear deterrence is central to the standard defense of nuclear deterrence. Because it appeals to the factors of strength and provocativeness, which are stressed in a traditional understanding of deterrence effectiveness, it is also the implicit basis of the prudential and consequentialist arguments for nuclear deterrence from Chapters 1 and 2. But now it is time, as promised, to broaden this traditional prudential perspective.

The credibility problem

(2) Now we must consider the differences between nuclear and conventional deterrence concerning the second feature that distinguishes military deterrence from legal deterrence – the small number of parties involved in the threat relationship. Here another factor comes to the fore, one that has come to be of central importance with the advent of mutual vulnerability. This is threat credibility. Nuclear deterrence gives rise to a *credibility problem,* and this problem seems to call the effectiveness of nuclear deterrence into question, putting nuclear deterrence at a serious disadvantage by comparison with conventional deterrence. The credibility problem concerns the strength of the belief on the part of the threatened party that the threatener would be willing to carry out its threats. This belief is crucial for the success of deterrence. When this belief (in conjunction with the belief in the threatener's capability to carry out its threats) is strong, the threat is highly credible, and when it is weak, the threat is not. The credibility problem is the claim that nuclear deterrence suffers in effectiveness because nuclear threats cannot achieve a high level of credibility, the result being that the strength of this belief is seriously undermined.

The credibility problem is not, in general, as serious a matter for conventional deterrence, because there is usually some history of threat execution to demonstrate the threatener's dispositional willingness to carry out its threats. As Bernard Brodie says of conventional deterrence: "We should notice . . . the positive function played by the failures. The very frequency with which wars occurred contributed importantly to the credibility inherent in any threat."[27] In addition, even in the absence of such a history, there is usually a substantial basis for the threatened party's presuming that the threatener would be willing to carry out its threats, because nations frequently believe that they would be victorious in conventional war. The seriousness of the credibility problem for nuclear deterrence is the result of the threatened party's being unable, in general, to find the basis for either a demonstration or a presumption of the threatener's willingness to carry out its nuclear threats.

Consider first the possibility of a demonstration that the threatener would be willing to carry out its nuclear threats. A demonstration requires instances of threat execution. But under mutual vulnerability there are unlikely to be any threat executions, because one execution could bring about the end of the societies in question. Thus, there is unlikely to be any basis for a demonstration of the threatener's willingness to carry out its nuclear threats. The result is a credibility problem, for, as Kenneth Boulding points out: "If threats are not carried out their credibility gradually declines. Credibility, as it were, is a commodity which depreciates with the mere passage of time."[28]

Given that a demonstration of willingness requires behavioral manifestations, however, could there be some manifestations of a willingness to carry out nuclear threats other than a history of carrying out specifically nuclear threats? Could the carrying out of other kinds of threats serve to demonstrate a willingness to carry out nuclear threats? A willingness to carry out threats is the character trait of *resolve.* Can a resolve to carry out nuclear threats be demonstrated by behavior other than the carrying out of nuclear threats? Nations in general are often concerned to "show resolve," to be seen as tough, as unwilling to back down when challenged. Nuclear nations seem to believe that showing resolve in nonnuclear ways can demonstrate resolve to carry out nuclear threats. They seem to believe that resolve carries over from the one area to the other, or perhaps that resolve is of a piece, so that a show of resolve in one area is strong evidence for the existence of resolve across the board. On this view, a nation could show its willingness to carry out nuclear threats by carrying out other military threats. Schelling claims that "our threats are interdependent," and he gives a label to this interdependence: "'Face' is merely the interdependence of a country's commitments; it is a country's reputation for action, the expectations other countries have about its behavior."[29]

But is there an interdependence of threats such that a country's reputation for action in the conventional military area would be taken as an indication of its willingness to carry out nuclear threats? The kind of interdependence Schelling has in mind is primarily geographical, for the context of his discussion is "the difference between the national homeland and everything 'abroad'."[30] The interdependence between conventional and nuclear threats, on the other hand, is weak at best, however strong the interdependence may be among threats concerning different geographical areas.[31] Military threats are not interdependent across the nuclear firebreak, or at least not strongly so. The conventional and nuclear situations are so dissimilar, the stakes and nature of the conflict so different, that the threatened party is unlikely to draw strong conclusions about the willingness of the threatener to carry out its nuclear threats from its having demonstrated a willingness to carry out conventional threats. A situation in which a nuclear threat might be carried out would be so different in its potential outcomes from previous military situations that the threatener's past behavior would probably not be taken as a very reliable guide to predicting its response.

Resolve is not of a piece in this respect. It does not carry over well from conventional to nuclear threats. The attempt to produce such carry-over is as if a government tried to demonstrate its willingness to carry out its legal threat of capital punishment by its diligence in prosecuting parking violators. A nation's history of carrying out conventional threats may provide some basis to demonstrate its willingness to carry out its nuclear threats, but not much. The absence of a basis for a clear demonstration of the threatener's willingness to carry out its nuclear threats is indicated by Hans Morganthau: "While traditional force operates psychologically through the intermediary of actual physical employment, nuclear force has a psychological function pure and simple."[32] The psychology on which nuclear deterrence depends is not supported or reinforced by the actual employment of force, unlike the case with conventional deterrence. So much the worse for that psychology.

What about the other factor that can support the credibility of military threats, a presumption that the threatener would be willing to carry out its threats? The basis for such a presumption, like the basis for demonstration, is very weak in the case of nuclear deterrence. The execution of a nuclear threat under mutual vulnerability is very unlikely to be in the self-interest of the threatener. The general problem is made clear by Phil Williams: "Credibility is more difficult to achieve where both sides are able to inflict harm upon each other, since the implementation of a threat may then require that the deterrer himself is prepared to make certain sacrifices."[33] Because conventional military threat execution may be costly, it is not always rational. But in the case of nuclear deterrence, in particular, threat execution is almost never rational. Executing a nuclear threat is fighting a nuclear war. Fighting a nuclear war would be prudentially rational only if that war were limited, and a limited nuclear war is not reasonably foreseeable. If it is not rational to expect a nuclear war to be limited, it would not be rational to carry out a nuclear threat.

Consider this in the light of the factors that sometimes make it rational for a nation to carry out a military threat. First, the execution of a nuclear threat is much less likely than the execution of a conventional threat to have value in deterring future military conflict. The main reason is that the societal destruction that may result would rule out the achievement of any future deterrent value, special or general, because there would no longer be a nation against which aggression could be deterred. Second, the prospects for victory could not make rational the execution of a nuclear threat, in contrast with the execution of a conventional threat, given that a limited nuclear war is not reasonably foreseeable. Third, for the same reason, the prospects for denial are unlikely to make nuclear threat execution rational.[34] Nuclear deterrence is deterrence primarily by threat of punishment rather than by threat of denial. Denial is a battlefield notion, involving the idea of pushing back the aggressor's forces on the ground.[35] But a nuclear war may not involve a battlefield, and even if it does, nuclear violence is likely to be present at a higher order of magnitude on the homefront. Nuclear force could be used for denial, if it were counterforce targeted and if it involved relatively small, so-called tactical nuclear weapons, and a nuclear war may at least begin on a traditional battlefield. But the threat of denial posed by these capabilities is overshadowed by the threat of societal destruction, because it is not reasonably foreseeable that societal destruction could be avoided. A nation could reasonably expect to achieve prudentially advantageous denial from its nuclear threat execution only if it could reasonably expect the nuclear war to be limited.[36]

The point is not that there can be no basis for either a demonstration or a presumption of a threatener's willingness to carry out its nuclear threats. There may be cases, given the details, where the execution of a nuclear threat in a situation of mutual vulnerability would be rational. That it is not rational to expect a limited nuclear war does not imply that it may not be rational to run the risk of the war's not remaining limited, say, in a situation where the gains from executing the nuclear threat would be great.[37] Nor is it my point that nuclear threats, in the absence of a basis for either a demonstration or a presumption of the threatener's willingness to carry them out, have *no* credibility. Threat credibility is not all-or-nothing, but a matter of degree. The argument does not imply that nuclear threats have no credibility, but rather that they cannot achieve a high level of credibility. Nuclear threats may well achieve some middling amount of credibility.[38] In any case, the main point of the argument is simply that the basis for threat credibility is much weaker for nuclear deterrence than for conventional deterrence. Given the importance of credibility in deterrence effectiveness, nuclear deterrence is at a significant disadvantage by comparison with conventional deterrence in this regard.

Some have suggested that one way a nation could make its nuclear threats more credible would be for it to make its opponent believe that it is irrational. Schelling asserts: "It is not a universal advantage in situations of conflict to be inalienably and manifestly rational in decision and motivation."[39] Glenn Snyder claims: "The deterrer may increase the credibility of a seemingly irrational response by creating the general impression that he is prone to act irrationally."[40] This approach to deterrence credibility is an admission that there is little basis for a presumption of willingness. In recognition of this, and perhaps also in recognition of the general point that demonstration takes precedence over presumption, this approach is, in effect, a suggestion that a nation attempt a demonstration of its willingness to carry out its nuclear threats by showing that it has a "disposition" to act contrary to the way a nation normally would be presumed to act – that is, in its own rational self-interest. By putting on a show of irrationality, a nation seeks to demonstrate not a specific resolve to carry out nuclear threats, but a tendency to act when challenged in ways contrary to its best interests, which the lack of a presumption of willingness shows the execution of nuclear threats to be. Cultivating an image of irrationality may bolster the credibility of nuclear threats to some degree, but it is not an adequate solution to the credibility problem. A demonstration of irrationality has the same shortcoming as a demonstration of resolve. Irrationality, like resolve, is not of a piece. That a nation, like a person, disregards its best interests in less important matters does not entail that it will do so in matters of monumental importance. Again, the prospect of societal destruction concentrates the mind.

Nuclear threats and nondeliberative conformity

(3) The third feature distinguishing military deterrence from legal deterrence is that military deterrence is a nondomestic institution. Does this feature indicate any differences between conventional and nuclear deterrence relevant to the prudential comparison? The general implication of the fact that military deterrence is a nondomestic institution is that there is a weakness in its ability to sustain habits of nondeliberative conformity. Conventional and nuclear deterrence share this weakness. Neither kind of deterrence is likely to be perceived as legitimate, because, since neither is a domestic institution, neither involves a threatener with authority to threaten the other. In addition, both kinds of deterrence will suffer from perceptions of lack of fairness, because, unlike the case of legal deterrence, the threats apply not to everyone, but only to one's adversaries. But there is one feature of nuclear deterrence that would make it less likely than conventional deterrence to be perceived as fair. Nuclear threats hold hostages, so they are unfair in a way that conventional threats are not. Nuclear threats are threats of punishment, but, unlike the case of legal threats, the punishment would involve harming those who are not responsible for the nonconforming behavior.[41] For the reasons discussed in Chapter 2, such punishment is unfair, so that a form of deterrence that threatens it is less likely to be perceived as fair. To that extent, nuclear deterrence is less likely to sustain habits of nondeliberative conformity than is conventional deterrence, and this represents another comparative disadvantage for nuclear deterrence.

This may be illustrated by the analogy of "the gunman writ large." If a gunman takes over a territory and rules it for some time, his threats become institutionalized, yet they lack legitimacy, because the assumption is that gunman's rule is not (not yet, at least) a government. In such a situation, the gunman's threats are like military threats, and have the same problem in sustaining habits of conformity – namely, that the threats are likely to be perceived as neither legitimate nor fair. But the gunman would make it even less likely that his threats would be perceived as fair were he to direct them against innocent third parties, the result being that habits of nondeliberative conformity would be less likely to be sustained. The argument does not show that habits of nondeliberative conformity could not be sustained in the case of nuclear deterrence. Such habits might exist. The claim is that they are less likely to be sustained, so less likely to exist or more likely to be weak, than such habits in the case of conventional deterrence. Nuclear deterrence is, in this respect, at another prudential disadvantage by comparison with conventional deterrence.

Potency and credibility divorced

Thus, there are two kinds of prudential disadvantage suffered by nuclear deterrence by comparison with conventional deterrence – the credibility problem and the lesser ability of nuclear deterrence to sustain habits of nondeliberative conformity. But the credibility problem is by far the more serious of the two, because no form of military deterrence does very well in sustaining habits of nondeliberative conformity. So, when speaking of the comparative disadvantages of nuclear deterrence, I will give primary attention to the credibility problem. Assessing the relative effectiveness of nuclear deterrence involves, then, comparing this disadvantage of the policy with its comparative advantages – namely, the crystal ball effect and reassurance. The comparative advantages of nuclear deterrence are what make it seem so obviously better than conventional deterrence in the terms in which the effectiveness of military deterrence was traditionally assessed. Conventional deterrence involves a trade-off, in terms of effectiveness, between strength and nonprovocativeness. But nuclear deterrence, through its capacity for reassurance, obviates the need for this trade-off. Nuclear deterrence eliminates the tension between the need for military potency and the need to avoid provocation that traditionally undermined the effectiveness of military deterrence. Nuclear deterrence is at once an effective policy in both respects. But then there is the problem with credibility.

Credibility was not traditionally a major focus of concern in assessing the effectiveness of military deterrence. One reason is that the willingness of nations to carry out their military threats could often be presumed, and nations would demonstrate that willingness by sometimes carrying out the threats, all because executing the threats was often prudentially rational. But a more important reason is that under conventional deterrence, credibility is not, in general, an independent consideration. The most important consideration is military strength, and threats are credible to the extent that the military forces are potent. In other words, the other factors that make deterrence effective – the capability of the threatener to carry out its threat and the amount of harm threatened – also make conventional deterrent threats credible. Under conventional deterrence, the more potent a nation's forces are, the less damage the opponent could do in war, so the more reason the nation had to carry out its threats, so the more credible were the threats.

But nuclear deterrence changes all this. Considerations of military potency, creating the crystal ball effect, are now at odds with credibility. This is the prudential problem of nuclear deterrence. It is a problem new with nuclear weapons. Because prudential evaluations of military policy prior to mutual vulnerability did not find credibility to be at odds with other factors making for effective deterrence, credibility did not need to be given independent consideration. But the broadened prudential perspective of our theory of deterrence effectiveness shows that nuclear weapons bring into being a tension between credibility and other factors determining deterrence effectiveness. This is because deterrence itself is a derivative consideration where conventional forces are concerned. The deterrent effectiveness of conventional forces is, in general, a function of their effectiveness in fighting a war, because conventional deterrence is primarily deterrence by threat of denial. So the credibility of a conventional deterrent is dependent on the war-fighting effectiveness of the forces, which is based on factors such as the capability of the threatening nation to carry out its military threats and its ability to inflict harm that would clearly constitute an overriding disadvantage to the nation threatened. But in the condition of mutual vulnerability, these factors, though they support the effectiveness of deterrence, no longer make for effective war fighting. So, rather than supporting the credibility of the deterrent, they undermine it. The great destructive power of nuclear weapons is an advantage in that it reconciles strength and non-provocativeness, but it is a disadvantage, in that it puts strength at odds with credibility.

The prudential problem is that nuclear deterrence brings prudence into conflict with itself, as the moral problem is that nuclear deterrence brings morality into conflict with itself. The main prudential disadvantage of nuclear deterrence is a consequence of its prudential advantages. One advantage is the crystal ball effect, by virtue of which nonconforming behavior seems thoroughly irrational. But the crystal ball effect also implies that retaliation for such behavior is irrational, thus undermining credibility. Nuclear deterrence joins together potency and nonprovocativeness, but at the cost of driving apart potency and credibility. Reassurance is a form of self-deterrence and self-deterrence entails problems with credibility. That the prime disadvantage of nuclear deterrence is a function of its advantages is what makes the prudential evaluation of nuclear deterrence problematic. Nuclear deterrence does not simply happen to have advantages as well as disadvantages. But they are logically linked, the disadvantages having the same source as the advantages in the uniquely destructive character of nuclear weapons.

DOES NUCLEAR DETERRENCE HAVE MARGINAL DETERRENT VALUE?

Now is the time to attempt an overall comparison between nuclear deterrence and conventional deterrence to determine whether nuclear deterrence has marginal deterrent value. In prudential terms, nuclear deterrence has both significant advantages and a striking disadvantage compared with conventional deterrence. On the one hand, nuclear threats seem much superior to conventional threats in deterrent value due to the crystal ball effect and reassurance. On the other hand, nuclear threats seem much less effective than conventional threats due to the credibility problem. It is easy to see how those who study nuclear deterrence could be led to sharply diverging positions on its prudential value. Focusing on the advantages leads one to view nuclear deterrence as very effective, whereas focusing on its prime disadvantage leads one seriously to question its effectiveness. Attempting to take account of the factors on both sides may leave one in great uncertainty.

The prudential problem, like the moral problem, results in our being pulled in opposite directions. For this reason, the prudential problem, like the moral problem, is often represented as a paradox, a paradox of (prudential) rationality.[42] One formulation of this paradox is the following:

(1) It is rational to make nuclear threats, but it is not rational to carry them out.

(2) If it is not rational to carry out a threat, it is not rational to make that threat.

This is a paradox in the sense that it is two incompatible statements, each of which seems evidently true. But the prudential problem, like the moral problem, is a puzzle for practice rather than for mere reflection, so it is better called a dilemma than a paradox. It is not a true dilemma, however, for, unlike the moral problem, it is not even in appearance a conflict of obligations. It is not a conflict because it is solved by showing what the prudential obligation is, not by showing where the overriding obligation lies. The prudential obligation is found not by establishing a precedence order between existing obligations, as with the moral conflicts, but by considering what the factors represented in the conflicting claims, taken together, show the single obligation to be. This is the logical difference between the prudential problem and the moral problem.

The rationality paradox represents our argument in the following way. Claim (1) is a recognition of the crystal ball effect, as a result of which the nuclear threat is effective but its execution dangerous. Claim (2) is closely related to the credibility problem, according to which, if the threat is too dangerous, hence irrational, to carry out, then there is an inadequate basis for presuming the threatener's willingness to carry it out, which in turn implies that the threat is ineffective.[43] If the threat is ineffective, there is no reason to make it, hence it is not rational to make it. But seeing the paradox in this way points toward its solution. If some factors (the crystal ball effect and reassurance) tend to make nuclear deterrence more effective than conventional deterrence, whereas others (primarily the credibility problem) tend to make it less effective, the solution to the prudential problem is simply to determine the impact of all the factors taken together on deterrence effectiveness. This would indicate the overall effectiveness of nuclear deterrence by comparison with conventional deterrence. The paradox is simply a misleading way of stating the problem of finding the net marginal deterrent value of nuclear threats. This finding will show either that (1) is false, given (2), or that (2) is false, given (1), and so remove the seeming paradox. But determining where the balance of greater effectiveness lies is no simple matter.[44] Though possible in principle, it is extremely difficult in practice. It is hard to see how these factors could be quantified so that a metric could be established between them. Without such a metric, adequate comparison seems impossible.

General failure

There is, however, a way to finesse this difficulty. There is a way to establish, in the face of the seeming impossibility of determining whether or not the advantages outweigh the disadvantages, a prima facie conclusion on the question of the prudential preferability of nuclear deterrence, a conclusion only partly dependent on the question of net marginal deterrent value. To reach this conclusion, we must consider not just the likelihood of war under the two different forms of deterrence, but the destructiveness of such war. A full-scale nuclear war would be vastly more destructive than a full-scale conventional war, but this is a factor that has so far not been included in the discussion. The effectiveness of deterrence policy has until now been cast, as it generally should, simply in terms of the likelihood of war under that policy, not in terms of what that war would be like. I will now argue, however, that the overwhelming destructiveness of nuclear war is not a consideration completely independent of comparative effectiveness. The destructiveness of nuclear war is relevant to the effectiveness question. Introducing the issue of destructiveness into the argument will also allow the argument more adequately to determine overall prudential preferability, because the comparative destructiveness of the two kinds of wars is certainly relevant to which form of deterrence is prudentially preferable. To see how these concerns are joined, I must recall some of the discussion of legal deterrence from Chapter 3.

If the number of instances of nonconforming behavior under a legal system becomes great enough, the social order of which that legal system is a part completely breaks down. Because a central social purpose of the law is to maintain the social order, a legal deterrence system that is unable to keep the number of instances of nonconforming behavior low enough to prevent this from happening is a general failure. Recall that the general failure of a legal deterrence system is to be distinguished from its particular failures. An important implication is that whether or not a legal deterrence system is a general failure is not dependent exclusively on its particular failures – that is, on the number of instances of nonconforming behavior under that system. The tendency of the social order to break down, its robustness or fragility in the face of instances of nonconforming behavior, is a factor as well. If a social order is fragile in this sense, a legal deterrence system would have to allow fewer instances of nonconforming behavior in order to avoid complete social breakdown than if the social order were more robust. Because a deterrence system that is a general failure is an ineffective system, deterrence effectiveness is not exclusively a matter of the number of instances of nonconforming behavior, but is also dependent on the fragility or robustness of the social order of which that system is a part.

In the light of this, one can see how a deterrence system might *necessarily* be a general failure. It would be, if it did not have a positive instability tolerance. Instability tolerance, as defined in Chapter 3, is the distance on a scale of instances of nonconforming behavior between the point of maximum deterrence-induced stability for a deterrence system (the point of its maximum effectiveness in terms of reducing instances of nonconforming behavior) and the breakdown point (the point at which instances of nonconforming behavior are frequent enough to result in a complete breakdown of that social order). Instability tolerance would be a negative or a nonpositive quantity when the latter point is at or below the former. This would be a situation in which the deterrence system cannot, due to the fragility of the social order, reduce the number of such instances low enough to preserve the social order. In such a situation, a deterrence system would necessarily be a general failure. Social orders, as discussed earlier, are normally quite robust in the face of particular failures of legal deterrence – that is, they have a high positive instability tolerance of instances of illegal activity. But this need not always be the case. When a social order is on the verge of violent revolution, for example, it might, for extra-legal reasons, be so prone to break down that the contribution that legal deterrence could make to stemming the rising tide of social chaos would be insufficient to avoid the destruction of the old social order.[45]

Social orders are extremely fragile in the face of nuclear attack. However robust nuclear deterrence may be, it is meant to provide security for a social order that is extremely delicate in the face of the destruction it threatens. The point is often made that nuclear deterrence can tolerate no failure – that is, no particular failure, no instances of nonconforming behavior – because such an instance could initiate or lead to a war of mutual destruction. Bernard Brodie remarks that nuclear deterrence "uses a kind of threat which we feel must be absolutely effective, allowing no breakdowns ever." He continues: "The sanction is, to say the least, not designed for repeating action. One use of it will be fatally too many."[46] If there were an instance of nonconforming behavior leading to threat execution, there could be no reasonable expectation that the destruction of the society would not result. So, a policy of nuclear deterrence needs to be total rather than restrictive, avoiding not merely some instances of nonconforming behavior, but all. A single failure cannot be tolerated.[47] This is in contrast with conventional deterrence, where not only is a particular failure unlikely to lead to the destruction of the threatener's society, but the resulting war might be prudentially advantageous for the threatener. This difference between nuclear and conventional deterrence is due to the comparative fragility of social orders in the face of the destruction involved in each kind of war.[48]

A deterrence system is a general failure when the social order completely breaks down. Societal destruction brought about by nuclear war would be a most vivid example of complete social breakdown. Of course, the cause of breakdown in this case – massive destruction of human life and social infrastructure – differs considerably from the cause of breakdown resulting from a general failure of a system of legal deterrence, which is the social chaos brought about by widespread disregard for the law. One may be grimmer to contemplate than the other, but each form of social breakdown represents the general failure of a deterrence system. Nuclear deterrence is for the sake of national security, so it, like legal deterrence, has as a central social purpose to maintain the social order. If nuclear deterrence fails in this by leading to complete social breakdown, it is appropriately regarded as a general failure. In the case of legal deterrence, general failure usually results only when the number of particular failures is very large. But general failure can result from a single particular failure in the case of nuclear deterrence. As Richard Wasserstrom observes: "In the nuclear context, success is an all-or-nothing matter. There is no third way, as there is in thinking about the system of criminal law and deterrence, of viewing it as systemically successful even while it fails in some particular cases."[49] There is, then, little distinction, in the case of nuclear deterrence, between particular and general failure. Nuclear deterrence, Leon Wieseltier observes, "must be the only public arrangement that is a total failure if it is successful only

99.9 percent of the time."[50] There is no reasonable expectation that a particular failure will not amount to general failure.[51]

The special destructiveness of nuclear war makes nuclear deterrence prone to general failure (because it may take only one particular failure), and the judgment of comparative effectiveness must take account of this, as well as of marginal deterrent value. The alternative approach that would keep matters of effectiveness and destructiveness separate is suggested by Jonathan Schell: "The problem with deterrence is not that it doesn't 'work' – it is, I am sure, a very effective (though far from infallible) way of restraining the superpowers from attacking one another, should they be inclined to do so – but that we must pay an inconceivable price if it fails."[52] This approach is misleading, because it fails to recognize that the tendency of a deterrence system to destroy the society of which it is a part is an important factor in a comparative assessment of how well it works. Thus this factor should appear along with that of net deterrent value in the judgment of effectiveness. More generally, of course, both the net deterrent value of nuclear deterrence (if any) and the destructiveness of its particular failure are relevant to the question of prudential preferability.

How are the two factors to be combined? Considerations of general failure carry greater weight than considerations of marginal deterrent value, because complete social breakdown is a more serious matter than individual instances of nonconforming behavior. If a form of deterrence is a general failure, it is, clearly, less effective than a form of deterrence that is not, even if the former has marginal deterrent value by comparison with the latter. It is possible for a form of deterrence that is a general failure to have marginal deterrent value by comparison with a form of deterrence that is not, because whether or not a deterrence system is a general failure depends not only on the likelihood of particular failure under that system, but also on the fragility of the social order in the face of those particular failures. Particular failures of one form of deterrence may have more serious consequences for a social order than particular failures of another form of deterrence. It may take fewer particular failures to result in complete social breakdown in the one case than in the other. This is what we find in the comparison between nuclear and conventional deterrence. In this sense, nuclear deterrence may be less effective than conventional deterrence, even if it is nuclear deterrence that has marginal deterrent value.

Two easy arguments

As a result of the close connection between particular failure and general failure in the case of nuclear deterrence, there are two easy arguments that nuclear deterrence is necessarily a general failure, and hence less effective than conventional deterrence, which is not. The first is a dilemma: Nuclear deterrence is either a general failure because it has particular failures or it is a general failure because it does not. The first horn of the dilemma is based on the connection between particular and general failure. If nuclear deterrence has any particular failures, it is likely to be a general failure. The second horn is based on the argument (from the last chapter) that no deterrence system can reduce the number of instances of nonconforming behavior to zero, because of the role of such instances in demonstrating that the threatener is willing to carry out its threats. One might think that this argument is inapplicable to military deterrence, because a presumption of the threatener's willingness to carry out its threats can replace such a demonstration. But this may not be so. It may be that whereas a presumption of willingness can bolster credibility when there is a weak demonstration of willingness, the former may not be able completely to replace the latter. A presumption of willingness may be able to extend the time that a threat would retain an adequate level of credibility in the absence of any threat executions, but not postpone forever the need for some demonstration of willingness.

The second (related) argument is this. Nuclear deterrence is necessarily a general failure because it does not have a positive instability tolerance. Because of human fallibility, no deterrence system can escape particular failure indefinitely, forever avoiding instances of nonconforming behavior. Because institutions depend on human choices, none can be expected to function perfectly. As a result, there is, in the case of nuclear deterrence, no positive distance from the point of maximum deterrence-induced stability to the point of complete social breakdown. At best, the value of each is one. Nuclear deterrence cannot guarantee less than one particular failure, and one particular failure is likely all that is needed for general failure. To get from the conclusion of these two arguments to the conclusion that nuclear deterrence is less effective than conventional deterrence, one need only add that conventional deterrence is not necessarily a general failure. Because conventional deterrence does not involve a condition of mutual vulnerability, it often fails in particular cases without being a general failure. These two arguments that nuclear deterrence is not prudentially preferable to conventional deterrence completely bypass the question of marginal deterrent value.

But these two easy arguments are too easy. Each assumes that nuclear deterrence would eventually result in a particular failure, which would likely amount to a general failure. But if the likelihood of there being a particular failure of nuclear deterrence over an extended time period is low enough, it may be treated as negligible. If the likelihood of nuclear deterrence failing over, say, fifty years is very small, there may be, given the other considerations involved, a case for saying that that likelihood, in practice, need not be treated as decisive. The prospects that nuclear deterrence would eventually become a general failure may not weigh so heavily if the "eventually" is likely to be measured in centuries. In a similar manner, certain activities, such as genetic engineering, are seen as prudent despite their involving some, presumably very small, risk of a catastrophe of similar magnitude. If the risk of catastrophe with nuclear deterrence is very small, that risk should not override all other factors in determining the comparative effectiveness of nuclear deterrence.

The question whether the likelihood of nuclear deterrence's failing is negligible is one that our discussion of marginal deterrent value can help to answer. Conventional deterrence has a long history of particular failure. Clearly, the likelihood that a conventional deterrence system will have a particular failure is far from negligible. So the likelihood that a nuclear deterrence system will have a particular failure is negligible only if nuclear deterrence is substantially more effective than conventional deterrence – that is, only if it has a *substantial* marginal deterrent value in comparison with conventional deterrence. The question, then, is not simply whether nuclear deterrence has any marginal deterrent value, but whether it has substantial marginal deterrent value.

The argument of this chapter provides no support for the claim that nuclear deterrence has substantial marginal deterrent value by comparison with conventional deterrence. Indeed, the argument provides reason to think that it does not. For the argument leaves open whether nuclear deterrence has *any* marginal deterrent value at all by comparison with conventional deterrence. For all the argument implies, it may be conventional deterrence that has the marginal deterrent value. There are important factors on both sides, the crystal ball effect and reassurance favoring nuclear deterrence and the credibility problem favoring conventional deterrence. The prudential problem of nuclear deterrence leaves us unable to decide which form of military deterrence has marginal deterrent value in comparison with the other. If all the factors favored nuclear deterrence, there would be no reason to conclude that nuclear deterrence did not have substantial marginal deterrent value. But in the light of the important factor favoring conventional deterrence, there is reason to believe that if it is nuclear deterrence that has the marginal deterrent value, its marginal deterrent value is only marginal. The argument is that if nuclear deterrence had substantial marginal deterrent value, there would be no prudential problem with nuclear deterrence – that is, it would not be unclear which form of deterrence has the marginal deterrent value.

The prima facie argument

Thus, the argument implies that nuclear deterrence does not have substantial marginal deterrent value in comparison with conventional deterrence. If so, the likelihood of particular failure for nuclear deterrence is not negligible. It follows that the likelihood of general failure is decisive in determining comparative effectiveness. Nuclear deterrence is less effective than conventional deterrence. Conventional deterrence is prudentially preferable to nuclear deterrence. In other words, even if nuclear deterrence has some marginal deterrent value, a possibility the argument leaves open, nuclear deterrence would not be prudentially preferable to conventional deterrence, for unless the marginal deterrent value were substantial, the prospect that nuclear deterrence would be a general failure would be the overriding consideration. Given the differential effects on the social order of their particular failures, nuclear deterrence is prudentially preferable to conventional deterrence only if it is much less prone to particular failure, which is the case only if it has substantial marginal deterrent value. The argument provides a basis for thinking that this is not the case.

This argument is not conclusive. But it does amount to a *prima facie argument* that nuclear deterrence is not prudentially preferable to conventional deterrence. At the least, it shifts the burden of proof to supporters of nuclear deterrence. If their rebuttals should prove ineffective, the conclusion would stand. Nuclear deterrence is sometimes said to involve a great trade-off, in that it lessens the likelihood of war in exchange for increasing war's destructiveness.[53] The question is, of course, whether the exchange is worth it. Are we better off with nuclear deterrence, or would we be better off under conventional deterrence. Some argue that it is a trade worth making. The argument here is, at least prima facie, that it is not.[54] The rebuttals offered by supporters of nuclear deterrence, however, remain to be heard.

The abstractness of the argument

But a cautionary note about the abstract nature of the argument is in order. Assume for the moment that the rebuttals fail and that the conclusion of the prima facie argument stands. What does that tell us? The argument does not get us as far as we had thought it would. It does not yet provide a resolution of the conflict between prudence and morality and the conflict within morality. The argument, in its current form, is too abstract to establish that prudential revisionism is the correct approach to resolving these two conflicts, because it does not directly imply that the prudential and the consequentialist arguments from Chapters 1 and 2 are unsound. The argument, even assuming the rebuttals fail, is not yet sufficiently developed to show these arguments unsound. To appreciate this, consider the argument in the context of the following three questions:

(1) Is it a good thing prudentially that nuclear weapons were invented and that the condition of mutual vulnerability came into being?

(2) When nations are in a condition of mutual vulnerability, is there sufficient prudential reason to seek to escape that condition by replacing nuclear deterrence with conventional deterrence?

(3) From a prudential point of view, what military policy should some particular nation adopt when facing some particular opponent with an assured destruction capability?

These questions are at different levels of abstraction, (1) being the most abstract and (3) the least.

The only one of these questions on which the prima facie argument, as presently developed, has immediate bearing is (1). The argument, if unrebutted, shows that (1) should be answered in the negative. But an answer to this question has no direct relevance to our current situation, because mutual vulnerability has become actual, and, as many have pointed out, nuclear weapons cannot be "disinvented." The moment cannot be recaptured when it would have been possible to choose not to have nuclear weapons invented, if it ever was practically possible to stop their invention, given the seemingly inexorable growth in human scientific and technical skill. The claim that conventional deterrence is prudentially preferable, in the sense implied by a negative answer to (1), does not, by itself, tell us what to do. This is why the prima facie argument, does not, in its present form, show the prudential and consequentialist arguments to be unsound. Rather than being part of current debates over nuclear weapons policy, question (1) relates to a much less practical concern about the abstract desirability of the existence of nuclear weapons. Some believe that nuclear weapons are desirable in this sense, because in making great-power war so horrible, they have succeeded in banishing it from history. Such thoughts, though they may not often be expressed, are an important undercurrent in the nuclear debate. But though an answer to (1) has no direct implications for policy, it has important indirect implications.

Only an answer to (2) will join the discussion from Chapters 1 and 2. Question (2) is the one that must be addressed in order to determine the soundness of the prudential and consequentialist arguments. An answer to (2) speaks of our historical situation, our need to choose within a condition of mutual vulnerability, and so would have policy implications for us. If the answer to (2) is yes, prudential revisionism is the correct approach to resolving the two conflicts. If the answer is yes, the implication is that we should abandon nuclear deterrence. If the answer to (1) is no, as the prima facie argument concludes, this would support an affirmative answer to (2), but not conclusively. The argument needs to be further developed before one can know whether or not its conclusion necessitates an affirmative answer to (2). The discussion of the rebuttals will help in this development in two ways. First, now dropping the assumption that the rebuttals fail, we need to determine whether they succeed or fail in order to know whether or not the conclusion of the prima facie argument, and the implied negative answer to (1), stand. Second, if the rebuttals do fail, the additional detail brought into the argument by the discussion of them may allow us to put on firmer footing the implications for question (2) of the negative answer to (1). In particular, we may be able to determine not only whether the abstract prudential preferability of conventional deterrence implies that we should abandon nuclear for conventional deterrence given the actuality of mutual vulnerability, but also, if we should abandon nuclear deterrence, whether we ought to do this unilaterally or attempt it only bilaterally.

Because of the general character of the argument in this book, I will not consider the policy implications the argument may have regarding question (3). My concern is the difference nuclear weapons make, and this difference, though it originated in the vicissitudes of the post-war relationship between the United States and the Soviet Union, clearly transcends that or any other particular nuclear relationship. Any two nations that are adversaries and have a certain, now relatively minimal, technological capability can bring themselves into a condition of mutual vulnerability. My question concerns what one can say about any two nations in a condition of mutual vulnerability, in abstraction from the particular nature of their relationship. Nuclear weapons make a difference in the general case, and this difference has some bearing on the policy choices that should be made in particular cases. The general case is worthy of attention.

DEFENSES OF NUCLEAR DETERRENCE

To be successful, a rebuttal to the prima facie argument must show that nuclear deterrence has substantial marginal deterrent value by comparison with conventional deterrence. To show this, it must successfully argue either (a) that the factors favoring nuclear deterrence over conventional deterrence – the crystal ball effect and reassurance — are stronger and carry more weight in the prudential calculus than indicated in the discussion so far; or (b) that the chief factor favoring conventional deterrence — the credibility problem – is weaker than so far indicated. Either argument would show that the factors favoring nuclear deterrence strongly outweigh the factor favoring conventional deterrence, from which one could conclude that nuclear deterrence has substantial marginal deterrent value. But it is important to insure that if (a) is adopted, the argument does not at the same time show that the factor favoring conventional deterrence is stronger than so far indicated, or that if (b) is adopted, the argument does not at the same time show that the factors favoring nuclear deterrence are weaker than so far indicated. For otherwise the advantage the argument gains for nuclear deterrence on the one hand might be lost on the other. The concern must be net deterrent effect. In any case, (a) and (b) each suggests a line of rebuttal. The first argues that the factors favoring nuclear deterrence should be recognized as having greater weight than so far indicated, whereas the second argues that the factors favoring conventional deterrence should be recognized as having less weight than so far indicated.

These rebuttals rely on the fact that there are different kinds of nuclear deterrence, different ways to practice nuclear deterrence – that is, different deterrent strategies. Each line of rebuttal, (a) and (b), argues that there is some strategy under which nuclear deterrence would have substantial marginal deterrent value by comparison with conventional deterrence. Different nuclear strategies involve different kinds of nuclear threats, so it would not be surprising if the effectiveness of nuclear deterrence differed depending on what strategy was adopted. It is plausible that there is a kind of strategy under which nuclear deterrence is more effective than conventional deterrence, even though it is less effective than conventional deterrence under another kind of strategy.[55] The military relationship between the United States and the Soviet Union during the Cold War saw different kinds of nuclear threats representing different kinds of nuclear strategies. Out of this historical parade, one can discern two main kinds of strategy, which may be taken as the two main ways in which strategic relations between opponents under a condition of mutual vulnerability may be structured.[56] One kind of strategy emphasizes what is distinctive about nuclear weapons, while the other emphasizes the continuity between nuclear and conventional weapons as military implements. One line of rebuttal appeals to the first of these kinds of strategy, while the other appeals to the second.

Rebuttal (a), which argues that the factors favoring nuclear deterrence carry greater weight than so far indicated, appeals to the kind of strategy that emphasizes what is distinctive about nuclear weapons. Emphasis is put on the deterrent advantages afforded by the condition of mutual vulnerability – namely, the crystal ball effect and reassurance. The argument for the claim that these advantages substantially outweigh the disadvantage of the credibility problem is that the advantages create a deterrent strong enough to succeed in the face of uncertainty about whether or not the threatener would carry out its threat. Societal destruction is such a horrific prospect that merely the chance that it would come about is more than sufficient to deter nonconforming behavior. The ruggedness or great stability of nuclear deterrence is not dependent on beliefs about the threatener's willingness to carry out its threats. Rather, stability is "a technical quality and is inherent in certain configurations of force structure."[57] This rebuttal appeals to the idea that war can be eliminated if it is made horrible enough, in Churchill's words, that safety can be "the sturdy child of terror."[58] Those adopting this general approach label the strategy they recommend in different ways, sometimes calling it minimum deterrence or finite deterrence, other times talking of existential deterrence, but in all cases emphasizing the great deterrent efficacy inherent in mutual assured destruction.

Rebuttal (b) argues that the chief factor favoring conventional deterrence – the lack of credibility of nuclear threats – is less important than has been so far indicated. This line of rebuttal appeals to important continuities between nuclear and conventional weapons. The argument is that nuclear deterrence based on counterforce targeting can be highly credible, thereby greatly reducing or eliminating the prudential advantage conventional deterrence seems to enjoy over nuclear deterrence in this regard. Under a counterforce strategy, limited nuclear war, contrary to the argument in Chapter 1, could be reasonably foreseeable, which would mean that nuclear retaliation could be rational, and hence that there could be a presumption that the threatener would be willing to carry out its nuclear threat. What is continuous between conventional and nuclear weapons is the possibility of advantageous war outcomes. Nuclear threats are not credible if a nuclear war is unlikely to remain limited, but counterforce strategy can alter what is reasonably foreseeable, and in so doing, largely solve the credibility problem. This rebuttal does not see nuclear deterrence at a prudential disadvantage in relation to conventional deterrence, because it emphasizes the respects in which nuclear and conventional weapons are alike. In the words of Hans Morganthau, this approach "conventionalizes" nuclear weapons – that is, it treats them as usable in the way that conventional weapons are usable.[59]

The rebuttal offered by proponents of counterforce deterrence will be the first one discussed. Before discussing this rebuttal, however, the time is right to take up another thread of the argument. This chapter and the last have been an initial exploration of one approach to the moral problem of nuclear deterrence, prudential revisionism. But there are two other approaches, strategic revisionism and moral revisionism. Proponents of counterforce deterrence argue not only that counterforce targeting can solve the prudential problem by showing how nuclear threats can be quite credible, but also that it can resolve the moral problem by showing how a system of nuclear threats can avoid holding hostages. This attempt to resolve the moral problem is strategic revisionism, and it will be explored in the next chapter, prior to the discussion of the counterforce rebuttal in Chapter 6. Chapter 7 will discuss both the other line of rebuttal and the related notion of moral revisionism.

Chapter 5

Moral counterforce

Where should a nation aim the nuclear weapons with which it makes its deterrent threats? What kind of nuclear threats should it make? Some argue for a strategy based on aiming the weapons exclusively at the opponent's military forces and military assets, its counterforce targets, whereas others argue that at least some of the weapons should be aimed at the opponent's population and social and economic infrastructure, its countervalue targets. What a nation values most fundamentally is its social order, and it deploys its military forces primarily to protect that order. Thus the key elements of that order, the population and the social and economic infrastructure, being that on which the nation places the highest value, have traditionally been referred to as countervalue targets.[1] But countervalue and counterforce targets are not always neatly separable. For example, destruction of counterforce targets can do countervalue damage, because the destruction of military forces will often do significant indirect or "collateral" damage to human and economic elements of the social order. In any case, *counterforce deterrence*, based on a counterforce strategy, is here understood as a form of deterrence in which the nuclear warheads are aimed exclusively at counterforce targets, whereas *countervalue deterrence*, based on a countervalue strategy, is understood as a form of deterrence in which the warheads are aimed primarily though not necessarily exclusively at countervalue targets. A form of nuclear deterrence in which a major portion of the weapons are aimed at counterforce targets and a major portion at counterforce targets will be referred to as a *mixed strategy*.

Advocates of counterforce strategy argue on both prudential and moral grounds. In prudential terms, they argue that a counterforce strategy is necessary to make nuclear deterrence effective, because only counterforce threats can be sufficiently credible. Whereas countervalue attacks would almost inevitably lead to a countervalue retaliation, counterforce attacks might not, so counterforce attacks might be rational in some circumstances. This implies that a counterforce strategy could create a presumption that the threatener would be willing to carry out its threats. This would make a counterforce strategy credible in cases where a countervalue strategy would not be. If so, this prudential counterforce argument would constitute a successful rebuttal to the prima facie argument that nuclear deterrence is not prudentially preferable to conventional deterrence. This rebuttal is explored in the next chapter. If the prudential counterforce argument is successful, this would support the claim that prudential revisionism fails as an approach to resolving the conflict between morality and prudence and the conflict within morality. The failure of prudential revisionism would open the way for an alternative approach to resolving the conflicts. One of these alternatives is strategic revisionism, which maintains that the deontological argument against nuclear deterrence is unsound. The moral argument for counterforce deterrence makes the case for strategic revisionism.[2]

The moral counterforce argument is that a nation seeking to deter its opponent with a counterforce nuclear strategy need neither intend to kill civilians nor hold them hostage. If this is correct, it would show that there is a form of nuclear deterrence that is acceptable on deontological grounds.[3] Arthur Burns points out: "If and only if every practicable use we could now make of nuclear weapons obliterated the combatant/non-combatant distinction would the traditional ethics of armed force forbid the deployment of nuclear weapons as such." Counterforce strategy is put forth as a use of nuclear weapons that would not obliterate this distinction. It is, Burns reminds us, the use of an instrument that is evil, not the instrument itself.[4] Though some uses or threatened uses of nuclear weapons are morally unacceptable, others may not be. If the moral counterforce argument proves sound, then strategic revisionism would be the correct approach to resolving the two conflicts. This chapter examines the moral counterforce argument to determine the success of strategic revisionism. Before taking up the argument, however, I will present a general overview of counterforce strategy, which will serve as an introduction to both the moral argument of this chapter and the prudential argument of the next.[5]

COUNTERFORCE STRATEGY

If ought implies can, then, before one considers whether a nation ought, on either prudential or moral grounds, to adopt a counter-force strategy, one should first ask whether a counterforce strategy is possible. This is a complex question, turning both on technical considerations and on one's understanding of the goals of a counterforce strategy.[6] The most basic point is that if a nation's goal for its counterforce strategy is its having the ability to destroy all or almost all of the opponent's strategic nuclear forces, then a counterforce strategy that would achieve that goal is not possible. If a nation had such an ability, the opponent would be unable to retaliate effectively, and the nation would have overcome its own vulnerability. The condition of mutual vulnerability would no longer hold. The ability to destroy almost all of an opponent's strategic nuclear forces in an initial counterforce attack is referred to as a capacity for a *disarming first strike,* and it is the most important feature of the nuclear situation that in a situation of mutual vulnerability a disarming first strike is not possible.[7] If counterforce strategy requires the capacity for a disarming first strike, it is not possible.[8]

A disarming first strike is not possible despite the dramatic improvement in the technology of counterforce targeting that the arms race between the United States and the Soviet Union has produced. Some elements of a nation's strategic forces, such as military airfields, can be successfully targeted even with primitive nuclear weapons and delivery systems. But there are a number of factors, either inherent in the military situation or deliberately introduced, that make the successful targeting of strategic forces difficult and the problem of achieving the capacity for a disarming first strike intractable. First, strategic nuclear forces are often hard to locate, and hence to target successfully. Reconnaissance satellites partially solve this problem. But ballistic missile submarines remain practically unlocatable when on patrol. Land-based missiles may be made less vulnerable to attack by being buried and hardened, although improved accuracy in missile guidance systems can largely negate this advantage. But these missiles can be made mobile, so they, like submarine-based missiles, would not be easily locatable.

The factors making a disarming first strike impossible also pose serious difficulties for a counterforce strategy with less ambitious goals. In addition, there are other technical impediments. For example, assuming at least rough parity in strategic forces between superpower opponents, for a counterforce attack to leave the attacker relatively better off than its opponent would require that the attacker have a favorable "exchange ratio" – that is, a guarantee that it would destroy more of the opponent's forces than the forces it used in the attack. A favorable exchange ratio is not easy to achieve, though this problem can be at least partially overcome by technology allowing a single missile to launch several independently targeted warheads. Moreover, even if counterforce strategy had a less ambitious goal, a successful counterforce attack would probably require a command and control structure and an intelligence gathering network that could, in the midst of a nuclear war, achieve a high level of coordination of a nation's forces and acquire timely and reliable information about the opponent's military situation. This may not be possible.

An additional technical consideration making counterforce strategy difficult is the problem of effective discrimination – that is, the problem of destroying military targets without causing high levels of civilian damage. Advocates of counterforce strategy believe that it is important, for both prudential and moral reasons, to destroy military targets discriminately, avoiding significant collateral countervalue damage. Improvements in missile guidance systems, leading to great increases in accuracy, have done much to lessen, at least in theory, the potential collateral damage of a counterforce attack. For example, a modern cruise missile is three orders of magnitude more accurate than early ballistic missiles. Partly as a result of increases in accuracy, the total explosive power of the United States nuclear arsenal declined significantly during the Cold War: In 1980 it was one-quarter of what it was in 1960.[9] In addition, it is possible to design nuclear weapons so as to reduce nonlocalized effects such as radioactive fallout.[10] But the major difficulty with discriminate targeting is that some of the most important counterforce targets are in or adjacent to large cities, where even the most accurate nuclear attack would cause a large number of civilian deaths.

The extent to which the technical considerations concerning discrimination affect the possibility of counterforce strategy depends, of course, on how discriminate the strategy needs to be. In this regard, a broad distinction may be drawn between pure and impure counterforce strategies. A *pure counterforce strategy* is one in which the number of civilian casualties resulting from the attacks threatened against military targets would be (relatively) small. An *impure counterforce strategy*, on the other hand, is one in which the number of civilian casualties resulting from the attacks threatened against military targets would be very large. Given the destructiveness of nuclear weapons, this means, in practice, that the military targets under a pure counterforce strategy would have to be at a distance from cities, whereas the military targets under an impure counterforce strategy would include those in and near cities.[11] As a result, an impure counterforce strategy is distinguished from a mixed strategy simply on the basis of the intentions involved. An impure counterforce strategy and a mixed strategy would not differ in what kind of destruction would occur as a result of the threatened attacks, because in each case cities would be attacked. The distinction is that in the case of mixed strategy, the attacks would be intended to destroy the cities, whereas in the case of the impure counterforce strategy, they would not. Whether this is a distinction without a difference – that is, whether an impure counterforce strategy would be any more morally acceptable than a mixed strategy – remains to be seen. On the other hand, there is the question whether a pure counterforce strategy, which may successfully avoid the moral difficulty, could be effective in consequentialist or prudential terms.

Declaratory and operational policy

The nuclear weapons policy practiced by the United States has had a strong counterforce component.[12] Has the policy been pure counterforce, impure counterforce, or mixed strategy? It has not been pure counterforce strategy, because cities in the Soviet Union were targeted.[13] It is unclear whether it has been impure counterforce or mixed strategy. On the one hand, the United States threatened the Soviet Union with "unacceptable damage," which seems clearly to be a countervalue threat.[14] On the other hand, there is evidence that the targets of U.S. nuclear warheads have been uniformly assigned on the basis of counterforce considerations.[15] Moreover, the U.S. government claims that it does not target cities "per se."[16] This discrepancy might be explained in terms of the distinction between *declaratory policy* and *operational policy*.[17] Declaratory policy is publicly announced policy, whereas operational policy informs actual military deployments and plans for weapons use, which are often secret. In terms of declaratory policy, the United States seems to have been practicing a mixed strategy, whereas in terms of operational policy, it seems to have been practicing an impure counterforce strategy. So in the case of the United States, declaratory and operational policies appear to have diverged.

If declaratory and operational policies have diverged, why is this the case? Divergence may be explained, in part, by political considerations, external to those of military effectiveness. But there may also be reasons for divergence in terms of military policy. There is an important tension potential in nuclear weapons policy that such a divergence may serve to accommodate or to paper over. The main goal of declaratory policy is deterrence, because the effectiveness of deterrence depends on successful communication of the threats to the opponent, and declarations are a prime means of communication. Moreover, there seems to be no deterrent reason to allow operational policy to diverge from declaratory policy, because the coincidence of the two would tend to increase the credibility of the threats. But operational policy, because it concerns actual rather than merely stated plans for the use of weapons, is relevant not so much to the goal of avoiding war (which is why the plans can be secret), but to the goal of producing the best outcome should war come. It is this potential tension between the goals of *war avoidance* and *war waging* that the divergence between declaratory and operational policy may represent.

Military policy, in general, must be concerned with both war avoidance and war waging. A nation wants both the best deterrent of war and the means to produce the best outcome should war come.[18] Either the goals of war avoidance and war waging conflict or they do not, in the sense that either what is best to threaten declaratively for the sake of deterring war conflicts with what would be best to do operationally in war or it does not. If these goals do not conflict, there is no reason in terms of military effectiveness for declaratory and operational policy to diverge, but if they do conflict, there is. That the goals do conflict is suggested by Bernard Brodie, who speaks of "the sharp differences in character between a deterrence capability and strategy on the one hand, and a win-the-war strategy and capability on the other."[19] If what is best threatened to avoid war is different from what actions are best done should war come, then, other things being equal, a nation should make those threats as declaratory policy but plan those actions as operational policy.

Counterforce strategists tend to regard war avoidance and war waging as goals that do not conflict, whereas countervalue strategists tend to regard these goals as conflicting. This is important in understanding the differences between the two kinds of strategy. The perception that the goals conflict can be clearly seen in the position often taken by countervalue strategists known as deterrence only. According to this position, the only purpose that nuclear weapons can serve is to deter their use by others. Nuclear weapons can deter war, but have no effective use in war. Nuclear weapons policy should be purely deterrent. At the extreme, the logic of this strategy yields a policy of nuclear bluff: Because nuclear weapons have no use in war, a nation should never choose to use them. Non-use would then be the operational policy. (This is the conclusion of the prudential impossibility argument of Chapter 1: If nuclear war comes, the best outcome is likely to be produced by a nation's not carrying out its nuclear threat.) A less extreme view is that though nuclear weapons have no military use, they might be used in war as symbolic gestures or as demonstrations of resolve. Operational policy would then reflect this potential use. In either case, what one threatens to do to avoid war is not what one should do if war comes.

Counterforce strategists see things differently. *Si vis pacem, para bellum.* The opponent will be most effectively deterred from war when a nation threatens to do what would be in its best interests to do in the event of war. But the nuclear weapons policy a nation adopts must not only be the policy that would be most effective in fighting a war. It must be so potentially effective that it promises to allow the nation to achieve advantage from the war. Counterforce strategists believe this is possible, and thus they challenge the argument of Chapter 1 that nuclear war is prudentially impossible. A nation can threaten a war in which it would achieve advantage, and those threats would secure the highest level of deterrence of war, because they would be the most credible. A militarily effective use of nuclear force is possible only through an attack on counterforce targets, because an attack on countervalue targets would yield no military advantage and would likely bring on countervalue retaliation. Thus, for the counterforce strategist, the goals of war avoidance and war waging are not in conflict. As Colin Gray claimed: "There is no necessary tension between a realistic wartime strategy (and the posture to match) and the prewar deterrence of undesired Soviet behavior."[20] If a nation practices a deterrence policy that treats these goals as conflicting, as it does when its declaratory and operational policies diverge, it is not sufficiently committed to a counterforce strategy, and its policy is to that extent lacking in effectiveness.

Counterforce strategy places nuclear weapons policy in a traditional military context, wherein the deterrence of war has always been regarded as a byproduct of, and best achieved by, the ability to wage war successfully. The traditional task of the military was to develop a capacity to defeat the military forces of the other side, and the threat that this provided is what deterred war. Traditional military policy regards the capacity to wage war successfully as primary, with the capacity to deter war resulting from this. As Bernard Brodie points out: "The military have long been fond of saying that the best deterrence force is a war-winning force."[21] The counterforce strategist sees military force in the same terms, seeking what Hans Morganthau calls the *conventionalization* of nuclear weapons.[22] The capacity to deter nuclear war derives from a capacity to fight nuclear war. A single policy can achieve both. For the countervalue strategist, on the other hand, neither capacity follows from the other. Because the two goals are in conflict, no policy can achieve them both. As a result, the policy chosen would have to give preference to one of the goals (generally, that of war avoidance) over the other, and would represent some kind of compromise between them. It is this need for compromise that is partially avoided, partially masked, by the distinction between declaratory and operational policy.

Countervalue strategists believe that the goals of war avoidance and war waging conflict because they believe that a nuclear war cannot be fought to achieve advantage (or, rather, that it is not possible to "fight" a nuclear war at all), whereas threats of nuclear war can achieve deterrence. In contrast, counterforce strategists believe that advantage can be achieved in a nuclear war, and it is precisely this possibility that allows nuclear threats to deter. Countervalue strategists believe that nuclear deterrence must be deterrence by threat of punishment, whereas counterforce strategists believe nuclear deterrence, like conventional deterrence, can and must be deterrence by threat of denial. In war, inflicting punishment would not achieve advantage, whereas inflicting denial would achieve advantage. As a result of this difference, countervalue and counterforce strategists see the credibility question differently.

For the counterforce strategist, the lack of credibility that appears to haunt nuclear deterrence is not inherent in the policy, but is a function of the mistaken perception that in the case of nuclear weapons, there is a conflict between the goals of war avoidance and war waging. When nuclear weapons policy treats these goals as consistent, the credibility problem will be solved. These goals can be made consistent only if a fully counterforce strategy is practiced. Because the threatened party's presumption that the threatener is willing to carry out its threat depends on the rationality of threatener's doing so, credibility is achieved only when what is threatened is what prudentially should be done if war comes. It is the seeming inability to use nuclear weapons to advantage in war that makes the goals of war avoidance and war waging appear to conflict, and so creates the credibility problem for nuclear deterrence. Thus, a credible deterrence policy requires what a counterforce strategy promises: a militarily effective way to use nuclear weapons in war. The subject of the next chapter is the soundness of the argument that counterforce strategy can provide this.

Intra-war deterrence

Counterforce strategists regard the deterrence of war as an extension of *intra-war deterrence* – that is, deterrence in war, the deterrence of the other side from continuing a war already underway. (In contrast, the deterrence of war has been labeled by counterforce strategists as *pre-war deterrence*.[23]) Intra-war deterrence is achieved through exercise of the capacity for war waging. The use of nuclear weapons in war is militarily effective when it causes the other side to break off the nuclear hostilities, and it does so by the threat of further effective use of military force if the war were to continue. Because an effective capacity for war waging is, for the counterforce strategists, the best way to achieve war avoidance, a capacity for pre-war deterrence is derivative from a capacity for intra-war deterrence. In fact, intra-war deterrence may be regarded as the genus, with pre-war deterrence as one of its species. Pre-war deterrence, in this view, would be a kind of limiting case of intra-war deterrence, in the sense that nuclear opponents, even when not firing on each other, are in a state of incipient war (cold if not hot). As a result, in this view, all deterrence would be deterrence in war, its point being to keep the opponent from escalating the conflict to a higher level of hostilities.

Counterforce strategists sometimes claim that countervalue strategy is not a strategy at all, because it tells us nothing about how to use nuclear weapons in war, or at least nothing about how to use them in a militarily effective way. Benjamin Lambeth claims that assured destruction is "the antithesis of strategy."[24] The response of the countervalue strategist is, of course, that there is no such thing as a strategy for using nuclear weapons in war, because they cannot be used to military advantage. The best that one can hope for from a strategy is war avoidance. A reciprocal criticism made by countervalue strategists is that counterforce strategy, because of its focus on war waging, is not a theory of deterrence at all. But the response of the counterforce strategist is, of course, that a nation can most effectively avoid war through having a capacity to wage one successfully.[25] Similarly, critics often claim that counterforce strategy is based on overkill. But because there are many more counterforce targets than there are countervalue targets, a counterforce strategy requires a much larger arsenal. Nuclear arsenals developed by the United States and the Soviet Union would be grossly redundant under a countervalue strategy, but not under a counterforce strategy. What underlies all of these criticisms is the basic issue whether a counterforce strategy would be more effective at avoiding war than a countervalue strategy.

In counterforce strategy, the notions of intra-war deterrence and limited nuclear war are closely related. Because no military advantage could be achieved in a large-scale nuclear war, the claim that nuclear weapons could be used to military advantage requires that the war be limited. Mutual vulnerability – the practical removal of all capacity limitations – entails that a limited nuclear war is possible only through the exercise of restraint, and it is the task of intra-war deterrence to induce the opponent's restraint. Intra-war deterrence is a more important notion in the nuclear age than previously. Traditionally, a nation could win a war by destroying the military capacity of the opponent. The opponent's will to fight would then be irrelevant. Because the opponent would lack the means to keep fighting, there would be no need to deter it from doing so. The condition of mutual vulnerability makes it impossible for either side to destroy the military capacity of the other. So using weapons to military advantage in war is now possible only if the opponent ceases to fight while it still retains the military capacity to continue. Moreover, if the nation is to come out of a nuclear war advantaged, it may well be that the opponent must be willing to cease fighting in a situation militarily unfavorable to itself. The bargain for mutual restraint that is the limitation of the war would then be a bargain unfavorable to the opponent. This is what victory and defeat in a limited nuclear war would amount to. It is intra-war deterrence that is supposed to induce the opponent to accept such terms. Intra-war deterrence, like pre-war deterrence, seeks to work on the opponent's will.

Following on the discussion of nuclear war limitation from Chapter 1, the limited nuclear war envisioned by counterforce strategy must have two characteristics. First, it must be limited not merely in the sense that substantial portions of the nuclear arsenals go unused (relative limitation), nor merely in the sense that societal destruction does not occur (absolute limitation). It could be limited in both these senses, yet the damage not be prudentially, nor morally, justifiable. The proper question is not whether nuclear war could be limited, but whether it could be *appropriately* limited – that is, limited to the right extent and in the right way so as to make it prudentially (or morally) justifiable. (The appropriate limitation is different, depending on whether one is considering the prudential or the moral perspective.) Second, the bare possibility that a nuclear war would be appropriately limited, a possibility no one would deny, is not enough. As argued earlier, for a nuclear war to be prudentially or morally justifiable it must be reasonably foreseeable that it would remain appropriately limited. This is true in the prudential case because the presumption of willingness on which credibility depends requires that threat execution be in the threatener's perceived self-interest, which would likely not be the case if it were not reasonably foreseeable that the war would be appropriately limited.

In prudential terms, limiting a war, whether nuclear or conventional, is a process of bringing the military means by which the war is fought and the political ends for which it is fought into adjustment with each other, so that each is appropriate or proportional to the other.[26] But the direction of adjustment, so to speak, is different depending on whether the war in question is conventional or nuclear. In the case of conventional war (between non-nuclear powers), the political ends would normally be set by national policy, and the process of properly limiting the war would be one of adjusting the military means so that they are proportional to these ends. In the case of nuclear war, however, there is an overriding prudential interest in limiting the military means, due to the potential for societal destruction. As a result, the political ends would have to be adjusted in an effort to keep the military means severely within bounds. Bernard Brodie observes: "We should be willing to limit objectives *because* we want to keep the war limited, and not the other way around."[27] Limited war theory in the nuclear age, Lawrence Freedman asserts, is "not a theory about the primacy of political objectives over military means, but of the primacy of military realities over political objectives."[28] If a nation is not free to choose its ends in war, but must instead adjust the ends downward from the politically desirable in an effort to keep the conflict from escalating to societal destruction, this suggests that prudential justifiability, which requires that the value of the ends outweighs the cost of the means, is even harder to achieve.

Nuclear strategists differ not only on what a nuclear war could achieve, but also on what nuclear deterrence can achieve. They disagree on how broad a range of the opponent's behavior can be successfully influenced by nuclear threats. In general, one's view of how much nuclear deterrence can achieve depends on one's view of the credibility of nuclear threats. Those who have doubts about whether nuclear threats can achieve a very high level of credibility see at most a limited role for nuclear deterrence, believing that the threats can effectively deter the opponent only from the most serious form of aggression – nuclear attack. On the other hand, those who believe that nuclear threats can be highly credible see a wide role for nuclear deterrence, believing that nuclear threats can be used to deter a broad range of the opponent's behavior. Because they believe that nuclear threats can be highly credible, counterforce strategists tend to see a much wider role for nuclear deterrence than many countervalue strategists do, assuming, of course, that it is counterforce strategy that is practiced. At the extreme, some counterforce strategists believe that nuclear threats can achieve compellence as well as deterrence.

Counterforce strategists, believing in a wider role for nuclear deterrence, see a positive political role for nuclear weapons in peace, as they see a positive military role for nuclear weapons in war. Nuclear threats alone can advance a nation's political interests. This shows, again, how counterforce strategy places nuclear weapons policy in a traditional military context. Traditionally, nations have used superior military force in peacetime to influence and coerce their opponents for political advantage. Nuclear force, with credibility restored by a superior counterforce capability, could do the same. In contrast, countervalue strategists often believe that in a condition of mutual vulnerability, nuclear weapons can provide no political advantage. This belief, critics charge, results in self-deterrence, because it makes a nation reluctant to use its nuclear forces in defense of its interests. As Albert Wohlstetter puts it, Western countervalue threats "paralyze the West, not the East."[29] Counterforce strategists see self-deterrence as a bad thing, but avoidable through the adoption of a counterforce strategy. Countervalue strategists see self-deterrence as inevitable, and a good thing too, because both sides are self-deterred and the risk of war is thus lessened. Self-deterrence is reassurance, which, as we have seen, helps to make the nuclear balance stable.

Counterforce and countervalue strategists also differ on the role of defense in nuclear weapons policy. Deterrence and defense are seen by countervalue strategists as exclusive notions. Defense is no longer possible, because the condition of mutual vulnerability entails that an effective defense against nuclear attack is impossible. All that a nation can do is to seek to deter an attack by threatening nuclear retaliation. In contrast, because counterforce strategists see the goals of war avoidance and war waging as consistent, they believe not only that both defense and deterrence are possible, but that deterrence is achieved through a capacity for defense. To wage nuclear war effectively, a nation must have an effective capacity for defending against nuclear attack, a capacity for *damage limitation*, even if this falls short of a capacity to eliminate its vulnerability to societal destruction. The difference between countervalue and counterforce strategists on the role of defense is, then, part of their disagreement over whether there is advantage to be had in nuclear war.

Counterforce strategy is purported to provide a way in which nuclear deterrence can avoid both the moral disadvantage of the threats being directed against civilians and the prudential disadvantage arising from their apparent lack of credibility. Each problem has the same form. The apparent (moral or prudential) unacceptability of nuclear war infects deterrence policy, making nuclear threats seem (morally or prudentially) unacceptable as well. The moral unacceptability of nuclear use infects the nuclear threat, because both use and threat are directed against civilians. The prudential unacceptability of nuclear use infects the nuclear threat, because the unacceptability of use (its disadvantageousness) makes the threat incredible, and hence ineffective. Counterforce strategists would agree that if the use of nuclear weapons were unacceptable in these ways, then nuclear threats would be as well. But they deny the antecedents. In the prudential case, they argue that there may be advantage to be had in nuclear war. In the moral case, to which I now turn, they argue that nuclear war may be morally justifiable.

THE MORAL CLAIMS OF COUNTERFORCE

In the debate over nuclear weapons policy, counterforce strategists ardently claim the moral high ground. The moral heights may appear to be theirs because they offer a resolution of the conflicts nuclear deterrence generates. Counterforce strategists are strategic revisionists because they conclude that the deontological arguments against nuclear deterrence are unsound. Changes in strategic policy can create a form of nuclear deterrence that involves neither intending to kill civilians nor holding them hostage. The possibility of such a form of deterrence would show that the conflict between morality and prudence and the conflict within morality are merely apparent. James Turner Johnson suggests: "If the use of force is justified in response to threats against value, but the only means of force available are such that they contravene important values themselves, then the preferred moral alternative is the development of different means of force."[30] These different means of nuclear force have already been developed, according to counterforce strategists. They are nuclear delivery systems of greatly improved accuracy, requiring weapons of less explosive power, and allowing for a more discriminating attack with less collateral damage.[31]

Counterforce strategists vigorously proclaim the immorality of deterrence based on countervalue threats. They have used, with significant rhetorical effect, the acronym for mutual assured destruction, proclaiming that threats against cities are not only strategically mad, but morally mad as well. They have proclaimed the moral absurdity of a policy based on mutual vulnerability, by virtue of which: "Offense is defense, defense is offense. Killing people is good, killing weapons is bad."[32] Paul Ramsey refers to countervalue strategy as "the most politically immoral nuclear posture imaginable."[33] Speaking of the civilians who are threatened by nuclear retaliation, Fred Iklé claims: "Tomas de Torquemada, who burned 10,000 heretics at the stake, could claim principles more humane than our nuclear strategy; for his tribunals found all his victims guilty of having knowingly committed mortal sin." Further:

"Our method for preventing nuclear war rests on a form of warfare universally condemned since the Dark Ages – the mass killing of hostages."[34] Donald Brennan criticized our "bizarre" nuclear policy "that appears to favor dead Russians over live Americans." He asserted: "We should prefer live Americans to dead Russians, and we should not choose deliberately to live forever under a nuclear sword of Damocles."[35]

The moral difference between the strategies lies in the fact that counterforce strategy is based on the threat of denial, whereas countervalue strategy is based on the threat of punishment. The threat of denial, a threat to deny the opponent any aggressive gains it might attempt to achieve, is a threat of attacks on military forces. The threat of punishment is a threat to punish the opponent by retaliating against what it most values, its population and economic assets. Because the nuclear threat of denial is directed against military assets rather than civilians, it is said to avoid the moral objections to the nuclear threat of punishment. Legal deterrence, like countervalue nuclear deterrence, is based on threats of punishment rather than denial, because it involves threats to deprive law breakers of what they value most, such as their freedom, rather than attempting simply and directly to deny them the gain from their illegal behavior. But legal deterrence by threat of punishment is morally acceptable, because the person who would be harmed by the punishment is the agent responsible for the nonconforming behavior, whereas this is not the case for deterrence by countervalue nuclear threats.[36]

There are other moral advantages claimed for counterforce strategy, in addition to its avoidance of threats against civilians. One of the most important of these is that counterforce strategy is required by the obligation a nation has to do all it can to insure the safety of its citizens. What if deterrence fails? War may come despite a nation's best efforts to avoid it, and if it comes, the nation should be prepared to attack the military forces of the opponent in order to provide the maximum protection for its own citizens. One of the main purposes of a counterforce strategy is to limit the damage to the nation should war come, and a damage-limitation capability is what a nation needs to protect its citizens in war. A damage-limitation capability not only serves to meet this obligation, but it is what makes nuclear threats credible, hence effective, hence of consequentialist value as well. In the view of the counterforce strategists, all moral considerations support counterforce strategy. The

strategy that avoids threats against civilians and best protects a
nation's citizens should war come is also the strategy that best
promotes the interests not only of the nation but of humanity as
a whole, because it best avoids war. But there is reason to doubt
this purported happy confluence.

The moral case for counterforce strategy, like the prudential case,
depends on the prospects that a nuclear war would remain appropriately limited. Nuclear war is appropriately limited in a prudential sense only if the amount of damage done to the nation is
kept low enough that the nation can emerge from the war overall
advantaged. But nuclear war is appropriately limited in a moral
sense only if the damage done to the opponent does not involve
intentional attacks on civilians. There may be an indirect relation
between these two kinds of limitation, in that a nation's avoiding
attacks on the opponent's civilians may be helpful in inducing the
opponent to exercise the restraint necessary to make the war prudentially justifiable for the nation. In an actual nuclear war, a nation
would have a strong prudential incentive to avoid attacks on the
opponent's cities, in order to avoid reciprocal attacks on its cities.
But there is no necessary connection, because a nuclear war might
be appropriately limited in the prudential sense without being appropriately limited in the moral sense, and conversely.

What would make a counterforce strategy morally justifiable in
a deontological sense is not what would make it prudentially justifiable. There are two important differences between the kind of
prospectively limited nuclear war required to make a counterforce
strategy morally justifiable and the kind required to make it prudentially justifiable. First, the appropriate limitations from a moral
point of view are partly qualitative, in that they involve no intentional attacks upon civilians, whereas in the prudential case, the
limitations are purely quantitative. Second, a nation fights a war
appropriately limited in a moral sense only if the nation limits the
damage it does to its opponent, whereas it fights a war appropriately limited in a prudential sense only if the opponent limits the
damage it does to the nation. This implies a difference in the kinds
of nuclear threat that each may involve. A morally justifiable counterforce strategy precludes threats against the opponent's civilians,
whereas a prudentially justifiable counterforce strategy does not.

But I will argue, more strongly, that a counterforce strategy cannot be prudentially justifiable unless in includes threats against the
opponent's civilians.[37] That is not to say that a counterforce strategy

including such threats is prudentially justifiable. Whether counterforce strategy is prudentially justifiable – that is, whether counterforce nuclear deterrence is prudentially preferable to conventional deterrence – is a matter to be taken up in the next chapter. The point is that threats against civilians are a *necessary condition*, though perhaps not a sufficient condition, for a counterforce strategy to be prudentially justifiable. The reason is the role that threats against civilians play in intra-war deterrence. As a result of this role, we shall see, a counterforce strategy without such threats suffers a low level of threat credibility, and, according to the discussion of the last chapter, a counterforce strategy can show nuclear deterrence to have a substantial marginal deterrent value, and hence be prudentially preferable, only if that strategy has a high degree of threat credibility. This is the sense in which threats against the opponent's civilians are a necessary condition for prudential justifiability. In the remainder of the chapter, I will make the point by claiming that a counterforce strategy without threats against civilians is not *effective*, meaning that it does not satisfy a necessary condition for prudential justifiability in the sense just described. If it is true that a counterforce strategy without threats against civilians is not effective, and that a counterforce strategy with such threats is not morally acceptable, it follows that no counterforce strategy can be both prudentially and morally justifiable.

But things are a bit more complicated. Recall that in addition to pure counterforce strategy and mixed strategy, there is impure counterforce strategy. Pure counterforce strategy may be morally justifiable, because it involves no threats against civilians, though for that reason it is not effective, or so I will argue. On the other hand, mixed strategy is effective in this sense, because it involves threats against civilians, but it is for this reason not morally justifiable. But perhaps impure counterforce strategy could secure the virtues and avoid the vices of each of these. It might be effective, because its threats against military targets in cities would have the deterrent effect of threats against civilians. It might also be morally justifiable, because the threats would be directed against only military targets, so there would be no intention to kill civilians or hold them hostage. The possibility that such a policy might be both morally and prudentially justifiable is based on an ambiguity in the notion of threat. Threats may be direct or indirect. A *direct threat* is a threat considered in relation to its explicit target, whereas an *indirect threat* is a threat considered in relation to other harm that its execution would bring about. Unmixed (pure or impure) counterforce strategy, by its nature, involves no direct threats against civilians, but if it is impure it involves extensive indirect threats against civilians, in that the threatened attacks against military targets in cities would result in the deaths of a very large number of civilians. The question is the moral status of indirect threats. An impure counterforce strategy that is effective because it threatens cities indirectly might also be morally justifiable because its direct threats are against only military targets. But this is not the case. Impure counterforce strategy is not a middle way in which moral and prudential justifiability can cohabit in a single form of deterrence.

The argument for this may be cast as a dilemma. Only an unmixed (pure or impure) counterforce strategy could be morally justifiable. But pure counterforce strategy, though it may be morally justifiable in deontological terms, is not effective, so cannot be prudentially justifiable. On the other hand, impure counterforce strategy, though it may be effective, does not in the end avoid the deontological argument against nuclear deterrence. This dilemma is, in fact, simply another instance of the conflicts we seek to resolve. So, if it stands, it represents the failure of strategic revisionism. The strategic revisionist presents counterforce strategy as a way to resolve the conflicts between the deontological arguments on the one hand and the prudential and consequentialist arguments on the other. Pure counterforce strategy may avoid the deontological disadvantages of other forms of nuclear deterrence, but it would not be effective, so it would fail to achieve the prudential and consequentialist advantages they achieve. An impure counterforce strategy may secure the prudential and consequentialist advantages, but it would not avoid the deontological disadvantages. In either case, the conflicts created by nuclear deterrence remain unresolved.[38] Anthony Kenny asks: "Must it be the case that any threat which is sufficient to act as a deterrent to our potential enemies must be a threat whose execution would be immoral?"[39] The answer is yes. But to make the case for this, each horn of the dilemma must be examined in some detail.

THE EFFECTIVENESS OF MORAL COUNTERFORCE

The first horn of the dilemma is the claim that pure counterforce strategy, though it may avoid the deontological disadvantages of other forms of nuclear deterrence, would not be effective. The threats of pure counterforce strategy, in contrast with those of impure counterforce strategy, do not put at risk the lives of a large number of civilians. So it appears that a nuclear war prosecuted under such a strategy could be similar in morally relevant respects to a justifiable conventional war. As a result, I will assume, at least for the sake of argument, that a pure counterforce strategy would be morally justifiable.[40] But a pure counterforce strategy would be effective only if the opponent could be successfully deterred without a large number of its civilians being put at risk. Would the threat to destroy only military targets far from cities provide effective deterrence? In general, a form of deterrence is effective only to the extent that the expected loss it threatens is perceived by the opponent to outweigh the expected gain from the aggression it is meant to avoid. So the effectiveness of a pure counterforce strategy is, in part, dependent on the value the opponent places on the targets whose loss would be expected from the counterforce retaliation, compared with the value it places on the expected gains from some contemplated aggression. Because counterforce strategy involves threats of denial, the calculations of expected gain from the aggression must, of course, take into account that the counterforce retaliation would make the success of the aggression less likely.

One way to criticize the effectiveness of pure counterforce strategy is to focus on the role of this calculation of gain versus loss in determining how likely the opponent is to be deterred. The great difficulty in predicting how the opponent might make this comparison – including uncertainty about how it would perceive the military situation, what its relative value preferences would be, and what its attitude would be toward risky ventures – has led some to reject pure counterforce strategy on the grounds that the amount of damage such a strategy threatens would not provide a sufficient margin of safety to guarantee effective deterrence. For example, Gregory Kavka, rejecting the policy he calls scrupulous retaliation, similar to our pure counterforce, says: "We want our nuclear deterrence policies to be extremely *robust* – that is, effective under the greatest possible variety of circumstances."[41] Due to the uncertainties involved, a nation can never be sure what amount of threatened damage will be enough to provide effective deterrence, so it is better, other things being equal, to threaten more rather than less. To put the point differently, the effectiveness of deterrence is a matter of degree, varying in part with the amount of damage threatened. So, again, it is better, other things being equal, to threaten more rather than less. In constructing a bridge, an engineer will calculate the stresses likely to be placed on it and then, given the high value we place on bridges not collapsing, multiply this by a factor of two or more in deciding how strong to build the structure. Nuclear deterrence should, likewise, be designed to provide the highest levels of assurance that it will be effective.

But this line of criticism is incomplete, for the effectiveness of a deterrence policy is based not only on the magnitude of the damage threatened, but also on the credibility of the threat. The argument that increasing the amount of damage threatened increases deterrence effectiveness applies only if that increase does not lead to a greater decline in threat credibility. If pure counterforce strategy is more credible, perhaps this offsets any loss in effectiveness resulting from the lesser damage it threatens. Kavka's policy of scrupulous retaliation, Jeff McMahan suggests, "may gain back through the greater credibility of its threats at least some of the deterrent value it loses through the fact that its sanctions are often less severe."[42]

Pure counterforce and credibility

But the requirements of intra-war deterrence show that pure counterforce strategy is less credible, not more credible, than forms of nuclear deterrence that threaten massive civilian damage. The credibility of counterforce strategy depends on the prospects for limited nuclear war under that strategy, which depend on that strategy's capacity for intra-war deterrence. If pure counterforce strategy cannot meet the requirements of intra-war deterrence, its credibility suffers. A nation has the capacity for intra-war deterrence when the opponent can be dissuaded from escalating a nuclear war by the nation's threat that it will respond to the escalation by retaliating against the opponent at that level or a higher level of nuclear violence. But if a nation adopts pure counterforce strategy, it forfeits this mechanism for dissuading its opponent from attacking its cities. For the nation does not threaten corresponding targets on the opponent's side. The nation has no effective way to deter the opponent from escalating the nuclear war to the destruction of its cities. If a nation practices pure counterforce strategy, it is less able to induce its opponent's restraint, so less able to keep a war limited. Hence the presumption of its willingness to carry out its nuclear threats would be weaker. As a result, its threats would be less credible.

This argument should be compared with the argument of Chapter 4 that nuclear deterrence in general lacks credibility. The same kind of credibility problem is involved in each case, but the problem is more severe for pure counterforce strategy than it is for forms of nuclear deterrence that involve threats against cities. The adoption of pure counterforce strategy would replace mutual vulnerability with one-sided vulnerability. A nation choosing such a strategy would deny itself the capacity to destroy the opponent's society, rendering the opponent no longer vulnerable. The argument of Chapter 4 is that in a condition of mutual vulnerability, nuclear threats would lack credibility because a limited nuclear war would not be reasonably foreseeable. But in a condition of one-sided vulnerability, the basis for attributing credibility to the nuclear threats of the side that is vulnerable would be even weaker. Under mutual vulnerability, the threat each side holds against the other's cities may, in war, keep each from attacking the other's cities, even if such a limited nuclear war would not be reasonably foreseeable. But in a condition of one-sided vulnerability, the vulnerable nation would lose even this check on the opponent's countervalue attacks, making even less likely a war limited in the damage done to the vulnerable nation. This is why threats against civilians are a necessary condition for the prudential justifiability of a counterforce strategy.

A version of the argument that a pure counterforce strategy lacks credibility is presented by John Finnis, Joseph Boyle, and Germain Grisez, who claim: "At certain levels of escalation, credible deterrence depends not only on the threat against enemy forces but also on the threat against cities." They ask rhetorically: "How can X, by legitimate threats restricted to Y's forces, deter Y from responding to any attacks on Y's forces with a retaliation unacceptable to X?"[43] Jeff McMahan criticizes this argument on the grounds that "it assumes a chessplayer's model of rational decision making" and that "it is implausible to suppose that those in charge of the deterrent would actually think in this way in a crisis."[44] But this misses the force of the argument, which is not dependent on the claim that nations would reason in an abstract way. A desert-island analogy makes the point better. If X and Y are alone on an island, X having a gun but Y having thrown his away, Y's threat to retaliate against X's aggression is unlikely to have much credibility, because X is likely to believe that Y believes that should a fight start, Y is likely to end up dead, because Y cannot threaten X with death in response. X's belief does not attribute any especially abstract thinking to Y, because Y need not mentally run through all the intermediate steps of the potential escalatory process to appreciate what would obtain near the end of that process. Of course, Y might retaliate in any case, but the point is that retaliation would be clearly imprudent, so that the threat to retaliate would lack credibility.

A second objection of McMahan's is that the argument of Finnis, Boyle, and Grisez's that a pure counterforce strategy would lack credibility begs the question because it mistakenly assumes that what is threatened under such a strategy would not be unacceptable damage.[45] He is correct to point out that a nation practicing pure counterforce strategy might well be able to inflict damage that the opponent finds unacceptable. But questions about credibility are distinct from questions about the unacceptability of the threatened damage, as indicated in the analysis of deterrence effectiveness in Chapter 3, where beliefs about credibility came under (1) and beliefs about the unacceptability of damage came under (2). What is crucial for the credibility question in this case is not the status of the threatened damage as acceptable or unacceptable, but rather a comparison of the amount of damage each side threatens. The vulnerable side threatens only contingently unacceptable damage, whereas the invulnerable side threatens the necessarily unacceptable damage of societal destruction.

The relevance of this difference is that credibility is a function of the strength of the presumption that a nation would likely be willing to carry out its threats. In the midst of nuclear war, toward the end of the escalatory process, the vulnerable nation would have no way to deter the opponent from attacking its cities, hence the presumption that the opponent would be willing at that stage to attack the nation's cities would be strong. The strength of this presumption makes it less rational for the nation to carry out its nuclear threats, because to do so would move the situation up the escalatory ladder. Hence it weakens the presumption that the nation would be willing to do so. It is the special character of societal destruction that determines the credibility issue. The analogy illustrates this. Y may threaten, at the worst, to break X's arm, and this damage may be unacceptable to X in relation to what she could gain from aggressing against Y (Y's coconut, say). But the fact that Y threatens X with damage that would be unacceptable does not assure the credibility of Y's threat. The argument is not that Y's threat lacks credibility because it is not a threat of unacceptable damage, but rather that it lacks credibility because X's threat of death represents a kind of ultimate threat in relation to the mere broken arm that Y threatens, even though a broken arm is unacceptable damage.

Paul Ramsey, a proponent of counterforce strategy on moral grounds, gives much attention to the question of whether a counterforce strategy could be effective or, as he puts it, feasible. He claims that strategic thought must address "the question of how what is morally right in war and deterrence can be made feasible." He contrasts "graduated deterrence," which he recommends, with "suspended deterrence," which includes the threat of "ultimate indiscriminate destruction" and is suspended from such a threat in the sense that its "effectiveness is supposed at all lower levels to be indivisibly connected with a conditional willingness to invoke that final political immorality."[46] Graduated deterrence, he argues, is feasible, so a nation need not practice suspended deterrence.

> War today becomes a *disproportionate* means to any substantive political purposes long before it need be judged to have become *indiscriminate* (if non-combatant immunity from direct attack is properly understood). This being so, if one starts from the bottom and moves upward in the scale, there would seem to be sufficiently powerful ways to persuade an opponent by the deterring effects mentioned that do *not* give and take hostage populations or reverse the relation between arms and society.[47]

By claiming that nuclear war would become disproportionate before becoming indiscriminate, Ramsey is presumably suggesting that threats against military targets can be effective as a deterrent because they can threaten more than the opponent would gain from an attack – that is, they threaten unacceptable damage.[48] But if this is understood as an argument for the effectiveness of pure counterforce strategy, it faces the problems just discussed. If the point is that counterforce threats can effectively deter because they threaten more damage than what the opponent could hope to gain from aggression, then the argument is inadequate because it fails to show that the amount of damage threatened is sufficient, given the various uncertainties involved, to guarantee effective deterrence. If the point is that counterforce threats can effectively deter because the unacceptability of what they threaten makes them credible, then the argument is inadequate for the same reason as McMahan's second objection to the argument of Finnis, Boyle, and Grisez's. In focusing only on the question whether a counterforce threat can be a threat of unacceptable damage, it fails to consider the complexity of factors involved in the judgment of threat credibility – in particular, the relevance of the distinction between contingently and necessarily unacceptable damage.

The disproportionate damage the threat of which Ramsey relies on, however, is not counterforce damage, but "collateral civil damage." He is, in fact, not morally opposed to threats that put at risk large numbers of civilians, for he argues that the principle of discrimination cannot be violated "by numbers [of non-combatant deaths] or amount of destruction." Rather, it can be violated only in terms of the intention of acts of war, which is a matter "of their direction or thrusts in the world, of their targets and objectives, the planned design of the war to be executed."[49] This suggests that graduated deterrence is not pure counterforce strategy, but rather impure counterforce strategy. Apparently, graduated deterrence, like suspended deterrence, puts at risk large numbers of civilians. The difference between them is the difference between impure counterforce strategy and mixed or countervalue strategy. The "ultimate indiscriminate destruction" that distinguishes suspended deterrence is best understood not as referring merely to massive civilian destruction, but to such destruction brought about through countervalue attacks – that is, attacks where the civilians are themselves the direct targets. Societal destruction is threatened in either case, directly with suspended deterrence, indirectly with graduated deterrence. Under the assumption that Ramsey advocates impure counterforce strategy, I will examine his position further when the second horn of the dilemma is taken up.

Military forces as countervalue targets

A number of strategists claimed that nuclear threats by the United States against Soviet military targets could be expected to have a significant deterrent effect because Soviet leaders valued their military capability a great deal. One such strategist, Bruce Russett, proposed what he called a countercombatant strategy, which is a

distinctive version of pure counterforce strategy.[50] Under this strategy, nuclear threats against the Soviet Union would have been
directed at domestic security forces as well as conventional military
targets such as troop concentrations, rather than at strategic nuclear
forces.[51] The point of the strategy is to have posed a threat to the
ability of the Soviet state to rule by threatening to destroy its ability
to repel foreign invasion and to suppress domestic dissent. In Russett's view, the Soviets would view such a threat with the gravest
of concern, and hence would be effectively deterred by it. But this
proposal faces the same problem encountered with other versions
of pure counterforce strategy. Russett shows how his version of
pure counterforce strategy would threaten unacceptable damage,
but this is not enough to show that it would be effective, given
the Soviet threat to destroy U.S. cities.

Moreover, there is a significant moral problem with Russett's
strategy of countercombatant targeting. This strategy moves away
from the notion of denial, which is at the heart of most forms of
counterforce strategy. In a nuclear war, counterforce attacks against
the opponent's strategic military targets would be a form of denial,
because this would prevent those forces being used against the
nation. But attacks on conventional military forces, with the exception of those that are fighting with the nation or its allies, would
not be a form of denial, because those forces would not be engaged
in aggression. The notion of denial, however, underlies what is
morally relevant in the distinction between innocents and nonin-
nocents. Military personnel who are not engaged in aggression
should not be subject to attack any more than should ordinary
civilians.[52] If military violence is justified only on defensive
grounds, then it should not be used against those who are not
themselves posing an aggressive threat, even if they are military
personnel. This problem arises even more sharply in the case of
the targeting of domestic security forces, which do not even have
the capability to engage in aggression. Russett's proposal seems,
therefore, to lack the main moral advantage claimed for counterforce strategy.

But putting this moral problem aside and returning to the issue
of effectiveness, there are two arguments that might be used to
show that a strategy like Russett's could be effective. Each argument purports to show that what pure counterforce strategy can
threaten would be as unacceptable to the opponent as what countervalue strategy threatens. The first is offered by Paul Ramsey:

"A real threat to an essential ingredient in a nation's capacity for further independent action is a threat to its life in the international system." The threat to destroy an opponent's conventional military capability would be such a threat, "a threat as serious to the integrity of a nation's life as, or more serious than, the technical taking of certain hostage cities."[53] A threat to a nation's ability to protect itself is, indirectly, a threat to its very life, so the damage that is threatened would be seen to be as unacceptable as that threatened under a strategy that puts cities at risk. Both would be necessarily unacceptable. This may be the kind of point Russett had in mind when he referred to his strategy as "a strategy of assured destruction of the military and police powers of the Soviet state, rather than the population and civilian industry."[54] But this argument has two serious problems. For one, the connection between an attack on a nation's conventional military capability and its fall to foreign invaders may be too speculative for such an attack to be perceived as being equivalent in its effects to foreign domination. Nations have often fought off foreign invasion while having to rebuild their military capability in the midst of the war. Another, more important point is that foreign domination itself is the death of the regime, not the death of the society. Thus it would not be perceived as the kind of ultimate loss that societal destruction would.

The second argument addresses this last point. Those who made this argument believed that it applied to the Soviet Union in particular, rather than to nuclear superpowers in general. It is based on the claim that the leaders of the Soviet regime not only cared dearly for their military capability (or, more generally, for their instruments of power and control), but that they cared more for this than they did for their people.[55] They cared more for their military capability and means of control because they cared more for maintaining their own power. James Child, arguing for the effectiveness of a pure form of counterforce strategy against the Soviet Union, claimed that threats against cities "would probably not be effective," because "it is not at all clear that the Soviet leadership places sufficient value on the lives of its civilian population."[56] Wohlstetter asserted: "The Soviets value military power and the means of domination at least as much and possibly more than the lives of Russian civilians." As a result: "Prudence does not force us to rely for deterrence on even *unintended* damage done to civilians."[57] If the Soviets valued their power as much as or more than their civilians, they would have perceived the loss of that power as an ultimate loss. This would falsify the claim, at least in the case of deterrence practiced against the Soviet Union, that a counterforce strategy without a threat against cities would be less credible. The distinction between counterforce targeting and countervalue targeting would tend to disappear.[58] Pure counterforce strategy could then be a form of assured destruction in the full sense.

The claim that the Soviet leaders cared more for their power than their people often goes along with the Cold War claim that there is a basic "moral asymmetry" between East and West, in that lives are valued more highly in the liberal West than in the totalitarian East.[59] But the first claim does not depend on the second, because the first is an instance of a general claim that transcends the particular political and moral differences that existed between the United States and the Soviet Union. The moral Manichaeanism represented by the second claim, which in any case is of historical interest only, can be ignored.[60] The general claim, which is relevant to our inquiry, is that given the nature of political power, all regimes have a tendency to be willing to sacrifice the lives of large numbers of their people rather than to surrender their power, or the military capability that insures it.[61] From the leaders' perspective, of course, such sacrifice would seem to be in the best interests of the nation as a whole, because the continuance of their regime is in the best interest of the nation as a whole. But, from the outside, it would appear that the leaders value their power more than their population. In any case, assuming for the sake of argument that this general claim is true, the question is, does it show that pure counterforce strategy need not be lacking in credibility?

To answer this, one must measure the threat of loss of military and domestic-control capability against the threat of societal destruction. Societal destruction is more than the threat to kill large numbers of civilians. The crucial point is that societal destruction entails the leaders' loss of control. As Robert Art observes: "Political leaders do not value political control mechanisms per se; they value the power over others that such mechanisms yield. If there is no one left (or very few) to control, what, precisely, can be the point of the machinery of control?"[62] Moreover, the prospect of societal destruction means for leaders the loss of their power not to an alternative regime, but rather to the dissolution of the possibility of central authority of any kind. This means that societal destruction would seem a greater loss to the leaders than the loss of their power, for societal destruction is the loss of their power as well as the loss of their national community. Even if leaders prefer losing a large number of their people to losing their own power, they would not prefer the destruction of their society to the loss of their power, if only because societal destruction would also result in a lose of their power, and much more in addition. As a result, leaders would regard societal destruction as a graver threat than the mere loss of their power. Societal destruction is, in an important sense, an absolute, unique, incomparable kind of loss or harm. If one nation can threaten another with it, the other's nuclear weapons policy will lack credibility unless it is willing and able to reciprocate that threat.

So there is good reason to think that pure counterforce strategy would not be effective, first, because it threatens less damage, and, second, because it lacks credibility in comparison with other forms of nuclear deterrence. As the argument has shown, these two are related, because the reason that pure counterforce lacks credibility is that it threatens less damage, in particular that it does not reciprocate the opponent's ultimate threat of societal destruction. As a result, the switch from a form of nuclear deterrence threatening cities to pure counterforce strategy would entail a significant loss of prudential and consequentialist advantage. So, pure counterforce strategy, though perhaps morally acceptable in deontological terms, would not resolve the conflicts, for a nation is required on prudential and consequentialist grounds to choose another form of nuclear deterrence, one that threatens cities and hence is not acceptable in deontological terms.

It seems, then, that in a situation in which a nation is vulnerable to destruction by its opponent, that nation's nuclear threats will not be effective unless they put the opponent's cities at risk. If the opponent's cities are not threatened directly, then they must be threatened indirectly. A deontological perspective precludes cities being threatened directly, as they are in mixed strategy or countervalue strategy. The question for the next section is whether indirect threats against cities are precluded as well. So the focus of attention must shift from pure to impure counterforce strategy.

But before taking up this question, it is important to make clear that when nuclear strategies that involve threats against cities are claimed to be effective in comparison with pure counterforce strategy, this implies nothing about how effective such strategies are in comparison with conventional deterrence. That impure counterforce strategy is more credible than pure counterforce strategy does not imply that impure strategy is credible enough to show that there is a successful rebuttal to the prima facie argument from Chapter 4. The question whether (impure) counterforce strategy could be sufficiently credible to show that there is a successful rebuttal will be taken up in the next chapter. This chapter has shown that a nuclear strategy that involves a threat against cities is more credible than one that does not. But such a strategy still might be substantially less credible than a policy of conventional deterrence. Although threats against cities yield a credibility advantage for a nation's deterrence policy when the opponent threatens the nation's own cities, the conclusion of the prima facie argument is, in effect, that the mutual threat against cities itself gives rise to a serious credibility problem. The claim examined in the next chapter is that when a threat against cities is augmented into a full array of counterforce threats, the resulting strategy does avoid the credibility problem of mutual assured destruction.

THE MORALITY OF EFFECTIVE COUNTERFORCE

The second horn of the dilemma is that a counterforce strategy that indirectly threatens cities by directly threatening military targets in or near them does not avoid the deontological objections against a policy that threatens cities directly. The important point in establishing this claim is that the risks of urban destruction under impure counterforce strategy would be welcomed, even if not directly intended, by the threatener, because the threat of such destruction would be seen as essential for the effectiveness of the deterrence policy.

It is true that in a nuclear war fought under impure counterforce strategy, the threats against cities might never be carried out. For the sake of intra-war deterrence, a nation with such a strategy would practice "city-avoidance." It would refrain from attacking cities, so long as the other side did so, in order that its threat to attack cities would induce the other side to break off the conflict.[63] If the war remains limited, attacks on cities might be avoided altogether. But cities may be deliberately struck. Finnis, Boyle, and Grisez observe: "City-sparing will be relative to, and conditional upon, the deterrent's requirements at particular stages of nuclear conflict."[64] Threats against cities cannot be regarded as morally acceptable from a deontological perspective simply because they might not be carried out in a war.

Is a threat against cities morally acceptable by virtue of being indirect rather than direct? Consider the question in terms of the just-war tradition. There, the moral relevance of the distinction between direct and indirect threats is captured in the doctrine of double effect.[65] According to this doctrine, actions should be more stringently assessed in terms of their intended effects than in terms of their foreseen but unintended effects (that is, their merely foreseen effects). In particular, the just-war principle of discrimination applies to an action only in terms of its intended effects, not its merely foreseen effects. Using this doctrine, some would argue that when a threat is carried out, the damage that had been directly threatened is intended, whereas the damage that had been indirectly threatened is merely foreseen. Because impure counterforce strategy threatens cities only indirectly, the urban destruction resulting from the execution of that threat would be merely foreseen rather than intended. As a result, the principle of discrimination would not be violated by the threats of impure counterforce strategy, so that that strategy, in contrast with mixed or countervalue strategy, would be acceptable in deontological terms.

Some would reject this argument on the grounds that when the lives of a very large number of civilians are threatened, it is the number who would be killed, rather than whether their deaths would be intended or merely foreseen, that should be the basis for the moral evaluation of the threat. Robert Tucker claims: "The prospect held out by nuclear war threatens to make of the issue of intent a grotesque parody." He continues: "If we are instead to preserve a sense of realism in these matters, we must acknowledge that the significance of intention decreases roughly as the destructiveness of war increases."[66] This is a rejection of Ramsey's claim that the principle of discrimination cannot be violated in quantitative terms. The argument may seem to be consequentialist in form, so that it would better be cast in terms of proportionality rather than discrimination. But it is deontological in spirit. The argument continues to treat the principle of discrimination as central, because it is concerned with threats to civilians. It simply rejects the claim that the difference emphasized by the doctrine of double effect between intending civilian deaths and merely foreseeing them is morally determinative, at least when the number of civilian deaths becomes very large. There is much to be said for this line of response. But the argument based on the doctrine of double effect can be met on its own terms.

Depending on the countervalue threat

In assessing the argument for the moral acceptability of indirect threats against civilians, the guiding moral intuition should be that it is wrong to adopt a policy whose effectiveness is believed to depend on the threat against civilians, whether that threat is direct or indirect. That there is such a dependence can be seen in Ramsey's argument. Ramsey bases his claim that a counterforce strategy could be effective on the claim that nuclear attacks would produce disproportionate damage before they became indiscriminate. But the disproportionate character of the threat resides in the "collateral civilian damage" the counterforce attacks would cause. In terms of the doctrine of double effect, Ramsey would say that this damage is merely foreseen, not intended. "Collateral civilian damage is certainly an unavoidable indirect effect and, in the technical sense, an 'unintended' result . . ."[67] But if, as Ramsey believes, the prospect of this civilian damage is necessary for effective deterrence, leaders practicing deterrence would depend on the threat of that damage for the deterrent effect. Presumably if all the military targets in or near cities were magically transported to remote areas far from population centers, Ramsey's view would be that counterforce strategy, no longer able indirectly to threaten massive civilian damage, would lose its effectiveness.

Because the nation depends on the threat of civilian damage to achieve the main purpose of the policy, the nation bears full moral responsibility for threatening such damage, even if it is only indirectly threatened. As Michael Walzer puts it: "Surely anyone designing such a strategy must accept moral responsibility for the effects on which he is so radically dependent."[68] This means that the principle of discrimination should apply to the threat. Walter Stein makes the case forcefully. The doctrine of double effect, he claims, "is a way of analyzing predicaments in which radically unwanted, often tragic effects cannot be precluded" from our otherwise morally acceptable actions. As such, the application of this doctrine is subject to "the principle of moral dissociation," according to which for an effect to be counted as a second effect – that is, as merely foreseen rather than intended – it must be unconnected with or dissociated from what the actor wants to achieve.

Stein argues: "I cannot morally dissociate myself from what I want, from what I cannot avoid wanting as a means to achieving my purpose, if in fact I choose to achieve my purpose by these means."[69] A nation practicing impure counterforce strategy wants that strategy to be effective and believes that threatening civilian damage in necessary for its effectiveness. As a result, the civilian damage is not unwanted, not dissociated from the nation's purposes in adopting the policy. The civilian damage threatened is not a second effect. Impure counterforce strategy fails to satisfy the principle of discrimination, and thus, in just-war terms, is not morally acceptable.

A different version of Stein's criticism is offered by Finnis, Boyle, and Grisez. They accept the moral relevance of the distinction between intended and merely foreseen effects, but argue that the risk to civilians posed by nuclear threats is intended, even under a counterforce strategy. The intent involved in a sincere threat of attack is determined not by what the specific targets are, because "targeting does not define intent," but by what the threatening nation desires to achieve. Nations adopting impure counterforce strategy desire that the opponent fear the civilian damage that is threatened. But this shows that the damage is intended. "What they desire the other side to fear is what they threaten, and (unless they are bluffing) what they threaten is what they intend, so they intend the killing of innocents." Further: "The inter-relations between desire, making a threat, and intention, being conceptual, are inescapable."[70]

This argument is criticized by McMahan, who responds that Finnis, Boyle, and Grisez are wrong to claim "that we conditionally intend to bring about whatever we sincerely threaten to bring about."[71] A nation's purpose in making a threat may be different from its purpose in carrying out the threat. In the case of a counterforce threat whose execution would result in massive civilian damage, the prospect of the civilian damage is, indeed, desired for its deterrent effect. But if war comes, the sole purpose of carrying out the threat would be the destruction of the military targets. In the midst of war, the civilian damage would serve no purpose, and so would not be desired. Only prospective, not actual, civilian damage is wanted. Ramsey makes the same criticism in response to Stein. He also distinguishes between what is wanted in prospect, as part of a threat, and what would be wanted were the threat ever to be carried out. Because the civilian damage would not be wanted were the threat carried out, the civilian damage that is threatened is dissociated from the purpose with which the threat would be carried out, and hence is not intended. Ramsey argues: "There is no reason why we should not want the immediate and direct *deterrent* effects of the prospect of extensive collateral damage, which itself remains unavoidable yet is and remains radically unwanted in *fighting* a modern war."[72]

There are, however, serious problems with this defense of impure counterforce strategy. It fails to recognize the role that intra-war deterrence would play in the execution of counterforce threats. The countervalue damage in the execution of a counterforce nuclear threat would have intra-war deterrent value. Nuclear attacks would not have as their sole purpose the defensive or damage-limitation goal of impeding the opponent's military offensive, because in a nuclear war neither side could avoid the destruction of its society by attacks on the opponent's military capability alone. The attacks would have a deterrent purpose, in that they would be designed to dissuade the opponent from continuing the war in order to keep the war appropriately limited. To this extent their purpose would be continuous with the purpose of threats in pre-war deterrence. For both pre-war and intra-war deterrence, the deterrence is achieved, in part, by threatening civilian damage. In the case of intra-war deterrence, the infliction of civilian damage becomes an important mechanism through which further civilian damage is threatened, dramatically bringing to the opponent's attention the threat of further civilian damage in store should the war continue. Robert Jervis points out: "Inflicting pain on the other side by destroying some hostages [makes] more credible the threat to continue and to increase the punishment."[73] Thus, in a nuclear attack, both the civilian and the military damage would be wanted, hence the civilian damage cannot be dissociated from the purpose with which the threat would be carried out.[74]

This moral criticism of impure counterforce strategy has been conducted in just-war terms, but a hostage-holding analysis yields the same conclusion. Impure counterforce strategy is morally unacceptable under a hostage-holding analysis, because the risk to civilians is seen as necessary for the effectiveness of the threat. As in the case of a countervalue strategy, the civilians who are put at risk under impure counterforce strategy are held hostage to the good behavior of their leaders. Those who seize a civilian airliner and threaten to blow it up unless their demands are met are holding the passengers hostage so long as they regard the threat to the passengers as instrumental in getting their demands met, even if the threat of the destruction of the aircraft is also seen as instrumental to this end and the immediate target of the threatened explosion would be the plane itself, the hostages dying only as a result. In fact, the argument goes through more easily using a hostage-holding analysis, because the wrongness of hostage-holding depends only on the threatener's creating a risk to the hostages to achieve its ends. Under a just-war analysis, the wrongness of the threat is dependent on the intention with which the threat would be carried out. As a result, there appears to be room under a just-war analysis, as McMahan's argument suggests, to avoid the moral objections to impure counterforce threats by driving a wedge between the purpose behind the making of the threats and the intention that would be involved in their execution. Though this attempt fails, in the case of a hostage-holding analysis, there is not even a gap into which such a wedge might be successfully driven.

What about the other moral advantage claimed for a counterforce strategy, that should war come, a damage-limiting capability would provide some protection for the nation's civilians? Such an advantage cannot salvage strategic revisionism, for it cannot show that impure counterforce strategy avoids the deontological objections to nuclear deterrence. Nor can it show that a pure counterforce strategy preserves the consequentialist advantage of nuclear deterrence, because, given a situation of mutual vulnerability, the consequentialist value of damage-limitation in war pales besides the consequentialist disvalue of the increased risk of war resulting from the ineffectiveness of pure counterforce strategy. More generally, assuming that the adoption of a counterforce strategy has a significant effect on the likelihood of war, one way or the other, the value of its capacity for damage-limitation will not be decisive in the overall consequentialist assessment. If a counterforce strategy can solve the credibility problem, hence lessen the likelihood of war, as counterforce strategists claim, the value of its damage-limitation capability will be a relatively insignificant addition to its overall consequentialist value. If a counterforce strategy makes war more likely, as critics claim, then the value of its damage-limitation capability will be overwhelmed by the disvalue of the increase in the likelihood of war.

The conclusion of the chapter is not that all forms of counterforce strategy are necessarily morally unacceptable in deontological terms. The conclusion is rather that counterforce strategy cannot resolve the conflicts between the deontological arguments opposing nuclear deterrence and the consequentialist and prudential arguments favoring it. Pure counterforce strategy, though it may be morally acceptable, would be substantially less effective than a strategy involving threats against cities, and impure counterforce strategy would not be morally acceptable. So strategic revisionism fails. Ironically, its failure is due to the role of intra-war deterrence in counterforce strategy, a role strongly emphasized by proponents of that strategy. It is the requirements of intra-war deterrence that show that pure counterforce strategy is not effective and that impure counterforce strategy is not morally acceptable. The fact that it is the requirements of intra-war deterrence – the importance of which is emphasized by those arguing for counterforce on prudential grounds – that lead to the failure of the moral arguments for counterforce shows that despite initial appearances, there is a deep underlying tension between the moral and the prudential case for counterforce. The discussion now returns to a consideration of prudential revisionism, in particular to the question whether impure counterforce strategy, though more effective than pure counterforce strategy, is effective enough to establish a rebuttal to the prima facie argument that nuclear deterrence is not prudentially preferable to conventional deterrence.

Chapter 6

Prudential counterforce

Spade flung his words out with a brutal sort of carelessness that gave them more weight than they could have got from dramatic emphasis or from loudness. "If you kill me, how are you going to get the bird? If I know you can't afford to kill me till you have it, how are you going to scare me into giving it to you?"

Gutman cocked his head to the left and considered these questions. ... "Well, sir, there are other means of persuasion besides killing and threatening to kill."

"Sure," Spade agreed, "but they're not much good unless the threat of death is behind them to hold the victim down. See what I mean? If you try something I don't like I won't stand for it. I'll make it a matter of your having to call it off or kill me, knowing you can't afford to kill me."

"I see what you mean." Gutman chuckled. "That is an attitude, sir, that calls for the most delicate judgment on both sides, because, as you know, sir, men are likely to forget in the heat of action where their best interest lies and let their emotions carry them away."

Spade too was all smiling blandness. "That's the trick, from my side," he said, "to make my play strong enough that it ties you up, but yet not make you mad enough to bump me off against your better judgment."

Gutman said fondly: "By Gad, sir, you are a character!"

Dashiell Hammett, *The Maltese Falcon*[1]

Counterforce strategists see the credibility problem, often expressed by the question what happens if deterrence fails, as the central intellectual problem of nuclear strategy and the chief impediment to an effective policy of nuclear deterrence. They agree with Lawrence Freedman: "The question of what happens if deterrence fails is vital for the intellectual cohesion and credibility of nuclear strategy.''[2] If deterrence fails, a nation wants to have the capability that would guarantee the best outcome from a military point of view. But it is not simply the desirability of producing the best outcome should war come that makes an answer to the question of such vital importance to nuclear strategy. Unless a nuclear strategy provides an appropriate answer to this question, unless a nation has something that is in its interests to do if deterrence fails, its threats will lack credibility, and the strategy will not be effective in achieving its deterrent end. Counterforce strategists believe that effective pre-war deterrence flows from an effective war-waging capability. In order that the threats be credible and that deterrence not fail, a nation should be able, should deterrence fail, to wage a limited war to its advantage. As William O'Brien puts it: ''Without the capability of waging a limited nuclear war if deterrence fails, deterrence ultimately may indeed fail.''[3]

Showing that counterforce strategy solves the credibility problem – that is, showing that counterforce deterrence can achieve a high level of credibility – is crucial for establishing that this strategy is prudentially preferable to countervalue strategy. More importantly, in solving the credibility problem, counterforce strategy would avoid what was seen in Chapter 4 to be the chief prudential disadvantage of nuclear deterrence. This would seem to rebut the prima facie argument that nuclear deterrence is not prudentially preferable to conventional deterrence. The ability of counterforce strategy to solve the credibility problem is central to claims about the prudential preferability both of counterforce strategy in particular and of nuclear deterrence in general. The two claims are related and may stand or fall together. But they do not stand or fall on the credibility issue alone. For even if counterforce strategy solves the credibility problem, it may weaken nuclear deterrence in other prudentially relevant respects. The net deterrent effect of a strategy is what is important. In assessing counterforce deterrence, we must attempt to reflect the actual complexity of the prudential judgment.

The concern about the credibility of nuclear deterrence is often posed in the context of worries about the demands of a policy of extended deterrence, such as the policy practiced by the United States during the Cold War to deter Soviet aggression, nuclear or conventional, against key allies, especially those in Western Europe. Freedman sees as an underlying theme in the history of nuclear policy ''the attempt to develop a convincing strategy for extended deterrence, to make the United States' nuclear guarantee

to Europe intellectually credible rather than just an act of faith."[4]
Once the Soviet Union had acquired an assured destruction capability, the U.S. nuclear threat to protect Western Europe was
thought to be no longer credible. Who would believe, de Gaulle
observed, that the United States would trade Chicago for Paris?
The problem appeared especially acute because the United States
threatened to use nuclear weapons first, in response to a Soviet
conventional attack. It may seem, then, that the credibility problem
would not arise in the case of a nation's efforts to deter attack on
its own territory, what is called basic deterrence.[5] But extended
deterrence simply reveals more vividly the credibility problem inherent, though to a lesser degree, in basic deterrence as well. For
example, the credibility problem arose in regard to the U.S. threat
to retaliate for a Soviet attack on U.S. land-based missiles. It may
not have been rational for the United States to retaliate for such
an attack because the next round of escalation might have involved
the destruction of U.S. cities.[6]

The argument that counterforce strategy can restore credibility
is that it allows the threat of retaliation in kind, especially measured
and proportional retaliation for a limited attack. The credibility
problem arises more acutely in deterring attacks that avoid hitting
cities, as the example of a Soviet attack against U.S. missiles suggests. What counterforce theorists see as most lacking in credibility
is the threat of countervalue retaliation in response to a counterforce attack.[7] In a situation of mutual vulnerability, such retaliation
would not be prudentially rational. But retaliation proportional to
a limited attack might be prudentially rational.[8] As a result, nuclear
deterrence can be credible only if it includes the capacity for proportional retaliation. The counterforce critique is that countervalue
strategy is not credible because it allows retaliation only at the
highest level. On the other hand, as the last chapter made clear,
nuclear deterrence can be credible only if it includes threats to
destroy cities. Pure counterforce strategy is not credible because it
does not threaten retaliation at the highest level. So, credibility can
be achieved only if both kinds of threats are combined, as in impure
counterforce or mixed strategy, so as to include the threat to attack
at any level. A strategy that threatened to destroy only cities or
only military targets away from cities would not be sufficient to
achieve a high level of credibility.

The ability to retaliate or respond at lower levels is clearly essential for the prospects of limited nuclear war, because a nuclear

war could not remain limited unless both sides are able to attack in a limited way. The need for intra-war deterrence shows the connection between credibility and the threat to respond at all levels. Counterforce strategists argue that in a war, if there were some levels at which a nation was unable to respond, the opponent would be less likely to be deterred from escalating the conflict to those levels, so that intra-war deterrence would suffer. Pre-war deterrence would also suffer. If there are any gaps in the series of levels at which the nation is able to respond, these may be exploited by the opponent in war to its military advantage, which would lessen the credibility of the nation's threats. Thus the capacity to respond at all levels, from the highest to the lowest, is necessary for deterrence credibility.[9] But due to the condition of mutual vulnerability, it may not be sufficient. Because there is no possibility of a disarming first strike, a nation's counterforce capacity cannot deny the opponent its capacity for assured destruction. Some counterforce theorists have stressed the potential of new weapons technologies to allow nuclear attacks with minimal collateral damage, but making minimal civilian damage possible does not make maximal civilian damage impossible. If mutual vulnerability implies that a limited nuclear war is not reasonably foreseeable, as Chapter 1 argues, it would seem to imply that a counterforce strategy cannot provide nuclear threats with high credibility.

With an important class of exceptions, counterforce strategists have generally recognized that the condition of mutual vulnerability cannot be overcome by technology. But some proponents of the ballistic missile defenses, following Ronald Reagan, have argued that defenses could render nuclear weapons "impotent and obsolete."[10] Most proponents of missile defenses recognize, however, that such defenses could not be effective enough to overcome the vulnerability of a nation's society.[11] Counterforce strategists, by and large, believe that defenses can be effective not at overcoming vulnerability, but at enhancing the ability of a nation to wage nuclear war in spite of mutual vulnerability.[12] They argue that defenses would enhance deterrence by increasing the opponent's uncertainty about the results of a contemplated counterforce attack. This is simply to say that defenses would make the opponent's counterforce capabilities less militarily effective, thus making one's own comparatively more militarily effective. It is, again, the basic counterforce idea that better war-avoidance comes through better capability for war-waging.

Defenses, when understood in their proper strategic role, are simply another counterforce weapons system.[13] The distinction drawn between offensive and defensive weapons is of no special strategic significance, because they are all meant to enhance war-waging capabilities. Offensive counterforce weapons can be used defensively, in that they can destroy weapons before they are used in an attack. Defensive weapons can be used offensively in that they can improve the chances for aggression by inhibiting or interfering with the opponent's military response. This also applies to passive defensive efforts, such as programs for hardening offensive weapons from attack or making them mobile, or plans for civil defense by sheltering or relocating civilian populations to protect them from attack. Defensive and offensive capabilities do differ in the way they promote military effectiveness, defenses shielding a nation from, or protecting it from the effects of, weapons already launched against it, and offensive forces disabling those weapons before they are launched, but this is not a strategically important difference.[14] Both defensive and offensive capabilities are best understood under the genus of war-waging capabilities.

The argument of this chapter is that the prima facie case against the prudential preferability of nuclear deterrence cannot be successfully rebutted by appeal to the alleged advantages of counterforce strategy. Here is a sketch. Proponents of counterforce strategy do not succeed in showing to be unsound the argument of Chapter 1 that it is not reasonably foreseeable that a nuclear war would remain limited. As a result, counterforce strategy does not provide a basis for solving the credibility problem. Nonetheless, a nation's adopting a counterforce strategy may avoid the credibility problem, because it may lead the opponent to believe that the nation believes, despite the lack of an adequate objective basis for such a belief, that a nuclear war would remain limited, hence that nuclear retaliation could be rational. If the opponent believes this, the nation's threats may achieve sufficient credibility. But a dilemma then arises. A impure counterforce strategy may be more or less ambitious, and how ambitious it is determines the extent to which it is likely to lead the opponent to such a belief. A strategy that is more ambitious is more likely to lead the opponent to such a belief, but such a strategy is also likely seriously to undermine the central prudential advantage of nuclear deterrence, resulting in little or no gain in net deterrent value. A strategy that is less ambitious is unlikely to lead the opponent to such a belief, so it would not solve the credibility problem. Either way, the prima facie argument is unrebutted.

LIMITED NUCLEAR WAR

Recall some points made earlier about the prospects for limited nuclear war and its relation to deterrence credibility. First, not just any limitation will do. In prospect, the nuclear war must be appropriately limited, meaning that it must be prudentially rational for the nation to engage in, which requires that what the nation would achieve in the war be sufficient to outweigh the damage it would suffer. Second, nuclear war can be appropriately limited only through the opponent's restraint. Given mutual vulnerability, a capacity for damage limitation is not a capacity for unacceptable-damage limitation. Third, it must be reasonably foreseeable, not merely possible, that a nuclear war would remain appropriately limited. As Freedman puts it, a counterforce strategy, in order to be credible, "requires more than the design of means to wage nuclear war in a variety of ways, but something sufficiently plausible to appear as a tolerably rational course of action which has a realistic chance of leading to a satisfactory outcome."[15] In the light of these points, the question could be put in this way. Is it reasonably foreseeable that a nation in the midst of a nuclear war can, through the use and threat of use of its counterforce capability, induce its opponent to practice restraint to the extent that the war remains appropriately limited?

Counterforce strategists argue that a nation cannot count on its opponent to practice restraint as a matter of course, rather that the nation must be able to impose conditions forcing the opponent to choose restraint. This is achieved through intra-war deterrence, and it is the nation's counterforce capability that provides effective intra-war deterrence. By using its counterforce capability to force the opponent to choose restraint, the nation can have an effective way of achieving an appropriately limited nuclear war. There are two aspects to this process of forcing the opponent to exercise restraint. First, as discussed in Chapter 1, the ending of the war is through a bargain, most likely informal or implicit, struck by the belligerents in the midst of war, whereby both sides agree to cease attacking short of mutual destruction.[16] The bargain is achieved through intra-war deterrence, and it is akin to the implicit bargain that constitutes successful pre-war deterrence whereby each side tacitly agrees not to attack if the other side does not.[17] By analogy, the bargain limiting a nuclear war is an agreement not to attack any more if the other side does not. In a nuclear war, matters cannot be resolved by military means without such a bargain, because neither side is able to disarm the other. Expressing this view, Freedman says that it is "in contributing to bargaining positions that the utility, if any, of nuclear weapons" resides.[18]

Burden of restraint

The second aspect of the imposition of restraint involves the crucial role played by counterforce capability in the nature of the bargain that is achieved. Thomas Schelling asserts that "in limited warfare, two things are being bargained over, the outcome of the war, and the mode of conducting the war itself."[19] Though "it is in the interest of both sides to keep the war limited," Robert Jervis observes, "each could want to use the chance of escalation as a means of extracting concessions from the other."[20] A counterforce capability assists in this effort, being useful not simply in ending the war, but in ensuring that its outcome is favorable to the nation. Glenn Snyder notes: "Counterforce strikes do not contribute *directly* to 'winning the war' . . . they contribute only indirectly by improving the attacker's relative bargaining power."[21] A limited war can end on terms that are more favorable to one side than the other. The bargain limiting the war might be unequal, in the sense that it favors one side more than the other. It is in the interest of each side to attempt to end the war on favorable terms by imposing a bargain unfavorable to the opponent – that is, by getting the opponent to assume a larger portion of the burden of restraint.[22] Counterforce strategists argue that with an adequate counterforce capacity, a nation can impose a bargain unfavorable to the opponent.[23] Through the intra-war deterrent that counterforce capacity provides, a nation can get its opponent not only to cease attacking, but to do so on terms that are to the nation's relative advantage. Given the damage that even a very limited nuclear war would do, only if a nation could get the opponent to accept a larger portion of the burden of restraint would there be prospects that the war would be appropriately limited, that is, be of prudential advantage to the nation.

An argument of Chapter 1 is that a limited nuclear war is not reasonably foreseeable. Counterforce strategists must be able to show that this argument is unsound, if they are to establish that nuclear threats can achieve a high level of credibility. They would claim that this argument is unsound because it does not appreciate, first, how a sufficient counterforce capability could keep a war limited and, second, how that capability could achieve advantage for the nation in the war by getting the opponent to accept an unfavorable bargain for restraint. To consider whether these claims can be sustained, we must revisit the question of limited nuclear war, asking again whether an appropriately limited nuclear war is reasonably foreseeable. We must expand on the Chapter 1 argument, considering the notion of appropriate limitation and the role that counterforce capability would be able to contribute to its achievement. As argued earlier, these matters cannot be considered by arguing from experience or analogy. They must be addressed in terms of the general conditions that would need to be satisfied, in practice, for the opponent to exercise restraint in nuclear war to the extent that the war would be appropriately limited for the nation. There are three general conditions, each of which must be satisfied for the prospects of an appropriately limited nuclear war to be reasonably foreseeable: (1) The opponent must have the capacity to practice restraint. (2) The opponent must have sufficient reason to practice restraint. (3) The opponent's restraint must be sufficient to bring about a war appropriately limited for the nation.

The question whether these three conditions would be satisfied in an actual nuclear war is largely an empirical one, but it also has an important conceptual dimension. Both of these aspects are suggested by Harold Brown:

> Counterforce and damage-limitation campaigns have been put forward as the nuclear equivalents of traditional warfare. But their proponents find it difficult to tell us what objectives an enemy would seek in launching such campaigns, how these campaigns would end, or how any resulting asymmetries could be made meaningful.[24]

Brown here poses three questions. First, what ends could be reasonably sought in a nuclear war? Second, how would a nuclear war be brought to a conclusion? The third question, though not clear, I take to be: If one side achieves a relative advantage in the war, how could this count as a meaningful victory? The first and third of these questions are largely conceptual (and normative), whereas the second is mainly empirical. In discussing the three conditions for the reasonable foreseeability of an appropriately limited nuclear war, I shall understand conditions (1) and (2) as raising largely empirical questions, akin to Brown's second question, and condition (3) as raising primarily conceptual questions, akin to Brown's first and third questions.

Capacity for restraint

(1) Considering the first condition, the question is whether opponents in a nuclear war would have the capacity to restrain themselves. Nuclear weapons create severe problems for the exercise of restraint. In a recent study of nuclear operations, Ashton Carter, John Steinbruner, and Charles Zraket assert: "In devising weapons that concentrate destructive power to an unprecedented degree, governments have also created managerial problems more demanding than any previously encountered."[25] Managing military activities in the midst of nuclear war would be extremely difficult, if not impossible, because the system by which these activities are controlled is fragile and subject to serious disruption and degradation in war. According to Desmond Ball: "The command-and-control network is the most vulnerable component of the U.S. strategic forces." This vulnerability imposes "very severe physical limits to the extent to which a nuclear war could be controlled."[26]

The command system might be deliberately attacked in war. Carter, Steinbruner, and Zraket point out that attacks on the command system "appear to be the single most consequential thing that an attacker can do to blunt the military effectiveness of an opponent's retaliation," thus creating "a strong impulse to begin a nuclear war with attacks on the command system." As a consequence, hopes for limitation might well be lost. "The unsystematic retaliation that the damaged command system could carry out would be less damaging to protected and dispersed military targets but quite devastating to unprotected populations and economic assets."[27] The irony is that in attacking the opponent's command system, a nation, while attempting to achieve an advantage by doing what is militarily most effective, would end up guaranteeing an unlimited war where its damage would be necessarily unacceptable. Recognizing this, a nation might not attack the opponent's command system, deliberately avoiding doing what is militarily most effective, in an attempt to keep the war limited. But the nation would likely disrupt the opponent's command system in any case. Crucial command-system components are quite vulnerable to the environmental disturbances caused by nuclear explosions. As Ball says: "Control of a nuclear exchange would become very difficult to maintain after several tens of strategic nuclear weapons had been used, even where deliberate attacks on command-and-control capabilities were avoided."[28] Whether or not the command system were deliberately attacked, it is unlikely to survive the early stages of a nuclear war.

Moreover, efforts to overcome the inherent vulnerabilities of the command system are not only technologically difficult, but at least partially self-defeating, due to the trade-offs such efforts involve. For example, decentralizing authority in the command system would lessen the risk that the nation would be unable to respond due to damage to the command system, but by lessening the role of a single central authority, this would, at the same time, weaken the coordination of the system as a whole, lessening the degree of control that the system would be able to maintain in war.[29] The vulnerability of the command system seems to be an aspect of the confusion inherent in all war. The problem, as mentioned earlier, is that in the case of nuclear war, this confusion works to keep the war from being limited, rather than working to keep the war limited. The conclusion must be that there are serious doubts about the capacity of a nation's opponent, as well as the nation itself, to exercise restraint in the midst of nuclear war.

Reason for restraint

(2) Considering now the second condition, would the opponent have sufficient reason in the midst of a nuclear war to restrain itself, at least so that the damage to the nation would not escalate to the point of necessary unacceptability? Because a nuclear war could be limited only through a bargain, there is reason for each side to practice restraint, in order to induce restraint from its opponent. Self-restraint is the means by which a nation can limit damage to itself. But the problem is that the bargain for restraint need not be equal. Overall limitation of the war is of value to both parties, but each side will perceive its own restraint in the pursuit of that overall limitation as a burden, in the sense that it thereby forgoes an opportunity to achieve a military advantage or avoid a military disadvantage in relation to its opponent. Each side has a strong incentive to attempt to achieve a relative military advantage

by getting its opponent to accept an unfavorable burden of restraint. Indeed, the counterforce argument is that a nation can achieve an appropriately limited nuclear war precisely by getting its opponent to accept an unfavorable bargain.

Limited war is a "public good," at least by comparison with its unlimited alternative. But like other public goods, it can be achieved without all parties contributing their fair share. Counterforce strategy is concerned with the apportionment of the burden of restraint in war so that it is to the nation's relative advantage. But the efforts of each side both to avoid assuming a larger portion of the burden of restraint and to impose this on its opponent can doom overall efforts at limitation. This is a logic that fuels escalation in a variety of conflict situations. In a nuclear war, Robert McNamara asserts, "it is highly likely that rather than surrender, each side would launch a larger attack, hoping that this step would bring the action to a halt by causing the opponent to capitulate."[30] The idea is that escalation may not be simply an uncontrolled process, as it is often taken to be in discussions of nuclear war, but rather it may be composed of a series of deliberate escalatory moves, each designed to achieve relative advantage by forcing the other side to accept an unfavorable bargain for restraint.[31] Because of its desire to avoid assuming a larger portion of the burden of restraint and to impose such a burden on the other side, the opponent may well lack what it takes to be sufficient reason to practice restraint, despite its desire to reach a bargain that would keep the war limited.[32]

Two ways in which this escalatory logic could play itself out in a nuclear war, to the detriment of prospects for its limitation, are suggested by Desmond Ball. "There are compelling military arguments both against the highly graduated application of force and for attacking the command-and-control infrastructure of the adversary's nuclear forces."[33] In both respects, a major escalatory move in war is tempting because it could secure a military advantage by getting the opponent to capitulate, thereby accepting a larger portion of the burden of restraint. But it could also lead to an unlimited war. On Ball's first point, a military argument against a gradual increase in the application of force is based on the belief that the way to get the opponent to withdraw from a war is to raise the level of violence suddenly and dramatically rather than gradually, as the way to get a frog to jump out of the pot of water is to increase the heat quickly rather than slowly. On this view, a nation's nuclear response should be large in order to shock the opponent into withdrawing from the war, rather than giving it a chance to adjust to that level of damage, as it might were the damage reached through a series of escalatory moves. According to Henry Kissinger: "Gradual escalation tempts the opponent to match every move." Rather than practicing such gradualism, a leader "must be prepared to escalate rapidly and brutally to a point where the opponent can no longer afford to experiment."[34] This approach might work, but if it does not, then the massiveness of both the attack and the retaliation it would call forth are likely to move the war past the point at which it could be appropriately limited.

On Ball's second point, an attack on the opponent's command system is, as we have seen, militarily tempting. Such an attack, Robert Jervis notes, "might be the only chance for victory, but it would also increase the chance that the adversary will launch an unrestrained counterattack."[35] Although an attack on the command system could force the opponent to accept a larger portion of the burden of restraint by destroying its capacity to respond, it would also undermine the prospects for limitation by destroying the opponent's ability to restrain its own forces. With no one in command of the opponent's forces, the possibility of reaching a bargain for mutual restraint disappears. The military hope is that a command-system attack would decapitate the opponent – that is, not only destroy its ability to coordinate its retaliation, but destroy its ability to retaliate altogether. Decapitation would be the elusive technological fix, a way in which counterforce capability could achieve, in effect, a disarming first-strike, eliminating the nation's societal vulnerability. But command systems can be designed to avoid the possibility of decapitation.[36] So, rather than suppressing retaliation, a command-system attack is likely to bring about an uncoordinated, massively destructive retaliation.

Escalation dominance

In response to such concerns, counterforce strategists claim that an adequate counterforce capability can keep the escalatory process from getting out of hand. Such a capacity, they claim, provides what is called *escalation dominance*, allowing the nation possessing it to control the escalation process. Escalation dominance is the way in which intra-war deterrence works, the way in which a nation gets its opponent to accept an unfavorable bargain, whereby it assumes a larger portion of the burden of restraint. The idea is that when a nation has a counterforce capability sufficient to provide escalation dominance, the opponent would not perceive escalation to be to its military advantage, as a result of which it would capitulate rather than escalate further. A nation has escalation dominance when its forces "can contain or defeat the adversary at all levels of violence with the possible exception of the highest."[37] A nation's ability to use force at any potential level of nuclear conflict to contain or defeat the opponent will allow the nation to threaten credibly to use force at any level. As a result, the opponent would expect that if it escalates the conflict, the nation would respond with an escalatory move of its own. Convinced that the nation would respond to any escalation, the opponent would recognize that escalation could gain it no military advantage, and so would exercise restraint, even if this meant accepting an unfavorable bargain whereby it assumed a larger portion of the burden of restraint. Thus, a nation's capacity for escalation dominance would provide the opponent with sufficient reason to practice restraint.

Again, the issue comes to the credibility of nuclear threats, this time intra-war threats rather than pre-war threats. Escalation dominance works only if the intra-war deterrent threats are credible. Counterforce strategists argue that the credibility of intra-war deterrent threats leads to the credibility of pre-war deterrent threats. If intra-war deterrent threats are credible, this would allow a nation to control the escalation process, establishing the reasonable foreseeability of an appropriately limited nuclear war, and hence the credibility of pre-war deterrent threats. But the question is whether the intra-war deterrent threats can themselves be credible. The problem with the credibility of pre-war deterrence is that the threat to retaliate is a threat to do something that could well lead to societal destruction. Thus, a nation's intra-war deterrent threat to escalate a war would be credible only if it were not a threat to do something that could well lead to societal destruction, and this would be the case only if the opponent would not be expected to escalate the conflict further in response to the nation's escalation. According to the counterforce strategist, what keeps the opponent from escalating further is its recognition that the nation could contain or defeat it at that new level of conflict. The ability of a nation to contain or defeat its opponent at some level of conflict is a matter of its relative military capability. Thus, the claim that the nation's counterforce capability can achieve credibility for its intra-war deterrent threats by depriving the opponent's threat to escalate of its credibility depends on the extent to which the credibility of intra-war deterrent threats depends on relative military capability.

The claim that nuclear threat credibility is a function of relative military capability is based on a misperception of the nature of nuclear war. Relative military capability may determine threat credibility in a traditional military situation. But in a situation of mutual vulnerability, what counts is not relative capability, but the absolute capability each side has to destroy the society of the other.[38] To draw the contrast between a traditional military situation and a situation of mutual vulnerability, Robert Jervis, following Thomas Schelling, has characterized nuclear war as a "competition in risk-taking." "When all-out war will destroy both sides, maneuvering short of that level of violence is very strongly influenced by each side's willingness to run risks," a willingness "not closely linked to the military balance, since military advantage cannot protect the state from destruction."[39] In a nuclear war, any escalation increases the risks that the war will not be limited, so in making escalatory moves, each side is competing with the other in running the risk of societal destruction.

In a situation of mutual vulnerability, each escalatory move has a dual context. Not only does it have an impact on the relative military balance (assuming it is a counterforce attack), but it also brings the whole conflict closer to mutual destruction. Because the stakes are so high, the latter context would play a more crucial role in the dynamics of a war than the former. The counterforce argument that an adequate counterforce capability can make a nation's escalatory threats credible considers only the context of relative military balance, ignoring the fact that nations would use escalation to compete in taking risks. In making an escalatory move, a nation would increase the risk of mutual destruction, and if it were more willing to run such a risk than its opponent, it could get the opponent to assume a larger portion of the burden of restraint, irrespective of the opponent's relative military capability. Instead of being a battle for military supremacy, a nuclear war would be a game of "chicken."[40] This is the dynamic that would be forced on the belligerents by the fact of mutual vulnerability. A nation's superior counterforce capability cannot establish the credibility of its intra-war deterrent threats, nor insure that the opponent would agree to end the war on terms favorable to the nation. By showing its greater willingness to run the risk of societal destruction, the opponent, though inferior in a traditional military sense, might well get the nation to end the war on the opponent's terms.

This argument is supported by some observations on the nature of the credibility of deterrent threats from Chapter 4. Threat credibility is demonstrated by the threatener's history of threat executions. But in the case of nuclear deterrence, where there is no such history, credibility is determined by whether there is a presumption that the threatener would be willing to carry out its threats, which is a function of whether it would be rational for the threatener to do so. But this is pre-war deterrence. In the case of intra-war deterrent threats, a nation does have a history of threat executions, with each escalation adding to that history. It is in a nuclear war that a nation can demonstrate what it cannot demonstrate prior to the war – namely, its resolve to carry out its nuclear threats. Because a demonstrated history of threat executions is, in general, a more reliable indicator of future behavior than is presumptive willingness, a nuclear war would be primarily a battle of resolve, a competition in risk taking, rather than a contest in which relative military capability would carry the day. The primary motive each side would have in its escalatory moves is showing that it has more resolve, that it is more willing to risk societal destruction, than the other side. This is why each side would have the hope that one more round of escalation on its part would cause the other side to capitulate. Despite the claims of counterforce strategists, then, counterforce capability does not obviate the logic of nuclear escalation, and cannot by itself insure that the opponent will have sufficient reason to cease attacking.

There is another set of problems facing the claim that an adequate counterforce capability can provide the opponent with sufficient reason to practice restraint. These problems, discussed in Chapter 1, result from the inherent confusion of nuclear war. This confusion would interfere with the belligerents' forming beliefs that could provide them with sufficient reason for restraint. One important factor in this regard is that nuclear attacks themselves would be part of the means by which the bargain for mutual restraint, whether equal or unequal, would be reached, and nuclear attacks are poor communication vehicles. An aspect of this problem is that there is a lack of obvious, recognizable limits in nuclear warfare that could provide the basis for the clear communicative content of a nuclear attack.[41] Such limits would provide the conventions that nuclear communication, like any communication, requires. A bargain limiting a nuclear war would involve an understanding of where the two sides would stop, what limits they would agree to observe. For the bargain to be reached, these limits would have to be jointly recognized, but it would be difficult tacitly to arrive at such a recognition in a nuclear war, because there are few conspicuous stopping points.

The most salient point of limitation is not internal to nuclear war, but is at the boundary between conventional and nuclear conflict, what is referred to as the nuclear firebreak. Apart from the geographical distinction between attacks on the opponent's territory and those outside of its territory – that is, the recognition of the so-called homeland sanctuary – there are no comparable firebreaks within nuclear war. The difference between the use of tactical and strategic nuclear weapons, to the extent that it is not a geographical distinction but one simply based on the size of the weapon, is not the basis for a clear distinction. According to two critics of counterforce, "the only meaningful 'firebreak' in modern warfare, be it strategic or tactical, is between nuclear and conventional weapons, not between self-proclaimed categories of nuclear weapons."[42] The problem is compounded by the related difficulty of applying in practice the idea, essential to the notion of limited escalation, of a response in kind. "What constitute[s] a response in kind? a similar number of casualties, an explosion of a similar yield, a delivery vehicle of similar type, or a target of equivalent significance and value (a regional capital or a naval base)?"[43] Since it is not obvious what constitutes response in kind, it is not likely that the belligerents in a nuclear war would come to a common understanding of what aspects of the conflict to limit, let alone where the limits to those aspects should be placed.

As a result of all of these problems, it is unlikely that the second condition would be satisfied. There is little basis to believe that the opponent would have sufficient reason in the midst of war to practice restraint.[44] The strong reason a nation has to avoid nuclear war as a result of its societal vulnerability does not necessarily translate into an overriding reason to stop at some particular point in the midst of a nuclear war. A nation's possession of a superior counterforce capability does not enable it to force the opponent to practice restraint, because at each point in the conflict, escalation holds out the prospect of the opponent's being able to end the war on its own terms, irrespective of deficiencies in its relative military capability, by showing greater resolve and willingness to run the risk of societal destruction. Escalation dominance cannot be achieved through an advantage in relative military capability. Moreover, even if escalation dominance were possible in theory, it would not work in practice because of difficulties in achieving the tacit bargain necessary to limit the war.[45] Given the discussion of the first two conditions, one should concur in the judgment of four former senior nuclear policy makers that "no one has ever succeeded in advancing any persuasive reason to believe that any use of nuclear weapons, even on the smallest scale, could reliably be expected to remain limited."[46] The answer to Harold Brown's second question (how would a nuclear war be brought to a conclusion?) is that although a nuclear war may end short of mutual destruction, there are no mechanisms nations can rely on to bring it to such an end, other than refusal to participate.

Appropriate limitation

(3) The third condition should now be considered. If conditions (1) and (2) were satisfied, this would show that it is reasonably foreseeable that a nuclear war would remain limited, but not that it would remain appropriately limited. To determine whether the third condition would likely be satisfied, one must determine how limited a nuclear war would have to be in order to be appropriately limited and how likely it is that a limited nuclear war would be that limited. Our efforts in this regard can be facilitated by our keeping in mind two of Brown's questions: What ends would be sought in a nuclear war and would the achievement of any of those ends count as a meaningful victory?

Michael Howard says of war scenarios described by counterforce strategists: "I ask myself in bewilderment: this war they are describing, *what is it about?*"[47] The force of asking what ends would be sought in a nuclear war is that it brings home the point that the value of any potential ends pales besides the damage that is risked. Indeed, the traditional sorts of ends for which wars are fought, various kinds of political advantage, would turn out to be of only secondary importance. As discussed in the last chapter, although limiting a war is normally a matter of adjusting means to ends, limiting a nuclear war would be a matter of adjusting ends to means. The primary focus of attention would be on controlling the means, stopping the fighting, in order to avoid societal destruction.

Though each side would treat the war as competition in risk-taking, and seek thereby to end the conflict on terms favorable to itself, it would recognize that a necessary condition for achieving this end would be putting an early end to the war, and it would view its controlled use of escalation as a means both of ending the war and achieving advantage. In large measure, then, the answer to Brown's question is that the end of the war would be the end of the war. There have been wars to end all (future) wars, but a nuclear war would be a war to end itself.[48]

This is not to say that some advantage of the traditional sort could not be achieved in a nuclear war. For example, even if the war resulted simply in a reaffirmation of the political status quo ante, the negative end of denying the opponent any gain would have been achieved and something of fundamental value would have been preserved. Aggression would have been defeated. Even a positive end might be achieved and fundamental interests advanced, if the nation won the competition in risk taking and imposed on its opponent a larger portion of the burden of restraint. In either case, there would be something to weigh against the damage suffered in the war. This raises Brown's question of whether the achievement of that kind of end could be regarded as a meaningful victory. In other words, would the achievement of that end be worthwhile compared with the damage suffered? That damage would not be necessarily unacceptable, because the assumption is that the war is absolutely limited, but what reason is there to think that it would not be contingently unacceptable?

There are two reasons for concluding that any political advantage a nation might gain in a limited nuclear war would not be sufficient to outweigh the damage it would suffer. First, because of the great destructive power of nuclear weapons, the amount of damage brought about by a limited nuclear war would be high.[49] Second, the political advantage achieved by a nation in a limited nuclear war, if any, is not likely to be very great. The more unequal the bargain a nation seeks to impose, the larger the portion of the burden of restraint it attempts to force the opponent to assume, the less likely the opponent is to accept the bargain. The opponent always has the option to escalate the war in order to attempt to avoid assuming the lion's share of the burden of restraint, and the larger that share, the more likely the opponent is to make that choice. Because total war is possible, total victory is not, and a nation's prospects for keeping a war limited depend on its willingness to accept, at best, the achievement of a limited political advantage. Pre-nuclear wars were limited by one side's achieving the end for which it was fighting, because achieving that end would mark for that nation the point at which it should stop. But in a nuclear war, the attempt to achieve even a very modest end is precisely what could make the war unlimited. War aims help insure limitation in pre-nuclear wars, but they promote lack of limitation in nuclear wars.

One objection to this line of argument is that it ignores the possibility, discussed in Chapter 1, that overall advantage should be measured in relative rather than in absolute terms. If overall advantage is measured in relative terms, then any advantage a nation achieves by imposing a larger portion of the burden of restraint on its opponent might be sufficient for the achievement of overall advantage, thus meaningful victory, given that the damage the nation suffers would be canceled out by the damage suffered by the opponent. This view can be seen in the claim that the United States would be the victor in a nuclear war if it were able to recover from the effects of the war more quickly than the Soviet Union.[50] But this understanding of meaningful victory fails to appreciate the distinction between the use of military force for denial (or aggression) and its use for punishment. When military force is used for denial or aggression, the idea of victory as overall relative advantage makes some sense because one side's gain implies the other's loss and vice-versa. The cumulative gain and lose for both sides is zero sum. But when military force achieves a significant level of punishment, the situation is not zero sum. Both sides can lose. This is ignored in any attempt to treat overall advantage in a nuclear war in relative terms.[51] It is the fact that both sides could lose in a nuclear exchange that makes possible a bargain to limit it, because otherwise the side with the military advantage would have no reason not to fight through to complete victory.

If overall advantage is understood in absolute rather than relative terms, how limited must a nuclear war be to be appropriately limited? The answer seems to be that it cannot be limited enough. Once it began, it would already be beyond the point at which it might be prudentially justifiable. In all likelihood, a nation in a nuclear war could not avoid suffering unacceptable damage, even though, assuming conditions (1) and (2) to be satisfied, the damage may be contingently rather than necessarily unacceptable. Thus, condition (3), like conditions (1) and (2), is unlikely to be satisfied.

According to Jervis, nuclear weapons have "brought an end to the proportionality between the means employed and the goals sought that used to characterize international politics."[52] This is the case whether the nuclear wars in question are limited or unlimited.[53] The point might be put by saying that the notion of limited nuclear war borders on incoherence. Because war is instrumental in the achievement of political objectives, the limits of the war are defined by those objectives. This is how it was with pre-nuclear war, where the achievement of the objective determined the point at which war stopped. But in the case of nuclear war, this essential relation between objectives and limitations is absent. Ian Clark makes this point by arguing that what is lacking in discussions of limited nuclear war is an appreciation of the relation that ought to hold between a theory of limiting war and a theory of war, understood as politically instrumental. Limited war theorists "have placed the cart of practical limitations before the horse of the theory of war."[54]

The conclusion must be that an appropriately limited nuclear war is not reasonably foreseeable. For good empirical and conceptual reasons, there is no adequate theory of nuclear war termination. A nuclear war may turn out to be limited, and there are things a nation can do to make it more likely that it would be limited, but a nation cannot by choice of a counterforce strategy make a nuclear war's limitation, let alone its appropriate limitation, a reasonably expectable outcome. The idea of using counterforce capability to fight a nuclear war that could be controlled so as to be kept deliberately limited is, according to Desmond Ball, "essentially astrategic." Ball goes on to suggest that "the use of nuclear weapons for controlled escalation is . . . no less difficult to envisage than the use of nuclear weapons for massive retaliation."[55] There is self-deterrence with a counterforce strategy as without, and the credibility problem remains. A counterforce strategy seems unable to establish the continuity between nuclear and conventional weapons needed to provide nuclear threats with high credibility.

Dashiell Hammett captures the logic of this problem in the detective-novel prose quoted at the start of the chapter. Spade and Gutman are in a kind of mutual vulnerability, in that Gutman can kill Spade and, although Spade cannot kill Gutman, he can deny Gutman the achievement of the objective to which he has devoted his life, possession of the Maltese Falcon. Both parties, of course, want to keep any conflict between them limited, but, as Spade explains, Gutman's efforts to get the bird from Spade and Spade's efforts to deny it to him, could easily lead to an unlimited conflict – Spade would be dead and Gutman would not get the bird. That their conflict could readily be kept limited is "the stuff dreams are made of."

A DILEMMA

But the move from the claim that an appropriately limited nuclear war is not reasonably foreseeable to the claim that the adoption of a counterforce strategy would not impart a high level of credibility to a nation's nuclear threat may be too quick. To say that an appropriately limited nuclear war is not reasonably foreseeable is to say that though such an outcome is possible, a nation should not expect it. But the credibility of a nation's nuclear threat is determined not directly by what one should believe about the prospects for limited nuclear war, nor even by what the opponent believes about such prospects, but primarily by what the opponent believes that the nation believes about such prospects. As Jervis points out: "What is crucial for the added credibility that the ability to carry out limited strikes brings is not the Russians' beliefs about whether nuclear war can be kept limited, but their beliefs about what the American decision-makers think about this question."[56] If the opponent believes that the nation believes that an appropriately limited nuclear war is reasonably foreseeable, even though it is not, the opponent would then believe that the nation is likely to carry out its nuclear threat, in which case that threat would be highly credible.

Given that credibility is dependent on beliefs, a counterforce strategist could argue that the nation's adoption of a counterforce strategy would be taken by the opponent as sufficient evidence that the nation believes that it could fight an appropriately limited nuclear war. If so, counterforce strategy could provide a highly credible form of both intra-war and pre-war deterrence. But there are strong objections to this argument. First, although the opponent might take the nation's adoption of a counterforce strategy as some evidence that the nation believes it could fight an appropriately limited nuclear war, it does not follow that the opponent would take this as conclusive evidence. One reason is that the opponent may find plausible other possible explanations for the nation's choice of counterforce strategy. One such explanation is suggested by Warner Schilling, who claims that the military capabilities of the United States may "owe more to the end products of the bureaucratic and Executive-Congressional politics of acquisition policy" than to the requirements of strategic doctrine.[57] Another reason is that there would probably be a considerable level of debate in the nation about the wisdom of adopting extensive counterforce deployments, which would clearly undermine the opponent's belief that such deployments indicate a firm belief on the nation's part that they could be effective in fighting an appropriately limited nuclear war. There would be an element of insincerity, bluff, or self-deception in any claim the nation made that its counterforce strategy could keep nuclear war appropriately limited, and this would show.

Second, for this argument to hold, the opponent must believe not only (1) that the nation believes that it could fight an appropriately limited nuclear war, but also (2) that the nation would act on this belief should war come. However likely the opponent is to believe (1), it is less likely to believe (2). Given the daunting prospects for a nuclear war's remaining limited, even if the opponent believes that the nation is confident before the fact that it could control escalation, the opponent may also believe that the nation would quickly lose this confidence should war become imminent. These two objections seriously undermine the argument that the nation's adoption of a counterforce strategy can establish the credibility of its nuclear threats via the opponent's beliefs about the nation's beliefs.

The argument supports, at best, a weaker conclusion: A nation's adoption of a counterforce strategy *may* impart some additional credibility to its nuclear threat, but not necessarily enough to overcome the credibility problem. Thus, as it stands, the argument is too weak to rebut the prima facie argument against nuclear deterrence, because this would require a definite showing that the credibility problem could be solved. But even if the stronger conclusion could be sustained, so that it would be clear that counterforce threats could achieve high credibility, there is a serious problem with the argument that would keep it from constituting a successful rebuttal to the prima facie argument. This is the need to consider net deterrent effect. Counterforce strategy carries a serious prudential liability, which would offset whatever prudential advantage it has in terms of improved credibility. The liability is the tendency of counterforce strategy to undermine the factor of reassurance. Moreover, although some forms of counterforce strategy increase credibility more than others, the forms that would do the most to increase credibility are precisely those that would do the most to undermine reassurance. In other words, the more a counterforce strategy appears able to remedy the prudential disadvantage of nuclear deterrence (its lack of credibility), the more it undermines one of deterrence's main prudential advantages (its capacity for reassurance).[58] But the prima facie argument could be successfully rebutted only if the disadvantage was remedied without the advantage being lost.

This may be cast as a dilemma. Different forms of counterforce strategy may be distinguished by the extent of the counterforce capability they require. Ambitious strategies of counterforce require a very extensive counterforce capability, whereas modest strategies of counterforce require a much less extensive counterforce capability. The dilemma is this. If a counterforce strategy is ambitious, then it increases threat credibility, but it also seriously undermines reassurance. If a counterforce strategy is modest, it does little to undermine reassurance, but it also does little to improve threat credibility.[59] In either case, the prima facie argument is not rebutted. Even if counterforce strategy could solve the credibility problem, the prima facie argument would not be successfully rebutted, because, as the dilemma indicates, the solution of the credibility problem would come only through adopting a form of deterrence that seriously undermines the prudential advantage nuclear deterrence has over conventional deterrence. To argue the dilemma, I will show in this section that only an ambitious counterforce strategy can do much to improve threat credibility and in the next section show that an ambitious counterforce strategy would undermine reassurance by creating *crisis instability*.

Modest counterforce

Consider, first, a modest form of counterforce strategy, which may be called *selective options strategy*.[60] This strategy involves a relatively small counterforce capability, one that allows a nation to respond at any level of force, but only in a modest way. Assuming that the opponent has a more ambitious form of counterforce strategy, selective options strategy would provide no expectation that the nation could challenge the opponent at any level with an amount of force equal to or greater than that used by the opponent. Thus, there would be no expectation among those committed to the counterforce perspective that the nation could, in a nuclear war, through the exercise of relative military advantage, impose on its opponent a larger portion of the burden of restraint. As a result, the adoption of a selective options strategy would not be taken by the opponent as an indication that a nation believes that an appropriately limited nuclear war is reasonably foreseeable. To that extent, selective options strategy would do little to contribute to threat credibility.

There is, however, a different justification for a selective options strategy. Even if such a strategy would not signal that the nation believes that an appropriately limited war is reasonably foreseeable, it could increase the chances, however slim, of a war's remaining limited. The idea is that a capacity for making limited, counterforce responses would slow the pace of a nuclear war, providing time in the midst of the war for the belligerents to come to their senses and strike a bargain for mutual restraint before the slide to mutual destruction.[61] A selective options strategy could thus play a *temporizing* role, increasing the likelihood of a limited war by giving the bargaining process more time. This would increase the chances that a nuclear war would remain limited, without an expectation either that the war is likely to remain limited or that, if it did, it would be appropriately limited. This would have some effect on increasing threat credibility, because it would make retaliation somewhat less irrational. Critics have charged that this kind of justification for counterforce strategy amounts to a call for "suicide on the installment plan," and so it does. But, still, it could improve credibility to some extent. After all, one of the points of installment plans is to get people to buy things they would be unwilling to purchase if they had to pay cash up front. But the increase in credibility would be small, because the signal that a nation believes that there is some chance for limitation is much weaker than the signal that it believes that an appropriately limited nuclear war is reasonably foreseeable.

A counterforce strategy of intermediate ambition is *countervailing strategy*. This strategy prescribes that a nation be able to respond at any level with an amount of force roughly equivalent to that of the opponent. Countervailing strategy, as understood here, is close to the declaratory policy, which goes by the same name, that the United States adopted in the late 1970s. This strategy seeks to deter the opponent by convincing it that it "could never gain anything amounting to victory on any plausible definition of victory, or gain an advantage that would outweigh the unacceptable price [it] would have to pay."[62] It seeks to demonstrate to the opponent that it "could not an any level of nuclear attack expect to gain a military advantage that would be useful in political terms."[63] The idea that countervailing strategy requires the capacity for a roughly equivalent response to the opponent at every level is implied by the goal of the strategy, denial of advantage to the opponent, and the traditional military assumption that an opponent can achieve a positive advantage – that is, impose a bargain advantageous to itself – only if it has a preponderance of forces. This feature is implicit in the view that was taken by proponents of countervailing strategy that the United States should maintain equivalence or "counterforce parity" with the Soviet Union in its nuclear weapons deployments.[64]

One important feature of countervailing strategy, consistent with its goal of denying the opponent an advantage, is its reactive character. According to Walter Slocombe: "It is *not* a first-strike strategy. It is a strategy of deterrence, which deals with what the United States could and (depending on the nature of a Soviet attack) would do *in response* to a Soviet attack."[65] The reactive character of the strategy is suggested by the sense in which it seeks to establish escalation dominance. George Quester distinguishes two senses of escalation dominance, as this notion applied to the potential escalation of a conventional war in Europe to the nuclear level. If escalation dominance applied in the first sense, the Soviets would "never see an advantage for themselves in escalating to the nuclear level." If it applied in the second sense, "Western nuclear escalation [would] look credible," in the sense that the West could threaten to initiate the use of nuclear weapons.[66] The first sense is the one appropriate to countervailing strategy. The initiative is left to the opponent, and the purpose of the strategy is to deter the opponent from taking it by making credible the nation's threatened reaction. Sometimes this is expressed by saying that the purpose of strategy should be to place the burden of escalation on the opponent.[67] By providing the capability to match the opponent's use of force at any level, countervailing strategy seeks both to place the burden of escalation on the opponent and to discourage its assumption.

The question is whether a nation's adopting a countervailing strategy would lead the opponent to believe that the nation believes that an appropriately limited nuclear war is reasonably foreseeable. Unlike selective options strategy, countervailing strategy is designed to allow a nation to achieve a traditional sort of end in a nuclear war, the negative end of denying an advantage to the opponent. But would the adoption of this strategy signal the opponent that the nation believes that it could achieve this end? The problem is that the reactive character of the strategy calls into question the nation's ability to deny the opponent the kind of advantage it would most likely seek to achieve in war. This is an advantage from successful aggression in conventional war, such as the seizure of valuable territory. Nuclear deterrence is supposed to avoid conventional as well as nuclear war by the threat that a conventional war could become nuclear. So, to deter conventional war and to deny the opponent any advantage from it, a policy of nuclear deterrence must include the threat to escalate a conventional war to the nuclear level. But the reactive character of countervailing strategy seems to preclude such a threat, because it envisions nuclear weapons being used only in response to their use by the opponent.

This problem is illustrated by the U.S. policy of extended deterrence, which was designed to deter what was thought to be the most serious Soviet threat, a conventional attack by the Warsaw Pact against Western Europe. But deterrence of this threat required the threat of the first use of nuclear weapons. From the standpoint of credibility, as critics argued, the reactive character of countervailing strategy cannot support a threat of the first-use of nuclear weapons. Under countervailing strategy, first-use threats would lack credibility.[68] The first-use threat requires escalation dominance in the first sense discussed above, whereas countervailing strategy provides escalation dominance only in the second sense. Stalemate at the strategic level would leave the opponent free to attempt to achieve advantage through conventional war.[69] The threat of Soviet conventional attack in Europe was thought to be exacerbated by the perceived weakness of NATO conventional forces, but parity in conventional forces would not have solved the problem. The problem of extended deterrence in Europe, Robert Tucker observed, "cannot be fully compensated for by greater conventional forces," but must be solved "at the strategic level by forces that are more than simply the equivalent of the Soviet Union's forces."[70] Nor is the problem limited to extended deterrence, because it applies to the opponent's threat of conventional attack against the nation itself, though, as noted earlier, this is not a serious threat for the United States.

Parity is not enough. It is not enough at the conventional level, because a simple equivalence of forces may not dissuade the opponent from using its conventional forces to attempt to achieve some advantage. That is why nuclear threats are seen as necessary to deter conventional war. But, then, parity is not enough at the nuclear level, because it does not support the required threat to initiate the use of nuclear weapons in the context of a conventional conflict. The problem also applies within nuclear war. Having parity of forces at some level of nuclear force does not insure that a nation's efforts to deny the opponent an advantage at that level will succeed, given the unpredictability of conflict. Parity is not a sufficient guarantor of denial. The opponent is not likely to believe that a nation with a countervailing strategy believes that it would be able to achieve the end of denying the opponent an advantage, so it is not likely to believe that the nation believes that an appropriately limited nuclear war is reasonably foreseeable.

An indication that countervailing strategy does not support prospects for an appropriately limited nuclear war is that proponents of the U.S. countervailing strategy admitted that a nuclear war is unlikely to remain limited at all (let alone appropriately limited). According to Harold Brown:

> [Countervailing strategy] implies no illusion that nuclear war once begun would be likely to stop short of an all-out exchange. But it does acknowledge that such a limited war *could* happen, and it seeks to convince the Soviets that if a limited nuclear attack by them somehow failed to escalate into an all-out exchange, they would not have gained from their aggression.[71]

This shows clearly the weakness of the strategy. If a nation adopting the strategy has no illusions that a nuclear war would remain limited, it could not convince its opponent of the credibility of its retaliatory threats. The conclusion is that countervailing strategy would not make a significant contribution to the credibility of the nuclear threat. Like selective options strategy, it would make some contribution to credibility as a result of the temporizing effect it would have in a nuclear war, but because it is not a reliable instrument for the achievement of an end in war, it would do little to signal that a nation adopting it believes that a nuclear war would be appropriately limited.

Ambitious counterforce

The most ambitious form of counterforce strategy is *prevailing strategy*.[72] A counterforce strategy would be credible only if it could succeed in getting the opponent to believe that the nation believes that it could achieve advantage in a nuclear war, and this is possible only if the strategy appears to allow the nation to be initiatory, not merely reactive, in its military relations with its opponent. This is the promise of prevailing strategy. If the nation had the ability to take the nuclear initiative, it could succeed not only in denying the opponent any advantage, but also in achieving positive advantage for itself. It could impose an unequal bargain limiting the war under which the opponent would assume a larger portion of the burden of restraint. To achieve this potential, prevailing strategy prescribes that the nation have a more extensive counterforce capability than its opponent. Prevailing strategy calls for counterforce superiority. Instead of shifting the burden of escalation onto the opponent, prevailing strategy would provide the nation with the capacity to assume that burden, giving it the prerogative to escalate a conflict to a higher level in pursuit of advantage, thereby imposing "escalation discipline" on the opponent.[73] The nation would, then, have escalation dominance in the first sense discussed above. If the opponent believes that the nation believes that the nation could take such a commanding position in a nuclear conflict, the credibility of the nation's nuclear threat would seem to be assured.

Before assessing the credibility claims, two basic questions about prevailing strategy should be considered. First, what would a prevailing strategy threaten? There are three answers to this question, representing related aspects of the strategy: victory, the opponent's political order, and compellence. First, of course, prevailing strategy threatens victory, which means, in the first instance, the achievement of overall advantage in war, not simply denial of advantage, as is the case with countervailing strategy. Colin Gray recommends "the wisdom of approaching a central nuclear war as one should approach (or did approach, in pre-nuclear days) non-nuclear war." He claims: "Wars are indeed terminated, but they are also won or lost."[74] But an adequate notion of victory requires an adequate notion of defeat. So, prevailing strategy requires a plan for the opponent's defeat. This provides the second answer to the question. Victory requires that the nation be able to impose on the opponent the ultimate defeat – the destruction of its regime – not the destruction of its society, but of its political order. Gray maintained that defeat of the Soviet Union "entail[s] the forcible demise of the Soviet state."[75] This does not mean that a nation can achieve victory in a nuclear war only if it destroys the opponent's ruling regime, but that it can achieve victory only if it can credibly threaten such destruction. That threat is what insures that the opponent would accept a larger portion of the burden of restraint.

The threat to the opponent's political order is "the functional equivalent" of the traditional threat of assured destruction.[76] There seem to be two main reasons why prevailing strategists choose to anchor their strategy in threats against the opponent's political order, rather than in threats against its social-economic order. First is the view, discussed in the last chapter, which is prevalent among prevailing strategists, that Soviet leaders, unlike Western leaders, cared more for their power than for their people. Gray was calling on U.S. policy makers to recognize this, when he criticized them for not knowing "what unacceptable damage means in Soviet terms."[77] Second, the destruction of the opponent's political order is seen as valuable, in its own right, as an end for a nation to achieve in a war, unlike the destruction of the opponent's social-economic order, which is not in itself to the nation's political advantage.[78] But, if the threat to destroy the opponent's political order provides an advantage in terms of credibility, this is due not primarily to the opponent's fearing this most, but to the fact that this would be, under prevailing strategy, a threat the opponent could not reciprocate, a point to be discussed shortly.

The third answer to the question what a prevailing strategy threatens is compellence. Under a prevailing strategy, nuclear forces "in addition to the negative task of dissuasion, also have laid upon them by foreign policy a range of possible 'compellence' duties."[79] Superiority in counterforce capability would allow a nation to advance its own interests by coercing its opponent short of war. The nation could use the threat to initiate nuclear war to compel the opponent to surrender something of political value, not merely to deter it from attempting to take something of political value. Compellence would be possible because the war the nation threatens would be one in which the opponent would be defeated. Threats to win a war can compel as well as deter. Prevailing strategy thus has a more expansive notion of what nuclear threats can accomplish than other nuclear strategies do. Not only can nuclear threats deter nuclear and conventional aggression as well as lesser challenges to the nation's interests, they can be used to pose challenges to the opponent's interests.

An end to vulnerability?

The second question about prevailing strategy is: What military capabilities are needed for the strategy? What constitutes the superiority that prevailing strategy requires? Like other forms of counterforce strategy, prevailing strategy calls for military forces that will avoid the nation's being self-deterred. It requires "nuclear employment options that a reasonable political leader would not be self-deterred from ever executing, however reluctantly." But prevailing strategy differs from the other counterforce strategies in the military capability it regards as necessary for the avoidance of self-deterrence. Having superiority does not imply simply possessing a more extensive counterforce capability than the opponent. Self-deterrence would be avoided only if the nation were adequately protected. "If U.S. strategic nuclear forces are to be politically relevant in future crises, the American homeland has to be physically defended."[80] Superiority implies the ability to avoid societal destruction. This is the point at which prevailing strategy departs in a fundamental way from other forms of nuclear deterrence.

In the view of prevailing strategists, so long as the opponent is able to inflict massive damage on the nation, to the point of societal destruction, the nation will be self-deterred from nuclear use and its nuclear threat will never achieve a high degree of credibility. To this extent, the proponent of prevailing strategy would agree with the criticisms of less ambitious forms of counterforce strategy discussed earlier.[81] Unlike other counterforce strategies, prevailing strategy calls for a very high degree of damage limitation. Other forms of counterforce strategy are based on the assumption that military forces can provide at best a modest amount of damage limitation. But for the prevailing strategist, intra-war deterrence can work only if the nation is able to avoid the destruction of its society through the exercise of its own military capability, for only then can its threats to continue the war be credible. All counterforce strategies count on mutual restraint to keep a war limited, but prevailing strategy holds that the opponent's restraint cannot be relied on unless the nation is able, in the absence of that restraint, to limit its damage to below the point of societal destruction. To secure the opponent's restraint, the nation must be capable of winning the war without that restraint. Destroying the opponent's political order would not count as winning the war unless the nation's own society remained intact.[82] Such are the requirements of a credible nuclear threat.

Prevailing strategy calls for a degree of damage limitation that will put an end to the vulnerability of a nation's society to destruction by the opponent's nuclear weapons. Prevailing strategists do not regard mutual vulnerability as unavoidable, but rather as a situation we choose to maintain by failing to develop and deploy the counterforce technology that could overcome our own vulnerability and make possible a credible form of nuclear deterrence. In this spirit, Fred Iklé refers to the situation of mutual vulnerability as one of "consensual vulnerability."[83] Gray and Keith Payne refer to our mistaken belief that our vulnerability is inevitable as the "Armageddon syndrome."[84] But as I have argued all along, a nation's societal vulnerability is not by its choice. A nation cannot by its own actions alone overcome its vulnerability. One way to appreciate this is to examine the possibility of defenses. Given the extent to which nuclear weapons delivery systems are invulnerable to attack, a high degree of damage limitation cannot be provided by offensive forces alone.[85] A disarming first strike with offensive forces is not possible, and would not, in any case, be sufficient to overcome the nation's vulnerability, because the opponent might strike first. If a nation can overcome its vulnerability, it can do so only if counterforce offensive forces are augmented with extensive defenses.

But defenses cannot be good enough. To argue for this, I will consider the kind of defenses most crucial to a nation's effort to overcome its own vulnerability, ballistic missile defenses.[86] The argument can be set out in three stages. First, destroying an attacking ballistic-missile warhead is very hard to do. Whether that warhead is still attached to its ascending missile, flying free through space, or descending through the atmosphere to its target, it is hard to locate it and to bring an interceptor to bear upon it in the very brief time in which this would have to be done, especially because the attack may come as a surprise. Some warheads no doubt could be intercepted, but the question is whether very many could. To this kind of criticism, defenders of ballistic missile defenses respond that one should not so cavalierly prejudge what is technologically possible, given examples of human accomplishments, such as flying or landing on the moon, which were once claimed to be impossible. But the remainder of the argument shows that this response carries little weight, because it is based on a bad analogy.

Second, to put an end to a nation's societal vulnerability, its ballistic missile defenses must destroy a very high percentage of their targets, because only a relatively small number of ballistic missile warheads detonating on urban areas would be enough to destroy the nation's society. This magnifies greatly the technical demands on ballistic missile defenses, and makes their success extremely unlikely. Prior to the age of mutual vulnerability, a military balance favoring the offense might shift to one favoring the defense with a minor improvement in defensive technology.[87] But the destructive power and efficient means of delivery of nuclear weapons places the current military balance so overwhelmingly in favor of the offense that a technological advance that could return the balance to the defense is extremely unlikely in the foreseeable future. Third, the task of the ballistic missile defenses is further confounded by the fact that the opponent would bend every effort to thwart the defenses. There are a number of effective countermeasures the opponent could take. As critics have argued, landing humans on the moon is a poor analogy, because the moon does not deliberately attempt to thwart our travel plans.

One response Gray makes to the criticism that societal vulnerability is inescapable is to dispute the notion of unacceptable damage involved in such a claim. According to Gray: "U.S. defense planners face an apparently intractable moral-philosophical-strategic problem: What is acceptable (or unacceptable) damage?"[88] How one defines unacceptable damage (what I am calling necessarily unacceptable damage – that is, societal destruction), or what one predicts would be the level of destruction at which it would occur, will determine whether or not one thinks that societal vulnerability is inescapable, and so will strongly influence whether or not one regards prevailing strategy as feasible. How much damage can a society take before it can be said no longer to exist? "There probably is some point of damage beyond which a society truly could not survive," Gray admits, and he acknowledges a number of ways in which the damage caused in a nuclear war would be distinctively more destructive of society than high levels of damage caused in other ways. Yet he suggests that an all-out nuclear war need not result in societal destruction, and makes a case for this by pointing to historical precedents: "Many societies have survived and eventually recovered from casualty lists well in excess of one-third their prewar population levels." He continues: "The 'civilized world' survived the Huns and the Mongols. There is reason to believe that it could survive nuclear wars."[89]

This argument was rehearsed in Chapter 1, and the response is the same. There are crucial disanalogies between an all-out nuclear war and the causes of destruction in the historical examples Gray has in mind. In the case of an all-out nuclear war, the destruction would take place all at once, happening everywhere in the society at the same time, and would involve not simply a very long casualty list, but the obliteration of essential elements of the social infrastructure. The historical examples lack these features, which are crucially relevant because of their effect on the ability of a society to recover from severe damage. In an all-out nuclear war, there would be no temporarily undamaged areas that could provide support for damaged areas, as was the case with cities destroyed in the Second World War. Moreover, because of the loss of social infrastructure, whatever healthy survivors remained would lack the means to help the devastated areas to recover. There are other unique features of nuclear devastation, especially the long-term effects of the resulting environmental degradation, that would further weaken the argument from analogy with the historical examples. There is no reason to think that societal destruction could be avoided in an all-out nuclear war.

The infeasibility of prevailing strategy illustrates once again the difficulty in making nuclear threats credible. Other types of counterforce strategy fail to solve the credibility problem because they accept the assumption that mutual vulnerability is unavoidable. Prevailing strategy seeks to achieve credibility for nuclear deterrence by abandoning this assumption, prescribing sufficient counterforce capability to replace mutual vulnerability with one-sided vulnerability, the vulnerability of the opponent alone. But the assumption is correct, so the need to turn to prevailing strategy to attempt to solve the credibility problem simply makes clearer the depth of the problem. Prevailing strategy is, in effect, an admission that nuclear deterrence cannot succeed, because the argument for the strategy implies that the credibility problem can be solved only by nuclear deterrence becoming what it cannot be. Prevailing strategy is a natural extension of the logic of counterforce, with its concern to found effective pre-war deterrence on a capacity for war-fighting and intra-war deterrence. In this way, the infeasibility of prevailing strategy is a token of the failure of counterforce strategy in general. Prevailing strategy shows the incoherence of counterforce strategy, by showing that the logic of counterforce is inconsistent with unavoidable vulnerability.

But given the role of beliefs in a threat's credibility, which is the present subject of the argument, it is too quick to claim that the infeasibility of prevailing strategy shows that it fails to solve the credibility problem of nuclear deterrence. The credibility problem is a function of the beliefs of the opponent about the beliefs of the nation, rather than of the objective realities that the nation's beliefs are about. If the opponent believes that the nation believes that the nation's prevailing strategy is feasible, the nation's nuclear threat is likely to be credible to the opponent, despite the falsity of the nation's belief. For if the nation believes that it could avoid societal destruction in an all-out nuclear war, it would believe that it could win a nuclear war whether or not the opponent exercises restraint, and this would make it more willing to carry out its nuclear threats than if it believed that its avoiding societal destruction depended on the opponent's restraint, as it would if it had adopted a more modest form of counterforce strategy. This is why prevailing strategy may do much more to strengthen credibility than modest forms of counterforce. So, if a nation's attempt to implement a prevailing strategy would be taken by the opponent as strong evidence that the nation believes such a strategy is feasible, then the strategy may work in achieving credibility for nuclear deterrence despite its infeasibility.

But there are two difficulties in this conclusion that prevailing strategy could be an effective form of nuclear deterrence. First, for the reasons proposed earlier, it is doubtful that the opponent would conclude with a high degree of conviction that because the nation has adopted a strategy involving extensive counterforce deployments, it believes that it could effectively fight a limited nuclear war. Thus, the credibility problem is truly insoluble. But I let this concern ride for the sake of the argument, in order to address the important concerns raised by the second difficulty. For even if prevailing strategy could solve the credibility problem, one cannot conclude that it would be a prudentially preferable form of nuclear deterrence. This is the second horn of the dilemma. To the extent that prevailing strategy solves the credibility problem, it would undermine the prudential benefits of nuclear deterrence.

The benefits of nuclear deterrence, in comparison with conventional deterrence, depend on mutuality. In its attempt to conventionalize nuclear weapons, prevailing strategy seeks to make nuclear deterrence asymmetrical rather than mutual. It seeks to replace mutual vulnerability with one-sided vulnerability. It seeks to make nuclear deterrence, in the words of Robert Holmes, not mutual, but preferential, "attempting to deter the enemy without being deterred oneself."[90] Even though the infeasibility of prevailing strategy entails that nuclear deterrence would remain mutual in any case, the opponent's belief, as the result of a nation's adopting a prevailing strategy, that the nation believes that deterrence is no longer mutual can negate the prudential benefits that mutuality provides. One of the chief prudential advantages of nuclear deterrence flowing from its mutuality is reassurance. But this advantage flows not directly from the objective reality of mutuality, but from each side's belief that the other believes that deterrence is mutual. It is this belief that the adoption of prevailing strategy undermines. The result of this is crisis instability.

CRISIS INSTABILITY

A situation of mutual vulnerability provides reassurance to each party that it can avoid being aggressed against by not aggressing against the other. Mutual deterrence supports the status quo, and this helps it be effective. But if a nation mistakenly believes that it has overcome its own vulnerability, it would believe that it could aggress against its opponent without needing to worry about the consequences implied by its vulnerability to societal destruction. That nation would view deterrence as mainly a one-way street. It would believe that it could afford to be provocative, to threaten to escalate conflicts to its advantage, because the opponent is more deterred than it is. Escalation would be rational for it, and its threats of further escalation credible, because the opponent's threats of retaliation and escalation would not be credible. In particular, the nation would believe that it could credibly threaten to initiate war. In the light of this belief, its deterrence policy would no longer be merely defensive, but would have become offensive or disarming.[91] With its extensive counterforce deployments, it would believe itself able effectively to disarm its opponent. The implications of the consequent lose of the reassurance nuclear deterrence normally provides is what must now be considered.

If a nuclear war between nations in a situation of mutual vulnerability were to happen, it would most likely occur as a consequence of a serious crisis in their relationship.[92] The crisis may be primarily political in nature or it may be immediately military, resulting from a conventional war between them. The crisis may have been deliberately provoked by one of them or it may have arisen as the unintended consequence of one or both of their actions. Whatever its nature or genesis, a crisis would carry an increased risk of nuclear war, and it is a prime virtue of a deterrence strategy that it keep the likelihood of nuclear war in a crisis low. This virtue is referred to as crisis stability. In general terms, a situation is stable when it is strongly resistant to basic change, when it is not easily upset or altered by environmental influences. A situation of crisis between nuclear superpowers is stable when it is not easily upset into a condition of nuclear war. For a war to start, one side has to initiate an attack, so crisis stability is, ideally, "a balance in which neither side has any incentive to strike first in a time of crisis."[93] If neither side has an incentive to strike first, neither side is likely to do so, and nuclear war is not likely to occur. In a crisis, one wants it to be the case that "the incentives on both sides to initiate war are outweighed by the disincentives."[94]

Incentives to initiate war

In a normal, noncrisis situation, the incentives to initiate nuclear war are far outweighed by the disincentives. Given the horror of nuclear war, peace is far preferable to war, and the way for each party to maintain peace is for it not to initiate war. But in a crisis, matters can appear differently. In a crisis, war may come to seem a real possibility, so that neither side can automatically assume that its not initiating war will insure its staying at peace. Then each side may begin to wonder whether or not it would be to its advantage to attack first rather than waiting to be attacked. Thus, there are three beliefs crucial for crisis stability. In order that the likelihood of war in a crisis remain low, each side (A) must, despite the crisis, believe the following three claims:

(1)   that the other side's (B's) initiating nuclear war is unlikely;

(2) that it (A) would not be significantly advantaged by initiating nuclear war in comparison with letting B initiate nuclear war; and

(3) that B does not believe that it would be significantly advantaged by initiating nuclear war in comparison with letting A initiate nuclear war.

In a crisis, unless these claims are strongly believed, it may not be that the disincentives to war will outweigh the incentives, as these are perceived by the parties. For a national leader in a crisis: "The smaller he judged the chances of avoiding nuclear war altogether, and the larger he judged the advantages of striking first rather than second, the more incentive he would have to strike first."[95] When these claims are strongly believed, crisis stability exists. When they are seriously doubted, the situation is one of crisis instability, for then, initiating war may come to seem for one side or the other to be the preferable course.

Thomas Schelling's discussion of "the reciprocal fear of surprise attack" shows how belief in these claims can weaken and so create incentives for the initiation of nuclear war.[96]

> If I go downstairs to investigate a noise at night, with a gun in my hand, and find myself face to face with a burglar who has a gun in his hand, there is a danger of an outcome that neither of us desires. Even if he prefers just to leave quietly, and I wish him to, there is a danger that he may *think* I want to shoot, and shoot first. Worse there is a danger that he may think that *I* think *he* wants to shoot. . . . This is the problem of surprise attack. If surprise carries an advantage, it is worth while to avert it by striking first. Fear that the other may be about to strike in the mistaken belief that we are about to strike gives us a motive for striking, and so justifies the other's motive.

In this crisis, neither party wants gunplay. Each would withdraw if he could, for example, if he had spotted the other before being spotted by the other. But each recognizes that there is an advantage to firing first in comparison with letting the other fire first. What each would prefer is neither to fire nor to be fired upon, but the confrontation may make the option of no gunplay seem unavailable. Schelling's point is that in such situations, a self-reinforcing set of expectations can generate sufficient motivation for one or the other to fire.

> It looks as though a modest temptation on each side to sneak in a first blow – a temptation too small by itself to motivate an attack –

might become compounded through a process of interacting expectations, with additional motive for attack being produced by successive cycles of "He thinks we think he thinks we think . . . he thinks we think he'll attack; so he thinks we will; so he will; so we must."

What Schelling's analogy shows is that the logic governing the way nations think about nuclear war can shift dramatically in a crisis. As mentioned, a nation is normally deterred from attacking its opponent by the belief that if it were to attack, it would be worse off than if it were not to attack, because it would suffer the punishment of nuclear war only if it were it to attack. The question for each side is whether attacking would leave it better off than continuing in a state of peace. The effectiveness of deterrence depends on the answer to this question being obviously no. But the impli- cation of the analogy is that in a crisis situation a different question can become relevant – namely, whether a nation's attacking and receiving retaliation would leave it better off than being attacked first. The first question is whether war is preferable to peace, but the second is whether a war in which the nation goes first is preferable to one in which it goes second, under the assumption that peace is not an option. The first question is relevant when leaders believe that their options are initiating war or remaining at peace, but the second becomes relevant when they believe that their options are limited to initiating war or allowing their opponent to initiate war.

To understand what causes the shift from the first to the second question and how this could lead to nuclear war, we must consider the role of belief in or doubt about the three claims mentioned above. What makes war likely in a crisis is one or both sides having serious doubts about both (1) and (2). If these doubts are so strong that one side believes both that the other side is about to initiate war and that it would be much better off striking first than waiting to be struck by the other, then it is likely to strike first. The role of doubts about (3) is their tendency to increase doubts about (1). The disposition to believe or doubt (2) and (3) exists prior to the crisis. What the onset of a crisis does is to begin to raise doubts about (1). Doubts about (1) make relevant any doubts about (2) and (3). Doubts about (1) actualize the disposition to doubt (2) and (3), if there be such, by creating a real-world situation to which claims (2) and (3) or their negations apply. For the falsity of (1) would make the option of peace seem less sure, and it is by this option that the truth or falsity of (2) and (3) have no application. Once the crisis leads to doubts about (1), doubts about (2) and (3) can generate the crescendo of reciprocal expectations of the sort described by Schelling, and thereby instigate a rapid process by which the leaders come to have so little faith in the truth of (1) that they may believe that the opponent is about to initiate a war. The way this happens is that each side's doubts about (3) strengthen its doubts about (1), which are further strengthened by its belief that the other side also doubts (3). Each side's doubts about (1) will grow as it comes to believe that the other side's doubts about (1) are growing. As the mutual doubts about (1) grow, they may become so firmly entrenched that one side or both come to believe that the other is about to attack, thus having, as a result of its doubts about (2), strong reason to itself attack. When there is already a disposition to disbelieve (2) and (3), the seed of doubt in (1) planted by the crisis can quickly bear the fruit of fear that the other side is about to attack. Once (1) comes to be disbelieved in a situation where (2) and (3) are already disbelieved, war can easily result. One party or the other could readily launch what it would believe to be a preemptive attack.

The role of reassurance

Nuclear deterrence should arrest this process through its capacity for reassurance. Reassurance would keep any doubt in (1) created by the crisis from becoming very great by supporting firm belief in (2) and (3). The point of mutual vulnerability is that a full-scale nuclear war would result in societal destruction for both sides, so that whether one goes first or second in the war would make no difference. If going first is seen to have no advantage over going second, the process of crescendoing expectations should be avoided and the parties would never seriously doubt (1), even in a crisis. In order to take account of this feature of mutual vulnerability, the burglar example may be modified. As the example is set up, there is no "guarantee that both would die in a gunfight – only the slower of the two." But consider how the parties would behave with "less deadly weapons, permitting one to shoot back before he died." As Schelling says: "If both were assured of living long enough to shoot back with unimpaired aim, there would be no advantage in jumping the gun and little reason to fear that the other would try it."[97] If each party believed that gunplay would result in both of their deaths, each would be reassured that the other would not shoot first. This modification of the example replicates the way in which nuclear deterrence promotes crisis stability. The mutual perception of mutually perceived vulnerability provides a high level of crisis stability.

It is the advantage of reassurance that could be thrown away through the practice of prevailing strategy. The argument against this strategy is that it can create instability in a crisis by creating a disposition on the part of the leaders to doubt (2) and (3), thereby, through the process discussed, inclining them to believe the other side may attack, resulting in a much greater likelihood that war will occur. First, a nation practicing prevailing strategy is disposed to doubt (2), because it would believe that the advantage in a counterforce nuclear war would go to the side striking first. Second, if its opponent is also practicing prevailing strategy, then the nation is also disposed to doubt (3).[98] Under these conditions, the opponent would be similarly disposed. In a crisis, as a result of the mutual disposition to doubt (2) and (3), each side may well believe the other is about to attack, and war could well result. Prevailing strategy fosters doubts about (2) and (3) because it is a first-strike strategy, not only by design, but by appearance. As Hans Morganthau asserts: "An effective counter-force strategy is inseparable from a first-strike strategy."[99] Prevailing strategy is based on the belief that nuclear weapons can adequately achieve their deterrent and compellent tasks only if a nation threatens a first strike, and the counterforce deployments it requires communicate that this belief lies behind it. In a crisis, mutual first-strike threats are likely to lead to an actual first strike.

Risks from modesty

But the adverse effect of prevailing strategy on crisis stability is not limited to situations where both parties are attempting to practice that strategy. It holds as well, though less strongly, when one of the parties is practicing a more modest form of counterforce. There are several reasons for this. One is that counterforce capabilities, in general, are designed to limit damage and to fight a limited nuclear war. This means that even a party practicing more modest counterforce would have some reason to believe that going first might be better for it than going second. It might perceive a first strike as preferable because it would be inclined to believe that the resulting war might be limited and that striking first would allow it to limit the total amount of damage it would suffer in the war. Of course, given that it is not practicing prevailing strategy, it is unlikely to believe that a limited nuclear war is reasonably foreseeable, so it should not expect a loss short of societal destruction. It might limit damage to itself by striking first, but end up with its society destroyed in any case. If societal destruction is seen as an infinite loss, damage limitation might be real, but inconsequential. Limiting one's damage in a war resulting in societal destruction would be like subtracting some finite quantity from infinity – the result is still infinity. When one is before a firing squad, stopping one or two of the bullets does not change the outcome. Still, the allure of damage limitation might lead the party practicing more modest counterforce to focus on the relative advantage of striking first rather than the absolute loss of societal destruction, disposing it to doubt (2), and its opponent to doubt (3), thus undermining crisis stability.

A second reason that crisis stability can be undermined even when one party is practicing more modest counterforce is that when both sides are practicing counterforce, there are a number of factors in a crisis that interfere with each side's making a fully rational decision about whether or not to strike first. In a crisis situation, misleading evidence impedes rational decision. In particular, there is evidence that inclines leaders in a crisis to doubt (3) and (1), when in fact they are true. For example, in a crisis a nation will often act tough in the hope of intimidating the opponent and winning concessions, while never intending to push the crisis into war. Yet the opponent could easily interpret such toughness as good evidence that the nation is about to start a war. Another example is the role of preparations for war in crisis dynamics. Such preparations, involving, for example, raising the alert status of forces, are prudent measures when a nation fears its opponent might initiate a war, but, because of their inherent ambiguity, the opponent could interpret them as indications that the nation was about to go to war. As Richard Betts notes: "Intelligence indicators that the enemy was preparing to strike . . . would be ambiguous because they would be identical with preparations for defense, enhancement of deterrence or signaling of resolve, or generation of forces and command networks to maximize retaliatory capability."[100] The parties in the burglar confrontation might each take careful aim as a defensive measure, yet thereby be misunderstood. What these two examples show is that a decision to go to war in a crisis can readily be, in Robert Tucker's words, "a miscalculation in the sense that if each party had sufficient information about the other party's intentions, there would be no nuclear war."[101]

A third reason is that crises not only impede rationality, in the sense of providing evidence that is misleading, they also degrade rational capacities, leading the parties to doubt (1) and (3), even when the evidence available to them does not support such doubt. This is due to dysfunctional psychological factors created or exacerbated by crisis. A list is provided by Lawrence Freedman: "the stress of crisis, the pressures of 'group think,' the need to make sense of confusing and perplexing situations, world-views that fix and limit understanding of the world, the human frailties which lead to excessive confidence in hunches or refusal to acknowledge evidence which undermines favoured theories, and so on."[102] Two related factors are worth noting. One is wishful thinking. Given the stakes involved, the need for rapid decisions, and the ambiguity of the evidence, it would be surprising if there were not a tendency for the wish to be parent to the thought that an appropriately limited nuclear war could be fought. The other factor is the strong desire leaders would have to keep control of the military situation, which they might feel they could do only by initiating war, given that the consequence of leaving the initiative to the opponent could be the destruction of the nation's military capability or the loss of the leaders' control over it.[103] In other words, the alternatives might be understood and acted upon primarily in terms of how they would be described militarily, ("use them or lose them") rather than in terms of the risk of societal destruction.

The discussion so far has concerned the effect on crisis stability of a situation in which at least one of the parties is practicing prevailing strategy. But the factors presented suggest that crisis stability might also be undermined if both parties are practicing more modest forms of counterforce strategy. There are two reasons for this. First, most forms of counterforce strategy provide a military advantage from striking first. There is such an advantage whenever counterforce deployments can achieve a "first-strike bonus" – that is, whenever a first strike by a nation could eliminate more of the opponent's weapons than were used in the attack, for then the side attacking first would come out ahead militarily in the exchange.[104] The danger is that the prospect of military advantage can come to overshadow a concern with political or overall advantage, thus displacing attention from the risk of societal destruction. As a result, each side might come to doubt (2), and so its opponent come to doubt (3), when, on the evidence, it ought not. Second, even when the parties are focusing on political rather than military advantage, the counterforce promise of limited nuclear war may blind them to the risk of societal destruction, again leading them to doubt (2). For example, each side may believe that its attack might be such a shock that the opponent would simply not retaliate, thereby accepting the larger portion of the burden of restraint and handing the nation a costless political victory.[105] The negative impact of these points on crisis stability is exacerbated by the factors discussed earlier that impede and degrade the capacities for rational decision making in a crisis.

One criticism often raised of ambitious counterforce is that it increases the likelihood of war by encouraging the idea that nuclear war can be kept limited. The risk is that "thinking about limited conduct of war might well hasten its initiation."[106] Counterforce strategy can increase "the danger that the weapons *will* be used because the parties may believe that the cost and risks are not out of proportion to the values at stake."[107] This kind of criticism is sometimes presented in terms of what is called the "usability paradox," the idea that by making nuclear weapons more usable for the sake of greater credibility, counterforce strategy makes it more likely that the weapons will be used.[108] The paradoxical flavor of this problem is captured by Robert Goodin, who speaks of nuclear deterrence as "a scheme for making nuclear war less probable by making it more probable."[109] In our terms, the criticism is that though counterforce strategy is designed to bolster deterrence by improving credibility, it can undermine deterrence by weakening the other of its chief prudential advantages, the crystal ball effect. Our discussion has been framed in terms of the effect of ambitious counterforce on reassurance, but, as this criticism shows, it can also have a negative impact on the crystal ball effect. Both of these considerations come together, however, in the criticism that ambitious counterforce undermines crisis stability. For the claim that this strategy weakens reassurance is the claim that it leads to doubts about (3), whereas the claim that it weakens the crystal ball effect is the claim that it leads to doubts about (2).

Counterforce response

Counterforce strategists are not without a response to the criticism that their strategy undermines crisis stability. They offer two objections. First, they argue that the critics misunderstand how ambitious counterforce strategy works, and when the strategy is properly understood, it is clear that it does not undermine crisis stability. Second, they argue that even if ambitious counterforce strategy does undermine crisis stability, it is still a more effective form of deterrence overall, in part because it lessens the likelihood that crises will arise.

According to the first objection, the criticism that ambitious counterforce undermines crisis stability misunderstands the way the strategy works. The capacity for escalation dominance provided by prevailing strategy would keep war from breaking out in a crisis. For it would tend to keep the side successfully practicing prevailing strategy (call it A) believing (3) and the other side (B) believing (2), because both A and B would recognize that A would win a war no matter who went first. Colin Gray, discussing the effects of the United States's adopting a prevailing strategy, observed: "Why the Soviet Union would be interested in starting a war that it would stand little, if any, prospect of winning is, to say the least, obscure."[110] If neither A nor B saw it as in B's interest to initiate war, then the reciprocal fear necessary to deepen doubts about (1) and thus heighten the risk of someone's choosing a preemptive attack would be lacking. Moreover, both A and B are likely to appreciate that A has no need to initiate a war, even though both believe A could win it. For, given its credible threat to win the war, it would believe that it could prevail short of war in the coercive contest the crisis involves. In addition, A's practicing prevailing strategy would not mask for it the horrors of nuclear war, so that it becomes likely to initiate war. In response to those who raised concerns about the tendency of current and proposed counterforce capacities to undermine crisis stability, Albert Wohlstetter asserted that "it is absurd to think that American or Soviet leaders are straining at the nuclear leash."[111]

Part of the response to this objection, following the earlier discussion of escalation dominance, is that the claims for the relevance of an asymmetry in counterforce capability, on which the objection is based, cannot be sustained. The objection depends on the assumption that it is clear to both sides that the military asymmetry resulting from one side's successfully practicing prevailing strategy would determine the outcome of the crisis. But whatever the parties had been earlier disposed to believe, the crisis would likely turn out to be a competition in risk taking, so that the military asymmetry would not dictate the outcome. The uncertainty of outcome would incline both parties to doubt (3), hence creating crisis instability. In addition, the military asymmetry would not, in the crisis situation, be as clear to the parties as the objection assumes. Both parties may be attempting to achieve prevailing strategies, so that they might disagree about where the counterforce advantage lies. More importantly, the advantage to the party striking first is a kind of counterforce equalizer. The side with inferior counterforce capability might, correctly or incorrectly, see itself as more than the equal of its better-armed opponent, if it could gain the advantage from striking first. Finally, the claim that military asymmetry would keep the crisis from erupting into war assumes a degree of rationality in the decision makers that the crisis may make impossible, given the factors discussed earlier that would impede and degrade rationality in the crisis situation. The basic point is that the opponent's response in a crisis to the threats implicit in the nation's prevailing strategy cannot be predicted, as the objection assumes they can. The threats could cut either way, inducing timid compliance, as the objection believes they would, or rash military action.[112] This unpredictability is sufficient to defeat the objection.

There is an interesting variant of this objection that takes a different tack, making it immune to the criticism just presented. This version of the objection, like the one just considered, asserts that the claim that ambitious counterforce undermines crisis stability misunderstands the impact of counterforce deployments in a crisis. But, unlike the other version, it makes no appeal to the role of military asymmetry and escalation dominance. As presented by Glenn Snyder, the objection is that "the act of pre-emption tends to convert the other side's target system from primarily counterforce to primarily countercity," the result of which could be "the pre-emptor's suffering more damage than he would have absorbed as a result of the opponent's first strike."[113] The point is that the opponent's first strike would be a counterforce strike, whereas its second strike would likely be a countervalue strike, so that neither side could be better off striking first. As a result, neither party is likely to doubt (2), hence neither is likely to doubt (3), the result being that serious doubts about (1) would not arise. This argument is supported by a reported study that concluded that there would be more American casualties in a nuclear war beginning with an American first-strike than in one beginning with a Soviet first strike.[114]

But there is reason to doubt the assumption on which this version of the objection is based. If both parties are practicing counterforce strategy, their nuclear doctrine is based on the idea of fighting a limited nuclear war against counterforce targets. So why would either one assume that the opponent's retaliation for its first-strike would be countercity rather than counterforce? If a nation launches a first strike, the opponent has very good reason not to destroy the opponent's cities in retaliation – namely, that its own cities, still largely intact after the counterforce first strike, would themselves then be destroyed by the nation's third strike. Moreover, as discussed earlier, a party considering striking first may well be focusing on relative military advantage, so that risks of societal destruction would be downplayed, perhaps to the point of the party's expecting that the first strike would cause the opponent to capitulate, offering no retaliation at all.

The likelihood of crises

The second objection grants that ambitious counterforce undermines crisis stability, but argues that it is still a more effective strategy overall, in part because it reduces the risk of crises arising. One cannot conclude that a strategy that increases the risk of war in a crisis increases the risk of war overall, unless one assumes that that strategy has no positive effect on the likelihood of crises occurring. "The probability of pre-emptive nuclear war," Charles Glaser notes, "also depends on the probability of crises."[115] Roughly, (a) the overall likelihood of war (assuming that all wars begin in a crisis) is (b) the likelihood of crises occurring multiplied by (c) the likelihood of war should a crisis arise. Proponents of ambitious counterforce argue that their strategy substantially decreases (b), so that one cannot conclude that it increases (a), even granting that it increases (c). The argument that ambitious counterforce substantially decreases (b) is that it is much better than other strategies at deterring the opponent from mounting lesser challenges to the nation's interests, as a result of the greater credibility of its threat to respond in a limited way, and that it is these lesser challenges that lead to crises. More precisely, it is the fact that ambitious counterforce creates crisis instability that results in its being more effective in keeping crises from arising. The authors of an Office of Technology Assessment report note: "It is quite possible that a leader's perception of the degree of crisis stability at a particular time could influence his willingness to risk actions that might cause a crisis to arise."[116] If leaders perceive that crises are especially risky, they will be very careful not to take actions, such as minor challenges to the other nation's interests, which could cause a crisis to arise.

The point can be made by considering how proponents of ambitious counterforce would reconstruct the usability paradox, the claim that counterforce strategy seeks to make nuclear war less likely by making it more likely. More precisely, and less tendentiously, counterforce strategy seeks to make nuclear war absolutely less likely by making it conditionally more likely. That is, by making nuclear war more likely *on* the condition of a crisis, it seeks to make it less likely overall, because that conditional riskiness will keep crises from arising. The decrease in (b) is not simply coincident with the increase in (c), but is due to that increase. Moreover, (a) decreases because the increase in (c) is conditional, so that the decrease in (b) dominates the calculation. In other words, making nuclear war conditionally more likely is precisely how deterrence works. Making nuclear war more likely if the nation is provoked makes it less likely that the nation will be provoked. As a result, not only is nuclear war deterred, but so also are lesser provocations. This is why counterforce strategy is a better form of deterrence. It is effective not only in deterring nuclear war, but also in deterring lesser forms of aggression, and it is effective in this by making nuclear war conditionally more likely – that is, by creating crisis instability.

This objection is flawed on two grounds. First, it is mistaken in its implicit assumption that crises arise only from deliberate actions of provocation or aggression on the part of the opponent. "A crisis could result from a deliberate act of aggression by the Soviet Union against the United States, but it could also arise from a dispute triggered by some third-country actions which involve the perceived vital interests of the superpowers."[117] In addition, a crisis can arise as the unintended consequence of the actions of the nuclear powers. The general point is that crises are not necessarily foreseen or foreseeable by the two parties in the nuclear confrontation, even when they result from their actions, so that a strategy designed to deter them cannot insure their nonoccurrence. Second, in practicing ambitious counterforce strategy, a nation seeks to deter the crises that arise from the opponent's provocation, but crises can also arise from the nation's actions. Indeed, ambitious counterforce encourages such actions because it is believed to provide compellence as well as deterrence. To seek to compel is to create a crisis. Of course, proponents of the strategy might respond that the advantage sought through compellence can be achieved in the crisis through escalation dominance, but this would be to concede the criticism of the second objection and revert to the first objection, which we have already found reason to reject. Taking these two points together, the claim that ambitious counterforce strategy could decrease (b) sufficiently to decrease (a), given the increase in (c), becomes highly dubious.

The conclusion is that even if one assumes that a nation's practice of ambitious counterforce would solve the credibility problem by getting the opponent to believe that the nation believes (incorrectly) that an appropriately limited nuclear war is reasonably foreseeable (an assumption there is good reason to reject, in any case), this would not be sufficient to rebut the prima facie argument against the prudential preferability of nuclear deterrence. The reason is that with the advantage of credibility would come the disadvantage of the loss of the restraining effect of reassurance and the crystal ball effect. Even if counterforce strategy provided some help in making nuclear deterrence more credible, its measure of help would come along with a measure of greater danger. In terms of net deterrent effect, ambitious counterforce strategy could provide little or no advantage over other forms of nuclear deterrence, so it cannot support the claim that nuclear deterrence has substantial marginal deterrent value compared with conventional deterrence. Moreover, as the discussion in this section shows, the extra danger seems to exist, in reduced measure at least, even in cases where it is clear that there is little or no help provided in terms of greater credibility – for example, when both parties are practicing less ambitious forms of counterforce strategy. As a result, counterforce strategy is not only unhelpful, in comparison with other forms of nuclear deterrence, in terms of the credibility problem, but, if practiced in any other than a modest form, would probably make matters worse. A modest form of counterforce strategy might be an overall advantage, in comparison with other forms of nuclear deterrence, as a result of its temporizing effect. But to adopt modest counterforce is to put aside any real hopes of solving the credibility problem, so the advantage of temporizing cannot serve to rebut the prima facie argument against nuclear deterrence.

If one recommends modest counterforce deployments merely for the sake of the capacity to temporize in a nuclear war, one has in effect abandoned counterforce strategy, understood as a strategy designed to solve the credibility problem. It is a recognition that the attempt to solve the credibility problem is both bound to fail and attended by a measure of danger. That danger, crisis instability, can be avoided only by the acceptance of what is in essence a countervalue strategy, even if some counterforce deployments are included for their temporizing value. In the words of Hans Morganthau: "Counter-city strategy, as it were, expresses the inner logic of nuclear war. On the other hand, counter-force strategy, by presuming to superimpose upon the dynamics of nuclear war a pattern appropriate to conventional war, increases the likelihood of nuclear war."[118] We turn now to explore this inner logic in order to consider the second challenge to prudential revisionism. Can countervalue strategy succeed where counterforce strategy has failed in providing the basis for a successful rebuttal to the prima facie argument?

Chapter 7

Madvocacy

The missiles have only to exist, and deterrence is the law of their existence.

Leon Wieseltier[1]

We do not need to threaten anything. Their being there is quite enough.

Bernard Brodie[2]

Counterforce strategy does not provide a satisfactory form of nuclear deterrence. Not only is it doubtful that it could solve the credibility problem, but even if it could, it would at the same time weaken nuclear deterrence in the respect in which it is superior to conventional deterrence, and so have little or no net deterrent value in comparison with other forms of nuclear deterrence. As a result, counterforce strategy cannot serve as a basis for a successful rebuttal to the prima facie argument. The superiority of nuclear deterrence over conventional deterrence lies in the reassurance against attack provided to the opponent and the crystal ball effect, both of which are a function of the belief each side has in the fact of mutual vulnerability. This chapter considers countervalue strategy, the approach to deterrence that fully acknowledges the novel implications of mutual vulnerability.[3]

Countervalue strategy, unlike counterforce strategy, embraces the condition of mutual vulnerability or mutual assured destruction. The argument is that mutual vulnerability is the basis for such a strong form of deterrence that the failure of nuclear deterrence to solve the credibility problem is not a bar to its being highly effective. This is the other rebuttal to the prima facie argument that nuclear deterrence is not prudentially preferable to conventional deterrence. Because the rebuttal offered by the counterforce strategists fails, the success of prudential revisionism depends on the failure of the rebuttal offered by countervalue strategists, or madvocates, as they are called.[4] If their rebuttal succeeds, prudential

231

revisionism fails, and the only approach remaining for resolving the conflicts is moral revisionism. Moral revisionism is a position advanced by some madvocates, and it will be considered in this chapter as well.

Madvocates believe that mutual assured destruction or mutual vulnerability should be taken not merely as descriptive of our situation, but also as prescriptive for our strategic choices. Although advocates of counterforce strategy accept at least the present reality of mutual vulnerability, they see it as a disadvantage to be overcome, because it is what gives rise to self-deterrence, and so to the credibility problem. In contrast, madvocates see virtue in mutual vulnerability. Mutual vulnerability is seen not as an obstacle to effective deterrence, but as something that helps to make nuclear deterrence effective. Though mutual vulnerability makes a high degree of credibility impossible to achieve, what counterforce strategists fail to realize is that mutual vulnerability obviates the need to solve the credibility problem.

In the view of madvocates, mutual vulnerability entails not only that nuclear threats can be effective, but that deterrence is all that nuclear weapons can achieve. Part of the madvocates' criticism of counterforce strategy is that nuclear threats cannot effectively achieve the goals of war fighting, such as denial and damage limitation. Because nuclear weapons cannot be put to effective military purpose, the only purpose remaining to them is deterrence. In this sense, MAD-based strategies are strategies of *deterrence only*.[5] Counterforce strategies, on the other hand, are strategies of both deterrence and war fighting. From the counterforce perspective, nuclear weapons can be used effectively to fight a war, because they can accomplish the ends of denial and damage limitation, and it is the fact that they can be so used that makes the threat to use them effective as a deterrent. But for madvocates, nuclear threats are primarily threats of punishment, the infliction of which achieves no military purpose, and so is not useful in fighting a war.[6] If nuclear weapons were used in war, their use would continue to be for the sake of deterrence, though intra-war rather than pre-war deterrence. Madvocates do not, of course, claim that nuclear weapons cannot be used in war, nor even that the use of nuclear weapons in war cannot contribute to some purpose (whether or not their contribution would be great enough to make their prospective use prudentially rational), but they do claim that that purpose can only be deterrence.[7]

To a counterforce strategist, the deterrence-only position is incoherent. If nuclear weapons are not useful for more than deterrence, they are not useful for that. If the use of nuclear weapons in war cannot be prospectively justified on the grounds of military effectiveness, the threat to use them is not likely to succeed in deterring. Counterforce and countervalue strategists divide on the question whether the usefulness of nuclear weapons in fighting a war – that is, their use for denial and damage-limitation – is necessary for effective deterrence. Counterforce strategists, emphasizing the credibility problem, believe that it is, whereas madvocates believe neither that nuclear weapons can be useful as war-fighting implements nor that such usefulness is necessary for effective deterrence. Consistent with their appreciation that nuclear weapons cannot be militarily effective, madvocates recognize that nuclear strategy cannot be strategy in a traditional sense. Traditionally, strategy was anchored in ideas about how a nation's military resources could be used effectively in battle, a connection counterforce strategists believe still holds. But madvocates make a deliberate break with such ideas. The very idea of a nuclear strategy is as fundamental a departure from traditional ideas of military strategy as nuclear weapons are different from conventional weapons. Leon Wieseltier admits that nuclear "deterrence, strictly speaking, is not a strategy," because it "teaches nothing about the manner in which nuclear weapons may be employed."[8] Theodore Draper argues that nuclear deterrence "is by its very nature not a strategy for waging war; it is rather a nonstrategy or an antistrategy."[9]

Madvocates often claim that mutual vulnerability has changed the traditional behavior of nations in a basic way. Some see this change as a realization of Einstein's hope that given the advent of nuclear weapons, we would fundamentally change our way of thinking.[10] But whereas Einstein apparently believed that some form of world government would be required to avoid nuclear catastrophe, madvocates often argue that the only change required is the one that has already occurred – namely, a change in how nations behave. Michael Mandelbaum asserts: "Political institutions are the same; political behavior has changed. So it is with the international system in the nuclear age. The system remains anarchical. War is still possible. The possibility of nuclear war, however, has encouraged the two principal rival powers to behave cautiously, carefully, and prudently where the interests of the other are concerned."[11] It is this cautious behavior, induced by mutual vulnerability, which shows the effectiveness of nuclear deterrence. The more optimistic among the madvocates see this change in international behavior as so far-reaching as to make nuclear deterrence virtually foolproof. Nuclear weapons have "imposed a technological peace."[12] By making war between the great powers so destructive, they have put an end to great-power war.[13] In Churchill's phrase, safety is seen as the sturdy child of terror. According to Robert Holmes, Alfred Nobel believed that "once the nations of the world acquired the capacity to annihilate one another – and he expressly included civilian populations here – war would disappear from the face of the earth."[14] This "technologist's dream" is now fully realized with the advent of mutual vulnerability. Robert Tucker observes: "Mutual assured destruction was the latest version of the very old idea that war would disappear once its destructiveness promised to become sufficiently great."[15] The latest technology has finally realized the old idea. Those who argue that nuclear war cannot be avoided over an indefinite length of time, because war has never been long avoided in the past, simply do not recognize the unique impact of the destructiveness of nuclear weapons on the behavior of nations. Nuclear weapons have deprived war of any point, making it impossible for war to function as a continuation of politics.[16] The political problem of war has received a technological solution. If war is too horrible, it will not occur, and nuclear weapons are the technological leap that has finally made war too horrible. This is the implication of the crystal ball effect. So long as nations adopt nuclear strategies that recognize the reality of mutual vulnerability, war between them can be avoided. This is why nuclear deterrence is substantially more effective than conventional deterrence.

MAD is not itself a strategy, but rather a condition nuclear weapons have brought into being, a background reality in the light of which strategy or doctrine must be formulated. A MAD-based strategy is a strategy that appreciates the condition of mutual vulnerability and its implications. Among the different MAD-based strategies that have been proposed, there are two main kinds.[17] Although they differ in important ways, they have in common an appreciation of mutual vulnerability and a consequent recognition that the credibility problem has no solution. Their differences center on the diverging implications they draw from the inability of nuclear threats to achieve a high level of credibility. Advocates of one kind believe that the inability of a nation reasonably to foresee an appropriately limited nuclear war does not greatly restrict what nuclear deterrence can achieve, and should be used to achieve, whereas advocates of the other kind of MAD-based strategy believe that this inability does greatly restrict what nuclear threats should be used to achieve. The two strategies, in other words, differ over the proper scope of nuclear deterrence. Because proponents of the first kind of strategy believe that nuclear threats can and should be extended to influence a wide range of the opponent's behavior, this strategy may be referred to as *extended deterrence*.[18] Because proponents of the second kind of strategy believe that nuclear threats should be used to influence a narrow range of the opponent's behavior, this strategy may be referred to as *minimum deterrence*. In the discussion that follows, these two strategies will be treated as idealized types, and it should not be assumed that all madvocates would fit neatly under one head or the other.

EXTENDED DETERRENCE

One advocate of extended deterrence is Robert Jervis. He contrasts the kind of MAD-based strategy he supports, which he refers to as MAD-4, with both counterforce strategies and inadequate forms of MAD-based strategy (which he labels MAD-1, MAD-2, and MAD-3).[19] On the one hand, MAD-4 contrasts with counterforce strategies because it recognizes that escalation in a nuclear war "cannot be controlled by a state's having a military advantage over its adversary" and that "it is almost inconceivable that either superpower could be confident that control would be maintained."[20] This would make any use of nuclear weapons in war, whether initiatory or retaliatory, very risky. On the other hand, MAD-4 contrasts with other MAD-based strategies in that it does not view escalation as automatic, so that a war's remaining limited is quite possible.[21] These other MAD-based strategies, Jervis argues, view a war's remaining limited as very unlikely or virtually impossible. In our terms, one might say, Jervis regards it as reasonably foreseeable *neither* that a war would remain limited *nor* that it would not. According to this view, I will say, the prospects for a war's remaining limited are *middling*, neither very good nor very poor. That the chances for a war's remaining limited fall somewhere between being very likely and being very unlikely is crucial for an understanding of the dynamics of nuclear deterrence.

If the prospects of a war's remaining limited were good, the threat to engage in limited war could be highly credible. This is the idea behind the notion of escalation dominance, but it is inadequate for an understanding of nuclear deterrence under mutual vulnerability. On the other hand, if the prospects of a war's remaining limited were poor, the threat to retaliate against a limited attack might have little credibility. But there is a *middling level of credibility* for nuclear threats to respond to a limited attack, resulting from middling prospects for a war's remaining limited. "The threat to use limited violence has at least some credibility; implementing it is not tantamount to committing mutual suicide."[22] Bernard Brodie argues: "It is precisely *because* the chance for total war is finite and real that we must think earnestly about limited war."[23] Extended deterrence asks us to think about limited war in a new way. A middling level of credibility is not sufficient to solve the credibility problem, which requires a high level of credibility. But it is sufficient to allow advocates of extended deterrence to postulate a distinct dynamic to the interactions that would be involved in a nuclear confrontation, a dynamic different from that of escalation dominance postulated by counterforce advocates and one on which an alternative theory of deterrence effectiveness can be hung.

Competition in risk taking

The postulated dynamic is competition in risk taking, which was discussed in the last chapter in criticism of the dynamic of escalation dominance. Competition in risk taking, according to Thomas Schelling, is "a military-diplomatic maneuver with or without military engagement but with the outcome determined more by manipulation of risk than by an actual contest of force."[24] Because there is a good chance that a limited war would escalate, a threat of limited nuclear retaliation is a threat to create or increase the risk of mutual destruction. But because there is also a good chance that a limited war would not escalate, a nation might choose to create or increase the risk of mutual destruction by carrying out its threats of limited nuclear retaliation, betting on its opponent's not responding militarily out of fear of increasing the mutual risk even further. Though the risk of destruction is shared, the dynamic of a nuclear war, a dynamic that may (or may not) be enough to keep it limited, is that each side would seek to get the other side to accept a larger portion of the burden of restraint required to keep the war limited by getting the other side to back down. It would do this not through any military advantage its forces could achieve, but through its greater willingness to increase the risk. It would do this by showing greater resolve.[25] A limited nuclear war would be a game of chicken.[26] The notion of competition in risk taking provides a new paradigm for understanding military interactions between nuclear powers, a new paradigm required by the novelty of mutual vulnerability.

That a nation might be willing to increase the risk by seeking to shift the burden of keeping the war limited onto its opponent is what gives the nation's nuclear threats middling credibility. This dynamic does not make the carrying out of nuclear threats pru-dentially rational, because, given that an appropriately limited war is not reasonably foreseeable, any prospective gain could not be expected to outweigh the potential loss. But although the nation would not have sufficient reason to carry out its nuclear threats, it would have some reason to carry them out – namely, its expec-tation that by so doing it might gain an overall advantage by suc-cessfully shifting the larger portion of the burden of keeping the war limited onto its opponent. Whatever hope of success this ma-neuver would have is based on the fact that the opponent's nuclear response to the nation's execution of its nuclear threat would be no more prudentially rational than the execution itself.[27] A nation's nuclear threats have some credibility because escalation to mutual destruction would require that *both* sides behave irrationally. So the opponent might believe that the nation would retaliate on the gamble that the opponent would be the one to accept the burden of putting a stop to the escalatory process by behaving rationally.[28] In contrast, the notion of escalation dominance implies that the carrying out of nuclear threats is not irrational on both sides, only on the side that is weaker militarily.

The nature of this dynamic shows how nuclear deterrence can be extended. Nuclear deterrence is extended when a nation uses nuclear threats to seek to deter behavior other than military attack or coercion against itself. Extended deterrence is extended geo-graphically, in that the nation uses nuclear threats to seek to protect its interests outside its own borders – in particular, to defend its allies. Viewed in terms of competition in risk taking, deterrence can be extended in this way because each of a pair of nuclear opponents in a limited conflict, whether conventional or nuclear, in defense of itself or its allies, could threaten with middling credibility to escalate the conflict in an effort to conclude it on advantageous terms. The threat of societal destruction is influential in conflicts between nuclear opponents even at the level of conventional military violence outside of their borders. The effect of mutual vulnerability is that levels of violence in conflicts between nuclear opponents, including geographical levels, cannot be sealed off from each other, and the potential for violence at the highest level makes itself felt all the way down the line.[29] Jervis summed up extendibility in this way: "Second-strike capacity can protect Europe and the Persian Gulf because the Soviets realize that even a conventional, let alone a nuclear, war could easily escalate, but escalation is not so certain as to make the Soviets confident that the West would not dare use force to resist their predations."[30]

Counterforce strategists also believe that nuclear deterrence can and should be extended, but their understanding of this is different. For them, deterrence is extended through escalation dominance, which depends on counterforce war-waging capability. But under mutual vulnerability, as advocates of extended deterrence see it, deterrence can be extended even if a nation's nuclear forces have little counterforce capability. For counterforce strategists, deterrence is extended because a limited nuclear war is reasonably foreseeable, whereas for advocates of extended deterrence, deterrence is extended because a limited nuclear war is *not* reasonably foreseeable. If one could expect the violence to remain limited, war-waging capability could extend deterrence, but, because one cannot reasonably expect this, war-waging capability is not relevant and it is the simple ability of each side to escalate the conflict that extends deterrence. Moreover, the counterforce method of attempting to insure that the violence stay limited would tend to undermine deterrence, in part, because it would create the kind of instability discussed in the last chapter. So extended deterrence is a more effective form of deterrence. Competition in risk taking is not only a more accurate model than escalation dominance for understanding the dynamics of deterrence under mutual vulnerability, but it insures more effective deterrence than would be the case if the other model were the more accurate one. It is because nuclear confrontation involves the distinct dynamic of competition in risk taking that nuclear deterrence can be more effective than conventional deterrence.

What if deterrence fails?

The model of competition in risk taking requires the possibility of a nuclear war's staying limited, so to practice extended deterrence, a nation must be able to engage in a limited nuclear war. As Schelling observes: "The correct name for the strategy is not 'assured mutual destruction,' but 'assured *capability* for mutual destruction,' the difference being that the capability does not have to be ineluctably exercised at the outbreak of even an intercontinental nuclear war."[31] Critics of MAD-based strategies have sometimes argued that such strategies are unacceptable because the only choice they offer should war come is "holocaust or humiliation."[32] In other words, the claim is that a nation with a MAD-based strategy could retaliate against limited aggression only by launching an all-out attack, so that if such aggression occurred, its options would be either surrendering or bringing about mutual destruction. But this is clearly a mistake, a false dilemma.[33] A nation with a MAD-based strategy could, and, if it were to retaliate at all, certainly would undertake limited retaliation in response to limited aggression in the hope (though not the reasonable expectation) that the war would remain limited. What madvocates deny is that limited retaliation can achieve an effective military advantage. Madvocates need not be embarrassed by the question pressed by counterforce strategists: What if deterrence fails? The alternatives are not holocaust or humiliation. If deterrence fails by the opponent's engaging in limited aggression, madvocates, like counterforce strategists, can recommend limited retaliation. Both groups of strategists believe that intra-war deterrence is possible.

What, more precisely, troubles counterforce strategists, however, is not that madvocates have no answer to the question what if deterrence fails, but that their answer is a poor one. The counterforce strategists' question might be better put: What is there useful to do, if deterrence fails? One cannot simply say that retaliation should be limited in the hopes the war would remain limited without having some idea of how limited retaliation would be useful in helping to limit the war, so providing a basis for the hopes. Of course, there is a trivial sense in which a limited retaliation provides hopes that the war will remain limited, insofar as that response, in being limited, does not itself make the war unlimited. This is temporizing and it is certainly a good reason for a limited, as opposed to a massive, response. (Though it may be a better reason for not retaliating at all.) But once the hopes for escalation dominance have been abandoned, is there anything in a limited response that could positively contribute to keeping the war limited? The purpose of the retaliation would, of course, be intra-war deterrence, but the question is: How, according to the advocate of extended deterrence, would limited retaliation achieve intra-war deterrence? What is the mechanism by which the retaliation could deter?

Advocates of extended deterrence answer in terms of their alternative paradigm – nuclear war as competition in risk-taking. The question is pressed by counterforce strategists because they believe that the answer must make sense, as the madvocates' answer does not, in terms of an understanding of nuclear war as a traditional sort of competition for military advantage. But the alternative paradigm offers an alternative mechanism for intra-war deterrence. A nation's limited retaliation could help to keep the war limited by raising the risks of all-out war to the point where the opponent would be unwilling to raise them any further. It would show the nation's resolve. It would be a move in a game of chicken. If military advantage cannot keep war limited, it may be that retaliation could not be prudentially rational. But just because a nation does not have, in this sense, sufficient reason to retaliate, does not mean it does not have some reason to do so, and that reason is the potential intra-war deterrent effect of a demonstration of resolve. Extended deterrence, unlike counterforce deterrence, need not provide a sufficient reason to retaliate because it does not pretend or require that nuclear threats can achieve a high level of credibility.

The alternative paradigm offered by extended deterrence is explained by Schelling this way: "War no longer looks like just a contest of strength. War and the brink of war are more a contest of nerve and risk-taking, pain and endurance."[34] Nuclear war would be a contest in pain and endurance rather than in military strength, because nuclear threats are primarily threats of punishment rather than threats of denial or damage limitation. This suggests that a limited nuclear war might involve attacks upon countervalue targets, not just counterforce targets. Because it is the threat of punishment that does the deterring, even the intra-war deterring, a limited countervalue retaliation, as suggested in Chapter 5, might serve intra-war deterrence by vividly making clear to the opponent what is in store should the war escalate further.[35] So a limited nuclear war might "take the form of measured punitive forays into the enemy's homeland, aimed at civil damage, fright, and confusion rather than tactical military objectives."[36] Such a war has been referred to as "city swapping." But the strategy of extended deterrence does not require that a limited nuclear war take this form, because any nuclear attack raises the risk of mutual destruction, whether or not those strikes are primarily punitive. A nation could show its resolve by counterforce strikes, as well as by countervalue strikes. According to Jervis: "Nothing about mutual vulnerability means that cities and other values must be the first or only targets in a war; nothing in it implies that military installations are immune; nothing in it implies that wars must be quick and unlimited."[37]

So a strategy of extended deterrence does not preclude some of a nation's nuclear weapons being targeted on military forces. The fact that the strategy recommends or tolerates some counterforce deployments does not make that strategy a counterforce strategy. What distinguishes a counterforce strategy is that it regards counterforce deployments as being able to solve the credibility problem – that is, it sees the use of counterforce weapons as potentially militarily effective and military effectiveness as the means to limit war. Under a MAD-based strategy, however, counterforce deployments should not become too extensive, for this could lead to the false belief that a meaningful military advantage could be attained in a war, which could, as discussed in the last chapter, cast doubt on mutual vulnerability and weaken crisis stability. But advocates of extended deterrence tend to regard mutual vulnerability as so resistant to alteration and our belief in it as so deeply entrenched that they view that belief as not easily undermined by even large counterforce deployments. As a result, advocates of extended deterrence often accept, and even encourage, substantial levels of counterforce deployments. Advocates of extended deterrence recommended little or no change in the size and composition of even the very large arsenals accumulated by the United States and the Soviet Union during the Cold War. In this sense, extended deterrence leaves everything as it was. In terms of deployments, if not doctrine, the practical recommendations flowing from the strategy of extended deterrence required little or no change from the superpower status quo of the 1980s.[38]

The threat that leaves something to chance

It is not yet clear, however, how nuclear threats under extended deterrence can be effective, given that they lack a high level of credibility. Granted the threats have middling credibility, but how is this enough to make them work? How can this strategy ignore the failure of nuclear deterrence to provide a solution to the credibility problem? The answer lies in understanding the nature of the *risk* in the claim that nuclear war would be a competition in risk taking. According to advocates of extended deterrence, the effectiveness of deterrence comes from the risk that a confrontation between nuclear powers might escalate to mutual destruction and the ability of each of the nuclear opponents to manipulate that shared risk. The risk can be manipulated because it can be increased by either side's engaging in provocative actions or making limited attacks, which is what makes such behavior able to demonstrate resolve. But what is the source of this risk and how do such actions increase it? Given that escalating a nuclear war to the point of societal destruction would be highly irrational, how can the risk that a confrontation would escalate to that point be significant?

Schelling characterizes the posing of this risk as a kind of threat, "the threat that leaves something to chance." He asserts:

> The key to these threats is that, though one may or may not carry them out if the threatened party fails to comply, *the final decision is not altogether under the threatener's control.* The threat is not quite of the form 'I may or may not, according as I choose,' but has an element of, 'I may or may not, and even I can't be altogether sure.'[39]

It is a threat that things may get out of control, that an incipient conflict could escalate to large-scale nuclear war, not as the result of a deliberate decision, but through an escalatory process that runs away with itself, through things getting out of hand. It is a threat by a nation to lose control. The threat deliberately to retaliate should the opponent engage in aggression, which is how threats involved in nuclear deterrence are normally understood, is clearly different from the threat that such aggression could lead to an uncontrolled escalatory process resulting in destruction of the opponent's (and the nation's) society. The former kind of threat is a threat that on condition of the opponent's aggression, the nation will do intentional harm to the opponent, whereas the latter is a threat that on condition of the opponent's aggression, the nation will harm the opponent through participation in a process of which the nation is not fully in control.[40]

I will refer to the threat of deliberate action as a *threat-1* and the threat to lose control (or the threat of loss of control) as a *threat-2*. A threat-1 differs from a threat-2 in the way a statement of intention differs from a prediction about one's own behavior.[41] A threat-2 is a threat that should a certain situation arise, by the nature of that situation, the threatener may no longer be fully in control. For example, if one becomes violent when drunk, then her threat of becoming drunk is a threat to lose control in a way that may be harmful to others. Threats-2 are made possible by the existence of situations which, given their nature, a party in them could lose effective control of its actions.[42] Being drunk is one such situation and being in a nuclear war is another. A nation's being in a nuclear war is its being in a situation in which it may lose control, for all the reasons, technical and human, that make escalation in a nuclear war difficult to control, such as the role of emotions and misinformation on the leaders' decisions or a breakdown in the chain of command. A threat-1 is a threat of controlled escalation, whereas a threat-2 is a threat of uncontrolled or explosive escalation.[43]

Threats-2 have an important role in deterrence because limited nuclear war is not reasonably foreseeable. In contrast, threats-1 suffer in importance from this fact, because it keeps threats-1 from achieving a high level of credibility. The significant role of threats-2 in the workings of deterrence goes hand-in-hand with the inability of threats-1 to achieve a high level of credibility. Whatever role threats-1 have is due to threats-2, because the dynamic that gives threats-1 their middling credibility results from the shared risk of uncontrolled escalation.[44] The single factor that explains both the diminished role of threats-1 and the central role of threats-2 is the *uncertainty* that exists about whether a confrontation between the nations would stay under control. Because of this uncertainty, threats-1 cannot achieve a high level of credibility, but because of it, nuclear deterrence works anyway. The opponent will be deterred not because it thinks that the nation's threats-1 are highly credible, but because it thinks that the apparatus the nation has set up to give it the capability to carry out its threats-1 (that is, the weapons, their control systems, and the decision-making structure) poses a significant risk of generating an uncontrolled escalation. By virtue of mutual vulnerability, uncertainty replaces certainty as the mechanism by which deterrence works. Once mutual vulnerability was achieved: "It was the fear of nuclear war itself that deterred, not the specific threat of nuclear retaliation. In this way all nuclear threats became threats that leave something to chance."[45]

Massive retaliation

In making a threat-1, a nation poses a correlative threat-2, and even if the former cannot effectively deter, the latter can. This is how deterrence can be effective despite its failure to solve the credibility problem. But what about the credibility of threats-2? For the effectiveness of threats-2, like the effectiveness of threats-1, is dependent on the perceived likelihood that they would be carried out (or, that what was threatened would happen). But it seems that threats-2 can no more achieve a high level of credibility than can threats-1, because the inevitable uncertainty about whether a confrontation would stay under control means that no one is sure what would happen.[46] Middling prospects for a war's remaining limited doom both kinds of threats to middling credibility. So why should threats-2 be any more effective than threats-1? The answer is that threats-2 can be effective at a middling level of credibility because what they threaten in response to a limited attack is much worse than what threats-1 threaten. Threats-1 threaten limited retaliation for a limited attack, whereas threats-2 threaten societal destruction for a limited attack, because what they threaten is an uncontrolled process with that outcome. Given what threats-2 threaten, "only a little credibility may be required" for their effectiveness.[47] By virtue of threats-2, the result of limited aggression may be suicide, and only a moderate risk of this outcome is sufficient to deter. Certainty of this outcome is not necessary, because "sane leaders do not play Russian roulette."[48]

Threats-2 are equivalent in what they threaten to threats-1 of massive retaliation – that is, threats of all-out retaliation in response to limited aggression. But in a situation of mutual vulnerability, threats-1 of massive retaliation would have little credibility, because an opponent would not believe that a threatener would deliberately bring on its own destruction in response to a limited aggression. So, given that the chances of uncontrolled escalation in a limited nuclear war are significant, the credibility of threats-2 is much higher than the credibility of threats-1 of massive retaliation

Madvocacy

(though not necessarily higher than threats-1 of limited retaliation). The doctrine of massive retaliation, adopted by the United States early in the atomic age, was rejected on the grounds that such threats are incredible. So they are, when they are understood as threats-1, but not when understood as threats-2. In fact, extended deterrence is a strategy of threatening massive retaliation, with the proviso that the threats in question are threats-2 (and hence that the all-out retaliation would come at the end of an escalatory process rather than immediately). The critics of John Foster Dulles notwithstanding, nuclear deterrence has always worked through the threat of massive retaliation. Nations can make explicit threats-1 of limited retaliation while implicitly making threats-2 of massive retaliation. As Jervis notes: "States need not threaten all-out war in order to have that specter loom large in the adversary's (and their own) mind."[49] The explicit threat need only be a threat-1 of limited retaliation.

So uncertainty replaces certainty as the guarantor of deterrence. Deterrence is insured not by highly credible threats of limited retaliation, but by middlingly credible threats of massive retaliation. The failure of threats-1 to achieve a high level of credibility is compensated for by threats-2, which, though also failing to achieve a high level of credibility, are able, because of what they threaten, to be effective at a middling level of credibility. It is the unique nature of nuclear weapons that both causes the problem (the credibility problem) and provides a solution. The horror of societal destruction both undermines the credibility of threats-1 and allows threats-2 of middling credibility to be effective. In a situation of mutual vulnerability, each party is aware that the other is making a threat-2, and this results in both parties being deterred. Counterforce strategies are dangerous because they attempt to reduce the uncertainty that supports threats-2 for the sake of the credibility of threats-1, the effect of which would be the undermining of deterrence. The incalculable risk of threats-2 is a more effective deterrent than the calculable risk of threats-1.[50]

One way to think about threats-2 is in terms of the notion of a doomsday machine, a device that would automatically destroy all life on earth should a nation be attacked with nuclear weapons.[51] In one sense, a doomsday machine would be the ultimate deterrent, because the opponent would be certain that societal destruction would follow even limited nuclear aggression. The threat inherent in a doomsday machine (which is a threat-2, because retaliation would be automatic or uncontrolled) would have the highest credibility. But, as Barrie Paskins and Michael Dockrill point out: "Deterrence at current technological levels is semi-automatic."[52] Graham Allison, Albert Carnesale, and Joseph Nye observed: "Current U.S. and Soviet strategic nuclear arsenals have virtually created the 'doomsday machine'."[53] What exists now, one may say, is a virtual doomsday machine. When societal destruction is automatic and certain, one has a doomsday machine. When it is semi-automatic and there is uncertainty over whether it would result, one has a virtual doomsday machine. But the middling credibility associated with the virtual doomsday machine of extended deterrence may work as well in insuring effective deterrence as the total credibility that would result from a full-fledged doomsday machine.[54]

The doomsday machine analogy makes clear that the claim that nuclear deterrence works through uncertainty about whether a confrontation would stay under control implies that beliefs about capability largely supplant beliefs about will in determinations of credibility. While credibility is normally a function of the threatened party's belief that the threatener has both the capability and the will to carry out its threats, the import of the uncertainty argument is that credibility is determined largely by beliefs about capability alone. Though the nuclear apparatus is designed to provide for the exercise of will to retaliate if the threat fails, the inherent propensity of that apparatus to respond "automatically" marginalizes the opponent's belief about the nation's will to retaliate in determining the credibility of the nation's threat.[55] The execution of a threat-2 would not be a matter of will, in the sense of an intentional response, but rather a manifestation of loss of control. In the execution of a threat-2, the human agents would not stand outside the apparatus and its capabilities as decision makers, but would be part of that apparatus and its responses, part of the machine. Hence, credibility is reduced to a concern exclusively with capabilities. The uncertainty argument shows that the doomsday machine is an apt device for understanding nuclear deterrence, though in a way that makes us see Herman Kahn's discussion of the doomsday machine as ironic. Albert Wohlstetter claims that Kahn intended the doomsday machine "as a reduction to absurdity of the view . . . that targeting population was the cheapest and best way to deter nuclear attack."[56] Although the threat of societal destruction may seem an absurd way to insure deterrence, the propensities of the nuclear apparatus make this threat the way deterrence works in fact.

Existential deterrence

One way to understand the role of uncertainty in insuring deterrence is through McGeorge Bundy's notion of *existential deterrence*. Existential deterrence is the view that deterrence is inherent in nuclear deployments of the sort possessed by the Cold War superpowers, that it is, in the words of David Lewis, "our military capacities that matter, not our intentions or incentives or declarations."[57] Deterrence is existential because the existence of the weapons alone deters. Deterrence is inherent in the weapons because "the danger of unlimited escalation is inescapable."[58] Existential deterrence is a result of "the terrible and unavoidable uncertainties in any recourse to nuclear war."[59] Herman Kahn, offering an earlier version of this idea, spoke of (and criticized) the view that "the deterrence of a rational enemy [is] almost a simple philosophical consequence of the *existence* of thermonuclear bombs."[60] In presenting the notion of existential deterrence, Bundy suggests that it might allow us to reach "a new level of common understanding of what nuclear deterrence is, what it is and is not good for, and how it relates to morals, to politics, and to the prospects for peace." Existential deterrence is distinct "from anything based on strategic theories or declared policies or even international commitments."[61] Like the uncertainty argument, existential deterrence is not itself a nuclear strategy, but rather a claim about how nuclear deterrence works, a claim that any strategy must take into account. Extended deterrence is seen as the best strategy because it is the one that best takes existential deterrence into account.[62]

The notions of uncertainty and existential deterrence correct a misleading inference that may be drawn from the idea, basic to extended deterrence, that a nuclear confrontation would be a competition in risk taking or a contest in demonstrating resolve. If this idea is correct, one might be surprised by the fact that the United States and the Soviet Union did not have more serious crises or go to war over the four decades of the Cold War. One would imagine that each side would have been more eager to seek to promote its interests by testing the other's resolve. But it is easy to see why this did not happen once one focuses, as existential deterrence does, on what is risked in a nuclear risk taking – namely, societal destruction. The magnitude of what is risked in such a competition makes the parties very unwilling to compete. Jervis claims: "While sophisticated bargaining theories might indicate that statesmen can and should behave differently, the oppressive possibility of total destruction is likely to continue to lead them to be sensible."[63] David Lewis suggests the following analogy for existential deterrence: "*You don't tangle with tigers* – it's that simple."[64] This suggests that what is uppermost in the mind of leaders who contemplate some action that might precipitate a crisis with their nuclear opponent is not that they would be in competition with a human agency for some advantage, but that they (as well as their opponent) would be up against a monster, an inhuman process of potentially inexorable escalation, where one's attempt to show resolve would only make matters worse.

What existential deterrence suggests, finally, is that the mode of prudential rationality likely to characterize the leaders of mutually vulnerable nations is not a calculating rationality that carefully totes up potential gains and losses, nor a poker-like rationality of competitors in a contest of resolve and bluff, but rather the kind of rationality in which the agent contemplates the abyss and simply decides never to get too close to the edge. What makes deterrence effective is a simple aversion to nuclear war. This kind of rationality is the basis of what Patrick Morgan calls sensible decision making. "The sensible decision maker . . . will be impressed by the risks and incalculables, his own and his advisors' limitations, and the unpredictability of the opponent's and the other states' reactions."[65]

This discussion of extended deterrence makes clear the rebuttal that at least some madvocates would offer in response to the prima facie argument that nuclear deterrence is not prudentially preferable to conventional deterrence. The claim that nuclear deterrence does not have substantial marginal deterrent value in comparison with conventional deterrence is shown to be false by the special strength of the factors that favor nuclear deterrence over conventional deterrence, reassurance and, in particular, the crystal ball effect. The crystal ball effect operates through nuclear threats-2, the uncertainty about whether a confrontation would stay under control, and it is strong enough to more than compensate for the failure of nuclear threats to achieve a high level of credibility. This is why the failure of nuclear deterrence to solve the credibility problem does not seriously compromise its effectiveness. Uncertainty dissolves the rationality paradox discussed in Chapter 4, because it shows, in effect, how it can be rational to make a threat without its being rational to carry it out. The reason is that in making a threat-1 a nation implicitly makes a threat-2, and the latter can be effective despite the irrationality of carrying out the former. Existential deterrence "solves the most perplexing problems of nuclear policy by rendering them virtually irrelevant."[66] Because a nuclear arsenal is an existential deterrent, there is no reason to think that nuclear deterrence does not have substantial marginal deterrence value in comparison with conventional deterrence. Nuclear deterrence may have put an end to great power wars.

MINIMUM DETERRENCE

Extended deterrence, based on the notion that nuclear deterrence works through uncertainty, seeks to show "what [deterrence] is and is not good for."[67] Nuclear deterrence, good for more than simply protecting the threatener against attack, is extendible. As a result of existential deterrence, David Lewis asserts: "Nuclear deterrence extends itself willy-nilly."[68] But this is to overstate the point, because there are limits to extendibility. Bundy points out: "Existential deterrence cannot do everything."[69] How much can nuclear deterrence do and how much should nations try to do with it? Advocates of minimum deterrence believe that nuclear deterrence should not be encumbered with the extra purposes recommended by advocates of extended deterrence. Nuclear deterrence should be minimal, not extended. Some advocates of minimum deterrence – in particular, Robert McNamara – seem to take the position that though nuclear threats ought not be used to deter conventional attack upon a nation's allies, they should be used to deter nuclear attack upon them. Thus McNamara's version of minimum deterrence appears to prescribe only a partial retreat from extendedness, not a full return to basic deterrence, because he allows that nuclear threats should be used in providing protection from nuclear attack beyond a nation's borders.[70] In any case, because I will be focusing on McNamara's arguments, I will treat his position, which is concerned with the contrast between nuclear and conventional aggression rather than the contrast between homeland and extra-territorial aggression, as the paradigmatic minimum deterrence position.

For advocates of minimum deterrence, nuclear deterrence should be treated as minimal not only in the sense that it should not be extended, but also in the sense that it should be practiced with a relatively small nuclear arsenal. For example, McNamara suggested during the 1980s that the United States could reduce its nuclear arsenal to 500 warheads.[71] (Minimum deterrence, whether viewed in terms of extendibility or arsenal size, is often referred to as finite deterrence.[72]) Although it is the idea of low numbers that is most often associated with minimum deterrence, I will focus primarily on the question of extendibility. McNamara offers two lines of argument for his version of minimum deterrence.

Presenting one argument, McNamara asserts: "With huge survivable arsenals on both sides, strategic nuclear weapons have lost whatever military utility may once have been attributed to them. Their sole purpose, at present, is to deter the other side's first use of its strategic forces."[73] The first sentence is a basic premise accepted by all madvocates, that nuclear weapons in a situation of mutual vulnerability cannot be used to military advantage. The second sentence is a claim peculiar to minimum deterrence, in that it implies that nuclear deterrence cannot be extended to protect the threatener's allies against conventional attack. This is a claim that advocates of extended deterrence deny. Robert Jervis's response to this argument of McNamara's is: "The second sentence does not follow from the first and a more politically sensitive version of MAD accepts the first but rejects the second."[74] It is, of course, extended deterrence, Jervis's MAD-4, which affirms the first sentence but denies the second. Jervis is correct that the first sentence, by itself, does not imply the second. There is a missing premise.

How does McNamara argue that the military disutility of nuclear weapons entails that they are useful abroad only to deter nuclear attack? What is the argument that, in this sense, deterrence only implies *nuclear* deterrence only?[75] McNamara deduces the claims in both the first and second sentences of the earlier quotation from another premise: "Any use of nuclear weapons by the United States or the Soviet Union is likely to lead to uncontrolled escalation with unacceptable damage to both sides. Therefore, nuclear weapons have no military use other than to deter first use of such weapons by one's adversary."[76] He then contrasts this position with one that agrees that there are risks of uncontrolled escalation but concludes, nonetheless, that nuclear weapons can be used to deter conventional aggression. To argue that the risk of uncontrolled escalation leads to his position rather than the other, he criticizes NATO's nuclear first-use policy, which was the threat to use nuclear weapons in response to a Soviet conventional attack against Western Europe. Because nuclear use in response to conventional aggression is likely to lead to uncontrolled escalation, "the threat of such an action . . . has lost all credibility as a deterrent to Soviet conventional aggression." He continues: "One cannot build a credible deterrent out of an incredible action."[77] His argument, then, is that the threat of nuclear retaliation against conventional aggression is not credible, and hence that that threat cannot be effective. So nuclear threats deter only nuclear use.[78]

Both McNamara and advocates of extended deterrence base their arguments about whether nuclear deterrence can be extended on claims that there is a risk of uncontrolled escalation. For advocates of extended deterrence it is the very likelihood of escalation – that is, the threats-2 – that does the extended deterring. In their view, the problem with McNamara's argument is that it focuses exclusively on threats-1, ignoring the impact of threats-2. McNamara acknowledges the critics and their emphasis on threats-2 in this way: "Those who assert that the nuclear first use threat serves to strengthen NATO's deterrent believe that, regardless of objective assessments of the irrationality of any such action, Soviet decisionmakers must pay attention to the realities of the battlefield and the dangers of the escalatory process." He responds: "There is less and less likelihood . . . that NATO would authorize the use of any nuclear weapons except in response to a Soviet nuclear attack." "As this diminishing prospect becomes more and more widely perceived – and it will – whatever deterrent value still resides in NATO's nuclear strategy will diminish still further."[79] This response misses the point, because it continues to focus on threats-1 without recognizing the role of threats-2. It seems that McNamara reaches a different conclusion than the advocates of extended deterrence about the impact of the likelihood of escalation on deterrence effectiveness because the latter appreciate the import of threats-2, and he does not.

In understanding McNamara's view, it is important to recognize that minimum deterrence and extended deterrence tend to involve different assumptions about how high the risk of uncontrolled escalation is. In general, advocates of minimum deterrence believe that the likelihood of a war's remaining limited is much smaller than advocates of extended deterrence believe it is. McNamara asserts: "It is inconceivable to me, as it has been to others who have studied the matter, that 'limited' nuclear wars would remain limited – any decision to use nuclear weapons would imply a high probability of the same cataclysmic consequences as a total nuclear exchange."[80] In contrast, four German authors, writing in criticism of an article by McNamara and three others advocating the no-first-use position implied by minimum deterrence, assert that whereas the risk of escalation is "a danger," the advocates of no-first-use policy wrongfully present it as "a certainty."[81] Although the advocates of extended deterrence believe that the prospects for a war's remaining limited are middling, advocates of minimum deterrence believe that the prospects for limitation are poor.[82] Although Jervis does not agree with McNamara that the prospects for uncontrolled escalation of a limited nuclear war are poor, he seems to agree with McNamara that if they were poor, extended deterrent threats would not be effective. If escalation were perceived to be very likely, "statesmen could not credibly threaten or rationally carry out actions that they believed would surely lead to all-out war."[83]

McNamara's belief that escalation is very likely explains why he regards threats-1 as having less than the middling credibility granted them by advocates of extended deterrence, but it does not imply that nuclear deterrence cannot be extended, because it ignores the role of threats-2. Indeed, what in McNamara's view makes the credibility of threats-1 low – namely, the meager prospects of a nuclear war's remaining limited – would boost the credibility of threats-2. Confusion on this point may result from a failure to appreciate the implications of the uncertainty argument for how one party views the other's threatened retaliatory behavior. If that behavior is prospectively seen as voluntary and deliberate, then the meager prospects of avoiding escalation make the credibility of the threat of retaliation low. But those meager prospects are the result of the high likelihood that things would get out of hand, and they imply that the likelihood of retaliatory behavior is fairly high, even though the retaliation is likely to be the result of a lose of control rather than being voluntary and deliberate.[84] The credibility of threats-2 result from the very factor that makes threats-1 incredible. Moreover, as we have seen, the credibility of threats-2 need only be middling for them to be effective. So McNamara's first argument for minimum deterrence – that nuclear deterrence cannot be extended because the threats that seek to extend it have low credibility – does not succeed. If nations should not use their nuclear threats to extend deterrence, it is not because the threats are unable to extend deterrence.

Accidental nuclear war

Perhaps in appreciation of the weakness of the first argument, McNamara offers a second argument for minimum deterrence. "Whether it contributes to deterrence or not, NATO's threat of 'first use' is not without its costs." One is that the threat leads to "a higher probability that if war actually began in Europe, it would soon turn into a nuclear conflagration."[85] In the same vein, another advocate of minimum deterrence, Morton Halperin, lists as the costs of NATO's first-use policy, a number of ways in which the policy could lead to "the unintended use of nuclear devices." These are "Soviet preemption, the use-them-or-lose-them syndrome, unauthorized use by battlefield commanders, and uncontrolled escalation."[86] There is, in brief, the danger that first-use policy increases the risk of an *accidental nuclear war* – that is, the risk of a nuclear war's beginning accidentally and escalating out of control. It is because advocates of minimum deterrence believe that the risk of uncontrolled escalation from conventional to nuclear war is high that they show a special concern for accidental nuclear war. On the second argument, then, the implication drawn from the claim that the risk of uncontrolled escalation is high is not that it undermines credibility, but that, whatever its effect on credibility, it creates an unacceptable risk that a large-scale nuclear war will occur. The second argument for minimum deterrence is that because of the risk of accidental nuclear war, though nuclear deterrence may be extendible, it should not be extended.

There is, of course, a risk of accidental nuclear war even if the likelihood of uncontrolled escalation is middling rather than high, so this risk is something that advocates of extended deterrence should recognize as well. Indeed, they do, but they welcome the risk rather than fearing it. For them, the risk is not merely some unintended byproduct of extended deterrence, but is rather the policy's very foundation, that on which it depends for effective deterrence. The risk of accidental nuclear war is part of the threat-2 that achieves extended deterrence. The prospects for things getting out of hand and causing a conventional war to become nuclear can be seen from two perspectives – as beneficial in its deterrent effects and as harmful in the dangers it poses. Advocates of extended deterrence believe that the benefits are worth the costs, whereas advocates of minimum deterrence believe that they are not. This is at least partly due to the fact that they differ over the extent of the costs, because they differ over the likelihood of uncontrolled escalation.

The second argument for minimum deterrence is preferable to the first. The first, claiming that nuclear deterrence cannot be extended, ignores the role of threats-2, whereas the second, claiming only that nuclear deterrence should not be extended, does not. In rejecting threats-2, the first argument rejects existential deterrence. But existential deterrence is necessary to explain how nuclear threats can be effective in achieving even basic (that is, nonextended) deterrence. If a high likelihood of uncontrolled escalation makes nuclear threats ineffective in deterring conventional attacks, it would also make them ineffective in deterring a limited nuclear attack, whether against allies or (as pointed out in Chapter 6) against the nation itself.[87] In either case the argument would be that fear of escalation to societal destruction would keep the nation from choosing to retaliate. Minimum deterrence cannot deny the role of existential deterrence in extended deterrence while embracing existential deterrence for the sake of an adequate account of basic deterrence.[88] So the first argument is inadequate. Moreover, advocates of minimum deterrence often implicitly reject the first argument by acknowledging that existential deterrence plays some extended deterrent role. For example, Harold Feiveson endorses existential deterrence, noting: "No matter how unsuited nuclear forces may be to any rational response, their use could never be altogether discounted by a country if the provocation being contemplated, such as an invasion of Europe by the Soviets, was extreme."[89] According to Morton Halperin, some extended deterrence was provided by the fact that "whatever the United States and its allies do, there will be some residual danger that any conflict in Europe would not end short of a strategic nuclear exchange."[90]

But if minimum deterrence acknowledges that existential deterrence makes nuclear deterrence extendible, what distinguishes minimum deterrence from extended deterrence? Minimum deterrence is distinguished by the attitude it takes toward existential deterrence. Halperin asserts: "The West cannot avoid . . . existential deterrence, but it should not exacerbate it or rely on it." Speaking of the threat-that-leaves-something-to-chance, he admits that "this

254

aspect of deterrence would be reduced" by the minimum deterrence posture he recommends.[91] Minimum deterrence does not deny that the uncertainty about whether a confrontation would stay under control bolsters deterrence in one sense, but it seeks to minimize the role uncertainty plays for the sake of avoiding the dangers of accidental nuclear war. The role of uncertainty can be minimized because the degree of uncertainty is not independent of what kind of nuclear deployments and doctrine a nation has. For example, adopting a policy of first-use of nuclear weapons and placing tactical nuclear weapons in the hands of local battlefield commanders (as advocates of extended deterrence often recommended) raises the level of this uncertainty by making it more likely that a war would escalate. On the other hand, adopting a no-first-use policy and eliminating tactical nuclear weapons (as advocates of minimum deterrence recommend) would lower the level of uncertainty, making it less likely that things would get out of hand. But no such measures could eliminate the uncertainty, because it is inherent in the nature of political and military confrontation under mutual vulnerability, whatever the doctrines and deployments may be.

Basic and enhanced uncertainty

Because the uncertainty that makes threats-2 effective is partially but not wholly dependent on doctrine and deployments, a distinction may be drawn between what I will call *basic uncertainty* and *enhanced uncertainty*. Basic uncertainty is the residual uncertainty inherent in military relations under mutual vulnerability that cannot be removed by alterations in doctrine and deployments, whereas enhanced uncertainty is the additional uncertainty that can be created by particular doctrines and deployments, such as the doctrine of first use and the deployment of tactical nuclear weapons. I will identify existential deterrence with the deterrence that results from basic uncertainty. This is consistent with Bundy's claim that existential deterrence is distinct "from anything based on strategic theories or declared policies."[92] It is particular strategic theories and declared policies that can enhance uncertainty, adding to the basic uncertainty of existential deterrence. When advocates of extended deterrence speak of the threat-that-leaves-something-to-chance, they usually understand an uncertainty that has been enhanced beyond the minimum provided by existential deterrence.

Minimum deterrence, then, recognizes the deterrent role of existential deterrence (which is unavoidable in any case), but avoids pursuing enhanced uncertainty out of concern for the risk of accidental nuclear war it entails.

Although advocates of minimum deterrence believe that existential deterrence is satisfactory for basic deterrence, they recognize that eschewing enhanced uncertainty entails loss of effectiveness for extended deterrence. But they argue, first, that the advantage of lowering the risk of accidental nuclear war is worth this price and, second, that the extra deterrence may not be necessary or may be achievable in other ways – for example, by relying more heavily on conventional forces. It is primarily because minimum deterrence eschews enhanced uncertainty that it prescribes the deployment of a much smaller nuclear force than does extended deterrence. Having a nuclear force significantly over the minimum size needed to insure the opponent's vulnerability could provide enhanced uncertainty, but, if so, it would also tend to increase the risk of accidental nuclear war. In contrast, extended deterrence is usually seen not just as permitting, but as requiring, a nuclear force much larger than what is needed to insure the opponent's vulnerability, partly because extra forces are needed for enhanced uncertainty.[93] As a result, whereas extended deterrence would leave the 1980s superpowers' nuclear arsenals roughly as they were, minimum deterrence would require radical reductions in such arsenals.

Another way to represent the contrast between the two forms of madvocacy is in terms of the notion of the nuclear threshold, the point at which nuclear use is likely to occur in the escalation of a conventional war between nuclear powers. Minimum deterrence prescribes a high nuclear threshold, and extended deterrence a low one. If the nuclear threshold is high, resort to nuclear weapons in a conventional war is less likely to occur. In order to reduce the risk of accidental nuclear war, minimum deterrence seeks to keep the threshold high. But for the sake of enhanced uncertainty, extended deterrence prescribes a low nuclear threshold, because conventional war is better deterred if it could easily become nuclear.[94] Advocates of minimum deterrence recommend that nuclear powers have strong conventional forces in order that the resort to nuclear weapons in a conventional war can be resisted and the nuclear threshold be kept high.[95] Many advocates of minimum deterrence believe that conventional forces may be more effective at deterring conventional war than are nuclear forces.[96] Minimum deterrence, prescribing a high nuclear threshold, places greater emphasis on lowering the risk of a conventional war's becoming nuclear, but (so the critics, at least, maintain) at the expense of increasing the risk that there would be a conventional war. Extended deterrence, prescribing a low nuclear threshold, places greater emphasis on avoiding conventional war, but at the expense of increasing the risk that a conventional war would become nuclear.

Minimum deterrence gives a response to the what-if-deterrence-fails question that is different from, though related to, the one extended deterrence provides. Advocates of both strategies believe that nuclear retaliation can serve intra-war deterrence, despite the ineffectiveness of nuclear attacks in achieving a military purpose. The difference lies in the intra-war deterrent goal each strategy emphasizes. Because advocates of extended deterrence understand nuclear war to be a competition in risk taking, they sometimes argue that a nation, through a greater show of resolve, can use nuclear attacks to achieve political goals, such as getting the opponent to withdraw from some recently occupied territory. In contrast, advocates of minimum deterrence tend to argue as Robert Tucker does: "If deterrence fails the only rational course is to end the conflict as quickly as possible and without regard to calculations of relative advantage."[97] As Leon Wieseltier puts it: "In a nuclear war, *war termination is a strategic objective.*"[98] In a nuclear war, Bundy suggests: "The least bad thing that the combatants can do is to stop."[99] The intra-war deterrent goal is simply the cessation of hostilities, without reference to the achievement of political objectives. The contrast between the two strategies' goals is suggested by Schelling, who argues that a limited nuclear war can have as a political goal "to intimidate the enemy and to make pursuit of his limited objectives intolerably risky to him," in which case the "supreme objective may not be to *assure* that [the war] stays limited, but rather to keep the risk of all-out war within moderate limits *above zero.*"[100]

But the view that the objective of a war should be its own termination raises explicitly the problem with nuclear weapons discussed in Chapters 1 and 6. If the use of nuclear weapons in a situation of mutual vulnerability is never prudentially rational, the most effective way to stop a nuclear war initiated by one's opponent is not to retaliate at all. As Robert Tucker asserts: "To do nothing in response to a nuclear attack would likely hold out the best prospect of bringing the conflict to an end in the quickest and least destructive way."[101] Yet advocates of minimum deterrence are, in general, reluctant to recommend nonretaliation. More often, they adopt the paradigm of nuclear war presupposed by extended deterrence. For example, they may follow Desmond Ball when he suggests: "Small, carefully conducted attacks designed to demonstrate political resolve could well have a salutary effect."[102] Or they may straddle the fence on the question whether retaliation should occur, as Halperin does: "If an opponent were to use nuclear weapons on the battlefield, the appropriate U.S. response would be to use, or to threaten to use, nuclear devices against targets of great value to that opponent."[103] But a forthright admission that the best response to nuclear attack would be not to retaliate at all would not make minimum deterrence an incoherent view, as some critics claim, for the credibility problem cannot be solved in any case and existential deterrence is there to do the basic deterring.[104]

Enthusiastic and reluctant madvocates

Advocates of minimum deterrence can offer the same rebuttal as advocates of extended deterrence to the prima facie argument that nuclear deterrence is not prudentially preferable to conventional deterrence, because both of these MAD-based strategies, in contrast with counterforce strategies, regard threats-2 as what makes deterrence effective. Both appreciate the role of existential deterrence and regard nuclear deterrence as having at least some extended deterrent effect. As a result, advocates of minimum deterrence can join advocates of extended deterrence in arguing that the crystal ball effect, operating through threats-2, is sufficiently strong to provide nuclear deterrence with substantial marginal deterrent value over conventional deterrence, despite the failure of nuclear deterrence to solve the credibility problem.[105] But because advocates of minimum deterrence do not believe that nuclear deterrence should be extended beyond the point to which it is inherently extended as a result of basic uncertainty, they are not able to present the rebuttal with the degree of assurance or conviction that advocates of extended deterrence can. For the less the extended deterrent effect of nuclear deterrence, the less plausible is the argument that nuclear deterrence can, by virtue of the crystal ball effect, do a much better job than conventional deterrence of deterring war.

An indication that advocates of minimum deterrence cannot present the rebuttal with as much force is that they are less likely to believe that nuclear weapons have put an end to great-power war. This is shown by the emphasis advocates of minimum deterrence place on the risk of a conventional war's accidentally becoming nuclear. Such a risk is worth worrying about only if one believes that nuclear deterrence has not put an end to the risk of conventional war. So advocates of minimum deterrence apparently do not believe that the risk of conventional war is negligible. The greater the likelihood of conventional war between nuclear powers, the less the likelihood that nuclear deterrence has substantial marginal deterrent value in comparison with conventional deterrence. But still, if, under minimum deterrence, both the risk of conventional war and the risk that a conventional war would become nuclear remain very small, the rebuttal to the prima facie argument could be successfully made. One need not go so far as to argue that nuclear weapons have banished great-power war in order to argue that nuclear deterrence has substantial marginal deterrent value in comparison with conventional deterrence.

But because advocates of minimum deterrence are, in general, less optimistic about the beneficial role of nuclear weapons, some of them would not believe that a rebuttal to the prima facie argument is possible. Some would not regard nuclear deterrence as sufficiently more effective at avoiding war to make it preferable to conventional deterrence. These individuals would not, however, argue for abandoning nuclear deterrence for conventional deterrence, because they would take the view that it is not possible to do this. All advocates of MAD-based strategies believe that MAD should be prescriptive for strategy, but, whereas most believe that MAD should be prescriptive because it is inherently valuable, the less optimistic (some of those advocating minimum deterrence) would claim that MAD should be prescriptive simply because it is unavoidable. The former see nuclear deterrence as an attempt to take advantage of the beneficial nature of MAD, whereas the latter see nuclear deterrence simply as an attempt to make the best of the situation MAD presents us with. One may be a madvocate either through believing that MAD is a great boon or simply through believing that MAD is something we are stuck with. The latter attitude is captured by Wieseltier: "Nuclear weapons are not there to create deterrence. Deterrence is there to cope with nuclear weapons."[106] Although MAD is our fate, one may view this fact as fortunate or merely as unavoidable.

There are, then, *enthusiastic madvocates* and *reluctant madvocates*. Enthusiastic madvocates, including most or all advocates of extended deterrence and many advocates of minimum deterrence, believe that MAD is beneficial in the sense that it makes nuclear deterrence preferable to conventional deterrence. Enthusiastic madvocates would hold that the prima facie argument against nuclear deterrence can be rebutted. Reluctant madvocates, on the other hand, would wish MAD away if they could, but believe it to be an inevitability of which we must take account. They do not see nuclear deterrence as preferable to conventional deterrence, but believe that we are stuck with nuclear deterrence whether or not we prefer it to conventional deterrence. The concern of this chapter is the enthusiastic madvocates and their rebuttal to the prima facie argument. The concerns and assumptions of the reluctant madvocates are taken up in the next chapter. Before considering whether or not the rebuttal offered by the enthusiastic madvocates succeeds, however, I will now consider what the implications of its success would be.

MORAL REVISIONISTS AND EXISTENTIAL MORALISTS

If the madvocates' rebuttal succeeds, then prudential revisionism fails. This would mean that neither prudential revisionism nor strategic revisionism can resolve the conflict within morality and the conflict between institutional morality and prudence brought about by nuclear weapons. The only approach to conflict resolution remaining would be moral revisionism, according to which, resolution lies in a change in morality. As discussed in Chapter 2, however, it is not clear that moral revisionism could be an adequate approach, because the prescription to alter morality may not be intelligible, and, even if it is, the approach may provide only an apparent resolution of the conflicts, especially the conflict within morality. The basic motivation to resolve the moral dilemma is that lacking a resolution, morality would be revealed to be incoherent. But to resolve the dilemma by altering morality may be implicitly to admit precisely the conclusion one is trying to avoid – that morality is incoherent. But the question now is whether there are arguments that can, in the face of these concerns, show moral revisionism to be at least a plausible approach to resolution. I will consider its plausibility first for the conflict between institutional morality and prudence, and then for the conflict within morality. Many writers on nuclear issues have recognized that nuclear weapons create normative conflicts between prudence and morality and within morality. Robert Jervis asserts: "Because the possibility of total destruction is inherent in a world with nuclear weapons, no policy can meet all our moral standards."[107] Michael Walzer claims: "Nuclear weapons explode the theory of just war. They are the first of mankind's technological innovations that are simply not encompassable within the familiar moral world."[108] Some regard the conflict as irresolvable and, as a result, are prepared to abandon moral standards altogether, saying, in effect, "so much the worse for morality."[109] The moral revisionist does not abandon morality as such, but seeks to resolve the conflict by abandoning traditional morality, by putting new moral standards in place of the old. Arthur Burns suggests that if "the traditional ethic is now impractical as politics," perhaps "the responsible citizen [should] be looking for another code."[110] In light of the situation created by nuclear weapons, Hans Morganthau recommends a "radical transformation" of "traditional moral values."[111] George Quester argues: "If the prospect of torturing and killing the innocent works to keep the prospectively guilty from becoming the actually guilty, perhaps we ought simply to adjust our morality." He suggests that we adopt "a new contingent morality." As nuclear weapons force us to recognize the "rationality of irrationality," we should also recognize "the morality of immorality."[112]

Relaxing discrimination

What changes in morality would moral revisionists recommend? Military morality must be brought into line with the prudential demand to practice nuclear deterrence. This requires that the deontological strictures of the just-war tradition – in particular, the principle of discrimination – be relaxed. Robert Foelber claimed: "Western democracies, if they are to survive as guardians of individual freedom, can no longer afford to provide innocent life the full protection demanded by the Just War morality."[113] This recommended shift in the center of moral gravity away from restraints on what may be threatened against civilians is reflected in the claim by Bundy, McNamara, and two of their colleagues that MAD-based threats are "in a deep sense more civilized" than nuclear threats based on limited-war scenarios.[114]

What is the argument that the institutional morality concerning military matters should be thus revised? Is there any argument for this other than the question-begging one that to revise it would resolve the conflict between morality and prudence. One argument is suggested, in different contexts, by both Quester and Jervis. It is based on the claim that "the nuclear revolution undermines the rationale for civilian immunity."[115] The reason for this is suggested by Quester: "What protects weapons is good, what protects people is bad: Such is the inverted moral wisdom of nuclear deterrence, and our traditional morality is a major obstacle to any full and deep acceptance of this."[116] As Jervis puts it: "The call for civilian immunity, while attractive at first glance, fails because it assumes that nuclear weapons help reach political goals in the same manner as do conventional weapons. Since this is not true, the morality, like the logic, no longer works." In a nuclear confrontation, he asserts: "Pressure would be brought to bear on the adversary not through weakening its military capacity but through the increased threat of all-out war. . . . Indeed, because states are deterred by the fear that their societies will be destroyed, it is credible threats to civilians that provide bargaining leverage before and even during a war."[117]

The argument seems to be this. The rationale for the protection afforded civilians by the traditional morality is that the purposes of war are, in general, served by attacks on military forces, not by attacks on civilians. With nuclear weapons, however, the truth is the reverse of this. Because of mutual vulnerability, attacks on the opponent's military forces cannot protect the nation, but attacks on civilians, or threats to attack them, can.[118] Because the old rationale for civilian immunity no longer works, civilian immunity should no longer be a moral standard.[119] Under this understanding of the old rationale for civilian immunity, the justification for the moral standards is tied to the question of military effectiveness. Specifically, civilian immunity is, in effect, a rule against causing a kind of harm that is largely gratuitous. The argument, then, is that given that mutual vulnerability makes the harm of (threatened) attacks against civilians no longer gratuitous, civilian immunity must be abandoned. Whether this argument works depends on whether it is correct, as the argument assumes, that the justification for the institutional, just-war moral standards is in terms of military effectiveness – specifically, the avoidance of militarily ineffective harm. An alternative is to see the justification for civilian immunity as based not on strictures against imposing a generally gratuitous form of harm, but on strictures against a nation's imposing harm on those who are not causally responsible for the immediate threat to the nation. Under this rationale, nothing about mutual vulnerability would lead one to abandon civilian immunity.[120]

The success of the argument that civilian immunity should be abandoned thus depends on the basis of justification for the standards of the just-war tradition. If the basis is military effectiveness, as Jervis and Quester assume, then the argument may succeed. If it is not, for example, if the justification turns on the question of who is causally responsible for the military threat, the argument fails. The principle of tolerable divergence, discussed in Chapter 1, might be taken to imply that the justification for civilian immunity is in terms of military effectiveness. According to this principle, the institutional demands of military morality do not diverge sharply from those of military prudence. In Chapter 1, the conflict between morality and prudence brought on by nuclear weapons was represented as a failure of this principle. But things may be the other way round. If the principle represents an underlying connection between the moral standards and matters of military effectiveness, it shows that a sharp conflict between institutional morality and prudence is impossible. It would follow that nuclear deterrence does not invalidate the principle, but rather, that by virtue of nuclear weapons, the principle invalidates the moral standards. The prudence/morality conflict would be apparent only, simply an indication that changing circumstances require that morality be altered to bring it back into line with prudence.

On the other hand, it may be that one should adopt a weaker interpretation of the principle of tolerable divergence, under which the conflict between morality and prudence is a genuine counterexample to it. In this view, the principle is simply the result of a rough, accidental confluence that has existed in the past between prudence and the just-war standards, a happy coincidence shattered by the advent of mutual vulnerability. This view of the principle of tolerable divergence is in accord with the alternative justification for the principle of civilian immunity. The real reason it is wrong to threaten or attack the opponent's civilians is that they are not causally involved in the harm threatened against the nation, and the coincidence giving rise to the principle of tolerable divergence is simply that in the past their noninvolvement has gone hand-in-hand with harm to them being gratuitous. With nuclear weapons, this coincidence is no longer. If so, the argument for revising the just-war standards offered by Jervis and Quester would be unsound.

In any case, even if the argument were sound, it would go only part way toward establishing the plausibility of moral revisionism. The argument would show how moral revisionism could resolve the conflict between military prudence and morality, but not how or if moral revisionism could resolve the conflict within everyday moral reasoning represented by the moral dilemma. The moral dilemma arises in a different, broader arena. The special institutional context of the conflict between just-war morality and prudence makes plausible the claim that morality is beholden to military effectiveness, as the stronger interpretation of the principle of tolerable divergence suggests. The history of the development of the just-war standards in close quarters with the overall prudential purpose of the institution makes it not unlikely that the latter would (and should) largely shape the former. The moral dilemma, however, occurs not in any special institutional context, but in the realm of everyday moral reasoning. It does not follow that because the just-war standard of civilian immunity should be abandoned, its counterpart in the realm of everyday moral reasoning – the prohibition against hostage-holding – should be abandoned as well.[121]

In attempting to argue for moral revisionism as an approach to resolving the conflict within morality, one could make an argument analogous to the one just presented about the conflict between institutional morality and prudence. There is a link between prudence and the standards of everyday moral reasoning in the idea that morality cannot demand too great a sacrifice of individual self-interest. If this idea were itself taken to be a principle of everyday moral reasoning, one could argue that the prohibition against hostage holding should, in the case of the practice of nuclear deterrence, be abandoned – that is, the prohibition should be qualified so as not to apply to that practice. For, given the prudential argument from Chapter 1, adherence to this prohibition by a nation facing a nuclear opponent requires a great sacrifice of its self-interest. The only way to avoid the moral demand that this sacrifice be made is to qualify the prohibition against hostage holding so that it does not apply to the nuclear policies of such nations. Because of the confluence between the prudential and consequentialist arguments, revising everyday moral reasoning in this way would remove the conflict within morality. So revising morality to accord with the prudential demand that morality not require too great a sacrifice of self-interest would, at the same time, bring the deontological considerations regarding nuclear deterrence into accord with the consequentialist considerations.

There may, then, be some good arguments showing that moral revisionism provides a plausible approach to the resolution of both conflicts, but doubts remain. If these arguments are successful, however, they would go some distance toward addressing the concerns raised earlier about the intelligibility of the approach and about the genuineness of the resolution it appears to provide. For these arguments would subsume the deontological principles that need to be altered under broader principles that would justify or explain the relevant alterations of the former. In any case, it is necessary to adopt moral revisionism only if the madvocates' rebuttal to the prima facie argument fails. Before assessing the success of the rebuttal, however, I wish to consider one other possibility for resolving the two conflicts, a possibility suggested by the discussion of existential deterrence.

Morality and existential deterrence

Some philosophers, whom I will call *existential moralists*, have seized upon the notion of existential deterrence as providing a new way of solving the moral problem presented by nuclear weapons. The possibility that existential deterrence has relevance for the moral debate is suggested by Bundy, who remarks that existential deterrence may provide "a new level of common understanding of what nuclear deterrence is . . . and how it relates to morals."[122] The approach of the existential moralists is, in effect, a form of strategic revisionism, because it is based on the view that a change in strategy can bring nuclear deterrence into line with morality, though it is different from the form of strategic revisionism discussed in Chapter 5. The moral implications of existential deterrence are linked to the implications it has for the credibility problem, because in both cases what is central is the role of will or intention in the nuclear threat. This connection is made clear by Robert Foelber, who, speaking of the problems of morality and credibility, says:

> Existential deterrence offers an elegant way out of two problems that have plagued philosophers of deterrence for years . . . With existential

deterrence these conundrums are dissolved, because deterrence can be maintained without threats or the resolve to carry them out. The question of the morality or credibility of nuclear threats and intentions is irrelevant for deterrence.[123]

By virtue of existential deterrence, Greg Kavka observes: "The existence of a nuclear retaliatory capability suffices for deterrence, regardless of a nation's will, intentions, or pronouncements about nuclear weapons use."[124] Similarly, David Lewis notes: "It is our military capacities that matter, not our intentions or incentives or declarations."[125] The implication concerning credibility, as discussed earlier, is that because intentions are irrelevant, the inability of nuclear deterrence to solve the credibility problem does not imply the ineffectiveness of the policy. The implication concerning morality is that because intentions are irrelevant, an effective policy of deterrence does not require that a nation have morally unacceptable intentions. (I will for now examine the relevance of existential deterrence to the just-war argument, considering later its relevance to the hostage-holding argument.) The nation need not intend to attack civilians in order for deterrence to be achieved, though it must, of course, have the capacity to attack civilians. As a result, the just war argument against nuclear deterrence is shown to be unsound and the conflict between prudence and morality is resolved. This is existential moralism.

Two types of existential moralism have been proposed. Using names suggested by Kavka, these are the policies of "scrupulous retaliation" and "no intention." Scrupulous retaliation is a policy "in which a nation intends to retaliate if subjected to nuclear attack, but only in a clearly moral fashion by limited strikes against military and economic assets located far from population centers." A no-intention policy "is one practiced by a nation having the capability to retaliate if attacked (i.e., survivable nuclear weapons and plans for their possible use), but having no definite intention about whether or not to use this capability."[126] Each is a form of existential moralism because it relies for deterrence on the capacity of societal destruction, and the risk that in a war things would get out of hand, not on the conditional intention to bring about societal destruction. One involves only morally acceptable intentions and the other involves no intentions at all. Because existential moralism is a form of strategic revisionism, it should not be surprising that these two types of existential moralism have important similarities to the two types of strategic revisionism discussed in Chapter 5. Scrupulous retaliation strategy is roughly equivalent to pure counterforce strategy.[127] No-intention strategy is not equivalent to impure counterforce strategy, but they have in common the important feature that the practice of each would pose a risk to civilians without involving the intention to harm them. It will then be helpful, after considering the moral arguments for scrupulous retaliation and no-intention strategies, to look at them in the light of the moral arguments advanced for pure and impure counterforce strategies.

David Lewis makes a case for a policy he calls "finite counterforce," which I take to be representative of the scrupulous retaliation form of existential moralism.[128] Lewis's concern is primarily with the credibility problem. He uses the idea of existential deterrence to argue for a form of nuclear deterrence that is effective in terms of its credibility, while avoiding the instability problem to which ambitious counterforce strategies are prone. But he argues that in the light of existential deterrence, his policy solves the moral problem as well.

> If existentialism is true, and it is not intentions but capacities that deter, then deterrence does not require us to cultivate intentions to do anything except what would at the time be right. The 'paradox of deterrence', in which supposedly it is intentions that deter, and intentions to do the right thing would deter inadequately, and therefore it is right to form intentions that it would be wrong to fulfill, does not arise.[129]

Lewis recognizes that for a finite counterforce strategy to be effective, the deployed forces must have the capacity for societal destruction. The nation would need two war plans, "one for whatever it would be right to do (or to intend to do), and one for destroying the enemy's cities." The second is needed because "our war plans are part of our capacities, even when they are not part of our intentions." Planning to do something, he suggests, need not involve intending to do it.[130]

One representative of the no-intention form of existential moralism is Anthony Kenny. Kenny accepts the existential deterrence argument. "It is a nation's power rather than its willingness to use nuclear weapons that is the essence of the deterrent." The implications are that a nation can have an effective deterrence policy without the intention, or even the willingness, to use the weapons in retaliation. Kenny proposed a "minimum transitional existential deterrent," which would involve "continuing to maintain the physical operability of the nuclear weapons with the sole purpose of using them as bargaining counters to secure balanced and eventually total reduction of Soviet forces." What is morally wrong is not the mere "maintenance of a power," but "the maintenance of a power plus a murderous strategy and a willingness to implement that strategy." His policy is morally acceptable because "the transitional maintenance of the existential deterrent for bargaining purposes need involve no such murderous element."[131] One of the necessary features of a genuine no-intention position is made clear by James Sterba, who notes that "if a nation is to avoid threatening altogether, while possessing a survivable force of nuclear weapons, there must be some legitimate and independent use for those weapons."[132] If a nation is to keep its nuclear weapons, it must have a use for them, a reason for keeping them, and if it has no intention or willingness to use them in retaliation, it must have some other reason. Kenny supplies another reason: The weapons are to be used as bargaining chips in seeking mutual force reductions.

Avoiding immoral intentions

How does the argument that scrupulous retaliation strategy avoids the moral problem of nuclear deterrence fare in the light of the criticism of pure counterforce strategy discussed in Chapter 5? The criticism was that pure counterforce strategy would not solve the moral problem, though its threats might be morally acceptable in deontological terms. The problem is it would not be effective, because the lack of city targets would deprive the threats of credibility. Given the argument for existential deterrence, however, scrupulous retaliation strategy avoids this criticism. Because capacities are sufficient for deterrence, credibility becomes irrelevant. What matters is not how the capabilities would be used, simply how they could be used and, in particular, how they might be used if things got out of hand. All that is necessary is that the counterforce capabilities involved would be sufficient, were they appropriately targeted, to destroy the opponent's society.[133] Lewis, for example, guarantees this by prescribing that the nation have an alternative, countervalue retaliatory plan. An early indication of this existential moralist's argument is found in Paul Ramsey. In Chapter 5, Ramsey was criticized because his policy of deterrence depended for its effectiveness on the collateral damage a counterforce retaliation would involve. But on some occasions he argues differently, that deterrence effectiveness can be achieved by the ambiguity, inherent in the possession of nuclear weapons, about how they might be used. For example, he asserts: "The dual use the weapons themselves have – the fact that they may be used either against strategic forces or against centers of population – means that *apart from intention* their capacity to deter cannot be removed from them."[134]

Now, consider no-intention strategy in the light of the criticism of impure counterforce strategy in Chapter 5. The two strategies are alike in that the advocates of each believe that deterrence can be achieved without the intention to harm civilians, because it would be clear to the opponent that should it engage in aggression, harm to civilians could result anyway. In the case of impure counterforce strategy, that harm could result because the nation intends to attack counterforce targets in or near cities. In the case of no-intention strategy, that harm could result because things might get out of hand. It is due to the propensity of things to get out of hand – that is, to existential deterrence – that no-intention strategy can be effective despite the absence of an intention to use the weapons. The criticism of impure counterforce strategy was that the expected and desired result of its intention to retaliate against counterforce targets (that is, the risk to civilians which guarantees deterrence) is not something for which the nation can deny moral responsibility. The no-intention strategy seems to avoid this criticism, for the risk to civilians that guarantees deterrence in the case of this strategy is not the result of a retaliatory intention, but instead of the prospect of things getting out of hand.

It seems, then, that existential moralism, in both forms, avoids the objections raised against other forms of strategic revisionism. Existential moralism appears to avoid both the deontological difficulty with impure counterforce and the prudential or consequentialist difficulty with pure counterforce. But appearances are deceptive. Setting aside the question of prudential and consequentialist acceptability, I will argue that existential moralism does not avoid the deontological objection to nuclear deterrence.[135] The main point is that though neither form of existential moralism relies on threats-1 that put civilians at risk, in relying on existential deterrence, each relies on threats-2 that put civilians at risk. Civilians must be put at risk for deterrence to be effective. The argument that these strategies avoid deontological criticism is, in effect, the argument that the difference between threats-1 and threats-2 is morally relevant. But this is not the case. One is morally responsible for the risk one poses to civilians, when that risk is a third-party threat designed to achieve deterrence, whether the risk is posed through threats-1 or threats-2. The argument is the same as that used against impure counterforce strategy in Chapter 5. A nation practicing an existential-moralist strategy desires the deterrence outcome, and hence desires the threats-2 against civilians that make it possible. The threats-2 are desired as a means rather than as an end, but this does not put them beyond moral criticism. In the words of Walter Stein, cited in Chapter 5: "I cannot morally dissociate myself from what I want, from what I cannot avoid wanting as a means to achieving my purpose, if in fact I choose to achieve my purpose by these means."[136]

The difference between an existential-moralist strategy and impure counterforce strategy is this. Impure counterforce strategy involves an indirect intention to attack civilians, because it is a threat to do something intentionally that would result in massive civilian destruction. An existential-moralist strategy, on the other hand, involves no intention, direct or indirect, to attack civilians, because it is not a threat that the nation would do something intentionally that would result in massive civilian destruction. It is, instead, a threat that things would get out of hand. But this difference is not sufficient to alter the moral verdict. For a nation practicing an existential-moralist strategy does do something intentional that has as its aim putting civilians at risk – namely, constructing and maintaining a nuclear apparatus that could get out of hand. The nation not only knows the apparatus has this feature, but the nation constructs and maintains the apparatus in order that it have this feature, because its having this feature is believed to be a means of achieving deterrence. It matters not to the moral argument that the apparatus may have other purposes as well, such as damage limitation (for Lewis) or disarmament bargaining leverage (for Kenny), for purposes can be multiple, and a multiplicity of purposes would not alter the moral unacceptability of the purpose of putting civilians at risk.[137]

If A is worried about B's aggression, A may threaten, should B aggress, deliberately to assault innocent members of B's family. Alternatively, A, knowing (and knowing that B knows) A's moodiness and propensity to get indiscriminately violent when drunk, may stock enough liquor at home so as to threaten that should B aggress, A would, in the intoxicated depression and anger that would surely follow B's attack, pay a drunken visit to B's family. In the first case a conditional intention to harm innocent persons is part of A's deterrence strategy, and in the second case it is not, because the former strategy relies on threats-1 and the latter only on threats-2. But in both cases there is the intentional posing of a risk to innocents, in the one case by a threat of intentional action and in the other by the stocking of the liquor cabinet so as to threaten that things could easily get out of hand. This is what makes both strategies morally unacceptable. The difference between the two is not relevant to the judgment of moral acceptability. Because the threat against innocent persons is, in each case, intentionally posed, one is morally responsible for it, even if, as in the one case, execution of the threat would involve no intentional action. By analogy, a scrupulous retaliation or a no-intention strategy is no more morally acceptable than an impure counterforce strategy. Neither satisfies the principle of discrimination. This is even clearer when one considers existential-moralist strategies in terms of the hostage-holding argument. Innocent persons are hostages when they are put at risk of harm to influence the behavior of another, and this is just as much the case whether the risk of harm comes from a threat intentionally to attack them or from a threat that they will be attacked as a result of things getting out of hand, so long as both threats are deliberately instituted to influence the behavior of that other.

Note should be taken of what this implies for the argument against pure counterforce strategy in Chapter 5. The conclusion remains the same, but the route to it is different. The argument was that pure counterforce strategy may be acceptable in deontological terms, but, because it would not be effective, it would not solve the moral problem, so would not be an adequate form of strategic revisionism. Existential deterrence shows that pure counterforce strategy might be effective, but, to that extent, it would then not be acceptable in deontological terms. Pure counterforce strategy would be effective if it involved enough invulnerable warheads to pose a threat-2 of societal destruction, and if, as Lewis suggests, it involved plans for such destruction. But to the extent that it exhibited these features, it would no longer be acceptable in deontological terms, for the reasons just discussed.[138] Thus the conclusion of the argument against pure counterforce strategy stands.

The existential moralists do not provide an adequate form of strategic revisionism. As George Quester remarks: "The moral issues remain in place as before."[139] Now our discussion turns to the prudential (and consequentialist) value of MAD-based strategies. Do existential deterrence and the uncertainty argument show that nuclear deterrence can be effective enough to allow a rebuttal to the prima facie argument that nuclear deterrence is not prudentially preferable? The argument of the existential moralists is that by virtue of existential deterrence, nuclear deterrence solves the moral problem it creates. The argument of the madvocates is that by virtue of the uncertainty about whether a confrontation would remain under control (of which existential deterrence is a part), nuclear deterrence solves the prudential problem it creates. It solves the problem by creating, via threats-2, such a serious risk from war that a high level of credibility is not necessary for the policy to be highly effective.

NONCRISIS INSTABILITY

Because a policy of deterrence seeks to influence the choices of the opponent, a theory of deterrence must, in part, be a theory of choice situations. A policy of deterrence seeks to avoid aggression by inducing the opponent to choose not to aggress, but there are different kinds of situations in which an opponent might choose aggression, different kinds of choices that would be involved. So an effective deterrence strategy must be constructed with an eye to the differences among these kinds of situations and choices and what the differences imply about what sorts of threats the nation should issue to achieve deterrence.[140] There are two general categories of choice situations, situations of severe crisis between the nuclear opponents and situations without a severe crisis between them. (For brevity, I will refer to these, respectively, as crisis and noncrisis situations. They are meant to be exhaustive and roughly mutually exclusive, "crisis situations" referring to situations of moderate to severe crisis and "noncrisis situations" referring to situations of no crisis or low to moderate crisis.) The requirements for deterrence effectiveness or deterrence stability in crisis situations (that is, crisis stability) were discussed at the end of the last chapter. In this section I consider the requirements for deterrence effectiveness in noncrisis situations, which I dub *noncrisis stability*.

The argument of this section is that the rebuttal to the prima facie argument offered by madvocates fails because the effectiveness of MAD-based strategies suffers in noncrisis situations. First, I discuss the form of stability appropriate to noncrisis situations. Second, I argue that crisis and noncrisis stability vary inversely – that is to say, if a deterrence strategy exhibits crisis stability it will, to that extent, fail to exhibit noncrisis stability, and conversely. Finally, I argue that despite the contribution that uncertainty about whether a confrontation would stay under control makes to deterrence effectiveness, the fact that the two forms of stability are inversely related leads to the conclusion that the madvocates' rebuttal fails. Once net deterrent effect is considered, MAD-based strategies no more provide the basis for a successful rebuttal than do counterforce strategies.

Stability is described in the last chapter as the characteristics that make a situation strongly resistant to basic change. But to flesh out this idea, one has to have an idea of what changes are relevant to the judgment of stability – that is, what changes count as basic. Clearly, during any given time, any situation is undergoing change in a number of respects and remaining unchanged in a number of respects, so a situation can be described as stable or unstable only relative to certain kinds of change. In general, we refer to situations as stable or unstable relative to changes that are important to us. The avoidance of the opponent's nuclear attack is, of course, very important to a nation, so in referring to a nuclear deterrence strategy or relationship as stable, one may be claiming that it is unlikely to undergo change from peace to nuclear war. Because a nuclear war would almost certainly begin in a crisis, stability in this regard is called crisis stability. But also important to a nation is the avoidance of the opponent's non-nuclear aggression, whether this be conventional military aggression or simply a serious political challenge to the nation's interests. A nation is concerned about nonnuclear aggression not only because it is undesirable in its own right, but also because such aggression can lead to a crisis and hence indirectly to nuclear war. As a result, a nuclear deterrence strategy or relationship may be referred to as stable or unstable also in respect of its propensity to undergo change from peace to a state of nonnuclear aggression by the opponent. Because such aggression may well occur in the absence of a severe crisis, stability in this regard may be referred to as noncrisis stability.

Discussions of the stability of a nuclear strategy or relationship are often limited to crisis stability.[141] Glenn Snyder helps to provide a more general picture. He points out that the traditional notion of stability in political and military affairs is the "tendency of a system to maintain itself at or near a state of equilibrium." There are several aspects to this idea of stability, two of which are (1) "tendencies either to stimulate or inhibit war," and (2) "the tendency of the process to preserve the independence of the major actors."[142] The first of these aspects, understanding the war that is stimulated or inhibited as nuclear war, is crisis (in)stability. The second is noncrisis (in)stability, because successful nonnuclear aggression compromises, to a greater or lesser extent, the independence of the nation. Richard Garwin similarly broadens the idea when he defines the stability of a nuclear regime as "its ability to prevent nuclear war and subnuclear conflicts that could lead to war."[143] Nuclear deterrence stability has two basic dimensions, crisis and noncrisis stability. But one must not assume, as the words of Garwin might suggest, that stability is univocal, in the sense that there is a single set of features by virtue of which a nuclear strategy or relationship would be both crisis and noncrisis stable. We want nuclear deterrence to be stable in both ways, but we must realize that the features that are stability making in one way differ from those that are stability making in the other.

To each strategy its own stability

The way to appreciate that these sets of stability-making features are different is to recognize how each of the two dimensions of stability is connected with a different strategic approach. Crisis stability, as we have seen, is connected with MAD-based strategies, because it results from the virtues of mutual vulnerability emphasized by these strategies – namely, reassurance and the crystal ball effect. Noncrisis stability is connected with counterforce strategies, because it results from the virtue claimed for these strategies – namely, high threat credibility. The connection between noncrisis stability and counterforce doctrine is made clear by Colin Gray. He claims that notions of deterrence stability are strategic theory-laden: "There can be no useful, doctrine-neutral exploration of the idea of stability." His notion of stability is that it would be achieved when the goals of ambitious counterforce strategy are achieved. "The strategic balance would be stable were it to permit Western governments to enjoy not-implausible prospects both of defeating their enemy (on its own terms) and of ensuring Western political-social survival and recovery." A nation needs "multilevel stability," which is "stability at every level of potential conflict."[144] What makes deterrence stable is the credible threat to respond to and to defeat the opponent at any level of violence. The connection between threats that are credible in this sense and the concern of noncrisis stability to avoid nonnuclear aggression is clear. Because nonnuclear aggression would occur at lower levels of violence, it can be effectively avoided only when there are credible threats to respond at those levels.

The basic criticism Gray has of the notion of crisis stability discussed in the last chapter is that it views stability as being determined simply by technical factors – namely, the factors involved in the second-strike capability that constitutes mutual vulnerability. Crisis stability is the idea that military force postures (such as those of ambitious counterforce) "should not comprise the proximate cause of war." But the proximate cause of nonnuclear aggression would not be such technical considerations, but political conflict, and this the notion of crisis stability ignores. Thus, Gray observes: "The vision of stability that pervades much of U.S. theorizing about deterrence questions is essentially static and absolute. It tends to be bereft both of the idea of competition and of the essential referents of foreign policy interests and geopolitical relationships."[145] A nation's military policy must be capable of deterring political and nonnuclear military challenges by the opponent, not simply the opponent's nuclear attack. Only a deterrence policy that effectively avoids such challenges can be regarded as stable. The point is that there is no merely technical solution (such as second-strike capability) to the political problem of conflict between nuclear adversaries.

Gray claims that the notion of stability he favors is better in all respects than the notion of crisis stability he rejects – that is, that his notion can best avoid both nuclear and nonnuclear aggression. He argues that the form of stability he recommends would be more effective in a crisis, because the traditional notion of crisis stability is defective. " 'The reciprocal fear of surprise attack' as the principal proximate cause of war merits probable identification as a U.S. 'mechanistic' fantasy."[146] But consistent with his claim that no account of stability is doctrine neutral, it is clear that he makes these claims because he rejects MAD-based strategies in favor of counterforce strategies.[147] He says, for example, that one of the goals of a stable deterrence policy is to minimize self-deterrence, when self-deterrence is seen by madvocates as one of the prime virtues of nuclear deterrence. But a more accurate picture of nuclear stability is suggested in other remarks of his. On one hand, he says that the notion of crisis stability he rejects "is fully compatible with policy paralysis in the context of what may be dangerous instabilities at lower levels of violence." On the other hand, he argues that if nuclear deterrence is to be extended, this "requires that there be a measure of instability at the central war level – translated as a potential for U.S. advantage."[148] In other words, some instability exists no matter which kind of policy one chooses. If a nation focuses on achieving stability at the highest level, this will lead to instability at lower levels, which is why Gray rejects the traditional notion of crisis stability. But if the nation chooses to focus on achieving stability at the lower levels – that is, noncrisis stability – the potential for military advantage this requires will come at the expense of stability at the highest level, because of the risk of preemptive nuclear attack in a crisis.

This discussion shows not only that crisis stability-making features are different from noncrisis stability-making features, but that these sets of features are incompatible. If a nation sets out to achieve crisis stability, it will undermine noncrisis stability, and vice-versa. The truth is, as Richard Betts remarks, that "the goal of eliminating the possibility of nuclear war conflicts with the goal of reducing the danger of conventional war."[149] The underlying reason for the incompatibility and conflict is that each type of stability depends on their being a lack of stability of the other type. The incompatibility is necessary. Crisis stability requires self-deterrence and reassurance so that the rush toward preemption in a crisis is unlikely to occur, but these features make it more likely that the opponent will engage in nonnuclear aggression, because they entail the nation's threats to respond to limited aggression will be less credible. On the other hand, noncrisis stability requires the credibility of such threats, which entails the kind of counterforce military posture that would make the rush to preemption in a crisis more likely. The bland prescription that nuclear deterrence should be designed so as to avoid war masks a fundamental tension. The prescription suggests that there is one way nuclear deterrence could be that would avoid war, and that we should figure out which way this is and design our nuclear weapons policy accordingly. The battle between madvocates and counterforce strategists is often seen as a dispute about what way this is. But war can come in different ways – in particular, a nuclear war can erupt in a crisis or a war may start, in the absence of a crisis, through a political challenge leading to conventional conflict, which in turn could lead to a crisis and nuclear war. Avoiding war's coming in one of these ways requires doing things that make it more likely to come in the other way.

The stability/instability paradox

This inherent conflict between the two dimensions of stability has come to be known as the *stability/instability paradox*. Glenn Snyder formulates it this way:

> The greater the stability of the "strategic" balance of terror, the lower the stability of the overall balance at its lower levels of violence. The reasoning is that if neither side has a "full first-strike capability," and both know it, they will be less inhibited about initiating conventional war, and about the limited use of nuclear weapons, than if the strategic balance were unstable. Thus firm stability in the strategic nuclear balance tends to destabilize the conventional balance and to activate the lesser nuclear "links" between the latter and the former.[150]

This is Robert Jervis's formulation:

> To the extent that the military balance is stable at the level of all-out nuclear war, it will become less stable at the lower levels of violence. That is, if an uncontrolled war would lead to mutual destruction, then neither side should ever start one. But this very stability allows either side to use limited violence because the other's threat to respond by all-out retaliation cannot be very credible.[151]

The stability/instability paradox implies that the more a strategy achieves one kind of stability, the less it achieves the other. The greater the credibility of a nation's nuclear threats, the less the likelihood of avoiding nuclear war in a crisis. The greater the likelihood of avoiding nuclear war in a crisis, the less the credibility of the nuclear threats. The ability of a strategy to avoid nuclear attack in a crisis is in inverse relation to its ability to avoid nonnuclear aggression. If crisis stability is achieved, then "each side's nuclear weapons cancel out the influence of the other's."[152] But then each side's nuclear arsenal is partially neutralized as an effective tool to deter nonnuclear aggression. If, on the other hand, noncrisis stability is achieved, a nation's nuclear weapons are no longer neutralized in this way, but nuclear war becomes more likely in a crisis. The stability/instability paradox, as the discussion makes clear, is not, strictly speaking, a paradox, because there is not one kind of stability that a policy of deterrence both has and lacks. There are two different kinds of stability, and if a policy has one to that extent it lacks the other. If it has one, it has that one because it lacks the other.

It is important to appreciate the double-edged nature of the problem represented by the stability/instability paradox. First, it represents the problem with counterforce strategy discussed in the last chapter, because it shows that attempting to achieve high credibility (that is, noncrisis stability) will come at the expense of crisis stability. But more important for present concerns, it shows the mirror-image problem faced by MAD-based strategies – namely, that their commitment to crisis stability necessarily comes at the expense of noncrisis stability. The argument of this section is that this shows that the madvocates cannot offer a successful rebuttal to the prima facie argument any more than the counterforce strategists can. The general form of the argument is the same: Nuclear deterrence cannot be shown to have substantial marginal deterrent value in comparison with conventional deterrence because the comparative advantages of nuclear deterrence are a direct function of its comparative disadvantages. The stability/instability paradox represents this general argument. As a result, both madvocates and counterforce strategists are concerned to counter it. The argument of the last chapter is, in effect, that counterforce advocates fail in this effort. Their effort could succeed only if a nation could unilaterally overcome its own societal vulnerability.[153] Now we must consider the response of the madvocates to the paradox and the success of their efforts to counter it.

The madvocate's response

If the stability/instability paradox could be successfully countered, this would show the possibility of what Herman Kahn called "multistability" – that is, in our terms, that a policy of nuclear deterrence could achieve both crisis and noncrisis stability.[154] How do madvocates respond to the stability/instability paradox? What are their arguments that multistability is possible under MAD-based strategies? They claim that those who argue that the stability/instability paradox shows the inadequacy of MAD-based strategies do not appreciate the deterrent impact of the uncertainty about whether a confrontation would stay under control. This response can take three different forms. (1) Some proponents of minimum deterrence argue that though the paradox shows that nuclear deterrence cannot be effective if it is extended, the paradox does not apply, given the uncertainty provided by existential deterrence, when nuclear threats are used for nonextended deterrence only. (2) Proponents of extended deterrence argue that uncertainty has such a strong deterrent impact, especially when enhanced, that the paradox does not apply even in the case of extended deterrence. (3) Some madvocates admit that the paradox does apply to MAD-based strategies, but argue, nonetheless, that uncertainty moderates its impact to the extent that a MAD-based strategy with adequate multistability can be achieved. If all three of these responses can be shown to be inadequate, the conclusion should follow that the paradox applies to MAD-based strategies as it does to counterforce strategies, such that they are unable to provide a successful rebuttal to the prima facie argument.

The first response, the one taken by many proponents of minimum deterrence, is that the stability/instability paradox is a problem only when a nation seeks to extend deterrence. This is suggested when Jervis claims, in formulating the paradox, that crisis stability "creates instability by making lower levels of violence relatively safe and undermining 'extended deterrence'."[155] Leon Sigal claims that stable deterrence, by which he seems to mean nuclear deterrence that combines both crisis and noncrisis stability, is possible at the "intercontinental nuclear level," but that this "does not ensure stable deterrence at the theater nuclear or conventional level."[156] This implies that the paradox applies to nuclear deterrence when it is extended but not when it is basic. Earl Ravenal claims: "There is an essential tension, not an easy complementarity, between achieving safety for ourselves through crisis stability and achieving safety for the objects of our protection in the world through deterrent stability."[157] Again, the suggestion is that there is a conflict between the different forms of stability only when nuclear deterrence is extended.

Most advocates of minimum deterrence hold, with Robert McNamara, that nations should not use nuclear weapons to extend deterrence, relying on conventional forces to deter conventional war.[158] If the paradox does not apply to minimum deterrence, then such a policy would avoid the conflict between the two forms of stability. The argument is that the conflict between crisis and non-crisis stability is not unavoidable, but arises only when a nation attempts to use nuclear weapons to extend deterrence. But the argument's appeal to the distinction between extended and non-extended deterrence seems untenable. As argued earlier, the credibility problem afflicts the efforts to use nuclear threats for both basic and extended deterrence. The fear that a nuclear response to a limited attack could lead to societal destruction, which is the fear leading to a lack of credibility for nuclear threats, is present whether the limited attack is made against the nation's allies or against the nation itself, and it is a lack of credibility which generates noncrisis instability. As a result, there is no reason to think that if extending nuclear deterrence results in noncrisis instability, such instability would disappear when nuclear threats were used for basic deterrence. The tension between crisis and noncrisis stability may be more acute when nuclear deterrence is extended than when it is basic, but one cannot conclude that a policy of minimum deterrence would succeed in avoiding the stability/instability paradox altogether.

The advocate of minimum deterrence would respond that by virtue of existential deterrence and the uncertainty it involves, noncrisis instability, and thus the paradox, can be avoided for nuclear threats used for basic deterrence. But this creates an opening for the advocate of extended deterrence. If the basic uncertainty of existential deterrence avoids noncrisis instability when nuclear threats are used for basic deterrence, why would not the enhanced uncertainty provided by a policy of extended deterrence allow noncrisis instability to be avoided as well when nuclear deterrence is extended. Thus the first response to the argument that the stability/instability paradox shows MAD-based strategies to be inadequate leads naturally to the second response, which is that enhanced uncertainty is sufficient to avoid noncrisis instability for nuclear deterrence, both basic and extended. This is Jervis's response to the paradox. He argues that the view that the paradox applies to MAD-based strategies overlooks "crucial considerations of risk and chance."[159] "Because escalation can occur although no one wants it to, mutual second-strike capability does not make the world safe for major provocations and limited wars." He says of the paradox:

> Although the logic is impeccable, the argument is flawed because it is too abstract... As long as we imagine a world of certainties – one in which decision makers can predict how the other side will react and have complete control over their emotions, subordinates, and military machinery – the argument works fairly well.

But this assumption is "not realistic." "People have been killed playing Chicken."[160]

Thus, extended deterrence can provide noncrisis stability by virtue of the threats-2 resulting from the uncertainty, which the strategy enhances, about whether a confrontation would stay under control. This is, in fact, a version of the argument, presented earlier in the chapter, that a MAD-based strategy can avoid the credibility problem, because the claim that a MAD-based strategy cannot achieve noncrisis stability is simply another way to put the credibility problem. This argument against the paradox is also offered by Glenn Snyder. After presenting the paradox, he asserts:

> But one *could* argue precisely the opposite – that the greater likelihood of gradual escalation due to a stable strategic equilibrium tends to deter both conventional provocation and tactical nuclear strikes – thus stabilizing the overall balance. The first hypothesis probably is dominant, but it must be heavily qualified by the second, since nations probably fear the possibility of escalation "all the way" nearly as much as they fear the possibility of an "all-out" first strike.[161]

The fear of escalation "all the way" is the fear engendered by threats-2. Snyder is saying, in effect, that MAD-based strategies may achieve noncrisis stability because of the uncertainty about whether a confrontation would stay under control. But Snyder's doubts about this, his claim that it is more likely (that is, the dominant hypotheses) that the paradox does apply, are instructive. There are weaknesses with the second response.

According to David Lewis, existential deterrence implies "that even if we try to make crises as safe as we can they will still look quite dangerous enough." If potential crises look dangerous, non-crisis stability will be achieved. But Lewis's way of putting the point reveals two difficulties with the second response. The first follows from his implication that it is the perception leaders have that crises are dangerous that makes the paradox inapplicable. Lewis points out that "well-deterred statesmen should have an exaggerated fear of crises."[162] If a strategy has crisis stability, leaders should have relatively little fear of crises, because there would be little chance one would lead to nuclear war. But according to proponents of extended deterrence, the uncertainty about things getting out of hand makes leaders fear crises in any case. Recall that the way ambitious counterforce strategy achieves noncrisis stability is to make crises in fact dangerous, through crisis instability, so that leaders will perceive them as dangerous and avoid them by not engaging in nonnuclear aggression. Extended deterrence seeks to avoid the paradox by achieving noncrisis stability through the perception of dangerousness due to uncertainty, while combining this with the reality of crisis stability. But to the extent that extended deterrence relies on this gap between perception and reality in order to avoid the paradox, it is open to the criticism that that gap could close over time.[163] As the opponent of a nation practicing extended deterrence gets used to the deterrence relationship, the uncertainty about what was initially unfamiliar, which is not unrelated to the uncertainty about things getting out of hand, may fade and the opponent come to see the risk of nuclear war as less, which, according to advocates of extended deterrence, it is, because they claim that the strategy is genuinely crisis stable. As a result, noncrisis stability would decrease, and the paradox would then apply.[164]

The trade-off

The second difficulty with the argument, which is more relevant to our concerns, is that, as Lewis's remark suggests, making crises safe – that is, creating crisis stability – does have some costs in terms of the perceived dangerousness of crises, which means that it undermines noncrisis stability to some extent. The argument seems to be that the costs crisis stability exacts on noncrisis stability are not high enough seriously to undermine deterrence effectiveness. We can try to make crises safe (for the sake of crisis stability) and they will still look sufficiently dangerous (to ensure an adequate level of noncrisis stability). Jervis makes this clear:

> But if an all-out war is simply "forbidden," does this not make "lesser wars" relatively safe? Of course "relatively safe" may not be safe enough and even a slightly credible threat of all-out war may be credible enough to deter the other side. But the paradox cannot be completely disposed of in this manner; there remains a trade-off between the perceived risk of total conflict and the possibilities for adventurism.[165]

When a nation seeks to make crises safe, this will lessen the perceived risk of total conflict, but the trade-off will be an increase in possibilities for adventurism – that is, an increased risk of nonnuclear aggression. That a trade-off of this sort must be made shows that the paradox does not go away. The argument, more precisely, is not that the paradox can be avoided, but that it does not apply with sufficient force seriously to compromise deterrence effectiveness. This shows that the second line of response (along with the first) reduces to the third, which is that as a result of the moderating influence of uncertainty, the paradox does not have a severe impact on the effectiveness of MAD-based strategies.

But there are serious doubts whether the third line of response is adequate to rebut the prima facie argument. According to the prima facie argument, nuclear deterrence could be shown to be prudentially preferable to conventional deterrence only if nuclear deterrence could be shown to have substantial marginal deterrent value, and this cannot be shown, because nuclear deterrence has significant disadvantages as well as significant advantages compared with conventional deterrence. Given the logic of this argument, a successful rebuttal would have to show that nuclear deterrence lacks the disadvantages while retaining the advantages. But whenever the stability/instability paradox applies, this cannot be shown, for the paradox implies that there is a trade-off such that any attempt to weaken or to eliminate the disadvantages will weaken the advantages, whereas any attempt to retain the advantages will keep the disadvantages. This is because the advantages of nuclear deterrence – reassurance and the crystal ball effect – are the elements of crisis stability, whereas its disadvantage – its lack of credibility – implies noncrisis instability. The stability/instability paradox is, in fact, a special version of the prudential problem presented in Chapter 4, and the applicability of the paradox to both counterforce and MAD-based strategies implies that the prudential problem stands in the way of any attempt to rebut the prima facie argument.

This is not to say that the uncertainty argument for MAD-based strategies may not succeed in showing that these strategies are superior to counterforce strategies, because it may show that the paradox has more of a negative impact on the latter than on the former. Moreover, the fact that the trade-off between crisis and noncrisis stability is, in the case of a strategy of extended deterrence, moderated by enhanced uncertainty might be enough to show that nuclear deterrence has some marginal deterrent value in comparison with conventional deterrence. But nuclear deterrence can be shown to be prudentially preferable only if it can be shown that the marginal deterrent value it has is substantial. Because there is a trade-off between crisis and noncrisis stability, even if the impact of the trade-off is moderated by the uncertainty, substantial marginal deterrent value cannot be clearly demonstrated. The burden of proof thrust upon supporters of nuclear deterrence by the force of the prima facie argument requires a clear demonstration. Thus it seems that the rebuttal fails.

The fact that fashioning a nuclear weapons policy requires compromises and trade-offs between incompatible concerns is well recognized. Jervis remarks that "no nuclear policy can be very good."[166] Leon Sigal asserts that "no solution can satisfy all the relevant dimensions of the problem simultaneously."[167] In such a situation, one does the best one can. Nuclear strategists argue over whether a counterforce strategy or a MAD-based strategy is the best we can do. But my point is that the telling criticism that each strategic camp makes of the other (which is, in effect, that the other is subject to the stability/instability paradox), seems to imply that, whichever one is preferable to the other, it cannot be demonstrated that either is preferable to conventional deterrence. Because the trade-off is in terms of stability, it does not seem possible to show that any nuclear strategy would be stable enough in all respects to establish its preferability to conventional deterrence. The set of alternatives we face in terms of which we must do the best we can may be broader than simply different policies of nuclear deterrence. A distinction can be drawn, Henry Shue suggests, between internal and external criticisms of nuclear deterrence.[168] My argument is that the internal criticisms nuclear strategists on each side offer of opposing nuclear strategies provide a basis for the external criticism that conventional deterrence is prudentially preferable to nuclear deterrence.

Because war or other forms of aggression could arise in different ways, nuclear deterrence could fail in different ways. In particular, it could fail in a severe crisis or it could fail outside of a severe crisis, and avoiding each kind of failure places different, incompatible demands on deterrence policy. Crisis and noncrisis stability are in inverse relation. Threats that would most effectively deter the choice of aggression in one kind of situation are different from those that would most effectively deter the choice of aggression in the other kind of situation. Deterrence may fail because the opponent chooses premeditated war or aggression or deterrence may fail because the opponent chooses preemptive war.[169] (Moreover, nuclear war, the direct result in the latter case, may be an indirect result in the former case.) But because different factors motivate premeditated and preemptive action, no policy of nuclear deterrence can adequately insure the absence of sufficient motivation for aggressive action in both kinds of case.

Whether an opponent is likely to choose aggression in a certain kind of choice situation is, of course, partly a function of the nature of that particular opponent, its "national psychology" or the individual psychology of its leaders. In terms of psychological types, a distinction is sometimes drawn between (1) those who are risk-averse loss minimizers and (2) those who are risk-prone gain maximizers, the claim being that what would deter the one would not necessarily deter the other.[170] Deterrence is said to be easy with (1) and difficult with (2). But what this means is that the level of noncrisis stability needs to be higher with (2) than with (1). On the other hand, crisis stability may need to be at a higher level with (1) than with (2), because if war is seen as inevitable and imminent, the motivation to preempt would be to minimize losses. So the balance a nation strikes in its choice of strategy between its concern with crisis stability and its concern with noncrisis stability will be determined, in part, by its perception of the psychological type of its opponent. But this supports the assumption of this book that the question whether nuclear deterrence is prudentially preferable can be profitably discussed in general and in the abstract, without reference to particular opponents. The particular opponent will influence where a particular nation determines that the balance should be struck in its choice of nuclear strategy, but it is the need to strike a balance, irrespective of where the balance is struck, which shows that the prima facie argument against the prudential preferability of nuclear deterrence cannot be rebutted.

NUCLEAR DETERRENCE – A TRIANGULAR AFFAIR

But the argument of the last section is not fully satisfying. It is open to proponents of extended deterrence to claim that the third line of response has not been adequately addressed. The discussion of the last section simply fails to appreciate that the enhanced uncertainty extended deterrence achieves moderates the force of the stability/instability paradox to such an extent that though the paradox still applies, the strategy represents a much superior form of nuclear deterrence. Admittedly, what extended deterrence achieves in terms of crisis stability carries a cost in terms of noncrisis stability. But nothing said in the last section shows that the enhanced uncertainty the strategy provides is not sufficient to drive down this cost to such an extent that extended deterrence would, nonetheless, have substantial marginal deterrent value in comparison with conventional deterrence. Thus, extended deterrence provides the basis for a successful rebuttal to the prima facie argument. An extended deterrence strategy is able to retain the advantages of nuclear deterrence (the crisis stability provided by reassurance and the crystal ball effect) while avoiding, to a large extent, the disadvantages of noncrisis instability posed by the credibility problem. The reason is that uncertainty is an independent factor, transcending the dimension on which the incompatibility between crisis and noncrisis stability plays itself out, and it is able to disrupt the inverse relation between these two forms of stability sufficiently for a successful rebuttal.

Accidental war instability

This attempt to defend the third line of response, however, does not succeed. To see why it fails, and to appreciate more fully the unavoidable tendency of nuclear deterrence toward instability, we must add to the discussion of the stability/instability paradox a consideration of the criticism of extended deterrence offered by proponents of minimum deterrence. Recall that this criticism is that the enhanced uncertainty achieved by extended deterrence is not worth the risk it creates of accidental nuclear war, the risk of a nuclear war's beginning accidentally and escalating out of control. Proponents of minimum deterrence make clear that the risk of accidental nuclear war is an important component in the complex trade-off scheme involved in the choice of a nuclear weapons policy. One way to recognize this complexity and its implications for the argument for extended deterrence is to view the risk of accidental nuclear war itself as a form of instability. It is a form of instability because it represents the propensity of a deterrence strategy or relationship to undergo change from a state of peace (or, at least, a state of nonnuclear war) to a state of nuclear war. It is a separate form of instability from crisis instability, which is also concerned with the change from peace to nuclear war. First, an accidental nuclear war would probably begin with a relatively small nuclear strike, whereas a preemptive nuclear war, resulting from crisis instability, would probably begin with a large-scale nuclear strike. Second, accidental and preemptive nuclear wars would result from different kinds of choices. Understanding "choice" in a broad sense, the choice of accidental nuclear war would be unintentional, whereas the choice of preemptive nuclear war, which is the concern of crisis instability, would be intentional (though probably not deliberate in the way that the choice of nonnuclear aggression would likely be). So, *accidental-war (in)stability*, as I will call it, joins crisis and noncrisis (in)stability as proper sources of analytical concern.[171]

The uncertainty about whether a confrontation would stay under control is a result of there being a risk of accidental nuclear war. The criticism of advocates of minimum deterrence is that extended deterrence, in enhancing uncertainty, creates too high a level of accidental-war instability. This means that we need to add a second dimension to the analysis, a dimension in addition to the one on which crisis and noncrisis stability inversely vary. We need to see the (in)stability trade-offs as two-dimensional rather than one-dimensional, and to this end, we must consider a trio rather than a duo of contending strategic approaches. Nuclear deterrence is a triangular affair.[172]

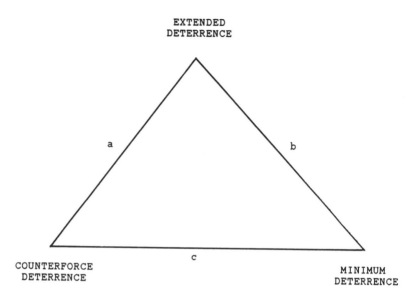

Each strategic approach emphasizes the achievement of one of the three kinds of stability. Extended deterrence emphasizes crisis stability, whereas counterforce deterrence emphasizes noncrisis stability, and minimum deterrence emphasizes accidental-war stability. This means that each strategic approach tends to be deficient in both of the other kinds of stability. This has important implications for the argument for extended deterrence and for an understanding of nuclear deterrence as a whole.

Other trade-offs

First consider the features that pair-wise combinations of the three strategic approaches have in common. The lower-case letters indicate the commonalities in the strategies at the ends of each line. (a) Both counterforce deterrence and extended deterrence strategists claim that deterrence should be extended. (b) Both extended deterrence and minimum deterrence strategists claim that mutual vulnerability is strategically beneficial. (c) Both counterforce deterrence and minimum deterrence strategists claim that credibility is a serious problem. The main criticism that each approach has of the other two is indicated by how the form of stability it emphasizes amounts to a rejection of the feature the other two have in common.

So the emphasis of extended deterrence on crisis stability is based on a rejection of (c), the claim that credibility is a serious problem. Similarly, the emphasis of counterforce deterrence on noncrisis stability is based on a rejection of (b), the claim that mutual vulnerability is strategically beneficial. Finally, the emphasis of minimum deterrence on accidental-war stability is based on a rejection of (a), the claim that nuclear deterrence should be extended. This means that each strategy tends to suffer from two different forms of instability, and the particular version of a strategy one chooses as policy is a matter of trading-off or balancing not only its preferred form of stability against the two forms of instability to which it gives rise, but also those two forms of instability against each other.

This shows why, in the end, extended deterrence cannot provide an adequate rebuttal to the prima facie argument. Because the crisis stability of the strategy leads to noncrisis instability, in order to try to lessen the latter, the strategy seeks to enhance the basic uncertainty provided by existential deterrence. But enhancing uncertainty is shifting the balance from noncrisis instability to accidental-war instability.[173] The greater credibility of the threats-2 resulting from enhanced uncertainty lessens noncrisis instability, but increases accidental-war instability. The greater noncrisis stability comes at the cost of greater accidental-war instability. This is a hidden cost when viewed from the perspective of the stability/instability paradox, because the paradox does not consider the third form of (in)stability. Hence there is a surface plausibility to the third line of response by advocates of extended deterrence in the last section. The cost is also hidden in the claim that extended deterrence achieves its moderate level of noncrisis stability as a result of the mere appearance that crises are dangerous. If crises are not really more dangerous, the extra noncrisis stability provided by the perception that they are seems cost free. But under extended deterrence, contrary to the argument in the last section, crises really are dangerous, not because of crisis instability, but because of accidental-war instability. In a state of serious tension, a nuclear war could start through accident as well as through preemption. Once the hidden cost is revealed, however, it becomes clear that extended deterrence cannot provide a successful rebuttal to the prima facie argument.

The risk of accidental war is a significant prudential disadvantage of nuclear deterrence in comparison with conventional deterrence. Some of the ways in which nuclear weapons differ from conventional weapons create a serious risk of accidental war. In particular, the destructiveness of the weapons and the speed of their delivery can generate intense pressures on decision makers and disrupt command-and-control systems so that accidental war becomes a significant possibility. Thus the list of factors discussed in Chapter 4 is incomplete. To the credibility problem must be added the risk of accidental war as a relative disadvantage of nuclear deterrence, in contrast with the relative advantages of reassurance and the crystal ball effect. Each of the disadvantages gives rise to its own form of instability, and because these two forms of instability are in inverse relation (as are the other two pair-wise combinations of the three forms of (in)stability), extended deterrence cannot avoid the disadvantages of nuclear deterrence while retaining its advantages. When the prudential problem of nuclear deterrence is understood to include the disadvantage of the risk of accidental war, it becomes clearer that a strategy of extended deterrence cannot avoid the problem to the extent necessary to rebut the prima facie argument.

It was mentioned earlier that the risk of accidental nuclear war could be seen in two different ways, with advocates of extended deterrence seeing it as a benefit to deterrence and advocates of minimum deterrence seeing it as a detriment. It is both. The risk benefits deterrence in lessening noncrisis instability, but it harms deterrence in increasing accidental-war instability. This is not paradoxical, because deterrence can fail in different ways. But it does help to reveal the implicit caveat in the optimistic claim of enthusiastic madvocates that nuclear weapons have put an end to great-power wars. After pointing out that nuclear weapons can deter conventional as well as nuclear wars, Bernard Brodie observes:

> It is a curious paradox of our time that one of the foremost factors making deterrence really work and work well is the lurking fear that in some massive confrontation crisis it may fail. Under these circumstances one does not tempt fate. If we were absolutely certain that nuclear deterrence would be 100 percent effective against nuclear attack, then it would cease to have much if any deterrence value against nonnuclear wars.[174]

The apparent ability of nuclear deterrence, under a strategy of extended deterrence, to deter all wars – that is, its apparent achievement of noncrisis as well as crisis stability – is the result of a lurking fear that deterrence may fail in a confrontation. But this fear is not cost free, because it results from the risk of accidental nuclear war. Thus, nuclear weapons do not put an end to great-power wars, for their ability to put an end to intentional war is a function of the risk they create of unintentional war.[175]

In addition to proclaiming an end to great-power war, enthusiastic madvocates often make the related claim that nuclear deterrence is so rugged or robust that one need not worry about its failing. Counterforce strategists sometimes claim, in contrast, that nuclear deterrence is delicate, so that a nation must be very careful to maintain the proper nuclear posture vis-à-vis the opponent to avoid deterrence failure. This difference of opinion concerns a disagreement over the requirements of maintaining noncrisis stability. Because advocates of extended deterrence believe that a good degree of noncrisis stability is consistent with crisis stability, they, unlike the counterforce strategists, see the maintenance of noncrisis stability as being not very difficult. Once again, however, an apparent advantage of the policy comes with a hidden cost in terms of accidental-war stability. If ruggedness means the ability to avoid any form of deterrence failure, then extended deterrence is not rugged, for the extent of a policy's ability to avoid intentional war varies inversely with its ability to avoid unintentional war.

The conclusion that the madvocates' rebuttal fails shows that nuclear deterrence is not prudentially preferable to conventional deterrence. This seems to imply that the consequentialist argument for nuclear deterrence from Chapter 2 is unsound. But this judgment would be too hasty. Important issues bearing on the soundness of that argument are raised in the next chapter. One can at this point, however, appreciate important weaknesses in that argument. The argument is divided into a positive case for nuclear deterrence (in P1) and a negative case against the alternative of complete nuclear disarmament (in P2 and P3). The weaknesses that are now apparent are in the positive case. This case relies heavily on the idea of stability, claiming that the stability of nuclear deterrence makes war between nuclear powers very unlikely. But now it is clear that stability is an ambiguous notion and that whatever gains nuclear deterrence provides in terms of one form of stability have their corresponding costs in terms of its other forms. This greatly weakens the positive case. But the strength of the negative case cannot be fully gauged at this point, because there are concerns it raises that have yet to be broached in our long discussion of the prima facie argument. These are the concerns of the reluctant madvocates, and to them we now turn.

Chapter 8

Conflict resolution

Both rebuttals fail. The conclusion of the prima facie argument stands: Nuclear deterrence is not prudentially preferable to conventional deterrence. There is not sufficient reason to think that nuclear deterrence has substantial marginal deterrent value in comparison with conventional deterrence. In this sense, nuclear deterrence does not work. This seems to show that prudential revisionism is the correct approach to resolving the two conflicts, the sharp divide between institutional morality and prudence and the moral dilemma within the context of everyday moral reasoning. The apparent implication is that it is our prudential view, rather than our moral view, that nuclear weapons require we rethink. Nuclear weapons demand a new understanding of prudence, of what it prescribes, rather than a new understanding of morality.[1] But it is, in fact, too soon to draw these conclusions. For prudential revisionism is the correct approach to resolving the conflicts only if the prima facie argument shows that the prudential and consequentialist arguments favoring nuclear deterrence are unsound. Despite the defeat of the rebuttals, however, the prima facie argument does not by itself show this.

Putting the point more carefully, the success of the prima facie argument does show that prudential revisionism resolves the conflicts, but only at an abstract level, not at a level of direct practical relevance, not at the level of policy implications for those situated, as everyone now is, in the midst of the nuclear age.[2] Because the prudential and consequentialist arguments address the policy implications of nuclear weapons for nations situated in the nuclear age, the success of the prima facie argument is not sufficient alone to show that those arguments are unsound. If the prudential and consequentialist arguments were unsound, the policy implication, then endorsed by prudence as well as morality, would be that nuclear weapons be abandoned. But the prudential and consequentialist endorsement of nuclear disarmament does not follow straightway from the conclusion of the prima facie argument. There is a gap between that conclusion and that prescription. The purpose of this chapter is to explore that gap and to determine if it can be closed. The question is, what relevance does the success of the prima facie argument have for a nation already possessing nuclear weapons? The conflicts resolved at an abstract level by prudential revisionism are in danger of reasserting themselves at the level of policy implications. Despite the success of the prima facie argument, there is the prospect that both prudential and consequentialist considerations remain in conflict with deontological considerations. Conflict resolution gained at the abstract level faces serious pressure when one attempts to bring it to bear on the situation of nations already practicing nuclear deterrence.

The conflicts at the practical level cannot be resolved by alterations in the political relationship between nations. It is important to emphasize this point again. When the adversarial character of the political relationship between two nations is sufficiently high, those nations enter into a relationship of military deterrence, which is, if they are nuclear powers, also nuclear deterrence. The political tensions between two such nations may moderate to the point where, over time, they cease to be military adversaries. Such a fundamental alteration in political relationship occurred at the end of the Cold War with the dissolution of the Soviet Union. This change will temporarily make the world safer from the risk of nuclear war, but it will not thereby resolve the conflicts nuclear weapons create. It will remove a particular instance of nuclear danger – but not the potential for nuclear danger – the fact that that danger will exhibit itself in other adversarial political relationships. Because nuclear deterrence is a general relation, the U.S./Soviet relationship being only one of its instantiations, the ending of that adversarial relationship does not resolve the conflicts nuclear weapons create. Because the potential for mutual vulnerability will remain, conflict resolution can be achieved only by showing that the conflicts can be overcome *within* a relationship of nuclear deterrence, and it is the possibility of this that must now be explored.

The gap between the conclusion of the prima facie argument and its practical implications for nations in a relationship of nuclear deterrence arises because the form of conventional deterrence that the prima facie argument finds preferable to nuclear deterrence is different from the form of conventional deterrence that could be achieved by such nations. To distinguish these, I will refer to what the prima facie argument finds preferable to nuclear deterrence as *conventional-1 deterrence,* and what would result from the complete nuclear disarmament of nations practicing nuclear deterrence as *conventional-2 deterrence.*[3] Because the prima facie argument compares nuclear deterrence with conventional-1 deterrence, its success does not necessarily show that the prudential and consequentialist arguments, which compare nuclear deterrence with conventional-2 deterrence, are unsound. If conventional-1 and conventional-2 deterrence differ in relevant respects, then the fact that the conflicts are resolved when nuclear deterrence is compared with the former would not imply that they are resolved when it is compared with the latter.

As discussed in Chapter 4, the prima facie argument addresses the question whether nuclear weapons should have been invented. Conventional-1 deterrence is deterrence as it existed prior to the advent of nuclear weapons. On the other hand, the prudential and consequentialist arguments, directly addressing the situation we face in the thick of nuclear weapons, concern whether nations already practicing nuclear deterrence should switch to policies of conventional deterrence. Thus, conventional-2 deterrence is deterrence as it would exist after nuclear disarmament. As a result, there are two important differences between conventional-1 and conventional-2 deterrence. First, conventional-2 deterrence may not be mutual, in the sense that a nation practicing conventional-2 deterrence might face an opponent with nuclear weapons, whereas conventional-1 deterrence is necessarily mutual, in the sense that neither side can possess nuclear weapons because they have not been invented. Second, conventional-2 deterrence, unlike conventional-1 deterrence, is haunted by the possibility of nuclear rearmament. The first difference is relevant when a nation's policy of conventional-2 deterrence results from its unilaterally abandoning its nuclear weapons, whereas the second applies whether the nation's policy of conventional-2 deterrence results from its unilateral or from the multilateral abandonment of nuclear weapons.

UNILATERALISM

A policy of unilateral nuclear disarmament may not achieve the resolution of the conflicts that conventional deterrence achieves at the abstract level because such a policy may not bring about the congruence of the prudential (and consequentialist) perspective and the deontological perspective. The concern of the deontological arguments about the immorality of intending to attack civilians or of holding them hostage is the nuclear deterrence policy of individual nations. Although the deontological arguments condemning nuclear deterrence apply to all nations, they apply to them individually, irrespective of what other nations are doing. The wrongness of holding hostages, for example, is independent of whether or not other nations are holding hostages. Thus, the deontological arguments, in their opposition to nuclear deterrence, view unilateral nuclear disarmament favorably. On the other hand, the prudential perspective, as represented by the prima facie argument, finds conventional deterrence preferable to nuclear deterrence only on the assumption that the latter entails mutual vulnerability – that is, the situation of mutual nuclear threatening.[4] This suggests that the recommendation of the prima facie argument is mutual conventional deterrence, not unilateral conventional deterrence. Although the imperatives yielded by the prima facie argument and the deontological arguments have the same form (no nuclear weapons!), it seems that they differ in substance. The latter arguments imply that nonpossession of the weapons is preferable to possession for each nation considered by itself, whereas the former argument implies only that the state of mutual nonpossession is preferable to mutual possession. The prima facie argument seems silent on the preferability of unilateral nonpossession.

The abandoning of nuclear deterrence may have to be unilateral, because multilateral abandonment may not be possible. It is within a nation's power to abandon its own nuclear weapons, but it is not within its power, absent international cooperation, to bring about mutual abandonment.[5] The deontological imperative requires unilateral abandonment, but the imperative flowing from the prima facie argument does not directly concern unilateral abandonment. Thus, on the assumption that mutual abandonment is not possible, the success of the prima facie argument does not show the prudential and consequentialist arguments to be unsound, at least not directly. The latter arguments seem to stand, if it is the case that a nation can proceed toward the abandonment of nuclear deterrence only unilaterally. Thus it seems that prudential revisionism may fail as an approach to a resolution of the conflicts as they exist in practice.

One problem with unilateralism from a prudential or consequentialist perspective is that the consequences of a situation in
which a nation is practicing conventional deterrence while its opponent is practicing nuclear deterrence may be substantially different, both for the nation and humanity as a whole, than those
of a situation in which both sides are practicing conventional deterrence after mutual nuclear disarmament. It seems that the nation's deterrence policy would not work as well in the former case,
because the effectiveness of conventional threats would likely be
greatly diminished in a situation in which one's opponent is making
nuclear threats. Credibility is supposed to be the prudential advantage of conventional deterrence, but the threat of conventional
retaliation is much less credible when conventional retaliation could
call forth a nuclear response. This point is emphasized by critics
of unilateral nuclear disarmament. Greg Kavka argues: "If a modern superpower were willing to use nuclear attack on a nuclear-
disarmed foe to obtain concessions or capitulation, resistance with
conventional forces would be quite ineffectual."[6]
    Two kinds of factors cited in the consequentialist argument in
Chapter 2 (in P2) reflect this concern with conventional threat credibility. First, if a nation abandons its nuclear weapons, its conventional threat would not be sufficient to avoid the opponent's use
of its nuclear threat as a compellent to coerce political concessions
from the nation. This is the worry about nuclear blackmail. Second,
a related point, the conventional threat would not be sufficient to
deter a nuclear attack upon the nation. Such an attack might come
either as part of an effort at nuclear-blackmail enforcement or for
other reasons. Russell Hardin has argued that a nation that has
adopted a policy of unilateral nuclear disarmament might well be
subject to a nuclear attack launched by its opponent in order to
destroy the nation's capacity to rebuild its nuclear weapons and to
guarantee that it could not rearm.[7] Putting the general point more
strongly, James Child asserts: "Unilateral nuclear disarmament just
is the irrevocable alienation of our right to life and liberty."[8]
    But the judgment of preferability is a comparative one. What
needs to be shown is not merely that the consequences of unilateral
nuclear disarmament are worse than those of mutual nuclear disarmament, but that they are worse than those of a policy of retaining nuclear weapons. In making this comparative judgment,
the consequentialist argument, in addition to delineating the risks
of unilateral nuclear disarmament just mentioned, emphasizes (in

P1) the stability of mutual nuclear deterrence. But the discussion in the last two chapters has shown that stability claims for nuclear deterrence are problematic, and this provides a basis for criticizing the conclusion of the consequentialist argument regarding unilateral nuclear disarmament. The discussion has shown that the danger of nuclear war under a regime of mutual nuclear deterrence is higher than commonly thought, especially when the risk of accidental nuclear war is counted. This suggests that the danger may be sufficiently high that unilateral nuclear disarmament would be preferable to continuing to practice nuclear deterrence. The risk of nuclear war under mutual nuclear deterrence has been emphasized by proponents of unilateral nuclear disarmament. For example, Jeff McMahan argues that unilateral nuclear disarmament is preferable because "the present policy of nuclear deterrence . . . has a significant probability of leading to nuclear war."[9] Doug Lackey argues in favor of unilateral nuclear disarmament on the grounds "that the risk of nuclear war is large enough, and that the methods used to control the risk are questionable enough, to warrant careful consideration of radical changes in current methods of managing the risk."[10] McMahan and Lackey, in their arguments in support of these claims, discuss many of the factors examined in the last two chapters that call into question the reliability of mutual nuclear deterrence.

But although the stability problems of mutual nuclear deterrence call into question the claim that practicing nuclear deterrence is preferable to unilateral nuclear disarmament, they do not seem to provide a sufficient basis to demonstrate its falsity. The main reason is that the risk of nuclear war would remain even after unilateral nuclear disarmament. One source of this risk would, of course, be the continuing possibility that the opponent would launch a nuclear attack. Such a one-sided nuclear war, as proponents of unilateral nuclear disarmament point out, would likely be a relatively small-scale affair, perhaps involving only a few demonstration shots to enforce nuclear coercion, so that it would not be of the same order of magnitude, in prudential or consequentialist terms, as the large-scale nuclear war possible under mutual nuclear deterrence.[11] But the risk of large-scale nuclear war would remain as well.

A nation's policy of unilateral nuclear disarmament could bring about considerable upheaval and uncertainty in world affairs. As suggested in the consequentialist argument in Chapter 2, this instability could lead to nuclear war in two ways. First, nuclear war could result from the behavior of other states, especially those that had formerly seen themselves as receiving protection from the nation's opponent under the nation's "nuclear umbrella." Some of these states might well seek to acquire nuclear weapons, or to enlarge their arsenals if they were already nuclear powers, in order to provide better protection of their own against the opponent. Were such armament to occur, the uncertainties on all sides may make major nuclear war more likely than it was prior to the nation's unilateral nuclear disarmament.[12] The other way in which nuclear war could result is the possibility that the disarmed nation would have second thoughts, perhaps brought on by its opponent's attempts at nuclear coercion, and seek to rebuild its nuclear weapons. It is easy to imagine the uncertainties of that process making nuclear war between the two more likely than it was prior to the nation's initial abandonment of its nuclear weapons. In both cases, the risk of nuclear war would be due in large part to the fact that for a period of time after beginning to arm or rearm, a nation would not yet be in a relationship of mutual vulnerability with its opponent, generating pressures in a crisis for a preemptive strike. The general point is that though there are serious instability problems with nuclear deterrence, those resulting from unilateral nuclear disarmament seem to be worse.

The continuing risk of nuclear war following unilateral nuclear disarmament is in contrast with the absence of such risk in the case of conventional-1 deterrence. The failure of deterrence that occurs subsequent to a nation's unilateral nuclear disarmament, like the failure of deterrence that occurs when both sides have nuclear weapons, could result in a major nuclear war, whereas the failure of conventional-1 deterrence could not have this result. This is why the prima facie argument favoring conventional-1 deterrence succeeds while the prudential and consequentialist arguments favoring unilateral nuclear disarmament apparently fail. The logic of the prima facie argument is that nuclear deterrence is preferable to conventional deterrence only if nuclear deterrence has substantial marginal deterrent value in comparison. The requirement that the marginal deterrent value be substantial results from the fact that the failure of nuclear deterrence could be so much more catastrophic than the failure of conventional-1 deterrence. But the continuing risk of major nuclear war subsequent to unilateral nuclear disarmament shows that the failure of deterrence under this policy would not necessarily be less catastrophic than the failure of mutual nuclear deterrence. Thus the prudential comparison between a nation's retaining and unilaterally abandoning its nuclear weapons must be decided simply in terms of which of these policies has marginal deterrent value. The greater instability problems resulting from the unilateral abandonment of nuclear weapons seem to show that it is retention of the weapons rather than their unilateral abandonment that has marginal deterrent value. The conclusion is that retention is prudentially preferable to unilateral abandonment. But mutual abandonment may be an option.

MULTILATERALISM

Multilateral nuclear disarmament appears to be recommended by the prima facie argument, and it would avoid the risk of nuclear war resulting from the one-sided nuclear deterrence relationship that would follow unilateral nuclear disarmament. Thus it seems that the prudential and consequentialist perspectives should favor multilateral nuclear disarmament over retention of the weapons, even though they favor retention over unilateral nuclear disarmament. But this is not necessarily the case, because, as (P3) of the consequentialist argument indicates, the risk of major nuclear war remains. The risk of nuclear war is unavoidable with conventional-2 deterrence, whether it results from unilateral or from multilateral nuclear disarmament. Major nuclear war would be a significant possibility if nations mutually abandoned their nuclear weapons, as it would be if only one side did so, as it is when neither side does so. Doubtless the likelihood of major nuclear war will differ from one of these cases to the other, and on such differences the overall consequentialist assessments would largely rest. But it seems that these assessments are unfavorable to multilateral nuclear disarmament as they are to unilateral nuclear disarmament.

There are two ways in which a process of multilateral nuclear disarmament could bring about instabilities that could lead to major nuclear war. Such instabilities could arise, first, from the disarmament process itself and, second, from the state of mutual disarmament once it had been achieved.[13] The first concerns the process of getting from here to there, from mutual nuclear armament to mutual nuclear disarmament. George Quester claims that the prospect of mutual nuclear disarmament "is fraught with enormous problems of verification and reliability, so much that the chances of war might rise spectacularly as the powers approached the zero-arms goal." He goes on to argue that this danger would arise from the possibility that each side might cheat in the agreed-upon disarmament process, or might believe or fear that the other side is cheating. "The temptations when one nation alone had the ability to devastate someone else's cities and the tensions caused by a fear that the other side might strike when it alone had such an ability would raise the risks of World War III far above what they are today."[14] The stability inherent in mutual vulnerability would be lost as the number of nuclear weapons on each side is reduced below the minimum needed to sustain that state, at which point the risk of war would become much greater. Quester suggests, however, that things might be better once we got there, once mutual disarmament had been completely achieved. In this view, nuclear deterrence exists in a trough of relative safety above a foundation of greater safety. Attempting to escape the trough would be dangerous, but once nations had escaped, greater safety would be achieved.

Kavka labels this line of reasoning the "Dangers of Transition Argument," and he responds that "the main dangers can be contained within acceptable limits if nuclear disarmament is carried out in the proper way."[15] There are certainly better and worse ways to manage the transition, and Kavka may be correct that if it were managed well, the risk of war could be kept in check. Moreover, if the danger of nuclear war existed only during the disarmament process, the danger might be tolerable, even if it were as great as Quester suggests, because it would last a relatively short time and lead to a long-term state of greater safety. Even if the trough were deep, it might be worth attempting to escape from. But this is where the second set of difficulties becomes relevant. According to Kavka: "The strongest argument that a nuclear-disarmed world would be undesirable is based on the idea that possession of nuclear weapons deters (or limits the extent of) conventional wars among great powers." Without the fear of nuclear weapons, "there would be more large-scale conventional conflicts and resultant human suffering."[16] His response to this, in part, is that because a conventional war would be much less catastrophic than a nuclear war, the increased risk is worth running.

But this misses the potential nuclear dimension of war in a world in which mutual nuclear disarmament had occurred. This concern is expressed by Robert McNamara:

In a 'nuclear-free world' a single nuclear weapon, the introduction of which would be impossible to detect, could alter the military balance. . . . Thus, we would have a strong incentive to secretly stockpile some nuclear bombs to protect ourselves against such a threat. The Soviets would harbor the same fears and would take the same kind of actions . . . The small nuclear arsenals that could emerge under this scenario would be tempting targets in a crisis. Each side would have a strong incentive to launch a strike against the opponent's nuclear force or suspected nuclear facilities. In other words, crisis stability would be extremely low, and any conflict could quickly become a nuclear one. . . . Unless we can develop technologies and procedures to ensure detection of any steps toward building a single nuclear bomb by any nation or terrorist group, an agreement for total nuclear disarmament will almost certainly degenerate into an unstable rearmament race.[17]

The potential for such instabilities confirms the claim that the risk of major nuclear war would remain even after multilateral nuclear disarmament.[18]

Weaponless deterrence

That nuclear war remains a risk even after multilateral nuclear disarmament is the basic truth underlying the clichés that nuclear weapons cannot be "disinvented" or that the nuclear genie cannot be put back into the bottle. The most important implication of the continuing risk of nuclear war is that the logical features structuring the military relationship under nuclear deterrence would continue to structure that relationship after nuclear disarmament. Nuclear threats would, in one sense at least, survive the mutual abandonment of nuclear weapons. Because the risk of nuclear war would continue to exist, a policy for managing that risk would still be needed. The risk of nuclear war in a world that had abandoned its nuclear weapons would result from the possibility of the weapons being rebuilt. So, in managing the risk, a nation would, as Jonathan Schell argues, seek to deter its opponent from rebuilding, and this would be achieved, at least in part, by the nation's having the capacity to follow suit and to rebuild its own nuclear weapons.[19] In the nation's capacity to rebuild its nuclear weapons would lie a threat, explicit or implicit, to rebuild them, and this threat, being a threat to make a nuclear threat, would itself be a nuclear threat of sorts. Because the weapons could be rebuilt, they would continue to cast their shadow over a world in which they had been eliminated. The logic of nuclear deterrence would remain in force. This is the most important respect in which conventional-2 deterrence differs from conventional-1 deterrence.

Schell, however, sees the shadow that nuclear weapons would cast over a world that had abandoned them as an advantage. He argues that "within the framework of [nuclear] deterrence itself it may be possible to abolish nuclear weapons," for an "abolition agreement would represent an extension of the doctrine of deterrence."[20] We could rid the world of nuclear weapons and base national security on a form of *weaponless deterrence*.[21] If the role of nuclear weapons is simply to deter, Schell suggests, their purpose could be served by their being potential instead of actual. Weaponless deterrence is nuclear deterrence without nuclear weapons.[22] It is the potential for catastrophic destruction that deters, and that potential can lie in potential weapons. The nuclear threat can be a threat to rebuild, and the threat can be mutual, because both sides can maintain rebuilding capabilities. Turning the standard argument against abolishing nuclear weapons on its head, Schell argues:

> It is often been said that the impossibility of uninventing nuclear weapons makes their abolition impossible. But under the agreement described here the opposite would be the case. The knowledge of how to rebuild the weapons is just the thing that would make abolition *possible*, because it would keep deterrence in force.[23]

Schell makes a virtue out of the feature of mutual nuclear disarmament that had seemed its chief vice. The risk of major nuclear war continues, but it is this very risk that would make mutual nuclear disarmament an effective policy. What makes nuclear deterrence work is what would make weaponless deterrence work.

Schell claims not only that nuclear deterrence would remain without the weapons, but also that it would be more effective. Weaponless deterrence is more effective than weaponful deterrence. In contrast with our earlier argument, he finds mutual abandonment of the weapons preferable to their retention. The issue is one of comparative stability. As Schell recognizes, the central logical feature of the military relationship that carries over when a world with nuclear weapons becomes one without is (in)stability.[24] Thomas Schelling and Morton Halperin observed a number of years ago: "Even with zero armaments, there is still a problem of deterring rearmament; and the stability of this deterrence may depend on much the same considerations that stabilized nuclear deterrence depends on in an armed world."[25] The role of stability in both situations, they suggest, shows that the goals of disarmament and arms control are not fundamentally different. Traditionally, these goals have been seen as opposed, that of arms control being not to eliminate the weapons, but merely to stabilize the nuclear balance.[26] But, at a deeper level, the goals of arms control and disarmament are the same – namely, greater stability. Each is concerned to lessen the likelihood of the catastrophic destruction of nuclear war. The fact that we cannot escape the risk of nuclear war shows that whether the policy prescription be to keep nuclear weapons or to get rid of them, it should be assessed in terms of the standard of stability. The question is whether retaining the weapons or abandoning them is more likely to bring about greater overall stability.

Weaponless deterrence is more effective, Schell claims, because it has greater stability. For this claim to be sustained, he must be able to meet objections, such as those raised by McNamara, that abandoning nuclear weapons would lead to greater instability. In Schell's view, the chief stability benefit of weaponless deterrence is that it greatly lengthens the "nuclear fuse," the lead time needed to wage nuclear war, the time that would transpire between the decision to wage a nuclear war and the commencement of the nuclear destruction.[27] He claims that "the modest increase in lead time – from about seven minutes to a month or six weeks – would mark a revolution in stability," and "given the everlastingness of the knowledge of how to build nuclear weapons, an increase in the lead time of one length or another is technically the best we can do." The chief virtue of a longer lead time is that it would allow for temporizing, for the drawing out in time of events that could lead to a nuclear war, and of the war itself, so as to allow a greater chance that decisions could be made to halt the process before it led to catastrophe. The result would be "a stability that we cannot even dream of in our present world of huge nuclear arsenals."[28] A longer lead time is, indeed, an important gain, but there is more to stability than the length of the nuclear fuse.

Weaponless and weaponful nuclear deterrence should be compared in terms of the three kinds of stability discussed in the last chapter. The advantage Schell claims for weaponless deterrence is an advantage primarily in accidental-war stability. The longer lead time would greatly reduce or eliminate the possibility of a runaway escalatory process. But how would weaponless deterrence fare in terms of crisis and noncrisis stability? The extent of crisis stability is the extent to which a deterrence policy can create a firm belief in the minds of the opponent that striking first could not be advantageous under any circumstances. In the case of weaponful deterrence, crisis stability is due to mutual vulnerability, and it is the absence of mutual vulnerability when each side has few or no nuclear weapons that leads McNamara and others to argue that the attempt to abandon nuclear weapons would lead to crisis instability. The concern is that in a crisis, such as an imminent or actual conventional war, the nations would rush to rebuild their nuclear weapons out of the belief that the first nation to have the weapons would be able to use them to great advantage and out of the fear that the opponent, sharing this belief, will be hurrying to rebuild its own weapons. Under weaponless deterrence, as Schell outlines it, this belief and fear would be mitigated by the inability of either side to destroy by a first strike the capacity of the other to rebuild its nuclear weapons, because the capacity would be dispersed and protected by defenses against nuclear attack.

But the degree of crisis stability, because it is based on the strength of each side's belief that a first strike would not be to its advantage, is a function of the strength of its perception that a first strike against its opponent would be met, whether sooner or later, by a devastating retaliation. This perception would inevitably be stronger when the nation has an existing assured destruction capability than when it has no nuclear arsenal. The reason is that the potential for retaliation lodged in a rebuilding capacity is more easily destroyed than the potential for retaliation lodged in existing weapons. First, it is inherently easier to reduce the vulnerability of existing weapons than to reduce the vulnerability of a rebuilding capacity, if only because the weapons are much smaller and more easily hidden than the large-scale industrial facilities that would constitute the rebuilding capacity. Second, the opponent would have more time to destroy the potential when it resides in a rebuilding capacity than when it resides in actual weapons. Under mutual vulnerability, the opponent would likely have time for only one attack before the retaliatory attack would be launched, but under weaponless deterrence it may have time for a number of attacks before the weapons could be rebuilt and a retaliatory strike could be launched. Thus, crisis stability is much stronger under weaponful deterrence.

Noncrisis stability, according to madvocates, is provided by existential deterrence. Speaking of weaponless deterrence, Schell says: "The deterrence theory in use, however, would be 'existential deterrence,' rather than any of the more theoretically elaborate kinds."[29] But existential deterrence is based on the opponent's fear that a serious challenge to the nation's interests could result in things getting out of hand and escalating to mutual destruction. But this fear would not be as strong in the case of weaponless deterrence, because of the long series of steps involved in the rebuilding process before retaliation could occur. Given the extra steps, the opponent is more likely to believe that the escalatory process initiated by its aggression could be arrested prior to its own destruction. This belief is less likely under mutual vulnerability, where the process from initial aggression to destruction could be very short. The weaker the fear of inevitable escalation, the weaker the existential deterrent. Thus, lengthening the nuclear fuse to the point of mutual nuclear disarmament and beyond, although it has an important advantage in terms of accidental-war stability, has serious disadvantages in terms of crisis and noncrisis stability.

The shadow cast by nuclear weapons

These arguments show how it is that the logic of nuclear deterrence would remain in force in a world disarmed of nuclear weapons. The logic remains in force because abandonment of the weapons is to be compared with their retention in terms of the same prudential criteria by which different strategies of nuclear deterrence are compared with each other – namely, criteria of stability. From a prudential perspective, nuclear disarmament is simply a different form of nuclear deterrence, a different deterrence strategy. Nuclear deterrence can be practiced with or without the weapons. As a result, the prudential case for abandoning nuclear weapons must be based not on an external criticism of nuclear deterrence, as earlier assumed, but rather on an internal criticism, a criticism of alternative, weaponful forms of nuclear deterrence. The shadow cast by nuclear weapons over a world disarmed of them internalizes all seemingly external prudential criticisms of nuclear deterrence. Thus the point made in the discussion of unilateralism applies also in the case of multilateralism. The choice between retaining and mutually abandoning nuclear weapons is, in prudential terms, a matter of showing whether or not retention has marginal deterrent value in comparison with abandonment, rather than a matter of showing whether or not retention has substantial marginal deterrent value in comparison. The abandonment of nuclear weapons – that is, a policy of conventional-2 deterrence – does not entail, as does a policy of conventional-1 deterrence, the absence of a significant possibility of major nuclear war. To say that no alternative available to us excludes the significant possibility of major nuclear war is to say that all prudential criticism of nuclear deterrence is internal criticism. Because no alternative excludes this possibility, we must prudentially judge all alternatives merely in terms of their marginal deterrent value in comparison with each other. The judgment seems to be that given the stability problems with multilateral nuclear disarmament, as with unilateral nuclear disarmament, it is retention of the weapons which is preferable.

Weaponless deterrence should, in fact, be regarded as a version of minimum deterrence, because each has the same (in)stability profile. Each purchases accidental-war stability at the cost of crisis and noncrisis instability. The difference is that weaponless deterrence seems to involve greater costs. The unilateral abandonment of nuclear weapons should also be seen as a form of minimum deterrence, because it likewise strengthens accidental-war stability at the expense of crisis and noncrisis stability.[30] In general, then, the choice between retaining nuclear weapons and abandoning them, whether the abandonment be unilateral or mutual, is a matter of judging whether the version of minimum deterrence that would result from abandonment is more advantageous in prudential terms than any other form of nuclear deterrence, whether it be a weaponful version of minimum deterrence or some version of counterforce or extended deterrence. The apparent conclusion is that it is not. Other forms of minimum deterrence are prudentially preferable to weaponless deterrence, just as more modest forms of counterforce deterrence may be prudentially preferable to ambitious counterforce.

What does this new appreciation of the nature of the policy choices nations face under mutual vulnerability imply about the resolution of the conflicts? Does the choice between retaining and abandoning nuclear weapons, now that it is understood as a choice among strategies of nuclear deterrence, generate the conflict between institutional morality and prudence and the conflict within morality? Does the resolution achieved by the prima facie argument at the abstract level, where the opposition is between nuclear and conventional-1 deterrence, carry over when the opposition is at the level of policy choice, between nuclear and conventional-2 deterrence? For prudential revisionism to provide a resolution at the level of policy, the prudential and consequentialist arguments for retaining the weapons must be shown to be unsound. These arguments now seem weaker than they had seemed in Chapters 1 and 2, because the alternatives they compare are now understood to be two different forms of nuclear deterrence, weaponful and weaponless deterrence. Any stability advantage weaponful nuclear deterrence enjoys is now seen as being purchased at the price of a stability disadvantage. But though these arguments appear weaker, they still do not appear unsound. Thus, at the level of policy choice, prudential and consequentialist considerations favor retention of the weapons, whereas deontological considerations favor their abandonment. The conflicts seem unresolved.

But a distinction may need to be drawn at this point between the two conflicts. The conflict within morality differs in an important respect from the conflict between morality and prudence. The moral dilemma does not hold unless the consequentialist stakes are very high. If the consequentialist argument favoring retention of nuclear weapons is weak, the moral conflict would be resolved in favor of the very strong deontological objection to their retention. Given that the consequentialist argument now seems weaker than it then did, there may be no dilemma after all. The weighing of consequentialist and deontological factors may lead straightforwardly to the overall moral judgment that nuclear weapons ought to be abandoned and weaponless deterrence practiced. Even though consequentialist considerations continue to favor retention over abandonment, the stability trade-offs involved in the choice of a nuclear strategy may lead to the conclusion that the overall consequentialist advantage of retention would not be great enough to constitute a dilemma. As a result, everyday moral reasoning may well come down on the side of abandoning the weapons.

But this reasoning does not apply to the conflict between morality and prudence, which would remain unresolved even if the stakes on the prudential side in favor of retention of the weapons were less than overwhelming. Any significant prudential advantage in choosing retention over abandonment would leave this conflict standing. There would still be a serious opposition between morality and prudence. The principle of tolerable divergence would still be violated. So even though the prudential argument for retention now seems weaker than it earlier did, this does not imply that the conflict between prudence and morality is resolved at the level of policy choice. The conflict between prudence and morality persists, even though the moral dilemma may not. In any case, our efforts at conflict resolution must continue.

Other obstacles may arise, however, when one seeks a resolution of either conflict at the level of policy. The recognition of the shadow that nuclear weapons would cast over a world that had abandoned them – that is, the recognition that abandonment of the weapons is itself a form of deterrence – weakens the prudential and consequentialist arguments in favor of their retention, and thus leads to the conclusion that the moral conflict, at least, may be resolvable in favor of abandonment. But this assumes that the shadow that nuclear weapons would cast over a world disarmed of them would have no effect on the arguments on the deontological side. This assumption is open to doubt and must now be examined.

EXTRICATION

There are two problems on the deontological side that must be considered. Each is a result of the shadow that nuclear weapons would cast over a world that had chosen to get rid of them. This shadow may have important implications for the deontological arguments, as it does for the prudential and consequentialist arguments. First, the shadow suggests the interesting possibility that *no* policy choice a nation with nuclear weapons could make would satisfy deontological considerations. As it is appropriate, from the prudential perspective, to regard the abandonment of nuclear weapons as itself a form of nuclear deterrence, perhaps it should be so regarded from the deontological perspective as well. If this were the case, then the deontological objections that apply to retention of the weapons would presumably also apply to their abandonment. If no policy could avoid the deontological objections, it would be impossible for prudential revisionism to provide a resolution of either conflict.

But, second, even if the deontological objections do not apply to a policy of abandonment, another problem from the deontological side stands in the way of an actual resolution of either conflict. The deontological demand for abandonment of the weapons is, presumably, a demand for immediate abandonment. But even if, contrary to the earlier arguments, prudential considerations favored abandonment, they surely would not favor immediate abandonment, for immediate abandonment, whether unilateral or multilateral, would generate stability problems that gradual abandonment would not. The shadow nuclear weapons cast has stability implications not just for the end state of abandonment, but also for the process of getting to that state. As a result, the period of time that would be needed to implement disarmament, in order that it be achieved in a way that would fully secure its prudential and consequentialist benefits, being nonimmediate, would inevitably doom the policy to deontological unacceptability. If these problems cannot be avoided, prudential revisionism cannot be a successful approach to conflict resolution, even if nuclear disarmament were the prudentially and consequentially preferred alternative. Both problems are problems of extricating ourselves from the deontologically unacceptable situation in which our possession of nuclear weapons has placed us.

Is abandonment morally acceptable?

The first extrication problem is that the shadow cast by nuclear weapons may make it impossible for any policy alternative, including the abandonment of nuclear weapons, to escape the deontological objections to nuclear deterrence arising from the intention to harm civilians and the holding of hostages which nuclear threats involve. The point is not the one from Chapter 2 that because there are consequentialist factors in serious conflict with the deontological demands, no alternative policy is morally acceptable overall. The point, more narrowly, is that our situation may be such that no policy alternative is morally acceptable in specifically deontological terms. As we have seen, nuclear threats would, in a sense, continue to exist after nuclear disarmament. The question is, would they continue to exist in a deontologically relevant sense? Would the deontological objections to nuclear threats backed up by existing nuclear weapons apply as well after nuclear disarmament to the nuclear threats backed up by the potential to rebuild the weapons? We have seen that the prudential and consequentialist logic of nuclear deterrence would carry over into a world disarmed of nuclear weapons. The question now is whether the deontological logic of nuclear deterrence would carry over as well. Schell suggests that it would when he remarks that "any proposal that relies on a threat to use [nuclear weapons], including the proposal for weaponless deterrence, raises an ethical question."[31] If the deontological logic carries over, then the abandonment of nuclear weapons may be as deontologically unacceptable as their retention.

One might seek to deny that the deontological logic carries over by arguing that once a nation had abandoned its nuclear weapons, it would be making no explicit threats of civilian destruction. But our earlier discussion has shown that the deontological issue does not turn on whether or not nuclear threats are explicit. If a moral defense of impure counterforce deterrence or of existential deterrence on the grounds that no explicit threats against civilians are involved is not allowed, neither can such grounds be used to defend the nuclear threats inherent in the rebuilding capacity. The formula adopted in Chapter 5 applies: "In deterring one threatens what one wants the other side to fear."[32] The capacity of a nation to rebuild its nuclear weapons subsequent to nuclear disarmament would pose a risk to the opponent's civilians who could be killed if the weapons were rebuilt and used. Because the opponent could also rebuild and use its nuclear weapons, the nation would need a policy for avoiding this eventuality. As a result, the nation would want its opponent to fear that the nation would rebuild and use its nuclear weapons in order that the opponent be deterred from rebuilding and using its own nuclear weapons. In this way, the nation would continue to threaten civilian destruction after the weapons had been abandoned. The nation would still be posing a risk to innocents to influence the behavior of third parties, and so would still be holding hostages. Thus it seems that a policy of nuclear disarmament would not allow a nation to escape the deontologically objectionable features of other strategies of nuclear deterrence.

If this argument is sound, prudential revisionism cannot possibly resolve the conflicts, because the abandonment of nuclear weapons would not avoid the deontological objection to their retention. If nuclear disarmament cannot avoid the deontological objections to possessing the weapons, then a determination that abandonment is preferable to retention in prudential and consequentialist terms would still leave the conflict between institutional morality and prudence and the conflict within morality unresolved. The only approach to resolution that could then work would be moral revisionism, which would be required by virtue of the principle that "ought implies can." For unless the moral requirements were altered, it would be impossible for nations, whether they retained or abandoned their nuclear weapons, to do what they ought in deontological terms. If nothing a nation can do can avoid its intending to harm civilians or holding them hostage, then these cannot be moral requirements. As with our earlier discussion of moral revisionism, the conclusion would be that nuclear weapons have created a world in which one of our basic moral obligations must be altered.[33]

On the contrary, however, there is good reason to think that a nation can, through abandoning its nuclear weapons, avoid the deontological objection to their possession. The shadow cast by nuclear weapons over a world that has abandoned them may not apply from the deontological perspective. There are two reasons. First, one must consider what is threatened in the two cases. What a nation armed with an assured destruction capability threatens is civilian destruction. But when a nation that has abandoned nuclear weapons seeks deterrence by threatening to rebuild them, the threat could be said to be a threat of civilian destruction only in an indirect sense. The threat is, more precisely, a threat to do something (rebuild its nuclear weapons) that would then allow it to threaten civilian destruction. A nation disarmed of nuclear weapons threatens nuclear destruction only in an elliptical sense: "Threatening nuclear destruction" is elliptical for "threatening to threaten nuclear destruction." *This* distinction between directly and indirectly threatening nuclear destruction is morally relevant.[34] To threaten to hold hostages is not to hold hostages, so to threaten to threaten nuclear destruction is not to run afoul of the proscription of hostage holding. What puts civilians at risk is the existence of the weapons, so to threaten rearmament is not directly to put civilians at risk, but only to threaten to do so. When a nation threatens to rebuild its nuclear weapons, it does seek to influence the behavior of the opponent's leaders, but it does not do so by putting civilians at risk, only by threatening to put them at risk. What it wants the other side to fear is that it would put itself in the position, through rebuilding its nuclear weapons, to threaten the other side's civilians.

The second reason that nuclear disarmament may allow a nation to avoid the deontological objections to retaining the weapons is that the nuclear threats the nation threatens to make by rebuilding its nuclear weapons, unlike its nuclear threats prior to disarmament, could be effective as pure counterforce threats. If nuclear weapons are rebuilt, they are likely to be rebuilt in the midst of a conventional war, or in a situation where a conventional war seems imminent, with the intention that their use be threatened on the battlefield to achieve military advantage. This is different from a threat of battlefield use of nuclear weapons in an existing situation of mutual vulnerability, because this threat, as we saw in Chapter 5, must, for the sake of credibility, be backed up by a threat of societal destruction, given that the opponent is making its own threat of societal destruction. If a nation sets out to rebuild its nuclear weapons, it may correctly believe that it will have nuclear weapons before its opponent does, in which case, because the opponent would be unable to threaten the nation's cities, the nation need not make threats against the opponent's cities in order to make credible its threats of use of the weapons on the battlefield. The general point is that while in a situation of mutual vulnerability, the threat of societal destruction is necessary to neutralize the opponent's threat to one's own society. Outside of mutual vulnerability such a threat may not be necessary.

Thus the shadow the logic of nuclear deterrence would continue to cast even after the weapons had been abandoned is not relevant to the deontological assessment. Abandoning the weapons would leave a nation inside the logic of nuclear deterrence from a prudential or consequentialist perspective but outside of it from a deontological perspective. As a result, abandonment would satisfy the constraints of the deontological perspective, and a resolution of both conflicts under prudential revisionism is at least possible, because abandonment may satisfy the prudential and consequentialist perspectives as well.[35] But before we can move beyond this mere possibility, we must examine the other deontological obstacle to resolution.

Must abandonment be immediate?

The second extrication problem is this. Whereas the deontological demand is apparently for immediate nuclear disarmament, prudential and consequentialist considerations, even assuming they favored nuclear disarmament, would presumably require that the disarmament be carried out over an extended period of time in order to minimize the risk of harmful consequences during the transition. If so, the conflicts would be unresolvable, not in the sense discussed earlier, in which one perspective calls for abandonment and the other for retention, but in the sense that one perspective calls for immediate abandonment and the other calls for nonimmediate abandonment. Not only would the conflict between morality and prudence be unresolvable, but it is likely that the conflict within morality would be as well. The reason is that the instabilities brought about by immediate abandonment might well be quite severe, so that the negative consequences that would follow this policy would likely be high enough to generate the dilemma, even though the negative consequences of a relatively gradual abandonment (assuming they are negative rather than positive) might not be high enough to generate the dilemma.

Is there any way of overcoming this obstacle to conflict resolution? Assuming that there would be a high level of negative consequences from the immediate abandonment of nuclear weapons, conflict resolution seems possible only if some deontological reason, in addition to the consequentialist reasons, could be found for delay. Tony Coady, discussing what he calls extrication morality, argues that there is such a reason. "Moral choice must often operate in situations already enmeshed in evil so that a primary moral concern is how best to reshape the situation and change its dynamics in conformity to a moral imperative rather than how to fulfill the moral imperative *simpliciter*."[36] The moral imperative is not to hold hostages, and fulfilling it *simpliciter* would require immediate nuclear disarmament. Reshaping the military situation and changing its dynamic in conformity with that imperative would, presumably, involve a relatively gradual abandonment of nuclear weapons. The question is whether a deontological case can be made for the latter alternative in the face of the apparent deontological demand for immediate disarmament.

Barrie Paskins suggests, as a moral analogue to the practice of nuclear deterrence in the realm of individual actions, the behavior of a person engaged in an immoral adulterous affair with someone who is suicidally dependent on that relationship. Paskins suggests that the morally correct thing for the person to do in this situation is not immediately to break off the relationship, despite the apparent deontological demand that it be ended immediately, but rather to break it off gradually, so as to minimize the chances that the partner will commit suicide. He argues, by analogy, that nuclear deterrence is also a relationship where immediate disengagement would not be morally correct.[37] Paskin's use of this example is criticized by John Finnis, Joseph Boyle, and Germain Grisez, who claim that his argument assumes "that evil may be done for the sake of good."[38] This criticism would be appropriate if Paskin's argument reduced simply to the claim that consequentialist considerations regarding the potential suicide should override deontological constraints. But there is more to the example than this, and it is this extra element that Coady seeks to bring out.

Coady suggests, first, that the issue is clearer when the problem is considered in terms of the immoral behavior of a large social organization, because this is the sort of behavior involved in the practice of nuclear deterrence. With this kind of case, the decision to end the immorality immediately is "replete with institutional ramifications that themselves have moral significance." But the point is not simply the consequentialist one that the effects of change in institutional behavior tend to be more far-reaching than the effects of change in individual behavior. An institutional example Coady suggests is that of slavery, where "the government's policy has brought about a situation in which slaves could not cope with immediate freedom."[39] A similar example is colonialism. Should a colonial power, upon realizing that its policies are in violation of the deontological prescription against interfering with the autonomy of another national group, immediately end its colonial rule, even in the light of the inability of that group, given the political dependence colonialism has fostered, to practice effective self-governance should the foreign rule end immediately? The negative impact of immediate freedom for the slaves or the subjected nation must be seen as being of deontological as well as of consequentialist import.

The question is how one should understand morally the negative institutional ramifications of the immediate termination of an immoral policy. Speaking of the negative consequences that would result from a man's immediate termination of the sort of adulterous affair discussed by Paskins, Coady argues:

> The consequences in question are plausibly viewed as at least partly *his* immoral acts, and so his previous behavior has put him in a position whereby, whatever he does, he will be acting immorally – at any rate, for a time. Here he should choose the course that will have him acting less badly, but this choice situation is clearly different

from the characteristic dilemma posed for [deontologists] by utilitarian and other critics, where the choice is between acting immorally or allowing great evils to flow from someone else's action for which one has no responsibility but that contrived by the choice situation itself.[40]

The crucial difference is whether or not the negative consequences that would flow from the immediate termination of the immoral behavior should be regarded as the actions of the agent of that behavior. Should those consequences be regarded as results that define actions of the agent? If not, if, for example, they would be more properly regarded as the actions of someone else for which the agent had only some causal responsibility, their occurrence would be of consequentialist concern alone. But if they are the actions of the agent of the immoral behavior, and if there are deontological constraints against such actions, there would be a genuine conflict of deontological duties, with the result that deontological considerations alone might overall favor gradual rather than immediate termination.

How should the negative effects of immediate, as opposed to nonimmediate, nuclear disarmament be viewed? The negative effects in question are the greater risk to civilians resulting from the increased instabilities that immediate abandonment would bring. Should putting civilians at this increased risk be regarded as an action of the nation that immediately disarms? Given that the nation, in part, created the technical apparatus that would be a necessary condition for the increased risk, and given that it created that apparatus in order to put civilians at risk for the sake of deterrence, the answer seems to be yes. The nation could not deny responsibility, in a deontologically relevant sense, for the negative consequences. Its hands would not be clean. This is just as it is in the slavery and colonialism cases. Because it is the nation's subjugation of its slaves or its colony that is responsible for their being unable to cope with immediate freedom, the negative effects of that inability to cope should the nation grant immediate freedom would be the nation's responsibility. The harm that would result would be rightly attributable to the nation as something it did, as something it perpetrated on the victims, not merely as something for which its actions were a causal antecedent. Indeed, we morally judge former slave holders and colonial powers not only in terms of the unacceptability of those practices, but also in terms of the extent to which they sought, through a gradual process of disengagement from the practices to correct, by preparing their subjects for self-governance, the damage they had done. The implication is that immediate nuclear disarmament, as a result of the instabilities it would involve, would run afoul of a deontological constraint against imposing risk upon innocent persons (as well as the consequentialist concern to minimize expected harm). As a result, the choice of whether or not to engage in immediate nuclear disarmament involves a conflict of deontological requirements, the best resolution of which might well be to choose to extend in time the disarmament process, assuming that this would, indeed, avoid the increased instabilities that would follow immediate disarmament. The nuclear disarmament deontologically required may be nonimmediate nuclear disarmament. As Coady is concerned to emphasize, however, this possibility creates a situation open to easy abuse, where nations could, contrary to deontological demands, retain their nuclear weapons indefinitely, rationalizing the practice on the grounds that they were engaging in a slow disarmament process. But the possibility of abuse does not nullify the fact that it may be nonimmediate rather than immediate abandonment that is deontologically required.

What the arguments in this section show is that it is not impossible that prudential revisionism can resolve the two conflicts as they are faced in practice by those in the nuclear age. It is not impossible, first, because the abandonment of nuclear weapons is acceptable (and required) from a deontological perspective, and second, because nonimmediate nuclear disarmament, which is presumably the form of nuclear disarmament required in prudential or consequentialist terms, may also be required from the deontological perspective. That the resolution of the conflicts is possible through prudential revisionism means that the resort to moral revisionism may be avoidable, but the question remains whether prudential revisionism provides actual resolution, in the face of the earlier argument that it does not.

DELEGITIMATION

This is where things stand. The success of the prima facie argument shows that prudential revisionism is an approach that allows a resolution of the two conflicts at the abstract level, but not directly at the level of policy choice. The question is, can prudential revisionism serve to resolve the conflicts when the choice is between retaining nuclear weapons and abandoning them? The last section shows that such a resolution is possible, but for it to be actual, a finding that nuclear deterrence can be more effectively practiced without the weapons is required. Although the prima facie argument is not sufficient for such a finding, it does have some relevance for it, because the necessity for stability trade-offs in the choice of a deterrence strategy shows that the prudential and consequentialist arguments from Chapters 1 and 2 are weaker than they had seemed. This may be sufficient to show that one of the conflicts, the moral dilemma, is resolvable, but not, as we have seen, to show that the conflict between prudence and morality is resolvable. The latter conflict is resolvable through prudential revisionism only if the prudential argument can be shown not merely to be weak, but to have a false conclusion, for only then would the abandonment of nuclear weapons be seen to be the prudentially preferable policy.

If the conflict within morality is resolvable in this way, this would actually exacerbate the conflict between morality and prudence, because it would generalize it. For then, prudence would be in conflict not only with institutional just-war morality, but also with the overall prescription of everyday moral reasoning. Both special and general moral considerations would prescribe the abandonment of nuclear weapons, whereas prudence would prescribe their retention. Given the failure of the prima facie argument to provide a basis for a resolution of this expanded conflict between morality and prudence, we would be at a loss for a way to resolve it, short of turning to moral revisionism.

A reversal of the conclusion that abandonment of the weapons is not prudentially preferable might be possible, however, if there were some factor of prudential relevance, as yet unconsidered, which would, when introduced, weigh strongly in favor of abandonment in the prudential calculus. Such a factor may be what I will call the *delegitimation* of nuclear weapons. If nations become deeply committed to the belief that nuclear weapons are illegitimate, this might remove the prudential disadvantage of abandonment, and thus make abandonment clearly prudentially preferable. Delegitimation is a member of a family of notions discussed by various writers in their attempt to find a solution to the problem posed by nuclear weapons. One of these notions is what Thomas Schelling calls "the tradition of nonuse," which is "a jointly recognized expectation that [nuclear weapons] may not be used in spite of declarations of readiness to use them, even in spite of tactical advantages in their use."[41] Another member of the family is the "nuclear taboo." The revulsion against the prospect of nuclear use, George Ball asserts, "has enveloped nuclear weapons in a rigid taboo." Ball continues: "Any nation that first broke that taboo by using H-bombs would suffer universal condemnation."[42] Adding another notion, Morton Halperin argues that nuclear weapons should be "stigmatized," which they would be once they were recognized to be not instruments for fighting wars, but mere "explosive devices."[43]

The point behind these various notions is that the use of nuclear weapons should be unthinkable. If the belief that nuclear weapons were illegitimate were so deeply held that it represented a habit or a disposition of mind by virtue of which their use would not be regarded as a real alternative, then their use would be unthinkable. The mere proclamation that the use of nuclear weapons is illegitimate is not sufficient. The mere intellectual assent to the claim that their use is morally unacceptable, when that assent in not grounded in such habits or dispositions, does not make their use unthinkable in the relevant sense. What is required is the instilling of habits of thought and action that would insure that they would not be used, because their use would not be seriously entertained. As Robert Jervis remarks: "The most effective restraints are those in which certain actions are literally unthinkable – statesmen do not consider taking the actions and do not get to the stage of calculating what they would gain by doing so. Instead, the thought never enters their minds."[44]

Writers on nuclear weapons have pointed out that other social practices and institutions once thought to be ineradicable have disappeared as a result of their having become unthinkable. John Mueller discusses how the practices of dueling and slavery passed from the historical scene as a result of the growth of a deep-seated belief that they were simply unacceptable. Potential duelers "do not avoid dueling today because they evaluate the option and reject it on cost-benefit grounds." Instead "the option never percolates into their consciousness as something that is available – that is, it has become subrationally unthinkable."[45] Dietrich Fischer adds to the list of discredited institutions the practice of cannibalism. Although we cannot disinvent nuclear weapons, he argues: "We have not disinvented cannibalism either. But we abhor the practice. Why can't we develop a similar feeling of abhorrence against the idea of incinerating whole nations with nuclear weapons?"[46] Such a feeling of abhorrence would be reflective of the habits or dispositions that would preclude the use of nuclear weapons by precluding their use ever being regarded as a real alternative. This would constitute their delegitimation.

The delegitimation of nuclear weapons will have occurred when there is an objective basis in shared habits of mind for the mutual expectation that nuclear weapons would not be used by one's opponent, even in a situation where their use might seem prudentially appropriate. The habits or dispositions in question would make the use of nuclear weapons unthinkable in that either the thought of using them would never occur, or, should it occur, the abhorrence at the thought would be such that the idea of using them would be immediately dismissed without reaching the point of being considered a real alternative. In either case, one would never calculate the advantages and disadvantages of their use. As a result, the expectation of nonuse based on the existence of these habits or dispositions would effectively eliminate the prudential advantages of retention of the weapons as factors relevant to the choice whether or not to abandon the weapons. The result would be that the prudential advantages of abandonment – in particular, the advantage in terms of accidental-war stability – would carry the day, and abandonment would become prudentially preferable. The conflict between morality and prudence at the level of policy choice would have been resolved through prudential revisionism. The question, of course, is whether nuclear weapons can be delegitimated. Is there is any policy a nation can adopt that would bring about or at least encourage their delegitimation? What, if anything, can policy do to help to create and to support the requisite habits of mind, given that the habits cannot be brought into being by a mere declaration that the use of the weapons is illegitimate or mere assent to such a claim?

Nondeliberative conformity

Habits of delegitimation are equivalent to the habits discussed in Chapters 3 and 4, under the topic of nondeliberative conformity. In the case of the law, habits of delegitimation are equivalent to habits of nondeliberative conformity in the sense that one purpose of the law is to delegitimate certain forms of activity – that is, to create habits by virtue of which such activity is unthinkable – and this purpose has been achieved when the law has created habits resulting in widespread nondeliberative conformity with the threats by which it proscribes that activity. In the case of nuclear weapons, the two kinds of habit are equivalent in the sense that both habits of delegitimation of nuclear weapons and habits of nondeliberative conformity with nuclear threats would make the use of nuclear weapons unthinkable. In Chapters 3 and 4, I argued that because a large proportion of legal conformity is nondeliberative, much of the success of legal deterrence must be explained in terms of the existence of habits resulting in nondeliberative conformity with the law, but that there is a much weaker basis for the existence of such habits in the case of military deterrence. As a result, nondeliberative conformity was not considered as a factor in the prima facie argument comparing nuclear and conventional deterrence. If, on the contrary, delegitimation of nuclear weapons is possible, this earlier omission of nondeliberative conformity from the argument was a mistake.

If habits of delegitimation are to play their appointed role in prudentially justifying the abandonment of nuclear weapons, however, they must be equivalent to habits of nondeliberative conformity with nuclear threats in a fuller sense. Because nuclear threats are meant to deter all major forms of aggression, not just nuclear aggression, habits of nondeliberative conformity with nuclear threats would make all major forms of aggression unthinkable. So far, habits of delegitimation of nuclear weapons have been characterized as making the use simply of nuclear weapons unthinkable. But if such habits are to play their appointed role, they too must make all major forms of aggression unthinkable. The reason is that a confrontation sparked by a lesser aggression could escalate out of control to nuclear war. The unthinkability of the use of nuclear weapons may insure only that they would not be deliberately or intentionally used. So the unthinkability of their use does not guarantee their nonuse, if lesser aggression can occur, because the use of nuclear weapons resulting from an escalation process begun by a lesser aggression would not necessarily be deliberate, or even intentional. If the habits do not guarantee the nonuse of nuclear weapons, they would not support an expectation of their nonuse, which is necessary for the prudential justifiability of their abandonment. Thus the habits of delegitimation, in the sense required for successful conflict resolution, must share with habits of nondeliberative conformity the characteristic of making all major forms of aggression between nuclear powers unthinkable.

This points to an important disanalogy between the delegitimation of nuclear weapons and the delegitimation of other social practices. The habits of mind needed to insure the nonoccurrence of cannibalism, for example, concern cannibalism alone. There is no other kind of action whose occurrence could lead through "escalation" to cannibalism. Eating other kinds of flesh does not lead one in an unthinking frenzy to consume human flesh. There is no blind escalatory path to cannibalism, as there is to nuclear war. Thus the requirements for the delegitimation of nuclear weapons are much stronger than they are for the delegitimation of other morally abhorrent social practices. If habits of delegitimation of nuclear weapons are to show the abandonment of nuclear weapons to be prudentially preferable, and thus resolve the conflicts, they must ground an expectation of the nonoccurrence of any major form of aggression between nuclear adversaries.

Given the earlier arguments against the prospects for nondeliberative conformity in the military arena, the prospects for achieving the required delegitimation of nuclear weapons may be remote. But should delegitimation nevertheless be possible, the prima facie argument may have to be revised, because it was developed in Chapter 4 on the assumption that habits of nondeliberative conformity are not an important factor in the comparison between nuclear and conventional deterrence. If the delegitimation of nuclear weapons were possible, nuclear threats, like legal threats, would be able to achieve a high level of nondeliberative conformity. If, in addition, the earlier conclusion that conventional deterrence (that is, conventional-1 deterrence) is unable to achieve a high level of nondeliberative conformity were to continue to hold, nuclear deterrence would have another important prudential advantage (in addition to reassurance and the crystal ball effect) in comparison with conventional deterrence. This might well be sufficient to defeat the prima facie argument against nuclear deterrence, because the advantage of a high level of nondeliberative conformity could be enough to show that nuclear deterrence has substantial marginal deterrent value in comparison with conventional deterrence. That it would be enough to show this is suggested by the great importance of the role of nondeliberative conformity in legal deterrence. Because this line of reasoning depends on the assumption that the delegitimation of conventional weapons is not also possible, it depends on there being something special about nuclear weapons in comparison with conventional weapons by virtue of which delegitimation is possible.[47]

But it is important to note the following. If the prima facie argument were in this way shown to be unsound, the policy prescription would be, in practical effect, the same as what it would be if the argument were sound. The policy prescription would be that nuclear weapons be abandoned. It is true that the defeat of the argument would imply that nuclear deterrence is prudentially preferable to conventional-1 deterrence, and thus should be practiced. But the implication would be, more precisely, that nuclear deterrence should be practiced in that form under which nuclear weapons would be delegitimated, because it is only when nuclear deterrence takes this form that the prima facie argument is defeated. This form is weaponless deterrence, nuclear deterrence without nuclear weapons. The success of the prima facie argument would recommend conventional-1 deterrence, whereas its failure would recommend conventional-2 deterrence. In either case, the recommendation is no nuclear weapons.

The reason that weaponless deterrence (or conventional-2 deterrence) is the form of nuclear deterrence under which nuclear weapons would be delegitimated is not that abandoning nuclear weapons would, by itself, bring about their delegitimation. Abandoning the weapons would no more bring into being the requisite habits than simply declaring the weapons to be illegitimate would. But the abandonment of the weapons would be what prudence would require if they had been delegitimated. If the intentional use of the weapons were precluded, as delegitimation promises, the only risk of use remaining would be accidental use. There would presumably still be some risk of accidental use, even if the habits of delegitimation, in precluding all acts of aggression, had eliminated the primary source of this risk. But, as argued earlier, the abandonment of the weapons insures the highest level of accidental-war stability. If the intentional use of nuclear weapons and other major forms of aggression could be precluded, there would no longer be a risk of nuclear war from crisis and noncrisis instability, and a nation should then, on prudential grounds, adopt the policy that maximized accidental-war stability. An analogy with handguns makes this point. Widespread nondeliberative conformity with legal threats makes personal disarmament possible, as widespread nondeliberative conformity with nuclear threats (that is, delegitimation) would make nuclear disarmament possible, because in each case the weapons are no longer needed for self-defense. Moreover, once a high level of nondeliberative conformity has been achieved, disarmament is prudentially preferable because the greatest risk that remains is of accidental use.

Is delegitimation possible?

The central question is whether or not nuclear weapons can be delegitimated. Given the discussion of nondeliberative conformity in earlier chapters, it seems as if the delegitimation of nuclear weapons is not achievable. Because military deterrence is a non-domestic institution, I argued earlier, it cannot foster a high level of nondeliberative conformity. It cannot sustain habits of nondeliberative conformity, because it does not support the perception that the threats are legitimate or that there is fairness in their application. Moreover, nuclear deterrence is worse off in this regard than conventional deterrence. If the delegitimation of nuclear weapons is possible, this must be in the face of the fact that nuclear deterrence lacks those features that allow legal deterrence to sustain habits of nondeliberative conformity. This possibility would require that there be something distinctive about nuclear weapons that somehow exempts them from the general argument that military deterrence cannot support a high level of nondeliberative conformity.

In any attempt to discover such a distinctive feature, it is important to keep in mind that a tradition of nonuse of nuclear weapons, which is what delegitimation requires, is different from the mere fact of nonuse. A tradition of nonuse does not exist merely because the weapons have not been used in war over an extended period of time. The fact that a person has not performed some action in a long time does not entail that his or her nonperformance of that action is a matter of habit, in the strong sense of habit relevant here – that is, in the sense that performance of that action is unthinkable. The fact that nuclear weapons have not been used for some time does not imply that their use is unthinkable. A tradition of nonuse, which would be based on a strong habit of nonuse, would involve, in addition to the fact of nonuse, a normative element strongly prescribing nonuse. The fact of nonuse could be a mere regularity, whereas a tradition of nonuse would involve a rule. What distinguishes a rule from a mere regularity is that a rule involves what H.L.A. Hart refers to as an "internal aspect," which is the critical attitude taken toward behavior in respect of the rule.[48] Thus, as George Ball suggests, the existence of a nuclear taboo would imply that any nation using nuclear weapons would "suffer universal condemnation." So to show that delegitimation is possible, one must show that the fact of nonuse could become a tradition of nonuse. One must show that habits of delegitimation could be inculcated. But the dynamics familiar from our discussion of the stability/instability paradox and noncrisis instability make it difficult to see how the transition from fact to tradition could occur.

The problem lies in the fact that the habits of delegitimation, if they are to ground an expectation of nonuse of nuclear weapons, must preclude all aggression between nuclear powers, not only nuclear use. The stronger the expectation that nuclear weapons will not be intentionally used, the apparently safer, so the less unthinkable, and so the more likely, lesser aggression becomes. The habits that would preclude intentional nuclear use seem to undermine the prospects for habits that would preclude lesser aggression. One manifestation of this problem especially relevant to the possibility of a transition from fact to tradition concerns time. The degree to which lesser aggression is unthinkable may be a direct function of the level of fear of the nuclear war to which it might lead, and the level of this fear is, in general, an inverse function of the length of time nuclear weapons have not been used. Speaking of the fear of nuclear war, Michael Mandelbaum asserts: "Insofar as that fear is a product of human memory it necessarily fades over time. The longer the nuclear system succeeds in maintaining equilibrium, the more precarious, in this sense, it will become."[49] Habits of delegitimation are desirable because their existence would preclude the use of nuclear weapons into the indefinite future, but the longer that nuclear weapons are in fact not used, the less likely those habits will be formed or maintained.

So to show that the delegitimation of nuclear weapons is possible, one must, first, point to some factor, peculiar to nuclear weapons, by virtue of which the general argument that military deterrence does little to sustain habits of nondeliberative conformity would not apply to nuclear deterrence. If any factor can successfully play this role, it is the crystal ball effect. The crystal ball effect is a factor that is both distinctive of nuclear weapons and tends to promote habits of delegitimation. When one can foresee clearly and unambiguously the total ruin, the societal destruction, that a large-scale nuclear war would involve, the prospect of using nuclear weapons, or of engaging in lesser aggression that could lead to this ruinous outcome, tends to become unthinkable. The tendency is for leaders not even to consider aggression, or to dismiss the thought, should it occur, without doing the prudential calculations. Aggression comes to be seen as abhorrent. The point is that the crystal ball effect can play a double role. First, it can guarantee that should leaders do the prudential calculations, the result would come up against aggression. This is the role of the crystal ball effect discussed in the earlier chapters. But, second, the crystal-ball effect tends also to instill habits of mind such that the leaders never get to the point of doing the prudential calculations. This is the role it would play in supporting the prospects for delegitimation.

But to succeed in showing that delegitimation is possible, one must show, second, that the crystal-ball effect is sufficient for the existence of the habits, especially in the light of the tendency of a long period of nonuse of nuclear weapons to undermine the creation and maintenance of the habits.[50] Though the crystal ball effect tends to promote habits of delegitimation, it is not clear that it is sufficient to insure their existence. The success of the crystal ball effect, both in insuring that prudential calculations come out for nonaggression and in instilling habits of mind that would insure nonaggression by guaranteeing that the option of aggression would never even enter the prudential calculus, depends on the sharpness of the apocalyptic vision. But the fact of the nonuse of nuclear weapons dulls the apocalyptic vision, the more so the longer the nonuse lasts, by making that vision seem less immediate, more remote. The tendency of the fact of nonuse to cloud the crystal ball is especially acute concerning the need for the habits of delegitimation to insure the nonoccurrence of lesser forms of aggression. When the action being considered is a nonnuclear form of aggression, apocalyptic prospects would seem even more remote when nuclear weapons have not been used for a long time.

POLICY

Short of a resort to moral revisionism, the resolution of the conflict between prudence and morality can be assured only if delegitimation is possible, because only if the delegitimation of nuclear weapons were achieved would their abandonment, which morality requires, be prudentially preferable. So the policy imperative is to pursue the delegitimation of nuclear weapons. But, first, this pursuit must be undertaken in the recognition that it is not guaranteed of success. Delegitimation may not be possible, in which case resolution of the conflict requires a status quo affirming resort to moral revisionism. Second, the pursuit of delegitimation must be indirect. The inculcation of the requisite habits cannot be achieved by fiat. The habits can, at best, be indirectly nurtured by actions and policies that foster their development and maintenance. The question, then, is how can delegitimation be indirectly pursued? This question has a two-fold answer. Delegitimation can be promoted through the actions of individuals and through the policy of governments. At the individual level, persons, singly and in groups, should seek constantly to bring to the attention of the public and its leaders the consequences of nuclear war, to keep everyone's attention focused on the full implications of the potential destruction. At the governmental level, the proper policy choice is a strategy of minimum deterrence. Consider first the individual level.

The prospects for the delegitimation of nuclear weapons depend on the clarity of the crystal ball – that is, on the keenness and the immediacy with which the horrors of nuclear war are present in the minds of those who make decisions about military matters. When the vision is sharp, the mental connection between a possible act of aggression, whether nuclear or nonnuclear, and the potential for societal destruction, is clear, and when that connection is clear, the aggression will likely be unthinkable. When each side believes that this connection is clear and strong for the other, it comes to expect nonaggression from the other, and this allows its own inclination against aggression to become habitual. The problem is that time clouds the crystal ball, and an expectation that nuclear weapons would not be used by the other side in response to nonnuclear aggression clouds it further, and this weakens the connection. To promote the habits, one must counteract this obscuration. One way to do this is constantly to remind people in general, and leaders in particular, of the horrors of nuclear war. Leaders must be continually scared straight. There must be an ongoing educational campaign to keep the potential destructiveness of nuclear war ever-present in their minds. Those engaged in this campaign should not be deterred by critics who claim that the danger of nuclear war is something everyone knows about already and that talking about it succeeds only in frightening people.[51] What will promote the habits is not the mere abstract knowledge of the potential for nuclear cataclysm, but the vivid impression of that potential cataclysm, the clear-as-crystal image, about which there is an appropriate element of fear. For its vividness, this impression or image psychologically depends on constant reminders.

The delegitimation of nuclear weapons depends more on such reminders than does delegitimation of other forms of behavior. We need not constantly be reminded of the moral horror of slavery or of cannibalism in order for these practices to remain unthinkable, though some reminders are probably necessary. The difference is, again, at least in part, a function of the need for the habits of delegitimation of nuclear weapons to preclude not only nuclear aggression, but nonnuclear aggression as well. For it is in regard to nonnuclear aggression that the crystal ball is most likely to become clouded. But because there is, in the case of cannibalism, for example, no other behavior that the habits of delegitimation need keep us from in order to guarantee cannibalism's nonoccurrence, its nonoccurrence can be assured without its moral horror constantly being held up to us.

Minimum deterrence again

The proper governmental policy choice is minimum deterrence. To see why this is the case, one must show, on the one hand, why the policy should not be one of the other two forms of weaponful deterrence and, on the other, why it should not be weaponless deterrence. Consider, first, why weaponless deterrence is not the correct choice. For prudential reasons, nuclear weapons should not be immediately abandoned, as the earlier discussion shows. Moving immediately to the zero level could create serious instabilities because of the suddenness of the policy shift. In addition, even when the instabilities due to the suddenness of abandonment are ignored, abandonment is a source of instabilities that make retention prudentially preferable, unless nuclear weapons have first been delegitimated. But the achievement of delegitimation takes time. Time is required for the habits of delegitimation to form and to strengthen to the extent necessary for their full inculcation. So, from the prudential perspective, if nuclear weapons are to be abandoned at all, this should not be done immediately nor prior to the time required for delegitimation to be achieved. Moreover, as the discussion of extrication has shown, nonimmediate abandonment may not be inconsistent with deontological requirements.

The reason that abandonment prior to the achievement of delegitimation would be imprudent is that without delegitimation, abandonment would sacrifice too much in the stability trade-off. Absent delegitimation, abandonment's advantage in accidental-war stability would come at too great a loss in terms of crisis and noncrisis stability. If the conflict between morality and prudence is to be resolved, abandonment must be prudentially as well as morally preferable, and this would be the case only if the inverse links among the different forms of stability, by virtue of which the choice of strategy involves a trade-off among them, could somehow be broken, so that abandonment's gain in stability would not come also with a more-than-counterbalancing loss of stability. It is delegitimation that could sever these links. Delegitimation would create a high level of crisis and noncrisis stability, so that the accidental-war stability flowing from a policy of abandonment would by itself be enough to show abandonment to be prudentially preferable.

Consider, now, why the policy should not be some other form of weaponful deterrence. Here, the main argument is moral rather than prudential. Minimum deterrence, when compared with counterforce and extended deterrence, is usually recommended on prudential grounds. But the argument of Chapter 7 indicates that prudential considerations are not sufficient to show minimum deterrence to be preferable. The fact of stability trade-offs shows that the prudential arguments for any one of these three strategies can achieve plausibility only through emphasizing the strategy's stability advantages while ignoring its stability disadvantages. Once the advantages and disadvantages are counted together, in the light of a recognition of our limited foresight, the arguments are inconclusive. There is insufficient prudential reason to prefer any one of these kinds of strategy over the others. Although some versions of these strategies, like the weaponless version of minimum deterrence, the ambitious version of counterforce, and the early-use version of extended deterrence, may be rejected on prudential grounds, prudence cannot decide among the three general kinds. Instead, the grounds for adopting minimum deterrence are primarily moral. The grounds are that the adoption of minimum deterrence is a move in the direction of the only policy that is ultimately morally acceptable – namely, abandonment. For one thing, adopting minimum deterrence is moving toward the state of nonpossession in a numerical sense. A nation's switching to a minimum deterrence strategy from a counterforce or extended deterrence strategy would involve a significant reduction in the number of its nuclear weapons.

But the moral justification for minimum deterrence cannot be based merely on the fact that it is a move in the numerical sense toward a state of nonpossession. The reduction in the number of weapons involved in adopting a strategy of minimum deterrence does not insure – and it need not even make more likely – that a further reduction to the zero level would later occur, any more than a motorist's switching from a large gas guzzler to a fuel-efficient compact need indicate that he or she will later abandon the automobile completely. In fact, many advocates of minimum deterrence do not foresee a subsequent move to abandonment, just as many advocates of arms control do not see arms control as part of a policy leading to complete nuclear disarmament. Many of those referred to in the last chapter as reluctant advocates believe that though a nation should greatly reduce the number of nuclear weapons, it cannot eliminate them. For example, Morton Halperin, who advocates a minimum deterrence posture, argues that even after the posture had been achieved, "problems of verification and third party participation would still make complete nuclear disarmament impossible."[52] It is not the mere fact of reductions in weapons numbers that would morally justify minimum deterrence, but rather the fact that one adopted the strategy as part of a policy of moving to zero. There need not be a guarantee that adopting the strategy would lead inevitably to abandonment, but it must be clear, beyond the simple fact of reduction in numbers, how adopting it would be a significant help in making abandonment possible. To have a moral justification for adopting minimum deterrence, a nation must adopt the strategy in the reasonable belief that doing so will help it to bring about conditions that would later allow it to abandon the weapons. Many advocates of minimum deterrence do not believe that adopting the strategy could lead to abandonment. Many others speak in vague terms about moving to zero sometime after adopting minimum deterrence, but without any clear idea, beyond the numerical idea, of how adopting minimum deterrence would help to make this possible.

A nation's adopting a minimum deterrence strategy can have a moral justification, only if it is part of a policy that could lead, in clearly understood ways, to the abandonment of the weapons. Adopting the strategy would lead to abandonment of the weapons only if it would foster the conditions under which abandonment would be prudentially preferable. As a result, adopting a minimum deterrence strategy has a moral justification only if it has what I call a *hypothetical prudential justification*. A hypothetical prudential justification for a policy is a justification that shows that the policy would help to create conditions that would later make some other policy prudentially preferable when it had not been prudentially preferable before. Minimum deterrence has such a justification, if its adoption would help to bring about conditions that would make the abandonment of nuclear weapons prudentially preferable. Its adoption would do this, if it fostered the delegitimation of nuclear weapons. Thus the strategy's fostering of delegitimation, not its reducing the number of weapons, is what would provide moral justification for adopting the strategy, because its being adopted to foster delegitimation would show that it is being adopted as a step toward complete disarmament.[53] But it remains to be shown that minimum deterrence would foster delegitimation.

Toward abandonment

Minimum deterrence would foster delegitimation because it would involve, in the words of Richard Ullman, "the denuclearization of international politics." Minimum deterrence seeks to limit the role of nuclear weapons in the relations between nuclear states, denuclearizing much of their interactions. As a result, the nonextended character of minimum deterrence amounts to a partial delegitimation of the weapons. Minimum deterrence delegitimates nuclear weapons in some areas, while leaving them legitimate in others. As we have seen, advocates of minimum deterrence hold that nuclear weapons should be "retained in national arsenals solely to deter their use by other nations."[54] Halperin argues that a minimum deterrence posture is like a policy of abandonment in that both presume that a nation "can defend its interests without nuclear weapons."[55] But this is misleading. Minimum deterrence assumes that the nation still needs nuclear weapons to defend its interests in not being subject to nuclear attack, whereas a policy of abandonment does not keep nuclear weapons on hand even for this purpose. Under minimum deterrence, the use of nuclear weapons is not unthinkable, but it is less thinkable than it is under extended or counterforce strategy, because there are, under minimum deterrence, fewer circumstances in which it is thought that they might be used. In limiting the circumstances in which the weapons might be used, minimum deterrence does incline a nation toward their nonuse and, if the opponent has such a policy, toward the expectation of the opponent's nonuse, thereby fostering the habits which, when fully developed, would constitute the delegitimation of the weapons.

Perhaps the best way to appreciate how minimum deterrence fosters habits of delegitimation is to consider the role played in the strategy by self-deterrence, the idea that nuclear weapons should deter their possessor as well as its opponent from using the weapons. Minimum deterrence places more emphasis on self-deterrence than does counterforce or extended deterrence, both of which are more concerned about the effects of self-deterrence on noncrisis stability. But to be self-deterred from using nuclear weapons is to be at least on one's way to acquiring a habit of nonuse. A habit of nonuse is simply a very high degree of self-deterrence. It is self-deterrence based on the unthinkability of the use of the weapons. The role of individuals in educating the public and leaders about the horrors of nuclear war may also be seen in terms of its contribution to self-deterrence of the use of nuclear weapons, which, in time, could develop into a habit of nonuse. But it must be kept in mind that delegitimation involves not only a habit of nonuse of nuclear weapons, but also a more general habit of nonaggression. A nation must be self-deterred from all major forms of aggression, not simply nuclear use.

As this discussion suggests, however, minimum deterrence can succeed in achieving delegitimation only if the adoption of that strategy is mutual. The habits of delegitimation can grow for each party only if it comes to expect nonuse from the other. The habits must grow together. But each side's coming to expect nonuse from the other is very unlikely unless the other has adopted a minimum deterrence strategy, given that minimum deterrence, through its emphasis on denuclearization, is the only one of the three kinds of strategy that implies a partial commitment to nonuse. This implies that the policy prescription, more precisely, is that the nation adopt a strategy of minimum deterrence in a way that would lead to the opponent's adopting such a strategy as well. The obvious way to do this is through negotiated mutual arms reductions. But, of course, this may not always be possible. The opponent may be completely intransigent in the face of all reasonable arms-control proposals. If so, the policy prescription is for the nation to adopt minimum deterrence on its own. First, there is no strong prudential argument against this, because one cannot successfully make the case that counterforce or extended deterrence is prudentially preferable to minimum deterrence. Second, a nation's unilateral adoption of minimum deterrence may, by example, succeed in getting the opponent to adopt such a strategy as well, because the nation's commitment to the partial denuclearization that minimum deterrence represents may well lead the opponent to recognize that a more aggressive nuclear posture is unnecessary. The unilateral adoption of minimum deterrence can thus lead indirectly to its mutual adoption. As a result, even in cases where a nation cannot succeed in inducing its opponent to join it in adopting minimum deterrence, the nation's adoption of this strategy would still have the hypothetical prudential justification discussed earlier. So the policy prescription is for the nation to adopt minimum deterrence, in consort with its opponent when this is possible, or unilaterally when this is not.

The policy prescription, then, is the same in content as that proposed by the reluctant madvocates, but on different grounds. Their justification for minimum deterrence is prudential, whereas the proper justification is moral. But this difference represents a more important divergence. Reluctant madvocates, many of them anyway, seem not to recognize that there may be conditions, which the adoption of minimum deterrence could help to bring about, under which the abandonment of nuclear weapons would be prudent. Their pessimism needs to be leavened with some optimism. The abandonment of nuclear weapons may be a prudent goal. Moreover, the delegitimation of nuclear weapons, which would make abandonment prudent, would put an effective end to the risk of war between the adversaries. So reluctant madvocates, and counterforce advocates as well, may be wrong in their view that nuclear weapons cannot put an end to war between great powers. With the proper policy choices, leading to delegitimation, two adversaries may be able effectively to end the risk of war between them. But enthusiastic madvocates are too optimistic. Nuclear weapons do not, by the very existence of mutual vulnerability, put an end to great-power war. To end the risk of war, what must be achieved is not mutual vulnerability, but delegitimation. In addition, even if delegitimation is achieved, this would end the risk of war only between two particular adversaries, not between other nuclear adversaries. The promise of delegitimation is limited to particular instances of the nuclear-deterrence relationship, its achievement in one instance not insuring its achievement in another. The conflicts nuclear weapons give rise to may be resolvable, and the risk of war put to an effective end, but only at particular points of time with particular adversaries, not once and for all. The struggle to eliminate the nuclear danger and to establish a policy that is acceptable on both moral and prudential grounds must be waged anew in each instance of the nuclear deterrence relationship. In this sense, even the possibility of the delegitimation of nuclear weapons holds out no promise that the nuclear danger will not be with us forever.

Notes

1. Robert Jervis, *The Illogic of American Nuclear Strategy* (Ithaca, NY: Cornell University Press, 1984), p. 170.

2. See Harold Feiveson, "Thinking about Nuclear Weapons," *Dissent* 29, no. 2 (Spring, 1982), p. 191, and Albert Wohlstetter, "Bishops, Statesmen, and Other Strategists on the Bombing of Innocents," *Commentary* 75, no. 6 (June, 1983), p. 22. Another way to see the nature of the increase is this. The burning of a carbon atom in a conventional explosive yields roughly 4 electron volts of energy, whereas the fissioning of a uranium nucleus in a nuclear weapon yields roughly 180 million electron volts. For the latter figure, see Samuel Glasstone and Philip J. Dolan, *The Effects of Nuclear Weapons,* third ed. (Washington: United States Department of Defense, 1977), p. 13. The former figure was supplied to me by Larry Campbell.

3. As of 1989. See "U.S., Soviet Nuclear Weapons Stockpile, 1945–1989: Megatonnage," *Bulletin of the Atomic Scientists* 45, no. 10 (December, 1989), p. 52. The total megatonnage used to be higher, although the total number of warheads has grown throughout the period. The U.S. megatonnage had fallen by three-quarters since 1960, and the Soviet megatonnage has fallen by a third since 1974. This decline is due largely to higher-yield gravity bombs having been replaced by lower-yield, more accurate missile warheads. See Morton Halperin, *Nuclear Fallacy* (Cambridge, MA: Ballinger, 1987), p. 69. Even if the United States and the successor states of the Soviet Union were to reduce substantially the size of their nuclear arsenals from 1989 levels, as they seem committed to doing, the destructive power of those arsenals would still be orders of magnitude greater than that of conventional arsenals.

4. In large cities in the United States in recent years, the ready availability of semi-automatic weapons has been, in part, responsible for a significant increase in street violence. If this relatively modest in-

crease in firepower has had such an effect, one can well imagine what the impact might be were the increase in available firepower to be of several orders of magnitude.

5. The prudential norms are largely rules of thumb adopted on the basis of experience about what works in the use of military force. Some will be general and obvious rules, such as the prescription to protect one's military forces against surprise attack, and some will be more specialized rules developed through the discipline of strategic thought. As an example of the latter, Paul Nitze asserts: "It is a copybook principle in strategy that, in actual war, advantage tends to go to the side in a better position to raise the stakes by expanding the scope, duration or destructive intensity of the conflict." (Nitze is quoted in Jervis, *The Illogic of American Nuclear Strategy*, p. 57.) Jervis argues that this principle does not apply in the nuclear age. One of the main purposes of my book is to determine whether the traditional moral and prudential norms concerning military activity have been made inapplicable by nuclear weapons. Chapter 6 will take up the issues relevant to determining whether Nitze's principle is any longer applicable.

6. As Plato argues in the *Republic*, those who practice the professions, in so far as they are practicing them, have not their own interest at heart, but the interests of the party served, and the party the military serves is the nation.

7. Harold Brown, *Thinking about National Security* (Boulder, CO: Westview, 1983), p. 4. Brown is formerly United States Secretary of Defense.

8. For a discussion of the ambiguous nature of the notion of national security and how it can be expanded at the expense of both prudential and moral concerns, see Arnold Wolfers, "National Security as an Ambiguous Symbol," in his *Discord and Collaboration* (Baltimore: The Johns Hopkins Press, 1962), and Chapter 8 of Bernard Brodie, *War and Politics* (New York: Macmillan, 1973).

9. Whether military actions in defense of national interests are defensive in a morally relevant sense depends on the moral status of the interests in question. If the interests are morally questionable, so in general would the military defense of those interests be, and such defense would often more appropriately be characterized morally as aggression. I understand paradigmatically defensive military measures to be measures in defense of interests that are not morally questionable, and thus seek to avoid questions about the justifiability of measures in defense of, for example, an unjust regime.

10. When speaking of defensive wars or justifiable wars, one is, of course, distinguishing among wars in a more fine-grained way than is normal in other contexts. One is speaking of wars as fought by one side or

the other, rather than of wars as involving all of the belligerents, such that, for example, the Second World War was not one war but a set of at least two contemporaneous wars. Morally acceptable or unacceptable wars are individuated by belligerents or by alliances of belligerents.

11. In asking whether the defensive use of nuclear force is *justifiable*, rather than asking whether it is *justified*, I mean to indicate that the question is one of whether an adequate or successful justification could be given by us, not whether such a justification exists in the abstract. One might understand the question whether the use of nuclear force has justification as the question whether an adequate justification for it exists in the abstract, independent of human determination. But because of the major role of epistemic factors in questions about the justification of the use of nuclear force, there may be an important difference between whether an adequate justification exists in the abstract and whether we are able to offer one. Justificatory questions about nuclear weapons turn on predictions about the outcomes of actions or policies, predictions that are largely beyond our capacity to make with a high level of accuracy. Thus I ask whether the use of nuclear force is justifiable, meaning justifiable by us. This distinction has the most relevance when nuclear weapons are considered from a consequentialist moral perspective, which they are in the next and succeeding chapters.

12. In this vein, Kant distinguishes between a narrow sense of prudence, which concerns one's effectiveness in the pursuit of one's particular purposes, and a broad sense of prudence, which is "the ability to unite all [one's] purposes to [one's] own lasting advantage." *Foundations of the Metaphysics of Morals,* trans. Lewis White Beck (Indianapolis: Bobbs-Merrill, 1959), p. 33. Joseph Allen makes the point that military strategy is only a part of what he calls national strategy, in "The Relation of Strategy and Morality," *Ethics* 73, no. 3 (April, 1963), p. 168.

13. I agree with Henry Shue in preferring the term "mutual vulnerability" to "mutual assured destruction" on the grounds that the latter term "builds the failure of the policy into its name as if failure were its goal." Shue continues: "The policy is mutual *vulnerability,* which is, rightly or wrongly, intended to deter destruction." Henry Shue, "Having it Both Ways: the Gradual Wrong Turn in American Strategy," in Shue (ed.), *Nuclear Deterrence and Moral Restraint* (Cambridge: Cambridge University Press, 1989), p. 46n4.

14. Wolfgang Panofsky, "The Mutual-Hostage Relationship between America and Russia," *Foreign Affairs* 52, no. 1 (October, 1973), p. 110.

15. Robert McNamara, as quoted in McGeorge Bundy, *Danger and Survival* (New York: Random House, 1988), p. 546. This quotation is

337

from a speech given by McNamara in 1963 when he was the United States Secretary of Defense.

16. Spurgeon Keeney, Jr. and Wolfgang Panofsky, "MAD Versus NUTS," *Foreign Affairs* 60, no. 2 (Winter, 1981–82), pp. 303–4. The prospects for ballistic missile defense under the Strategic Defense Initiative have not altered this assessment. Among the many places this is argued is Union of Concerned Scientists, *The Fallacy of Star Wars* (New York: Random House, 1984), Chapter 7. The basic problem nuclear weapons pose for any attempt to achieve a successful defense is well described in the Keeney and Panofsky article on p. 298.

17. Robert McNamara, *The Essence of Security* (New York: Harper and Row, 1968), p. 53. This quotation is from a 1967 speech of McNamara's when he was United States Secretary of Defense.

18. Walter Slocombe, "Preplanned Operations," in Ashton Carter et al. (eds.), *Managing Nuclear Operations* (Washington: The Brookings Institution, 1987), p. 139.

19. Brown, *Thinking about National Security*, pp. 49–50.

20. The first writer to interject the claim that nuclear war is survivable prominently into the public debate was Herman Kahn in *On Thermonuclear War* (Princeton, NJ: Princeton University Press, 1960).

21. The phrase "large-scale nuclear war" may seen like a pleonasm, but "large-scale" should be understood as relative not to possible wars, but to possible nuclear wars – that is, it should be understood in terms of the portions of the nuclear arsenals that are used. The claim that a large-scale nuclear war would lead to societal destruction does not imply that a nuclear war that was less than large-scale (a limited nuclear war) would necessarily lead to societal destruction.

22. James Child, *Nuclear War: The Moral Dimension* (New Brunswick, NJ: Transaction Books, 1986), p. 36.

23. Brown, *Thinking about National Security*, p. 49.

24. Gregory Kavka, "Nuclear Deterrence: Some Moral Perplexities," in Douglas MacLean (ed.), *The Security Gamble* (Totowa, NJ: Rowman and Allenheld, 1984), p. 128.

25. See Thomas Schelling, *Arms and Influence* (New Haven, CT: Yale University Press, 1966), Chapter 1.

26. Brodie, *War and Politics*, p. 379.

27. For a discussion of this difference, see Leon Sigal, *Nuclear Forces in Europe* (Washington: The Brookings Institution, 1984), p. 17. Sigal suggests those who judge advantage in relative rather than absolute terms might not regard the destruction of a nuclear war as unacceptable. But this is, I believe, incorrect, as I argue later. For another discussion of relative advantage in the context of nuclear war, see Robert Jervis, *The Meaning of the Nuclear Revolution* (Ithaca, NY: Cornell University Press, 1989), pp. 16–19.

28. Office of Technology Assessment, *Strategic Defenses* (Princeton: Princeton University Press, 1986 reprint), p. 67.

29. The claim that it makes sense to talk of winning even a large-scale nuclear war is often based on the view that prudential advantage should be judged in relative rather than absolute terms. (Critics who claim that the idea of winning a nuclear war makes no sense are often implicitly criticizing such a view.) A variant on this view is the claim that the winner in a nuclear war would be the side that would recover faster from the effects of nuclear war. But both the view and its variant assume the nation would continue, which the condition of mutual vulnerability shows would not be the case.

30. In Sidney Hook et al., "Western Values and Total War," *Commentary* 32, no. 4 (October, 1961), p. 278.

31. Anthony Kenny, " 'Better Dead than Red'," in Nigel Blake and Kay Pole (eds.), *Objections to Nuclear Defense* (London: Routledge & Kegan Paul, 1984), p. 21. John Finnis, Joseph Boyle, and Germain Grisez seem to deny this claim, for they argue that there is no way to judge in terms of consequences whether or not nuclear devastation is worse than Soviet domination. *Nuclear Deterrence, Morality and Realism* (Oxford: Clarendon Press, 1987), pp. 240–42. One can imagine circumstances in which a large-scale nuclear war would represent a lesser prudential disadvantage for the citizens of a nation taken individually. This would be the case, for example, if the alternative were for each of the nation's citizens to be rounded up and subject to an extended period of brutal torture. But such circumstances are fantasy and so can be ignored.

32. On the misleadingness of this notion, see Lawrence Freedman, *The Evolution of Nuclear Strategy* (New York: St. Martin's, 1981), p. 247.

33. Given that it is *imaginable* that a nuclear war could involve acceptable damage – for example, if the alternative to the war were for all the citizens of the nation to undergo prolonged torture – the necessity involved here should be seen as practical rather than conceptual.

34. Michael Mandelbaum, *The Nuclear Revolution* (Cambridge: Cambridge University Press, 1981), p. 4. See also Hans Morganthau, "The Fallacy of Thinking Conventionally about Nuclear Weapons," in David Carlton and Carlo Schaerf (eds.), *Arms Control and Technological Innovation* (London: Croom Helm, 1977), pp. 255–264, and Richard Wasserstrom, "War, Nuclear War, and Nuclear Deterrence," in Russell Hardin et al. (eds), *Nuclear Deterrence: Ethics and Strategy* (Chicago: University of Chicago Press, 1985), pp. 15–35, esp. p. 20.

35. Hans Morganthau, "The Four Paradoxes of Nuclear Strategy," *The American Political Science Review* 58, no. 1 (March, 1964), p. 25.

36. The notion of limited nuclear war, discussed in the next several paragraphs, is taken up again more extensively in Chapters 5 and 6.

Although what is considered here is the implication of this notion for the justifiability of nuclear war, what is considered in those chapters (and briefly later in this chapter) is the implication of this notion for the justifiability of nuclear deterrence. These considerations are, of course, related.

37. Bernard Brodie, *Strategy in the Missile Age* (Princeton: Princeton University Press, 1959), p. 309.
38. Brodie, *Strategy in the Missile Age*, p. 311.
39. Jervis, *The Illogic of American Nuclear Strategy*, p. 12.
40. For a discussion of Clausewitz's notion of friction, see his *On War*, Book 1, Chapter 7.
41. For a discussion of the role of these and related factors in nuclear war, see Paul Bracken, *The Command and Control of Nuclear Forces* (New Haven, CT: Yale University Press, 1983).
42. Richard Bauckham, "Facing the Future: The Challenge to Secular and Theological Presuppositions," in Richard Bauckham and John Elford (eds.), *The Nuclear Weapons Debate: Theological and Ethical Issues* (London: SCM Press, 1989), p. 35.
43. These kinds of factors are discussed by Hans Morganthau in "Four Paradoxes," pp. 26–27. For a discussion of nuclear war as a bargaining process, see Schelling, *Arms and Influence*, pp. 131–41.
44. William Daugherty, Barbara Levi, and Frank von Hippel, "The Consequences of 'Limited' Nuclear Attacks on the United States," *International Security* 10, no. 4 (Spring, 1986), p. 42. See also Desmond Ball, *Can Nuclear War Be Controlled?*, Adelphi Paper no. 169 (London: International Institute for Strategic Studies, 1981), pp. 26–30.
45. See, Keeney and Panofsky, "MAD Versus NUTS," p. 293.
46. Jervis, *The Illogic of American Nuclear Strategy*, p. 168. Jervis's concern in this passage is not just the risk of total destruction from a limited nuclear war, but also the risk of total destruction from a confrontation short of war that could lead to large-scale nuclear war.
47. Nuclear retaliation in response to a nuclear attack would be defensive only in the sense that it would be a response to aggression. It is not defensive in the fuller sense because, given mutual vulnerability, it cannot succeed in defending the nation. Nor, as we shall see, is it defensive in a morally relevant sense.
48. The assumption that the opponent's nuclear aggression would involve a limited attack is a safe one. It is very difficult to imagine that an opponent in a condition of mutual vulnerability would begin a nuclear war by firing its weapons at the nation's cities, thereby destroying the nation's society, in large part because it would then have nothing left to threaten the nation with. The nation would then have little reason not to launch an all-out retaliation, destroying the opponent's society in turn.

49. For a discussion of the morality of nuclear war from a just-war perspective, see Anthony Kenny, *The Logic of Deterrence* (Chicago: University of Chicago Press, 1985), pp. 8–36.

50. Kenny, *The Logic of Deterrence*, p. 10. For a valuable discussion of the notion of innocence in war, see the exchange among George Mavrodes, Robert Fullinwider, and Lawrence Alexander in Charles Beitz et al. (eds.), *International Ethics* (Princeton: Princeton University Press, 1985), pp. 75–105.

51. Some of those who would normally be regarded as civilians, such as munitions workers, are not regarded as innocent in the just-war tradition. But there is little need to consider the fine points of the debate over who is or is not innocent, because a large-scale nuclear war would kill an unacceptable number of those who would be regarded as innocent on any account, such as children. So an unrefined use of the term "civilian" should suffice.

52. This point is made, in part, by James Turner Johnson, *Can Modern War Be Just?* (New Haven, CT: Yale University Press, 1984), p. 116.

53. This shows why it is no more appropriate from the moral perspective to call a nuclear conflict a war than it is to speak of it so from the prudential perspective. War is understood to be something that, when fought for defensive purposes, is generally morally, as well as prudentially, justifiable.

54. The two moral norms are on a different footing concerning the argument in this paragraph. In the just-war tradition, the harm that is understood to count in applying the principle of proportionality is the harm that is merely foreseen, whereas the principle of discrimination applies only when attacks on civilians are intended, not merely foreseen. Thus it is odd to say that foreseeing that one will later be drawn into a situation in which one will intend to attack civilians is itself a violation of the principle of discrimination. What is needed to make the argument work is a reconstruction of the principle of discrimination under which it prohibits risking later doing some action intentionally harmful to civilians. Such a reconstruction is offered by Jefferson McMahan, "Deterrence and Deontology," in Hardin et al., *Nuclear Deterrence*, pp. 141–160. In the next chapter, however, I offer some objections to McMahan's analysis.

55. For a discussion of the domestic analogy in the nuclear context, see Thomas Donaldson, "Nuclear Deterrence and Self-Defense," in Hardin et al., *Nuclear Deterrence*, pp. 161–72. See also Gregory Kavka, *Moral Paradoxes of Nuclear Deterrence* (Cambridge: Cambridge University Press, 1987), pp. 84–92. Kavka argues, in effect, that the argument that the domestic analogy fails to hold in the case of nuclear weapons is based on too expansive a sense of innocence (or civilian-

hood). I take issue with these claims of Kavka's about the nature of innocence in the next chapter.

56. Schelling, *Arms and Influence*, p. 16.
57. Another way to run the argument is to claim that the institutional goals themselves contain a moral dimension, so that prudence and morality must function together in the pursuit of these goals. This is suggested by Joseph Allen, who argues that morality and strategy must be involved together in pursuit of the goal (to use the words of Liddell Hart) of "a better state of peace." "The Relation of Strategy and Morality," p. 168.
58. Jervis, *The Meaning of the Nuclear Revolution*, p. 112.
59. Bernard Brodie, "Implications for Military Policy," in Bernard Brodie (ed.), *The Absolute Weapon: Atomic Power and World Order* (New York: Harcourt Brace, 1946), p. 76.
60. Russell Hardin, "Deterrence and Moral Theory," in Kenneth Kipnis and Diana T. Meyers (eds.), *Political Realism and International Morality* (Boulder, CO: Westview, 1987), p. 53.
61. Patrick Morgan, *Deterrence: A Conceptual Analysis*, 2nd ed. (Beverly Hills, CA: Sage, 1983), p. 33. The classic discussion of compellence is in Schelling, *Arms and Influence*, pp. 69–91.
62. The distinction between deterrence and compellence cannot, however, be captured with complete accuracy in terms of the distinction between inducing refraining and inducing action. For a good discussion of this (though using different terminology), see Jefferson McMahan, "Nuclear Blackmail," in Nigel Blake and Kay Pole (eds.), *Dangers of Deterrence* (London: Routledge & Kegan Paul, 1983), pp. 84–111.
63. Compellence will come up again in the discussion of doctrines of nuclear coercion in Chapter 6.
64. Such a prudential argument for nuclear deterrence should be distinguished from a moral argument that, unlike the institutional moral norms, is based exclusively on an evaluation of a policy's consequences. The consequentialist moral argument for nuclear deterrence will be discussed in Chapter 2.
65. National Conference of Catholic Bishops, *The Challenge of Peace: God's Promise and Our Response* (Washington: United States Catholic Conference, 1983).
66. President Reagan's speech is reprinted in the *New York Times* of March 24, 1983, p. A20. George Quester suggests that Reagan's proposal "may simply have been a political move intended to undercut the kind of moral objections to nuclear deterrence exemplified in the U.S. Roman Catholic Bishops' Statement." *The Future of Nuclear Deterrence* (Lexington, MA: Lexington Books, 1986), p. 138. But Reagan shared the basic moral objections of the bishops. What he strongly opposed

and sought to undercut politically was their prescribed remedy. He proposed moving away from nuclear deterrence not by reducing U.S. military efforts, but by increasing them.

67. Robert W. Tucker speaks of there having been in the early 1980s a "lapse of faith" in nuclear deterrence, and he discusses what he sees as both the moral and strategic (what I would call prudential) dimensions of this lapse. See his *The Nuclear Debate* (New York: Holmes and Meier, 1985). The moral dimension of this lapse is what is spoken of here as the common moral concern about nuclear deterrence. On the other hand, the strategic or prudential dimension of the lapse was largely restricted to a group of strategic thinkers and was not widely shared by the public. The strategic concerns of these thinkers will be discussed in Chapter 6.

68. Quester, *The Future of Nuclear Deterrence*, pp. 108, 109.

69. This interpretation of the bishops' letter would be an *ad hominem* criticism, if it were based on the view that the letter were a political document and were seeking their political motivations, seeing their position as a rationalization of a concern not to reach a moral conclusion at odds with the prudential view about nuclear deterrence common both inside and outside of the Church. But problems with their argument invite such a criticism. For a discussion of these problems, see Susan Moller Okin, "Taking the Bishops Seriously," *World Politics* 36, no. 4 (Summer, 1984), pp. 527–54.

70. For a discussion of realism, see Robert Holmes, *On War and Morality* (Princeton: Princeton University Press, 1989), Chapters 2 and 3.

71. Brodie, *Strategy in the Missile Age*, p. 271.

72. Jervis, *The Illogic of American Nuclear Strategy*, p. 26.

73. Jonathan Schell, *The Fate of the Earth* (New York: Avon Books, 1982), p. 202. Out of the answer to these questions, Schell goes on to explore one of the most important prudential criticisms of nuclear deterrence, that its threats are not credible. This criticism will be considered later in the book, especially in Chapters 4, 6, and 7.

74. This difference is discussed in Glenn Snyder, *Deterrence and Defense* (Princeton: Princeton University Press, 1961), pp. 41–51. See also Mandelbaum, *The Nuclear Revolution*, Chapter 3.

75. Schelling, *Arms and Influence*, p. 23. Schelling suggests that this is "the difference nuclear weapons make." The point of this chapter is that this difference implies another difference regarding our understanding of the relation between nuclear prudence and morality.

76. This distinction is offered by Snyder, *Deterrence and Defense*, pp. 14–16.

77. Punishment (and retaliation) become relevant concepts in virtue of the impossibility of defense. If a nation's military countermeasures cannot blunt the attack or avoid the opponent's infliction of harm,

they are naturally categorized as a form of punishment. But precisely because these countermeasures are not directed at blunting the attack, their victims are innocent. In this important respect it is incorrect to refer to societal damage as punishment, because administered harm is punishment only when the victim deserves or is believed to deserve the harm. The civilians who would suffer from a nation's nuclear attacks neither deserve nor are believed to deserve that suffering.

78. George Quester, "The Necessary Moral Hypocrisy of the Slide into Mutual Assured Destruction," in Shue, *Nuclear Deterrence and Moral Restraint*, p. 232.

79. As Jervis points out: "Unless the Soviets emerged from a war with their social fabric intact, they could not enjoy the fruits of victory." *The Illogic of American Nuclear Strategy*, p. 78. The traditional way in which civilian damage was thought to contribute to denial is through undermining morale, lessening the will to fight. (The principle of tolerable divergence implies, however, that its contribution to this end may not have been significant.) But, in practice, the only way in which civilian damage through nuclear attack would contribute to denial is by virtue of societal destruction making gain impossible. A nuclear war would in all likelihood be too short for civilian morale to have any influence on its course.

80. There is a serious prudential problem with nuclear deterrence – namely, the credibility of nuclear threats, which will be discussed extensively in later chapters. But it is a problem that has become a serious consideration only with the advent of mutual vulnerability. Hence it was not a major factor in traditional judgments of military effectiveness. Will to fight was seen to follow military capability in a generally unproblematic way.

81. This has been labeled by Kavka the "Wrongful Intentions Principle," in *Moral Paradoxes of Nuclear Deterrence*, p. 19. It seems to be held in some form by most of those arguing out of the just-war tradition, for example, by the Catholic bishops (*The Challenge of Peace*, para. 178). It is discussed by Finnis, Boyle, and Grisez, in *Nuclear Deterrence, Morality and Realism*, pp. 77–86.

82. For helpful discussions of the question whether nuclear threats could be bluffs, see Finnis, Boyle, and Grisez, *Nuclear Deterrence, Morality and Realism*, pp. 113–124, and Michael Dummett, "The Morality of Deterrence," in David Copp (ed.), *Nuclear Weapons, Deterrence, and Disarmament* (Calgary, Alberta: The University of Calgary Press, 1986), p. 121.

83. The question whether such a deterrence policy could be an effective alternative to a policy of assured destruction is discussed in Chapter 5.

84. Jonathan Schell, *The Abolition* (New York: Avon Books, 1984), p. 98.

85. Quester, "The Necessary Moral Hypocrisy of the Slide into Mutual Assured Destruction."

2. THE MORAL PROBLEM

1. The perspective of everyday moral reasoning is not being presented as a moral theory, but simply as a representation of the way in which most people reason about moral matters most of the time. When confronted by situations demanding moral choice, people have moral intuitions of different kinds – in particular, deontological and consequentialist intuitions – and recognize the need, when they conflict, to weigh them against each other in their moral deliberations. Although this perspective is not a moral theory, it is something that a moral theory should explain. At the level of theory, of course, one is free to attempt to reduce all moral considerations to one approach, be it consequentialist, deontological, or some other, or to recognize pluralism as fundamental. (Although there are other kinds of moral intuitions, representing other moral approaches, that are part of everyday moral reasoning, I will focus on the consequentialist and deontological approaches as the two most important.)

2. I use the term "consequentialist" rather than the more familiar "utilitarian" to emphasize that the approach focuses on the consequences. One feature of everyday moral reasoning is that people often are partial to those near and dear to them, which may seem contrary to the impartiality of the consequentialist approach. But the partiality of everyday moral reasoning does not show that such reasoning does not encompass an impartial consequentialist approach, because the partiality may be due to deontological considerations. Indeed, this is a plausible view, because people are seen as having special moral duties to those close to them.

3. The weighing is, of course, more complicated than this, not only because the pluralism of everyday moral reasoning encompasses more than two moral approaches, but also because there may be conflicts within the two approaches. For example, there may be conflicts of duties within the deontological approach or conflicts over what the measure of consequentialist value should be.

4. The just-war tradition is not unitary, and there may be some working in this tradition who would recognize an appeal to consequences as an independent moral consideration that could override deontological considerations. But this is not how the tradition is normally understood.

5. For an indication of the limited role a consideration of consequences plays in a just-war approach, see John Finnis, Joseph M. Boyle, Jr.,

and Germain Grisez, *Nuclear Deterrence, Morality and Realism* (Oxford: Clarendon Press, 1987), p. 239.

6. This point is suggested by Russell Hardin, "Deterrence and Moral Theory," in Kenneth Kipnis and Diana T. Meyers (eds.), *Political Realism and International Morality* (Boulder, CO: Westview, 1987), pp. 35–6. This objection does not beg the question against the just-war tradition by simply assuming that a moral perspective that does not give independent consideration to the consequences is inadequate, for the point is that the overwhelming magnitude of what is at stake in terms of consequences provides a special reason to regard the tradition as inadequate in this context, a reason that may not apply in other areas.

7. Though prudentialism is, strictly speaking, a form of consequentialism, because it evaluates actions in terms of their consequences for some persons, I reserve the terms "consequentialist" and "consequentialism" for the moral doctrine that what counts in evaluating an action is its consequences for all persons or all sentient beings.

8. Gregory Kavka, *Moral Paradoxes of Nuclear Deterrence* (Cambridge: Cambridge University Press, 1987), p. 76.

9. I shall assume that a nation's abandonment of nuclear deterrence requires its complete nuclear disarmament, though it could, of course, abandon its capacity for assured destruction without getting rid of all of its nuclear weapons. Contrary to this assumption, James Sterba argues that a nation can possess nuclear weapons without making nuclear threats against its superpower rival. "Between MAD and Counterforce," in Kipnis and Meyers, *Political Realism and International Morality*, pp. 122–36. This kind of position is discussed in Chapter 7.

10. The imprecision in our assessment of the likelihoods is, of course, the source of great controversy about whether or not nuclear deterrence has overall better consequences than its abandonment. For two consequentialist arguments that make a different assessment of the likelihoods and reach a conclusion opposite to the one presented here, see Douglas Lackey, "Missiles and Morals: A Utilitarian Look at Nuclear deterrence," *Philosophy and Public Affairs* 11, no. 3 (Summer, 1982), pp. 189–231, and Jefferson McMahan, "Nuclear Deterrence and Future Generations," in Avner Cohen and Steven Lee (eds.), *Nuclear Weapons and the Future of Humanity* (Totowa, NJ: Rowman and Allanheld, 1986), pp. 319–39.

11. There are alternative principles of choice under conditions of uncertainty that could be used in a consequentialist argument. For a discussion of some of these and problems that arise in applying them to the case of nuclear deterrence, see Lackey, "Missiles and Morals," pp. 193–206.

12. Of course, no individual agent – that is, no person – can alone change

the nuclear policy of even a single nation. But because we are evaluating the policies of nations, we may treat the nation as an agent, a corporate agent. A nation may be treated as an agent because it has a centralized authority, but there is no such authority at the international level. The question of the moral obligations of individual agents in respect of the nuclear weapons policies of their nations is related to, but at the same time distinct from, the question of the moral obligations of nations, which is my concern.

13. Douglas Lackey, "Ethics and Nuclear Deterrence," in James Rachels (ed.), *Moral Problems*, second ed. (New York: Harper and Row, 1975), p. 343. Arthur Burns argues: "The taking of hostages entailed by most nuclear deterrent policies [puts] seriously in question the state's moral right to acquire such weapons." *Ethics and Deterrence: A Nuclear Balance without Hostage Cities?* Adelphi Paper no. 69 (London: Institute for Strategic Studies, 1970), p. 2. Whether there are forms of nuclear deterrence that can avoid hostage holding, as Burns suggests, will be discussed in Chapter 5.

14. Hardin, "Deterrence and Moral Theory," pp. 35–60.

15. Kavka, *Moral Paradoxes of Nuclear Deterrence*, p. 21.

16. Hardin offers a number of other criticisms that are meant to apply not only to the just-war tradition but to deontological approaches to the evaluation of nuclear deterrence in general. They center primarily on the institutional nature of nuclear deterrence and the inappropriateness of not allowing the value of consequences to count as an independent moral factor. The analysis of nuclear deterrence as hostage holding may avoid these problems, because it can be applied to an institutional policy and because it functions in the context of a pluralistic moral perspective that allows consequences as an independent moral factor.

17. Douglas Lackey, "Immoral Risks: A Deontological Critique of Nuclear Deterrence," in Ellen Frankel Paul et al. (eds.), *Nuclear Rights, Nuclear Wrongs* (Oxford: Blackwell, 1985), p. 159.

18. Jefferson McMahan, "Deterrence and Deontology," in Russell Hardin et al. (eds.), *Nuclear Deterrence: Ethics and Strategy* (Chicago: University of Chicago Press, 1985), p. 158.

19. The party threatened in the case of a second-party threat may well be innocent in the sense that the behavior the threatener seeks to control would be morally permissible for the threatened party to engage in. But hostages are innocent in a stronger sense. Their lack of responsibility for the behavior the threatener seeks to control makes them innocent whether or not that behavior is permissible.

20. To bridge the gap between imposing a risk of harm and actually doing harm, which would help to explain why imposing a risk of harm is wrong even in cases where the harm is never done, Douglas

Lackey suggests that we introduce the notion of a "statistical death" or an "expected death," which is each whole number resulting from multiplying the imposed likelihood of death for each person by the number of persons upon whom that likelihood of death is imposed. Each statistical or expected death would then be regarded as morally equivalent to an actual death. But Lackey laments the fact that few seem to share his intuitions on this matter. "Immoral Risks," pp. 167–68.

21. It is a basic principle of Kant's moral philosophy that one must treat persons as ends and never as mere means. For a discussion of the Kantian objections to nuclear deterrence, see Richard Werner, "The Immorality of Nuclear Deterrence," in Kipnis and Meyers, *Political Realism and International Morality*, pp. 160–62.

22. But even if hostages consent to being hostages, their being hostages would probably be fully in respect of their choices only if they endorsed the goals the hostage holders were seeking to achieve.

23. Nuclear deterrence cannot be a bluff for the reasons mentioned in Chapter 1. Bluffing cannot be regarded as a feasible option, because the institutional arrangements that would have to be made to ensure that the nuclear threat would never be carried out might well be discovered by one's opponent, making the policy ineffective.

24. For an argument about the nonnegligible character of the risk of nuclear war under a policy of nuclear deterrence, see Lackey, "Immoral Risks," pp. 159–61.

25. Second-party threats would, in general, be morally justified only if the threatener was seeking to get the threatened party to behave in a way that the threatener had a moral right to expect.

26. William Shaw, "Nuclear Deterrence and Deontology," *Ethics* 94, no. 2 (January, 1984), pp. 248–60.

27. For example: Michael Walzer, *Just and Unjust Wars* (New York: Basic Books, 1977), pp. 271–72; Gregory Kavka, "Nuclear Hostages," in R.G. Frey and Christopher Morris (eds.), *Violence, Terrorism, and Justice* (Cambridge: Cambridge University Press, 1991), pp. 276–95; and Shaw, "Nuclear Deterrence and Deontology," p. 251.

28. Sterling Harwood has suggested to me that the term "holding" implies restraint or lack of liberty, so that the moral argument based on the analysis of nuclear deterrence as hostage holding derives illegitimate assistance from our intuitions about the moral wrongness of the deprivation of liberty. But, rhetorical considerations aside, the moral argument depends on neither the term nor the intuitions it may call up.

29. Walzer, *Just and Unjust Wars*, p. 271.

30. Thomas Schelling, "What Went Wrong with Arms Control?" *Foreign Affairs* 64, no. 2 (Winter, 1985–86), p. 233. See also Thomas Schelling

and Morton Halperin, *Strategy and Arms Control* (1961, reprint ed., McLean, VA: Pergamon-Brassey, 1985), p. 59. In the latter work, the authors argue that part of the reason the pedestrian is not terrorized by the fast-moving traffic is that "he can control his own actions." But this is another reason why the analogy carries no moral weight. Whereas pedestrians are in control of their decision when to cross the street, nuclear hostages are not in control of the behavior that could lead to their being killed in nuclear retaliation.

31. Walzer, *Just and Unjust Wars*, p. 271.
32. Shaw, "Nuclear Deterrence and Deontology," p. 252.
33. Robert W. Tucker claims: "The relations of nations have always been based on hostage holding, since these relations have always been based on the pattern of collective responsibility." *The Nuclear Debate* (New York: Holmes and Meier, 1985), p. 57n37. But this is misleading, because it ignores the fact that the traditional military threat has been of denial rather than punishment. Hostage holding has been a significant element in deterrence only in the nuclear age, because only with such weapons has come the military capability to threaten societal destruction, the threat of which requires a response in kind.
34. Kavka, *Moral Paradoxes of Nuclear Deterrence*, p. 91.
35. On this point see C.A.J. Coady, "Escaping from the Bomb: Immoral Deterrence and the Problem of Extrication," in Henry Shue (ed.), *Nuclear Deterrence and Moral Restraint* (Cambridge: Cambridge University Press, 1989), p. 172.
36. James Child, *Nuclear War: The Moral Dimension* (New Brunswick, NJ: Transaction Books, 1986), pp. 142–43.
37. For an example of such resistance, see John Ford, "The Morality of Obliteration Bombing," in Richard Wasserstrom (ed.), *War and Morality* (Belmont, CA: Wadsworth, 1970), pp. 15–41.
38. On the way in which nuclear war reverses the trend toward greater citizen involvement, see Michael McDonald, "Commentary: Non-combatants and Hostages," in Michael Fox and Leo Groarke (eds.), *Nuclear War: Philosophical Perspectives* (New York: Peter Lang, 1985), pp. 53–54, and Richard Wasserstrom, "War, Nuclear War, and Nuclear Deterrence: Some Conceptual and Moral Issues," in Hardin et al., *Nuclear Deterrence*, p. 23.
39. James Child argues that the political responsibility of the ordinary citizen for a nation's military policy applies even in the case of non-democratic states, in *Nuclear War*, pp. 143–48.
40. For a discussion of what might be said by way of justifying attacks or threats of attacks on children, see Richard Wasserstrom, "Non-combatants, Indiscriminate Killing, and the Immorality of Nuclear War," in Fox and Groarke, *Nuclear War*, p. 47; see also Child, *Nuclear War*, p. 143.

41. The argument from political involvement, though not sufficient to show all of those threatened by nuclear deterrence to be responsible for the behavior the threatener is seeking to control, may show a great many of them to be at least indirectly responsible. This may explain an interesting observation of Kavka's, that it seems intuitively more objectionable to seek to deter an opponent by threatening the society of some third country than by threatening the opponent's society. *Moral Paradoxes of Nuclear Deterrence*, p. 89. But to say that it is more objectionable to threaten a third country is not to say that it is acceptable to threaten the opponent. For a criticism of Kavka's point, see Coady, "Escaping from the Bomb," pp. 172–73.

42. Again, one source for this idea is Anthony Kenny, *The Logic of Deterrence* (Chicago: University of Chicago Press), p. 10.

43. But civilians' responsibility for the war might make them liable for punishment after the war, say in a war crimes trial. The point is that defensive violence is justified on different grounds than punitive or retributive violence.

44. Many have thought that this shows that nuclear deterrence could be justifiable in deontological terms if the threats were directed only against military targets. The moral justifiability of such a policy will be discussed in Chapter 5.

45. Thomas Schelling, *The Strategy of Conflict*, new ed. (Cambridge: Harvard University Press, 1980), p. 239.

46. Lackey, "Immoral Risks," pp 162–64. Lackey rejects this interpretation of the treaty.

47. Another way to understand the claim that a nation has given its proxy consent to nuclear risks being imposed on its civilians by another nation is to understand the civilians not as hostages but as shields. This notion of a shield is introduced by Robert Nozick, in *Anarchy, State, and Utopia* (Cambridge: Harvard University Press, 1974), pp. 34–35. The idea is that a nuclear superpower has allowed its civilians to be subject to risk of nuclear attack in order to lessen the likelihood of that attack taking place, because of the opponent's reluctance to actually attack civilians. The risk to the civilians is thus used by that nation as a kind of shield. The argument that this alters the moral status of the risk to civilians is made by Jonathan Schonsheck in "Hostages or Shields? An Alternative Conception of Noncombatants and its Implications as Regards the Morality of Nuclear Deterrence," *Public Affairs Quarterly* 1, no. 2 (April, 1987), pp. 21–34. But if one understands the argument as a form of the argument from proxy consent, it fails for the reason suggested here – namely, that the government is not morally entitled to consent to the imposition of this risk.

48. Gerald Dworkin, "Nuclear Intentions," in Hardin et al., *Nuclear Deterrence*, pp. 51–52.
49. For a discussion of hypothetical consent to the imposition of risk, see Douglas MacLean, "Risk and Consent: Philosophical Issues for Centralized Decisions," *Risk Analysis* 2 (1982), pp. 59–67.
50. One might object to the attempt to substitute hypothetical consent for real consent in the context of a deontological argument on the grounds that this makes the argument a disguised consequentialist argument. But as I argue next, the argument from hypothetical consent yields a conclusion different from that of the consequentialist argument, because the argument from hypothetical consent considers the best interests not of everyone, but only of some.
51. The risks posed by automobiles are compared to the risks posed by nuclear deterrence by Douglas Lackey in "Immoral Risks," pp. 159–60. The acceptability of the risks from automobile driving may not be a good example of hypothetical consent, because, given that the practice of driving is permitted and regulated by legislation, those put at risk may be said to have consented in a more direct sense through the political process.
52. This is in contrast with the point made earlier under (1), where the concern was whether or not nuclear deterrence creates risk. There the claim that the policy lowers the overall risk to the opponent's civilians was not taken as a decisive objection to the hostage-holding argument, because that argument is concerned with the imposition not just of any risk, but only of morally unacceptable risk. But here the question is precisely whether or not the risk is morally unacceptable. We are assuming that the risk would not be unacceptable if there were hypothetical consent, and the question of hypothetical consent turns on whether or not the hostages' overall risk has been lowered.
53. Gregory Kavka, "Nuclear Hostages," pp. 285–86. Kavka argues the matter in "Nuclear Hostages," pp. 286–90, and in *Moral Paradoxes of Nuclear Deterrence*, Chapter 4.
54. The idea of nuclear deterrence as risk redistribution is discussed by Kavka in *Moral Paradoxes of Nuclear Deterrence*, Chapter 2, and by Douglas Lackey in "Immoral Risks." Jeff McMahan suggests, in comments to me on an earlier draft of this chapter, that an appropriate moral principle concerning the evaluation of nuclear deterrence may be that "there is no decisive objection to redistributing risks away from one group of innocent people onto another group of equally innocent people as long as this reduces the overall level of risk" or does not "significantly increase the overall level of risk." If the consequentialist argument is correct, nuclear deterrence would satisfy

this principle. But as the argument later shows, such a blanket principle is not acceptable because the redistribution it allows is not always acceptable, and nuclear deterrence is one case where it is not.

55. Douglas Lackey, *Moral Principles and Nuclear Weapons* (Totowa, NJ: Rowman and Allanheld, 1984), p. 152.

56. Kavka, *Moral Paradoxes of Nuclear Deterrence*, p. 42, and "Nuclear Hostages," p. 284.

57. Another way to make the point is that the sense in which a person could as well expect to be the citizen of one nation as of another requires for its truth the assumption of a kind of Rawlsian "veil of ignorance," whereas the sense in which I could expect to be either quarantined or a person benefiting from the quarantining of someone else does not. I can know everything I in fact know about myself and still see myself potentially as both victim and beneficiary of the quarantine rule. But I could see myself potentially as both victim and beneficiary of some particular nation's policy of nuclear threatening, only if I did not know one of the most basic facts about myself – namely, my nationality.

58. On the reality or genuineness of moral conflicts under a pluralist moral scheme, see Christopher Gowans, "The Debate on Moral Dilemmas," in Christopher Gowans (ed.), *Moral Dilemmas* (New York: Oxford University Press, 1987), pp. 16–18.

59. Kavka, *Moral Paradoxes of Nuclear Deterrence*, especially Chapter 1. The quotations in this paragraph are from pp. 20 and 21.

60. Kavka, *Moral Paradoxes of Nuclear Deterrence*, p. 18. He means by "utilitarian" what I mean by "consequentialist."

61. Walzer, *Just and Unjust Wars*, pp. 269–74.

62. Hardin, "Deterrence and Moral Theory," p. 57.

63. Lackey, "Missiles and Morals", p. 192. Lackey himself has a different view than Kavka about which side of the issue a concern for consequences falls.

64. For brevity, I will from now on refer to merely apparent conflicts merely as "apparent" – that is, henceforth, the apparent should be understood to exclude the real.

65. On the two different senses of resolution, see Gowans, "The Debate on Moral Dilemmas," p. 18. Given the definitions of the notions involved, all apparent moral conflicts are resolvable. But as a matter of fact, not all real moral conflicts are resolvable.

66. This example shows how the second resolution strategy may lead to an action, like Jones's calling for help on the car phone, being morally required overall when it is not the action that is required either within the consequentialist approach or within the deontological approach. This may seem odd, but it also seems to be the way in which moral conflicts are often resolved within everyday moral reasoning. On

another point, none of the examples of moral conflict should be taken as implying that deontological norms must be understood as simple and exceptionless. The norms, or at least some of them, may be better construed as allowing various kinds of exceptions within the deontological approach itself. Even so, there is still great room within the context of everyday moral reasoning for conflict between the deontological and consequentialist approaches.

67. See Gowans, "The Debate on Moral Dilemmas," p. 29, for the idea that comparative judgments cannot always be made even when the values in conflict are commensurable. This is the possibility I mean to capture in the notion of weak commensurability.

68. There is not a sharp dividing line between tragic and nontragic moral dilemmas. These terms are simply labels for opposite ends of a continuous scale of moral seriousness.

69. For example, Kavka, "Nuclear Hostages," p. 278.

70. All three of these factors should be considered in determining the seriousness of the deontological wrong represented by nuclear deterrence, that wrong being, in some loose sense, a product of these factors. The risk of death or serious suffering imposed on each hostage, though significant, cannot be very great, otherwise the consequentialist argument would be unsound, but when the number of hostages and the length of time they are held are taken into account, the deontological stakes do rise very high.

71. For a discussion of the idea that consequentialist and deontological approaches to the morality of military activity can lead to a wider range of irresolvable dilemmas, see Thomas Nagel, "War and Massacre," in Charles Beitz et al. (eds.), *International Ethics* (Princeton: Princeton University Press, 1985), pp. 56, 73. (He refers to the approaches as utilitarian and absolutist.)

72. The policy choice regarding nuclear deterrence does not involve the worst imaginable choices in terms of either approach. There are morally worse policies in both respects. Starting a nuclear war would be more serious in terms of consequences than merely increasing the likelihood of its being fought, which is, according to the consequentialist argument, what the abandonment of nuclear deterrence would do. Also, as mentioned later, there are institutions or policies that are deontologically worse than nuclear deterrence, such as slavery or the Holocaust.

73. The nuclear superpowers are too strong to challenge each other militarily, because any military conflict between them risks escalation to societal destruction. Derek Linton has pointed out to me that the original logic of nuclear deterrence was even closer to the logic of individual terrorists, inasmuch as the policy was adopted because the United States and its Western European allies felt that they were

too weak militarily to challenge the Soviet Union in a traditional military manner. An implicit recognition of the logical link between the policies of the nuclear superpowers and the actions of individual terrorists may explain why so many people expect individual terrorists to pursue their goals by acquiring a nuclear weapon.

74. Richard Falk, "Nuclear Weapons and the End of Democracy," *Praxis International* 2, no. 1 (April, 1982), p. 7.

75. Each of these notions is characterized here in a rather vague way, because in neither case is it made clear what counts as "central." But the vague formulations should be adequate for the argument.

76. Some may find this claim controversial because it implies that political terror cannot, over the long run at least, be an effective method of domestic social control.

77. Although one might prefer a society in which everyone had a legal right to a job, or to a noninflating currency, it would be difficult to construe these legal rights as corresponding to deontological norms. I owe the inflation-unemployment example and the general line of objection to which I respond in this paragraph and the next to Greg Kavka.

78. Robert W. Tucker, *The Just War: A Study in Contemporary American Doctrine* (Baltimore: Johns Hopkins Press, 1960), p. 199.

79. The notion of a roughly just society may be compared with John Rawls's notion of a "nearly just society," which is "one that is well-ordered for the most part but in which some serious violations of justice nevertheless do occur." *A Theory of Justice* (Cambridge: Harvard University Press, 1971), p. 363.

80. There may be a potential for nonnuclear weapons, for example biological or chemical weapons, to create a condition of mutual vulnerability. If nonnuclear weapons are developed to the point where they could create such a condition, the nature of the moral problem to which they gave rise would be the same as the moral problem of nuclear weapons. In this sense, the moral problem of nuclear weapons may not be unique. But whereas the general problem may be realized in the form of other potential weapons, it is nuclear weapons that have brought the problem into the world.

81. David Hollenbach, "Ethics in Distress: Can There Be Just Wars in the Nuclear Age?" in William O'Brien and John Langan (eds.), *The Nuclear Dilemma and the Just War Tradition* (Lexington, MA: Lexington Books, 1986), p. 13.

82. There is a fourth approach, which would alter not our concern to respect innocent civilians, but our understanding about what effects of actions are valuable and disvaluable to humans. That is, it would alter the basic assumptions of prudential and consequentialist ar-

guments rather than of the deontological arguments. This approach, like the other, would make one of the conflicting obligations nonexistent, and so make the conflicts apparent. But this approach will not be considered. It seems a much more radical revision of our general normative scheme to propose a basic change in what we conceive to be of prudential and consequential value than to propose a change in how we treat innocent civilians under certain conditions. Though perhaps this claim is only a consequentialist prejudice.

83. A similar claim has been made in the area of environmental ethics, that the old anthropocentric moral perspective cannot serve to solve the environmental crisis and that our moral view must change so that the environment is seen to be of intrinsic moral value. See, for example, William Godfrey-Smith, "The Value of Wilderness," *Environmental Ethics* 1 (Winter, 1979), pp. 309–319.

84. George Quester, "The Necessary Moral Hypocrisy of the Slide into Mutual Assured Destruction," in Shue, *Nuclear Deterrence*, p. 263.

85. As quoted in Hollenbach, "Ethics in Distress," p. 14.

86. Robert Nozick, *Philosophical Explanations* (Cambridge: Harvard University Press, 1981), p. 402.

87. The embarrassment for our moral view resulting from a need to resort to the third approach to solving the moral problem can also be seen in the following point. If we are forced to adopt the third approach, this would be an admission that our everyday moral view is functionally determined, which I speculated in Chapter 1 is true of the institutional norms of the just-war tradition. In other words, the deontological norms of our everyday moral view would have their content altered as circumstances changed in order to insure that they are not in radical discord with consequentialist considerations.

3. THE LOGIC OF DETERRENCE

1. "Deter" is what Gilbert Ryle calls an achievement verb – that is, a verb whose use implies success. *The Concept of Mind* (1949, reprint ed., New York: Barnes and Noble, 1970), pp. 130–31. The point about deterrence being a success term is also made by Leslie Pickering Francis, "Nuclear Threats and the Imposition of Risks," in Kenneth Kipnis and Diana T. Meyers, *Political Realism and International Morality* (Boulder, CO: Westview Press, 1987), p. 153. The fact that "deterrence" is a success term shows that referring to a nation's policy as one of nuclear deterrence may work as a subtle form of persuasive labeling, begging the question of the policy's effectiveness.

2. There is a fourth possible line of argument, one that is narrow like

(3) but particular like (1). It claims that there was no work for nuclear deterrence to do in the U.S./Soviet relationship not because military deterrence was not needed, but because conventional deterrence is all that was needed. Someone who seems to have adopted this line of argument is John Mueller. He argued that war is obsolete between the two superpowers even in the absence of nuclear weapons, that peace between them is overdetermined. John Mueller, "The Essential Irrelevance of Nuclear Weapons," *International Security* 13, no. 2 (Fall, 1988), pp. 55–79.

3. This distinction is made by Franklin Zimring and Gordon Hawkins, *Deterrence – the Legal Threat in Crime Control* (Chicago: University of Chicago Press, 1973), p. 72.

4. The debate over the effectiveness of capital punishment is like the debate over the effectiveness of nuclear deterrence in a number of respects. One is that it seems intuitively obvious to many people that each form of deterrence works. Also, the debate over capital punishment makes the same kind of assumption as the one made here, that relations in civil society require legal deterrence, as relations in international society require military deterrence.

5. When I speak of conventional deterrence or conventional (military) threats, I refer to the military policies of nations without nuclear weapons. Because nuclear powers continue to maintain conventional forces, nations practicing nuclear deterrence also practice conventional deterrence. But I am not interested in this form of conventional deterrence. The question here is whether policies of nuclear deterrence are preferable to policies of military deterrence based exclusively on conventional weapons. So when I speak of the comparison between nuclear and conventional deterrence, I understand conventional deterrence to be the kind of military policy practiced by nations without nuclear weapons.

6. Another assumption, following the discussion in Chapter 1, is that the question of deterrence effectiveness is taken to exhaust the consequences of a deterrence policy relevant to the judgment of prudential preferability, so that, for example, the costs of the policy in relation to other social needs are not considered.

7. One important difference in the comparison is that whereas nuclear deterrence is normally expected to deter both conventional and nuclear war, conventional deterrence has to deter only conventional war. Nuclear weapons create the possibility both of nuclear war and of nuclear deterrence. The relevance of this difference will be taken up later, where I will argue that the greater destructiveness of nuclear war is a factor in judging the relative effectiveness of nuclear deterrence.

8. As many have pointed out, if a nation's goal were simply the avoid-

ance of war, its most effective policy might well be the complete surrender of its national sovereignty to its opponent. But few understand the goal of war avoidance in this way. Rather, this goal is understood to include not just the avoidance of military attack, but also the avoidance of the nation's need to go to war – that is, the avoidance of any fundamental challenge to its sovereignty that would lead the nation to resort to military means in its defense.

9. John Mueller, "Deterrence, Nuclear Weapons, Morality, and War," in Charles W. Kegley, Jr. and Kenneth L. Schwab (eds.), *After the Cold War: Questioning the Morality of Nuclear Deterrence* (Boulder, CO: Westview Press, 1991), p. 72.

10. Another example from Russell is that of the chicken who is fed by the farmer every morning and reasons that this will go on forever, when one morning the farmer wrings its neck instead. Nuclear deterrence may be like this example not only because one should not conclude that the policy successfully avoids war from the fact that there has been no war in the past, but also because there might be a different causal connection at work – namely, that disaster may be likely for one practicing nuclear deterrence, as for the chicken, partly because one is lulled into a false sense of security by the fact that things seem to have gone so well so far.

11. There has not been enough experience with nuclear deterrence to provide an adequate test of its alleged war-avoiding capability. Colin Gray suggests: "It is arguable, at least, that the system truly has never been tested: that neither superpower has ever felt a strong incentive to fight the other." "Reactions and Perspectives," in Ashton B. Carter and David N. Schwartz (eds.), *Ballistic Missile Defense* (Washington: Brookings Institution, 1984), p. 407. The conclusion that Gray would draw from this observation, however, is not that we cannot be sure that nuclear deterrence works, but rather that we cannot be sure that the particular form of nuclear deterrence the United States practiced works. His arguments for this are considered in Chapter 6.

12. Some have argued that nuclear deterrence was a learning experience and that we kept getting better at it as the Cold War wore on. See, for example, Robert W. Tucker, *The Nuclear Debate* (New York: Holmes & Meier, 1985), p. 56, and Joseph Nye, "Nuclear Learning and U.S.-Soviet Security Regimes," *International Organization* 41, no. 3 (Summer, 1987), pp. 371–402. There is considerable plausibility to this argument, but it implies only that the likelihood of war under nuclear deterrence may lessen the longer a regime of nuclear deterrence is in place, not that that likelihood, even at its lowest, is lower than it would be under conventional deterrence.

13. John Finnis, Joseph M. Boyle, Jr., Germain Grisez, *Nuclear Deterrence,*

Morality and Realism (Oxford: Clarendon Press, 1987), p. 241. Although the authors think there are special problems with a consequentialist analysis of nuclear deterrence, their objections go deeper, amounting to a rejection of consequentialism as such.

14. Gregory Kavka, *Moral Paradoxes of Nuclear Deterrence* (Cambridge: Cambridge University Press, 1987), p. 59. Kavka's criticisms are directed not against a consequentialist approach as such, but against a version of this approach based on expected utility. He endorses a different version of a consequentialist or utilitarian approach, one based on what he calls the "disaster avoidance principle" (p. 67).

15. Richard Werner, "The Immorality of Nuclear Deterrence," in Kipnis and Meyers, *Political Realism and International Morality*, pp. 164, 166.

16. Thomas Schelling, *The Strategy of Conflict*, new ed. (Cambridge: Harvard University Press, 1980), Chapter 1.

17. A good sample of the debate between proponents and critics of rational deterrence theory is featured in *World Politics* 41, no. 2 (January, 1989).

18. Robert Jervis, "Introduction: Approach and Assumptions," in Robert Jervis, Ned Lebow, and Janice Gross Stein (eds.), *Psychology and Deterrence* (Baltimore: Johns Hopkins University Press, 1985), p. 1.

19. Patrick Morgan, "New Directions in Deterrence Theory," in Avner Cohen and Steven Lee (eds.), *Nuclear Weapons and the Future of Humanity* (Totowa, NJ: Rowman and Allanheld, 1986), pp. 179–80.

20. Some of these case studies are collected in Jervis, Lebow, and Stein, *Psychology and Deterrence.*

21. A good general discussion of some of the problems involved in the case-study approach is in Patrick Morgan, "New Directions in Deterrence Theory," pp. 180–81.

22. James Blight, "The New Psychology of War and Peace," *International Security* 11, no. 3 (Winter, 1986–87), p. 185.

23. Kavka, *Moral Paradoxes of Nuclear Deterrence*, p. 59.

24. A good example of such case studies is Graham Allison, *The Essence of Decision* (Boston: Little Brown, 1971).

25. John Baylis, Ken Booth, John Garnett, and Phil Williams, *Contemporary Strategy: Theories and Policies* (London: Croom Helm, 1975), pp. 68–69.

26. Stipulating that deterrence involve a threat of force is more restrictive than some would prefer. John Mueller suggests that "the deterrence concept may be more useful if it is broadened to include non-military incentives and disincentives." But this would broaden the concept too much for my purposes. Mueller admits: "Under this approach, if two nations are not at war, then it can be said that they are currently being deterred from attacking each other." An implication, he rec-

ognizes, would be that there is a deterrence relationship between the United States and Canada as well as between Bolivia and Pakistan. "The Essential Irrelevance of Nuclear Weapons," p. 70, 70n30.

27. Derek Beyleveld, *A Bibliography of General Deterrence Research* (Westmead, UK: Saxon House, 1980), pp. 14ff.

28. John Mueller has also recommended a broader definition of deterrence in this respect. Under his definition, deterrence need not be responsible for the conforming behavior: "Deterrence may be defined as a state of being – the absence of war between two countries or alliances." "Deterrence, Nuclear Weapons, Morality, and War," p. 70. But such a notion is too broad if one is concerned to compare the effectiveness of alternative polices of deterrence for the sake of better policy choices.

29. For example, Hugo Bedau discusses the possible tendency of capital punishment to lead some people to commit murders that they otherwise would not have. "Capital Punishment," in Tom Regan (ed.), *Matters of Life and Death*, second edition (New York: Random House, 1986), p. 199.

30. Zimring and Hawkins, *Deterrence*, p. 71.

31. Robert Holmes, *On War and Morality* (Princeton: Princeton University Press, 1989), p. 243.

32. The need to include this clause was made clear to me by Jonathan Schonsheck, in conversation and in his unpublished paper "Nuclear Deterrence and Nuclear Deterrent Threats: Criteria of Success and Failure," which is a criticism of my earlier formulation of this analysis.

33. Because there is an extensive history of legal deterrence, in contrast with nuclear deterrence, one might think that the apparent success of legal deterrence in keeping social orders going could serve as a basis for arguing that legal deterrence is highly effective. But this may not do, for, as discussed later in the chapter, the range in degrees of legal effectiveness that social orders seem able to tolerate is quite high. Another possible line of argument is this. Liberal democratic social orders have by and large been able to maintain a set of legal procedures designed to protect the right of criminal defendants, despite the fact that these procedures are widely perceived to lessen the effectiveness of the legal system in maintaining social order. Given the responsiveness of such social orders to popular concerns, the fact that these procedures have been maintained shows that the level of discontent with the effectiveness of the legal system has generally not run very high. This suggests that the legal systems have been overall quite effective, even in the face of the procedural constraints.

34. This notion of belief strength measures strength in terms of the con-

tent of the belief rather than in terms of its modality – that is, how it is held. It is adjectival rather than adverbial. But these notions of belief strength may be interchangeable, in the sense that "Bernard believes that it is very likely the threat will be carried out" may be roughly equivalent to "Bernard strongly believes that the threat will be carried out."

35. As mentioned earlier, the assumption that legal deterrence is paradigmatically effective implies only that most legal systems are very effective in deterring violations of their central criminal statutes. Moreover, the assumption does not imply that a legal system could not be made more effective by, for example, the state's taking steps further to strengthen the belief that it has the capability, as well as the will, to carry out its threats.

36. This distinction is discussed in Beyleveld, *A Bibliography of General Deterrence Research*, p. xxii.

37. The degree of social and distributive justice in a society can determine how strongly these beliefs are held among a significant portion of the population. Those who are poor and discriminated against in a wealthy society may easily come to believe that the treatment they receive from the police is not much worse when they break the law than when they do not, nor, given the poor quality of their lives, that the legal penalties provide an expected overriding disadvantage from nonconformity.

38. The idea that the appropriate beliefs can bring about conformity indirectly is to be distinguished from the possibility mentioned earlier where the threats might bring about conformity in anomalous ways, such as through third-party bribery. The distinction is that in the anomalous cases, the beliefs are not part of the causal mechanism by which the threats bring about conformity.

39. Zimring and Hawkins, *Deterrence*, pp. 75, 77.

40. Nothing special is meant by the term "habit" here. It is simply a general term covering cases where an agent acts or thinks in a certain way or adopts a certain attitude not out of deliberation, but out of a tendency or disposition to act or think in that kind of way or to adopt that kind of attitude. In the case of deterrence, habits leading to conformity with the law are largely habits of refraining. To avoid appearing to embrace discredited theories, I should hasten to note that this appeal to habits of obedience is not meant to be an analysis of law.

41. Habits of obedience to the law may originate in other ways as well. They may result from a process of conditioning involving no deliberative conformity at all. Or they may originate in a kind of transference from another kind of habit, such as a habit of obedience to one's parents. There are certainly other possibilities.

42. The perception of fairness depends not only on whether the legal system is in this sense formally just – that is, whether it applies its rules fairly – but also on whether it is substantively just – that is, whether the content of the legal rules is fair.

4. THE PRUDENTIAL PROBLEM

1. The moral problem involves conflicting kinds of obligation, whereas the prudential problem involves simply conflicting arguments about a single kind of obligation. In other words, the moral problem is that obligations conflict, whereas the prudential problem is, roughly, that rules-of-thumb for determining an obligation conflict. This shows that the prudential problem is a conflict in a different sense than is the moral problem, and many of the points made about moral conflicts in Chapter 2 do not apply to the prudential conflict.

2. In my actual order of exposition, the broadening of the prudential perspective, undertaken in the last chapter and this, is presented as a way of determining whether the moral dilemma of Chapter 2 can be resolved through examining whether the consequentialist argument is unsound. The point here is that Chapters 3 and 4 could have been Chapters 2 and 3 – that is, the broadening of the prudential perspective, rather than the broadening of the moral perspective, could have constituted the initial attempt to resolve the morality/prudence conflict discussed in Chapter 1. The discussion in this chapter and the last will show whether the prudential argument is unsound.

3. Kenneth Boulding, *The Meaning of the Twentieth Century* (New York: Harper and Row, 1964), p. 80.

4. States may recognize the rights of citizens to challenge the legal actions of the state judicially, and in this limited sense the citizens may represent independent centers of power capable of issuing substantial counterthreats (such as, "if you arrest me for burning the flag, I will challenge your action in court").

5. There may be a problem of identification, however, if states take action against other states through their intelligence agencies or through quasi-independent terrorist organizations.

6. This factor is not completely absent in the case of legal deterrence, where it arises in proposals for preventive detention.

7. Thomas Schelling observes: "In threatening to hurt somebody if he misbehaves, it need not make a critical difference how much it would hurt you too – *if* you can make him believe the threat." *Arms and Influence* (New Haven, CT: Yale University Press, 1966), p. 36. It is the demonstration of willingness through an adequate history of threat

executions that would make him believe the threat. But in the case of military deterrence, such a demonstration is hard to come by.

8. Glenn Snyder, *Deterrence and Defense* (Princeton: Princeton University Press, 1961), p. 11. Synder is speaking of war in a situation of nuclear deterrence. But though his point applies to military deterrence in general, its application to the nuclear context is highly problematic.

9. Derek Beyleveld, *A Bibliography of General Deterrence Research* (Westmead, UK: Saxon House, 1980), p. xx.

10. If anything, the execution of a military threat seems to encourage, rather than deter, future nonconforming behavior, as nations seek to avenge past military defeats. For example, the Germans did this in 1939 and the Egyptians in 1973. Sterling Harwood suggested this point to me.

11. There is a third advantage from executing a military threat, of a different sort than these two. It is notoriously the case that a nation's getting into a war can sometimes be an advantage for those in power, helping them to keep their hold on power by distracting the people from domestic problems and getting them to "rally 'round the flag." Because the leaders make the decisions, this can be a factor supporting a presumption of their willingness to execute military threats, though it is often a prudential advantage to them alone, not to the nation as a whole.

12. Arthur Waskow, "The Theory and Practice of Deterrence," in James Roosevelt (ed.), *The Liberal Papers* (New York: Doubleday, 1962), p. 145. An indication of this difference is that those threatened under legal deterrence are regarded as fellow citizens, whereas those threatened under military deterrence are labeled as opponents or enemies.

13. Nations are, of course, institutionally related to one another by the United Nations and by a host of international conventions and treaties to which they have agreed to adhere. But these international institutions are not the parties issuing the threats, and they are not generally sufficient to provide nations with authority for the issuing of military threats. The extent to which the institutions fall short of being capable of providing such authority is the extent to which the United Nations falls short of being a true world government.

14. Patrick Morgan criticizes the literature in which military deterrence "is almost always discussed as if it were embedded in conscious deliberations and decisions" rather than being "an inadvertent and unconscious effect." This is, in his view, a result of a focus on what he calls immediate deterrence, which is using threats to oppose a particular potential act of aggression, to the exclusion of general deterrence, which is the background of military threats opponents use to keep their antagonism from breaking out into armed hostilities.

Deterrence: A Conceptual Analysis, 2nd ed. (Beverly Hills, CA: Sage, 1983), Chapter 2 (quotation from p. 34). The role of nondeliberative conformity would be in maintaining what he calls general deterrence.

15. Russell Hardin argues that the fact that there are many more parties involved in legal deterrence than in military deterrence is what explains why the success of legal deterrence depends on its failures. This is contrary to the view advanced in the last chapter that this dependence is characteristic of deterrence systems in general. A history of threat executions, he suggests, is not needed for deterrence to be successful when there is no problem of identifying the party responsible for nonconforming behavior, as is the case with military deterrence, including nuclear deterrence. "Risking Armageddon," in Avner Cohen and Steven Lee (eds.), *Nuclear Weapons and the Future of Humanity* (Totowa, NJ: Rowman and Allanheld, 1986), pp. 219–20. But this argument runs together concerns with the threatener's capability to carry out its threat and its willingness to do so. Doubtless, threat executions help strengthen the belief that the threatener has the capability to carry out its threats, in particular, regarding its ability to identify the agents of nonconforming behavior, especially when this is in doubt because of the large number of parties to be deterred. But they are also necessary to create and to sustain the belief that the threatener is willing to carry out its threat, and here the different number of parties involved in the two cases seems not to make a difference.

16. This metaphor was offered by Robert Oppenheimer, as quoted in Lawrence Freedman, *The Evolution of Nuclear Strategy* (New York: St. Martin's, 1981), p. 94.

17. Schelling, *Arms and Influence*, pp. 4, 74.

18. Michael MccGwire, "Deterrence: the Problem—Not the Solution," *International Affairs* 62, no. 1 (Winter, 1985/6), p. 56. "Reassurance," the term I will use, is better than "assurance," because, given that military deterrence is an ongoing, institutional arrangement, the threatener must continue anew to give its assurances that it does not intend attacking. It should be noted, as MccGwire points out, that "reassurance between adversaries is quite distinct from the role of a deterrent capability in reassuring one's allies" (p. 56). For a discussion of this other type of reassurance, see Michael Howard, "Deterrence and Reassurance: Western Defense in the 1980s," *Foreign Affairs* 61, no. 2 (Winter, 1982–83), pp. 309–24.

19. The reason that reassurance is sometimes treated as a different feature of military policy from deterrence is that reassurance avoids a different kind of war than the war deterrence is often viewed as avoiding. Reassurance avoids a war of preemption, whereas deterrence is

often designed to avoid a war of deliberate aggression. But if the purpose of deterrence is to avoid war in whatever form it may come, then clearly reassurance is an aspect of deterrence.

20. Thomas Schelling, "What Went Wrong with Arms Control," *Foreign Affairs* 64, no. 2 (Winter, 1985–86), p. 220.

21. John Mueller argues that modern conventional war, though much less destructive than large-scale nuclear war, is sufficiently calamitous to be seen as an overriding disadvantage. He offers this analogy: "It is probably quite a bit more terrifying to think about a jump from the 50th floor than a jump from the 5th floor, but anyone who finds life even minimally satisfying is extremely unlikely to do either." "The Essential Irrelevance of Nuclear Weapons," *International Security* 13, no. 2 (Fall, 1988), pp. 66–7. But the comparison is crucial. Nuclear war would be prospectively perceived as more of a disadvantage, or more likely an overriding disadvantage, than conventional war. Conventional deterrence may work quite effectively in many situations, but the question is whether or not it is overall more effective than nuclear deterrence. There may be situations where the extra terror of a 50th floor plunge would be needed to keep one from jumping.

22. Albert Carnesale et al., *Living With Nuclear Weapons* (New York: Bantam Books, 1983), p. 44.

23. Robert W. Tucker, *The Nuclear Debate* (New York: Holmes & Meier, 1985), p. 129.

24. Phil Williams, "Deterrence," in John Baylis et al., *Contemporary Strategy: Theories and Policies* (London: Croom Helm, 1975), p. 74.

25. These two elements of nuclear deterrence are discussed by Henry Shue. "Having it Both Ways: the Gradual Wrong Turn in American Strategy," in Henry Shue (ed.), *Nuclear Deterrence and Moral Restraint* (Cambridge: Cambridge University Press, 1989), pp. 15–16.

26. Albert Wohlstetter, "The Delicate Balance of Terror," *Foreign Affairs* 37, no. 2 (January, 1959). In one view, discussed in Chapter 6, nuclear deterrence remains delicate.

27. Bernard Brodie, *Strategy in the Missile Age* (Princeton: Princeton University Press, 1959), p. 272.

28. Boulding, *The Meaning of the Twentieth Century*, p. 81.

29. Schelling, *Arms and Influence*, pp. 55, 124.

30. Schelling, *Arms and Influence*, p. 36.

31. In fact, threats concerning different geographical areas may not be strongly interdependent for the same reason that conventional and nuclear threats are not – namely, that the execution of the threats in different areas would involve very different expected advantages and disadvantages. The potential prudential advantages from threat execution in some geographical areas (such as the homeland) are greater

than those in others, as the potential disadvantages in nuclear threat execution are much greater than those in conventional threat execution. On the problematic nature of the claim about the interdependence of threats geographically, see Lawrence Freedman, *The Evolution of Nuclear Strategy*, p. 362.

32. Hans Morganthau, "The Four Paradoxes of Nuclear Strategy," *The American Political Science Review* 58, no. 1 (March, 1964), p. 24.

33. Williams, "Deterrence," p. 75.

34. Another reason offered for carrying out nuclear threats is that this could serve as an intra-war deterrent, helping to keep the nuclear war limited by deterring the opponent from escalating the conflict. Intra-war deterrence may be seen as an aspect of a threat of denial, because denial could not be achieved unless the war were limited. But its potential role as an intra-war deterrent could make the execution of a nuclear threat rational only if a limited nuclear war were reasonably foreseeable. An extensive discussion of intra-war deterrence is presented in later chapters.

35. See John Mearsheimer, *Conventional Deterrence* (Ithaca, NY: Cornell University Press, 1983), p. 15.

36. The destruction of the aggressor's society might be seen as denial, in an extended sense, because a gain presupposes a gainer, so that to destroy the gainer is to deny the gain. But this is a perverse sense of denial, one that it would not be in a nation's interest to seek, given that it entails the destruction of the denier as well.

37. This was pointed out to me by an anonymous reviewer of the manuscript.

38. To say that a courtroom witness lacks credibility usually implies not that there is no credibility at all to what that person says, but merely that the level of his or her credibility is not high. The claim that nuclear threats lack credibility should be understood in the same way. Thus the import of the claim that nuclear threats lack credibility is not that they cannot work at all, but rather that they may not work so well. As a result, this claim concerns the marginal deterrent value of nuclear threats. It does not deny their absolute deterrent value.

39. Thomas Schelling, *The Strategy of Conflict*, new ed. (Cambridge: Harvard University Press, 1980), p. 18.

40. Snyder, *Deterrence and Defense*, pp. 23–24.

41. Indeed, as suggested in Chapter 1, it is misleading to refer to what nuclear threats threaten as punishment, because this term is normally understood to imply that the harm involved is imposed upon those believed to be responsible for the nonconforming behavior, such that punishment of the (known) innocent would be a contradictory notion. See, for example, Anthony Quinton, "On Punishment," *Analysis* 14, no. 6 (June, 1954). The phrase "vicarious punishment," sometimes

applied to nuclear deterrence, makes this terminological mistake explicit. Speaking of punishment in both the legal and nuclear contexts should not disguise the important moral difference between them.

42. A version of the rationality paradox is discussed by David Gauthier, "Deterrence, Maximization, and Rationality," in Russell Hardin et al. (eds.), *Nuclear Deterrence: Ethics and Strategy* (Chicago: University of Chicago Press, 1985), pp. 99–120.

43. As this construal suggests, (2) is concerned only with the question whether there is a presumption that the threatener is willing to carry out its threats, not whether the threatener has demonstrated such a willingness through past behavior. In cases where there is such a demonstration, (2) would be false. But nuclear deterrence is not one of these cases.

44. Some strategic analysts would argue that determining this is a fairly simple matter, because the factors on one side or the other can effectively be ignored. For example, supporters of what is called existential deterrence argue that the possibility that nonconforming behavior could lead to societal destruction is enough to make deterrence very effective and to show that it has substantial marginal deterrent value. This argument says, in effect, that concerns about credibility can be set aside. This and other arguments that imply that one side or the other in this comparative debate can be safely ignored will be discussed in later chapters.

45. The argument does not assume that a legal system is a neutral arbiter of social disputes rather than a tool for promoting the interests of those in power. If a social order is systematically unjust, the law will certainly be one of the main means by which that injustice is perpetrated. This is to say that the social order a legal system helps to maintain may or may not be of moral value.

46. Brodie, *Strategy in the Missile Age*, p. 272.

47. As the notion is understood here, a particular failure of nuclear deterrence occurs whenever there is a nuclear war (though not all failures of nuclear deterrence are or lead to nuclear wars). Sometimes the notion of failure is used more narrowly, so as to cover only those nuclear wars that are the result of deliberation, not those resulting from accident or an out-of-control escalatory process. For example, speaking of nuclear deterrence, Leon Sigal claims: "War can result not only from a failure of deterrence but also from its instability." *Nuclear Forces in Europe* (Washington: Brookings Institution, 1984), p. 9. Robert Holmes also seems to understand deterrence failure more narrowly. *On War and Morality* (Princeton: Princeton University Press, 1989), pp. 256–59. It seems, though, that the comparison between nuclear and conventional deterrence is best made in terms of the

broader notion of failure, because the concern is to avoid all nuclear wars, not only those begun deliberately.

48. The debate over whether a nation could survive a nuclear war, as discussed in Chapter 1, is, in part, a debate over the fragility of modern societies in the face of multiple nuclear explosions. Most of those who argue that a large-scale nuclear war is survivable simply mischaracterize modern societies as being much less fragile than they in fact are.

49. Richard Wasserstrom, "War, Nuclear War, and Nuclear Deterrence: Some Conceptual and Moral Issues," in Hardin et al., *Nuclear Deterrence*, p. 30.

50. Leon Wieseltier, *Nuclear War, Nuclear Peace* (New York: Holt, Rinehart, Winston, 1983), p. 75.

51. This notion of general failure is noncomparative, because the judgment of general failure does not consider whether alternative policies would do worse – for example, by bringing about social destruction more quickly. In a criticism of an earlier version of this argument, Jonathan Schonsheck has argued that nuclear deterrence should not necessarily be seen as a general failure even if it leads to destruction of society, because the best alternative policy might have led to the destruction of society sooner. This is to argue, in effect, that the notion of general failure is comparative. Jonathan Schonsheck, "On Nuclear Deterrence and Nuclear Deterrent Threats: Criteria of Success and Failure," unpublished manuscript. As a matter of linguistic practice, I do not believe that the notion of failure is comparative in this way, but, in any case, I choose to use the noncomparative sense, allowing the comparison between nuclear and conventional deterrence to emerge from the larger argument.

52. Jonathan Schell, *The Abolition* (New York: Bantam Books, 1984), pp. 139–40. The scare quotes suggest that Schell appreciates the point I am making.

53. For example, Robert Jervis, *The Illogic of American Nuclear Strategy* (Ithaca, NY: Cornell University Press, 1984), p. 49.

54. Jeff McMahan suggested to me the parallel between my argument and the trade-off argument. He argues that the trade-off is a bad deal in *British Nuclear Weapons: For and Against* (London: Junction Books, 1981).

55. In speaking of the kind of strategy a nation employs, however, one should not assume that it is the strategy itself that determines what weapons are built and how they are deployed. It may well be that the strategic doctrine is largely epiphenomenal, an after-the-fact rationalization for weapons decisions made on other grounds. Speaking of strategic doctrines, Desmond Ball suggests that "their role in U.S.

nuclear force structure development is as instruments to be employed in intra-mural bargaining rather than as signposts to illumine that development." Desmond Ball, "The Role of Strategic Concepts and Doctrine in U.S. Strategic Nuclear Force Development," in Bernard Brodie et al. (eds.), *National Security and International Stability* (Cambridge, MA: Oelgeschlager, Gunn, Hain, 1983), p. 60. Whatever its causal role in military policy, however, strategic doctrine may be essential to assessing the comparative effectiveness of nuclear deterrence.

56. In the discussion of nuclear strategies in the following chapters, the strategies I examine are meant to be ideal types. They are not meant to be accurate representations either of strategies that nuclear nations have actually practiced or of strategies that particular strategic thinkers have advocated, though I will make free use of the doctrinal writings of the nuclear strategists in presenting my ideal types. I am not interested in giving a history of strategic theory, but rather in discussing the logic of some concepts developed in that history.

57. Richard K. Betts, "Surprise Attack and Preemption," in Graham T. Allison et al. (eds.), *Hawks, Doves, and Owls* (New York: Norton, 1985), p. 70.

58. These words from a 1955 speech of Churchill are quoted in many places, including Robert Jervis, *The Meaning of the Nuclear Revolution* (Ithaca, NY: Cornell University Press, 1989), pp. 7–8n19.

59. Hans Morganthau, "The Fallacy of Thinking Conventionally about Nuclear Weapons," in Herbert Levine and David Carlton (eds.), *The Nuclear Arms Race Debated* (New York: McGraw-Hill, 1986), p. 13.

5. MORAL COUNTERFORCE

1. It is not uncontroversial to claim that its population and social and economic infrastructure are necessarily what a nation regards as its highest value. As discussed later, some have argued that what the leadership of the Soviet Union valued most highly was, instead, its means of political control. Because military forces are an important means of maintaining such control, this view effectively conflates the categories of countervalue and counterforce.

2. This suggests an interesting connection between the prudential and moral arguments for counterforce deterrence. If the prudential argument succeeds, the moral argument would have to succeed as well, on pain of otherwise forcing a resort to the third and most problematic approach to resolving the conflicts – namely, moral revisionism. On the other hand, if the prudential argument fails, then the moral argument may be superfluous, in that the success of prudential revisionism (which the failure of the rebuttal would help to insure,

though not guarantee) would recommend the abandonment of nuclear deterrence, even if the moral argument showed it to be permissible.

3. The moral counterforce argument may also show that nuclear deterrence could satisfy the demands of the principle of proportionality in the just-war tradition, which requires that the amount of force used or threatened be no more than proportional to the harm that would thereby be avoided. See Robert Jervis, *The Meaning of the Nuclear Revolution* (Ithaca, NY: Cornell University Press, 1989), p. 120. My earlier discussion has ignored the issue of proportionality in favor of a focus on the principle of discrimination and the hostage-holding argument on the grounds that the additional condemnation of nuclear deterrence provided by the principle of proportionality would be redundant. But it is important to note that if the moral counterforce argument is to succeed in showing that nuclear deterrence can satisfy the norms of the just-war tradition, it must deflect the moral objections based on both principles.

4. Arthur Burns, *Ethics and Deterrence: A Nuclear Balance Without Hostage Cities?* Adelphi Paper no. 69 (London: Institute for Strategic Studies, 1970), pp. 26 (emphasis removed), 25.

5. To repeat an important point made earlier, the strategies I discuss are meant to be ideal types. The account of counterforce strategy presented here is not meant to represent a strategy practiced by any particular nation or a strategy developed by any particular strategic thinker.

6. The relevant technical considerations are discussed, for example, in Kosta Tsipis, *Arsenal: Understanding Weapons in the Nuclear Age* (New York: Simon and Schuster, 1984).

7. If the impossibility of a disarming first-strike is taken as a necessary condition for a situation of mutual vulnerability, then this claim is trivially true. The substantive point would then be that nuclear weapons have made mutual vulnerability possible – that is, they have made it possible for a nation to make a disarming first strike against it impossible. Once nuclear opponents each have a sufficient number of nuclear weapons sufficiently well protected, each side cannot then remove its own vulnerability without the other side's acquiescence. In particular, a nation cannot remove its own vulnerability through developing a capacity for a disarming first strike.

8. Another kind of counterforce technology that, some believe, might, by itself or in conjunction with counterforce-targeted nuclear weapons, give a nation the capacity to destroy almost all of its opponent's strategic nuclear forces, thereby rendering the opponent unable to retaliate effectively, is ballistic missile defenses. But, as will be discussed in Chapter 6, such defenses, alone or with other counterforce

weapons systems, cannot remove the vulnerability of a nation in a condition of mutual vulnerability. References in this section to counterforce capability should be understood broadly so as to include missile defense technology.

9. Albert Wohlstetter, "Bishops, Statesmen, and Other Strategists on the Bombing of Innocents," *Commentary* 75, no. 6 (June, 1983), p. 18. See also Donald Cotter, "Peacetime Operations: Safety and Security," in Ashton Carter, John Steinbruner, and Charles Zraket (eds.), *Managing Nuclear Operations* (Washington: Brookings Institution, 1987), pp. 29, 31. See also the references in Chapter 1, note 2.

10. For a discussion of such weapons, see Theodore Taylor, "Third Generation Nuclear Weapons," *Scientific American* 256, no. 4 (April, 1987).

11. Distinguishing between a pure and an impure counterforce strategy in terms of whether or not military targets in or near cities are included is based only on a consideration of immediate fatalities. If may be that nonlocal effects of nuclear explosions, such as fallout, ozone depletion, nuclear winter, famine, disease, and so forth, would be so deadly that no nuclear attack of more than a few warheads could avoid a very large number of civilian deaths. If so, the pure/impure distinction is largely untenable.

12. This is obvious from the fact that the United States, along with the Soviet Union, sought, throughout the period of the Cold War, to make their nuclear warheads increasingly accurate. Accurate warheads are required for counterforce use, but not for exclusively countervalue use. Earlier in the nuclear age, before the development of the technologies that made greater accuracy possible, the strategy of the United States may have been, of necessity, countervalue.

13. For example, according to Desmond Ball, the United States has aimed nuclear warheads at approximately sixty targets within the city limits of Moscow. *Can Nuclear War Be Controlled?* Adelphi Paper no. 169 (London: International Institute for Strategic Studies, 1981), p. 30.

14. John Finnis, Joseph M. Boyle, Jr., and Germain Grisez, *Nuclear Deterrence, Morality and Realism* (Oxford: Clarendon Press, 1987), pp. 13–18.

15. Fred Kaplan, *Wizards of Armageddon* (New York: Simon and Schuster, 1983), pp. 318–19.

16. Finnis, Boyle, and Grisez, *Nuclear Deterrence, Morality and Realism*, pp. 18–27.

17. Desmond Ball, "U.S. Strategic Forces: How Would They Be Used?" in Steven Miller (ed.), *Strategy and Nuclear Deterrence* (Princeton: Princeton University Press, 1984), pp. 216–17. Ball distinguishes five kinds of policy, not just two, and what I call operational policy he calls force employment policy or action policy.

18. The distinction between war avoidance and war waging is like the

distinction drawn by Glenn Snyder between deterrence and defense. *Deterrence and Defense* (Princeton: Princeton University Press, 1961), pp. 3–5. Snyder also points out the potential tension between them.

19. Bernard Brodie, *Strategy in the Missile Age* (Princeton: Princeton University Press, 1965), p. 276.

20. Colin Gray, "Nuclear Strategy: the Case for a Theory of Victory," in Miller, *Strategy and Nuclear Deterrence*, p. 56.

21. Bernard Brodie, "The Development of Nuclear Strategy," in Miller, *Strategy and Nuclear Deterrence*, p. 12.

22. Hans Morganthau, "The Fallacy of Thinking Conventionally about Nuclear Weapons," in Herbert Levine and David Carlton (eds.), *The Nuclear Arms Race Debated* (New York: McGraw-Hill, 1986), p. 13.

23. Whenever I use the term "deterrence" without qualification, I mean pre-war deterrence. The term "pre-war deterrence" is used by Colin Gray in the passage quoted earlier from "Nuclear Strategy," p. 56. The term seems to connote the inevitability of war, though this is presumably not intended in its use. But given that this term has been introduced into the debate by advocates of counterforce strategy, this connotation might be taken by critics to support their claim that that strategy is not the best policy for war avoidance.

24. Benjamin Lambeth, quoted in Lawrence Freedman, *The Evolution of Nuclear Strategy* (New York: St. Martin's, 1981), p. 260.

25. As the counterforce strategist Colin Gray puts it: "The debate over nuclear strategy is really about the prevention of war." *Nuclear Strategy and National Style* (Lanham, MD: Hamilton Press, 1986), p. 9.

26. This idea is developed in Ian Clark, *Limited Nuclear War* (Princeton: Princeton University Press, 1982).

27. Brodie, *Strategy in the Missile Age*, p. 313.

28. Freedman, *The Evolution of Nuclear Strategy*, p. 105.

29. Wohlstetter, "Bishops, Statesmen, and Other Strategists," p. 15.

30. James Turner Johnson, "Threats, Values, and Defense: Does the Defense of Values by Force Remain a Moral Possibility?" in William O'Brien and John Langan (eds.), *The Nuclear Dilemma and the Just War Tradition* (Lexington, MA: Lexington Books, 1986), p. 44.

31. This is a theme of Wohlstetter's "Bishops, Statesmen, and Other Strategists."

32. This "frosty apothegm" is attributed to John Newhouse, by Wohlstetter in "Bishops, Statesmen, and Other Strategists," pp. 15–16.

33. Paul Ramsey, "A Political Ethics Context for Strategic Thinking," in Morton Kaplan (ed.), *Strategic Thinking and Its Moral Implications* (Chicago: University of Chicago Center for Policy Study, 1973), p. 136.

34. Fred Ikle, "Can Nuclear Deterrence Last Out the Century?" *Foreign Affairs* 51, no. 2 (January, 1973), p. 281.

35. Donald Brennan, "The Case for Population Defense," in Johan Holst and William Schneider (eds.), *Why ABM? Policy Issues in the Missile Defense Controversy* (New York: Pergamon Press, 1969), p. 116.

36. The analogy with legal deterrence, however, suggests a potential problem for counterforce strategy. The legal analogue of deterrence by threat of denial is deterrence by threat of restitution, the threat that the law breaker will be required to make the victim whole. The primary goal of both denial and restitution is to right the wrong rather than to punish the wrongdoer. But there are serious doubts about whether legal threats of restitution in the criminal law could serve as an effective deterrent, and there may be similar doubts about the deterrent effectiveness of military threats of denial.

37. This is not inconsistent with the fact that a nation operating under a prudentially justifiable counterforce strategy would, in practice, avoid attacking civilians in war, because the threats against civilians would be meant to be executed only after there was no longer hope of keeping the war limited.

38. If pure counterforce strategy avoids the just-war and deontological disadvantages of other forms of nuclear deterrence, this does not mean a nation is obligated to practice it, only that it is permissible to do so. So the conflict arises in that case not because one is obligated to practice this strategy on deontological grounds and obligated not to practice it on consequentialist grounds, but rather because one is obligated on consequentialist grounds to practice another strategy, one that, unlike pure counterforce strategy, one is obligated not to practice on deontological grounds.

39. Anthony Kenny, *The Logic of Deterrence* (Chicago: University of Chicago Press, 1985), p. 39.

40. As mentioned earlier, to claim that a pure counterforce strategy would put at risk only a relatively small number of civilians considers only deaths resulting from the immediate effects of the nuclear explosions. If there were a large number of civilian deaths from the long-term environmental effects of the explosions, the morally relevant difference between pure and impure counterforce strategy would be lost, and pure strategy, like impure strategy, would be shown by the argument soon to be presented not to be morally justifiable. On the other hand, if the pure strategy involved so small a number of warheads that the long-term effects could be discounted, the argument in this section about the strategy's ineffectiveness would have all the more force.

41. Gregory Kavka, *Moral Paradoxes of Nuclear Deterrence* (Cambridge: Cambridge University Press, 1987), p. 49. Kavka's scrupulous retaliation is not, strictly, a pure counterforce strategy, because it includes threats against isolated nonmilitary targets, such as, perhaps, hy-

droelectric facilities. But the point about ineffectiveness applies equally to pure counterforce and scrupulous retaliation strategies.

42. Jefferson McMahan, "Is Nuclear Deterrence Paradoxical?" *Ethics* 99, no. 2 (January, 1989), p. 411.

43. Finnis, Boyle, and Grisez, *Nuclear Deterrence, Morality and Realism*, pp. 138, 148.

44. McMahan, "Is Nuclear Deterrence Paradoxical?" p. 412.

45. McMahan, "Is Nuclear Deterrence Paradoxical?" p. 412.

46. Ramsey, "A Political Ethics Context," pp. 139, 135.

47. Ramsey, "A Political Ethics Context," p. 144. In claiming that suspended deterrence "reverse[s] the relation between arms and society" what he may mean is that suspended deterrence avoids the traditional use of military forces to defend society by attacking opposing military forces. Because they are not based on a capacity to attack opposing military forces, nuclear forces under suspended deterrence could not defend society.

48. The latter claim does not necessarily follow from the former, because proportionality is a measure of the harm done in comparison with the value of what the nation achieves, whereas the acceptability of damage is a measure of the harm done in comparison with the value of what the opponent achieves. It should also be noted that Ramsey does not regard the threat of disproportionate damage as necessarily morally unacceptable, despite his adherence to the norms of the just-war tradition. He says: "Not every threat of something disproportionate is itself a disproportionate threat." "A Political Ethics Context," p. 145. For a discussion of Ramsey's views on this matter, see Michael Walzer, *Just and Unjust Wars* (New York: Basic Books, 1977), p. 280.

49. Ramsey, "A Political Ethics Context," pp. 142, 133.

50. Bruce Russett, "A Countercombatant Alternative to Nuclear MADness," in Harold Ford and Francis Winters (eds.), *Ethics and Nuclear Strategy* (Maryknoll, NY: Orbis Books, 1977). I am assuming that Russett's strategy would count as pure counterforce strategy, although this is not completely clear.

51. Part of Russett's reason for avoiding the targeting of strategic nuclear forces is a concern that this would lead to crisis instability, a situation in which each side, in a crisis, fearing that the other may be about to attempt to disarm it, is more likely to initiate a war. (This notion will be discussed in the next chapter.) But as he recognizes, it is not clear that his strategy can avoid crisis instability, for, given the number and accuracy of the warheads the strategy would require, the Soviet Union would probably have assumed that the bulk of its strategic forces were targeted, despite U.S. declaratory policy to the contrary.

52. Finnis, Boyle, and Grisez argue that a morally acceptable counterforce strategy would be one in which "only the forces which would be used in a potential enemy's unjust aggression would be threatened." *Nuclear Deterrence, Morality and Realism*, p. 132. See, also, Robert Jervis, *The Meaning of the Nuclear Revolution*, p. 115.

53. Ramsey, "A Political Ethics Context," p. 141. Ramsey seems here to have abandoned the assumption he elsewhere appears to hold, and which I attributed to him, that the threat of collateral civilian damage is necessary for an effective deterrence policy. See, also, Burns, *Ethics and Deterrence*, p. 17.

54. Russett, "A Countercombatant Alternative," p. 126.

55. See Robert Jervis, *The Illogic of American Nuclear Strategy* (Ithaca, NY: Cornell University Press, 1984), pp. 71–72.

56. James Child, *Nuclear War—the Moral Dimension* (New Brunswick, NJ: Transaction Books, 1986), p. 166.

57. Wohlstetter, "Bishops, Statesmen, and Other Strategists," p. 27.

58. These claims need some qualification. If the destruction of the opponent's means of maintaining political control is to be regarded as part of a pure counterforce strategy, it must be the case that this destruction could be achieved without destroying cities, which is doubtful. In addition, to regard the threat of such destruction as a form of counterforce strategy at all, one must regard the so-called countercontrol targets of the domestic police apparatus as honorary military targets, which would raise moral questions of the sort discussed earlier.

59. The phrase "moral asymmetry" is borrowed from Patrick Blackett, quoted in Freedman, *The Evolution of Nuclear Strategy*, p. 143. Blackett uses the phrase to characterize the views of Wohlstetter.

60. Moral Manichaeanism – the view that the Cold War rivalry was a contest of good versus evil – is more or less present in the writings of many nuclear strategists. It can be the basis for a quite different approach to the morality of nuclear deterrence. If the West is righteous and the East evil, the nuclear weapons policy of the West may be justified not merely on defensive grounds, but as part of a crusade to rid the world of evil. Mutual vulnerability undercuts moral Manichaeanism, however, for the effort to rid the world of evil risks destruction of the righteous as well. For this reason, moral Manichaeanism is a dangerous view, because its proponents have a strong motivation to deny the existence or the implications of mutual vulnerability, if not on empirical grounds, then on theological grounds.

61. It should not be surprising, for example, to discover that British leaders were relieved during the Blitz when the Nazis shifted their bombing from military targets to the city of London. See George

Quester, *Deterrence Before Hiroshima* (1966, reprint ed., New Brunswick, NJ: Transaction Books, 1986), pp. 117–18.

62. Robert Art, "Between Assured Destruction and Nuclear Victory: The Case for the 'Mad-Plus' Posture," in Russell Hardin et al. (eds.), *Nuclear Deterrence: Ethics and Strategy* (Chicago: University of Chicago Press, 1985), p. 133.

63. In the nuclear target list that was developed by the United States, Soviet cities were categorized as "withholds." See Desmond Ball, "U.S. Strategic Forces," p. 221.

64. Finnis, Boyle, and Grisez, *Nuclear Deterrence, Morality and Realism,* p. 140.

65. For a discussion of the doctrine of double effect, see Alan Donagan, *The Theory of Morality* (Chicago: University of Chicago Press, 1977), pp. 157–64.

66. Robert W. Tucker, *The Nuclear Debate* (New York: Holmes and Meier, 1985), p. 44.

67. Paul Ramsey, *The Just War: Force and Political Responsibility* (1968, reprint ed., Lanham, MD: University Press of America, 1983), p. 252.

68. Michael Walzer, *Just and Unjust Wars,* p. 280.

69. Walter Stein, "The Limits of Nuclear War: Is a Just Deterrence Strategy Possible?" in James Finn (ed.), *Peace, the Churches, and the Bomb* (New York: Council on Religion and International Affairs, 1965), pp. 80–81, emphasis omitted.

70. Finnis, Boyle, and Grisez, *Nuclear Deterrence, Morality and Realism,* p. 92, emphasis omitted.

71. McMahan, "Is Nuclear Deterrence Paradoxical?" p. 414.

72. Ramsey, *The Just War,* p. 318.

73. Jervis, *The Meaning of the Nuclear Revolution,* p. 13.

74. Ramsey recognizes the role of the threat of civilian damage in the effectiveness of intra-war deterrence. *The Just War,* p. 252. But he apparently does not appreciate that this makes the actual civilian damage wanted, just as the prospect of civilian damage is wanted in pre-war deterrence.

6. PRUDENTIAL COUNTERFORCE

1. Dashiell Hammett, *The Novels of Dashiell Hammett* (New York: Alfred Knopf, 1965), p. 417.

2. Lawrence Freedman, *The Evolution of Nuclear Strategy* (New York: St. Martin's, 1981), p. 395.

3. William O'Brien, "The Failure of Deterrence and the Conduct of War," in William O'Brien and John Langan (eds.), *The Nuclear Di-*

lemma and the Just War Tradition (Lexington, MA: Lexington Books, 1986), p. 153.

4. Freedman, *The Evolution of Nuclear Strategy*, p. xvi.

5. This is the view of Bernard Brodie. *Strategy in the Missile Age* (Princeton: Princeton University Press, 1965), p. 273. One might think that this claim is more obviously true in the case of the United States, because its geographical position makes it effectively invulnerable to foreign conventional attack, so that it need not worry about the credibility of its nuclear threats to achieve basic deterrence of such an attack. But the United States can be brought under nuclear attack from overseas, and, as the text shows, the credibility problem arises here as well.

6. The argument for this is discussed in Freedman, *The Evolution of Nuclear Strategy*, pp. 387–92. Bernard Brodie recognizes the possibility of the kind of attack imagined in this scenario, but he, like Freedman, does not believe that it is a serious problem for deterrence effectiveness. *Strategy in the Missile Age*, pp. 292–93. The reason neither sees it as a serious problem is likely that they accept the argument discussed in the next chapter that nuclear deterrence is stable enough to overcome any deficiency in credibility.

7. No one seems to believe that there is much of a credibility problem regarding the threat of all-out countervalue retaliation for an all-out countervalue attack. Although such retaliation may not be rational, in that there may be no good reason to do it, it is clearly less irrational than countervalue retaliation for a limited counterforce attack, because, in the latter case, the nation's cities are still left to lose. On this issue, see Chapter 7, note 88.

8. Counterforce strategists believed that the credibility problem presented by the scenario of a limited Soviet attack against U.S. missiles would be solved if the United States had remaining a sufficient number of missiles capable of counterforce retaliation against Soviet strategic targets. In other words, they did not see the credibility problem as inherent in deterrence, whether basic or extended, but simply as a function of inadequate counterforce deployments. There was not in the late 1970s a permanent vulnerability of the United States to coercion because of the Soviet threat of limited attack, only a "window of vulnerability" until the required deployments were made, at which point the U.S. threat to retaliate for such an attack would no longer lack credibility.

9. Those making this argument generally recognize a continuum between nuclear and conventional weapons, such that the credibility of the nation's overall posture of military deterrence is lacking unless it can respond at any potential level of nuclear or conventional conflict.

10. This phrase comes from Reagan's 1983 speech proposing the strategic defense initiative. *The New York Times*, March 24, 1983, p. A20.

11. Counterforce strategists are not unanimous in their resignation to the view that mutual vulnerability cannot be overcome. This disagreement will be aired later in the chapter.

12. Although counterforce strategists are the main proponents of missile defenses, some strategists who are not committed to counterforce argue that missile defenses would be valuable if they could unambiguously protect strategic forces rather than population centers, because such defenses would decrease the vulnerability of those forces and so strengthen the stability of deterrence. See, for example, Thomas Schelling, "What Went Wrong with Arms Control?" *Foreign Affairs* 64, no. 2 (Winter, 1985–86), pp. 222, 232.

13. Steven Lee, "Morality, the SDI, and Limited Nuclear War," *Philosophy and Public Affairs* 17, no. 1 (Winter, 1988), pp. 15–43.

14. Is it a morally important difference? It may seem so, because offensive capabilities indirectly threaten civilians and defensive capabilities do not. But one must morally assess defenses not in isolation, but in the context in which they would be used. On this point, see Lee, "Morality, the SDI, and Limited Nuclear War."

15. Freedman, *The Evolution of Nuclear Strategy*, p. 395. Some counterforce strategists would deny that a nuclear war's remaining limited must be reasonably foreseeable in order to justify adopting such a strategy, arguing that the mere possibility that such a strategy would help to limit a war is sufficient to justify adopting it, because if the strategy did keep the war limited, lives would be saved. But this line of argument concentrates exclusively on the damage-limitation impact of a war-waging capability, ignoring the more important question of its impact on war avoidance. The contribution of a counterforce strategy to war avoidance depends on its solving the credibility problem, and this requires the reasonable foreseeability, rather than the mere possibility, of a war's remaining limited.

16. For a discussion of limited nuclear war as a bargaining process, see Thomas Schelling, *Arms and Influence* (New Haven, CT: Yale University Press, 1966), for example, pp. 131–141.

17. For successful intra-war deterrence, nations must have the capacity to keep from attacking further (that is, adequate control over their own forces) and sufficient reason to restrain themselves. Likewise, for successful pre-war deterrence, nations must also have the control over their forces to keep them from being used without authorization and sufficient reason not to authorize such use.

18. Freedman, *The Evolution of Nuclear Strategy*, p. 209.

19. Schelling, *Arms and Influence*, p. 135.

20. Robert Jervis, *The Illogic of American Nuclear Strategy* (Ithaca, NY: Cornell University Press, 1984), p. 110.
21. Glenn Snyder, "The Balance of Power and the Balance of Terror," in Paul Seabury (ed.), *Balance of Power* (San Francisco: Chandler, 1965), p. 188.
22. George Quester, *The Future of Nuclear Deterrence* (Lexington, MA: Lexington Books, 1986), p. 3.
23. Some counterforce strategists, whose view is discussed later, adopt the weaker position that a nation's counterforce capability can, if not impose a bargain unfavorable to the opponent, at least avoid the nation having to accept a bargain unfavorable to itself. But this position creates problems for the claim that counterforce strategy can make an appropriately limited nuclear war reasonably foreseeable.
24. Harold Brown, quoted in Freedman, *The Evolution of Nuclear Strategy*, p. 393.
25. Ashton Carter, John Steinbruner, and Charles Zraket, "Introduction," in Carter, Steinbruner, and Zraket (eds.), *Managing Nuclear Operations* (Washington: Brookings Institution, 1987), p. 1.
26. Desmond Ball, *Can Nuclear War Be Controlled?* Adelphi Paper no. 169 (London: International Institute for Strategic Studies, 1981), p. 2.
27. Carter, Steinbruner, and Zraket, "Introduction," p. 11.
28. Ball, *Can Nuclear War Be Controlled?*, p. 36. For a discussion of the advantages and disadvantages of deliberately targeting the opponent's command structure, see John Steinbruner, "Choices and Trade-Offs," in Carter, Steinbruner, and Zraket, *Managing Nuclear Operations*, pp. 545–46.
29. This problem is referred to as the trade-off between positive and negative controls. See Steinbruner, "Choices and Trade-Offs," pp. 539–43.
30. Robert McNamara, "The Military Role of Nuclear Weapons: Perceptions and Misperceptions," *Foreign Affairs* 62, no. 1 (Fall, 1983), p. 72.
31. For a discussion of these two ideas of escalation, see John Baylis et al., *Contemporary Strategy: Theories and Policies* (London: Croom Helm, 1975), p. 126.
32. The argument does not depend on the claim that it is rational to escalate. The conclusion that limited nuclear war is not reasonably foreseeable implies that in general it is not. The point is that the adoption of counterforce strategy can lead national leaders to believe that escalation can achieve advantage, and so lead them to believe that it is rational, even though, partly for the reason that they are led to such beliefs, it is not. There may be sufficient reason for each side not to escalate, but neither side may have sufficient reason for this, in the sense that it may not recognize that there is sufficient reason for this.

33. Ball, *Can Nuclear War Be Controlled?*, p. 2.
34. Henry Kissinger, quoted in Robert Jervis, *The Meaning of the Nuclear Revolution* (Ithaca, NY: Cornell University Press, 1989), p. 194.
35. Jervis, *The Illogic of American Nuclear Strategy*, p. 34.
36. For a discussion of the prospects for a decapitating strike, see Ashton Carter, "Assessing Command System Vulnerability," in Carter, Steinbruner, and Zraket, *Managing Nuclear Operations*, pp. 560–73.
37. Jervis, *The Illogic of American Nuclear Strategy*, p. 130.
38. Ibid, pp. 59–60.
39. Ibid, p. 130.
40. Ibid, pp. 132, 152.
41. The problem of recognizable limits to support the intra-war bargaining process is discussed by Thomas Schelling, *Arms and Influence*, Chapter 4, and *The Strategy of Conflict*, new ed. (Cambridge: Harvard University Press, 1980), Appendix A.
42. Spurgeon Keeny, Jr. and Wolfgang Panofsky, "MAD versus NUTS: Can Doctrine or Weaponry Remedy the Mutual Hostage Relationship of the Superpowers?" *Foreign Affairs* 60, no. 2 (Winter, 1981–82), p. 298.
43. Freedman, *The Evolution of Nuclear Strategy*, p. 382.
44. Another reason to think that the opponent is unlikely to have sufficient reason to practice restraint is the tendency of nations to adopt more ambitious war aims as a war progresses, especially in cases where their loses have been high. As the violence increases, the stakes may expand. Fred Iklé claims that escalation "may raise the ambitions on one or both sides and thus widen the gap between what one side would settle for and what the other demands." Fred Iklé, as quoted in Ian Clark, *Limited Nuclear War* (Princeton: Princeton University Press, 1982), p. 209.
45. Another complicating factor, so far ignored in my bipolar analysis, which would undermine the opponent's motivation for restraint in a nuclear war, is the role of other nuclear powers that might become involved in a nuclear war between two superpowers. Because the other nations would not be under the control of a superpower, even if they were bound to that superpower by an alliance, their existence could provide further reason for that superpower's opponent not to expect its restraint to guarantee reciprocal restraint in the weapons used against it.
46. McGeorge Bundy, George Kennan, Robert McNamara, and Gerard Smith, "Nuclear Weapons and the Atlantic Alliance," *Foreign Affairs* 60, no. 4 (Spring, 1982), p. 757.
47. Michael Howard, "On Fighting a Nuclear War," *International Security* 5, no. 4 (Spring, 1981), p. 9.
48. Clark, *Limited Nuclear War*, p. 199.

49. See William Daugherty, Barbara Levi, and Frank von Hippel, "The Consequences of 'Limited' Nuclear Attacks on the United States," *International Security* 10, no. 4 (Spring, 1986), pp. 3–45.
50. For a discussion and criticism of this kind of view, see Jervis, *The Meaning of the Nuclear Revolution*, pp. 16–19.
51. This is not merely a verbal issue over how to define the notion of victory. One could define winning a limited nuclear war in terms of relative advantage, but in that case, one would need to go on to make the distinction, suggested by John Mueller, between a war-winning and a war-profiting capacity. John Mueller, "The Essential Irrelevance of Nuclear Weapons," *International Security* 13, no. 2 (Fall, 1988), p. 69n28. Then the claim would be that an appropriately limited nuclear war is one which the nation not only wins, but also profits from.
52. Jervis, *The Illogic of American Nuclear Strategy*, p. 25.
53. This claim applies, more precisely, for strategic nuclear war. A tactical nuclear war that did not escalate might leave one side with an overall advantage, and hence be appropriately limited for that side, because its primary effect might be denial rather than punishment. But even if a tactical nuclear war could satisfy the third condition, it is unlikely to satisfy the first and second conditions. A nuclear war which began as tactical would be unlikely to remain such.
54. Clark, *Limited Nuclear War*, p. 189. Clark's book provides an extended argument for this conclusion.
55. Desmond Ball, *Can Nuclear War Be Controlled?*, pp. 36, 37.
56. Jervis, *The Illogic of American Nuclear Strategy*, p. 111.
57. Warner Schilling, "U.S. Strategic Nuclear Concepts in the 1970s: The Search for Sufficiently Equivalent Countervailing Parity," in Steven Miller (ed.), *Strategy and Nuclear Deterrence* (Princeton: Princeton University Press, 1984), pp. 200–01.
58. Thus I am not open to the charge, reported by Lawrence Freedman, that critics of counterforce strategy try to "have it both ways, arguing simultaneously that the strategic balance [is] so stable that counterforce options would provide no advantages while insisting that their introduction would be destabilizing." *The Evolution of Nuclear Strategy*, p. 380. My argument is that counterforce strategy may have advantages as well as disadvantages, but that the disadvantages vary directly with the advantages, so that it is unable to provide a basis for a rebuttal of the prima facie argument.
59. A similar argument is made by Henry Shue, "Having it Both Ways: The Gradual Wrong Turn in American Strategy," in Henry Shue (ed.), *Nuclear Deterrence and Moral Restraint* (Cambridge: Cambridge University Press, 1989), pp. 39–40, and also by Harold Feiveson, "Finite Deterrence," in the same volume, p. 281.

60. The label "selective options strategy" usually refers to the doctrine adopted by the United States in 1974 under Secretary of Defense James Schlesinger. See Freedman, *The Evolution of Nuclear Strategy*, pp. 377–79. My use of the term is not meant to indicate a strategy necessarily identical to the one proposed by Schlesinger.

61. Clark, *Limited Nuclear War*, pp. 186–87.

62. Walter Slocombe, "The Countervailing Strategy," in Miller, *Strategy and Nuclear Deterrence*, p. 245.

63. Harold Brown, *Thinking about National Security* (Boulder, CO: Westview, 1983), p. 245.

64. For a discussion and critique of the notion of counterforce parity, see Jervis, *The Illogic of American Nuclear Strategy*, pp. 111–18. For a discussion of the role of equivalence or parity in U.S. policy, see Warner Schilling, "U.S. Strategic Nuclear Concepts." Another argument for counterforce parity was that the United States should have nuclear forces essentially equivalent to those of the Soviet Union for political reasons, in order to create an impression of equality in the eyes of the world. See Harold Brown, quoted in Colin Gray, *Nuclear Strategy and National Style* (Lanham, MD: Hamilton Press, 1986), p. 246. See also Freedman, *The Evolution of Nuclear Strategy*, Chapter 24.

65. Slocombe, "The Countervailing Strategy," pp. 252–53. The reactive character here attributed to countervailing strategy is supposed to characterize nuclear deterrence in general, because a policy of deterrence is not a policy of initiation and aggression. I refer to countervailing strategy as reactive in order to contrast it with highly ambitious forms of counterforce, which, as we shall see, are interested in compellence as well as deterrence. The point is that a counterforce strategy could not do much for nuclear threat credibility unless it crosses over from deterrence to compellence.

66. Quester, *The Future of Nuclear Deterrence*, p. 93.

67. Freedman, *The Evolution of Nuclear Strategy*, p. 389.

68. Not everyone sees this difficulty. In the next chapter, I will discuss the position that holds that first-use threats can be effective despite the credibility problem.

69. This is a statement of what is called the stability/instability paradox, which will figure importantly in the argument of the next chapter.

70. Robert W. Tucker, *The Nuclear Debate* (New York: Holmes and Meier, 1985), p. 71.

71. Brown, *Thinking about National Security*, pp. 81–82. See also Slocombe, "The Countervailing Strategy," p. 251.

72. For a brief discussion of prevailing strategy, see Office of Technology Assessment, "Ballistic Missile Defense Technologies," in Office of Technology Assessment, *Strategic Defenses* (Princeton: Princeton Uni-

versity Press, 1986), pp. 85–86. The most thoroughgoing proponent and exponent of prevailing strategy is Colin Gray.

73. This term is from Colin Gray, "Nuclear Strategy: A Case for a Theory of Victory," in Miller, *Strategy and Nuclear Deterrence*, pp. 53, 55.

74. Gray, "Nuclear Strategy," pp. 47, 51.

75. Gray, "Nuclear Strategy," p. 30.

76. Colin Gray and Keith Payne, "Victory is Possible," *Foreign Policy*, no. 39 (1980), p. 25. This idea was discussed in the last chapter.

77. Gray, "Nuclear Strategy," p. 35n31.

78. Prevailing strategy faces a conflict similar to one faced by traditional countervalue strategy. One way to put the point about a countervalue threat's lacking credibility is that the threat has value only as a threat. Once it is carried out, there is nothing to stop the opponent from destroying the nation's society in retaliation. In the case of prevailing strategy, there would be political advantage in the nation carrying out the threat to the opponent's political order, but a similar problem arises nonetheless, because once that threat has been carried out, there would be no one left to bargain with, and so no way to keep the opponent from making the war unlimited. In either case, the ultimate threat lacks credibility. In other words, a credibility-undermining gap opens up between declaratory and operational policies for prevailing strategy, as it does for countervalue strategy. Threats to the political order are made for the sake of pre-war deterrence, but, for the sake of intra-war deterrence, they would never be carried out. Gray recognizes this kind of problem, but has no adequate response. Gray and Payne, "Victory is Possible," pp. 24–25.

79. Gray, *Nuclear Strategy and National Style*, p. 286.

80. Gray, "Nuclear Strategy," pp. 26, 53.

81. See Gray's critique of countervailing strategy, for example, in "Nuclear Strategy."

82. Earlier I quoted Jervis's assertion that a nation has escalation dominance when its forces "can contain or defeat the adversary at all levels of violence with the possible exception of the highest." Jervis, *The Illogic of American Nuclear Strategy*, p. 130. The prevailing strategist rejects the qualification.

83. Fred Ikle, "Nuclear Strategy: Can There Be a Happy Ending?" *Foreign Affairs* 63, no. 4 (1985), p. 810.

84. Gray and Payne, "Victory is Possible," p. 27.

85. Schilling, "U.S. Strategic Nuclear Concepts," p. 212.

86. For a criticism of the claim that ballistic-missile defenses can provide significant damage limitation, see Sanford Lakoff and Herbert York, *A Shield in Space: Technology, Politics, and the Strategic Defense Initiative* (Berkeley: University of California Press, 1989), Chapter 3.

87. See Hans Morganthau, "The Four Paradoxes of Nuclear Strategy," *The American Political Science Review* 58, no. 1 (March, 1964), pp. 31–32.
88. Gray, *Nuclear Strategy and National Style*, p. 253.
89. Gray, *Nuclear Strategy and National Style*, p. 252. A similar argument of James Child's is discussed in Chapter 1. *Nuclear War: The Moral Dimension* (New Brunswick, NJ: Transaction Books, 1986), p. 36.
90. Robert Holmes, *On War and Morality* (Princeton: Princeton University Press, 1989), p. 252.
91. The notion of offensive or disarming deterrence is suggested by John Mearshimer as a third alternative to deterrence by threat of denial and deterrence by threat of punishment. John Mearshimer, *Conventional Deterrence* (Ithaca, NY: Cornell University Press, 1983), p. 214n6.
92. Office of Technology Assessment, "Ballistic Missile Defense Technologies," p. 119. There are other possibilities. A nuclear war could begin through an accidental or unauthorized launch of nuclear weapons or it could begin with a "bolt from the blue," but these possibilities are considered much less likely.
93. Schilling, "U.S. Strategic Nuclear Concepts," p. 203.
94. Thomas Schelling and Morton Halperin, *Strategy and Arms Control* (1961, reprint ed., Washington: Pergamon-Brassey, 1985), p. 50.
95. Office of Technology Assessment, "Ballistic Missile Defense Technologies," p. 120.
96. Schelling, *The Strategy of Conflict*, p. 207.
97. Schelling, *Arms and Influence*, p. 23; Schelling, *The Strategy of Conflict*, pp. 232–33.
98. Both sides could not objectively succeed in practicing prevailing strategy at the same time, because success requires the asymmetrical relationship of counterforce superiority. But each side could believe that it has such superiority, and it is the belief that is crucial. More ominously, each side might believe that its ability to win a war depends on its striking first, because of the advantage this would give in cases where counterforce capabilities were closely matched.
99. Morganthau, "Four Paradoxes," p. 29.
100. Richard Betts, "Surprise Attack and Preemption," in Graham Allison, Albert Carnesale, and Joseph Nye, Jr. (eds.), *Hawks, Doves, and Owls* (New York: Norton, 1985), p. 67.
101. Tucker, *The Nuclear Debate*, p. 130.
102. Freedman, *The Evolution of Nuclear Strategy*, p. 368.
103. Jervis, *The Meaning of the Nuclear Revolution*, p. 93.
104. Betts, "Surprise Attack and Preemption," pp. 57–58. In general, the technology required for a first-strike bonus, in a situation of rough parity between nuclear opponents in numbers of nuclear warheads,

is multiple independently targeted reentry vehicles (MIRVs), which allow one missile to destroy several missiles. This was a technology achieved by both the United States and the Soviet Union.

105. Jervis, *The Illogic of American Nuclear Strategy*, p. 129.
106. Clark, *Limited Nuclear War*, p. 157.
107. Jervis, *The Illogic of American Nuclear Strategy*, p. 50.
108. Albert Carnesale, "Smart Weapons and Ordinary People: Implications of Increasingly Accurate Long-Range Missiles," in Joseph Nye, Jr., Graham Allison, and Albert Carnesale (eds.), *Fateful Visions: Avoiding Nuclear Catastrophe* (Cambridge, MA: Ballinger, 1988), pp. 44–45.
109. Robert Goodin, "Disarmament as a Moral Certainty," in Russell Hardin et al. (eds.), *Nuclear Deterrence: Ethics and Strategy* (Chicago: University of Chicago Press, 1985), p. 268. Goodin is aiming the criticism contained in this remark at nuclear deterrence in general, but our concern is its application to ambitious counterforce strategy in particular.
110. Gray, "Nuclear Strategy," p. 56.
111. Albert Wohlstetter, "Bishops, Statesmen and Other Strategists on the Bombing of Innocents," *Commentary* 75, no. 6 (June, 1983), p. 32 (emphasis removed).
112. Freedman, *The Evolution of Nuclear Strategy*, p. 398.
113. Glenn Snyder, *Deterrence and Defense* (Princeton: Princeton University Press, 1961), p. 107.
114. The study is reported in Theodore Draper, "Nuclear Temptations," *New York Review of Books* (January 19, 1984), p. 47, citing Alain Enthoven and K. Wayne Smith, *How Much Is Enough?*
115. Charles Glaser, "Defense Dominance," in Nye, Allison, and Carnesale, *Fateful Visions*, p. 246n21.
116. Office of Technology Assessment, "Ballistic Missile Defense Technologies," p. 120n5.
117. Office of Technology Assessment, "Ballistic Missile Defense Technologies," p. 119.
118. Morganthau, "Four Paradoxes," p. 30.

7. MADVOCACY

1. Leon Wieseltier, *Nuclear War, Nuclear Peace* (New York: Holt, Rinehart and Winston, 1983), p. 38.
2. Bernard Brodie, *War and Politics* (New York: Macmillan, 1973), p. 404.
3. Mixed strategy and impure counterforce strategy, discussed in Chapter 5, also recognize the novel implications of mutual vulnerability, because they acknowledge that countercity threats are nec-

essary for effective deterrence, though they may not fully appreciate the problem about crisis stability discussed in the last chapter. In any case, one of the kinds of countervalue strategy discussed in this chapter, extended deterrence, might take forms in which it is more properly regarded as a mixed strategy.

4. Advocates of MAD-based strategies were originally labeled "MAD-vocates" by Donald Brennan, who also introduced the label "MAD." Donald Brennan, "When the SALT Hit the Fan," *National Review* (June 23, 1972), pp. 685–92. Brennan meant these tendentious designations to be an embarrassment for those persons and positions to whom they were applied, much as did those who labeled the Strategic Defense Initiative "star-wars." But Brennan's designations have come to be embraced by those they were meant to embarrass.

5. For the reasons explained in this paragraph, I am using the label "deterrence only" to cover both of the kinds of MAD-based strategies discussed in this chapter, extended deterrence and minimum deterrence. This label is sometimes used more narrowly to cover only minimum deterrence.

6. The countercity bombing of the Second World War had a purported war-fighting rationale – namely, the undermining of civilian morale, which could lead to military defeat. But countercity nuclear attacks would not have even this rationale, because, as argued earlier, the war would be over too quickly for civilian morale to have any impact on the outcome.

7. Thus, Robert Foelber incorrectly claims that " 'no use' nuclear policy . . . is just another name for 'deterrence only'." "Deterrence and the Moral Use of Nuclear Weapons," in Henry Shue (ed.), *Nuclear Deterrence and Moral Restraint* (Cambridge: Cambridge University Press, 1989), p. 123. He fails to recognize that deterrence can be intra-war as well as pre-war.

8. Wieseltier, *Nuclear War, Nuclear Peace,* p. 52.

9. Theodore Draper, "Nuclear Temptations," *The New York Review of Books* (January 19, 1984), p. 43.

10. This imperative is implicit in his often-quoted remark: "The unleashed power of the atom has changed everything save our modes of thinking, and we thus drift toward unparalleled catastrophe." Otto Nathan and Heinz Norden (eds.), *Einstein on Peace* (New York: Schocken, 1968), p. 376.

11. Michael Mandelbaum, *The Nuclear Revolution* (Cambridge: Cambridge University Press, 1981), p. 9.

12. Colin Gray, *Nuclear Strategy and National Style* (Lanham, MD: Hamilton Press, 1986), p. 140. Gray criticizes this idea. Gray also argues that this sort of view about the "logic of technology" is a theme peculiar to American strategic culture. "Nuclear Strategy: The Case

for a Theory of Victory," in Steven Miller (ed.), *Strategy and Nuclear Deterrence* (Princeton: Princeton University Press, 1984), p. 29.

13. Early in the nuclear age, the atomic bomb was seen by some as potentially putting an end to war in a very different way – namely, by ending the conflict over resources, a central cause of war, by making inexpensive energy available through nuclear power. Paul Boyer, *By the Bomb's Early Light* (New York: Pantheon, 1985), p. 136.

14. Robert Holmes, *On War and Morality* (Princeton: Princeton University Press, 1989), p. 4.

15. Robert W. Tucker, *The Nuclear Debate* (New York: Holmes and Meier, 1985), p. 98.

16. Karl Kaiser, Georg Leger, Alois Mertes, Franz-Josef Schulze, "Nuclear Weapons and the Preservation of Peace," *Foreign Affairs* 60, no. 5 (Summer, 1982), p. 1159. What about wars not between great powers? The logic of the argument seems to be that any nation would benefit from being in a situation of mutual vulnerability with an opponent, so that universal nuclear proliferation could, other things being equal, abolish all war. This argument is considered by Kenneth Waltz, *The Spread of Nuclear Weapons: More May Be Better*, Adelphi Paper no. 171 (London: International Institute for Strategic Studies, 1981). The question, of course, is whether other things are equal.

17. Robert Levine has divided nuclear strategies in a different manner than I have. The basic distinction we both try to capture is that between counterforce strategies and MAD-based strategies. He seeks to do this with the labels "extenders" and "limiters," thus suggesting that the proper criterion of distinction is whether or not the policy in question is a strategy of extended deterrence. This leads him to ignore most of the strategists discussed in the next section and to include among the limiters some strategists (such as Graham Allison, Albert Carnesale, and Joseph Nye) who support extended deterrence. The preferable taxonomy is to base the counterforce/MAD distinction on how the strategy in question responds to the credibility problem and to recognize, as I do here, that the divide between extenders and limiters is internal to the category of MAD-based strategy. Robert A. Levine, *The Strategic Nuclear Debate* (Santa Monica, CA: RAND Corporation, 1987).

18. Counterforce strategists also believe that nuclear threats can be used to influence a wide range of the opponent's behavior. So the term "extended deterrence" is generally used to refer both to some MAD-based strategies and to counterforce strategies. The two forms of extended deterrence differ over the mechanism by which deterrence is extended. When I speak of extended deterrence in this chapter and the next, however, I mean to refer exclusively to the MAD-based strategies that hold that nuclear deterrence can be extended.

19. Robert Jervis, *The Meaning of the Nuclear Revolution* (Ithaca, NY: Cornell University Press, 1989), pp. 74–106.
20. Jervis, *The Meaning of the Nuclear Revolution*, pp. 80, 95.
21. In talking about extended deterrence, we must speak of the prospects that a *war*, rather than a *nuclear war*, would remain limited, because extended deterrence is an effort to deter conventional as well as nuclear war between nations in a situation of mutual vulnerability.
22. Jervis, *The Meaning of the Nuclear Revolution*, p. 81.
23. Bernard Brodie, *Strategy in the Missile Age* (Princeton: Princeton University Press, 1959), p. 356.
24. Thomas Schelling, *Arms and Influence* (New Haven, CT: Yale University Press, 1966), p. 166.
25. As discussed in the last chapter, in attempting to show resolve through limited nuclear attacks in a war, a nation would be trying to provide its opponent with evidence that it has a disposition to carry out its nuclear threats, and thereby to achieve effective intra-war deterrence. (In Chapter 1, we saw that a nation is unable to do this outside of war.) Thus such attacks might boost the credibility of the nation's threats of attack on the next round of escalation, despite the continuing prudential irrationality of such attacks. If the credibility is sufficiently boosted, the opponent may accept the burden of restraint by not escalating the conflict further. But, as we shall see, there is more to the risk than the prospect that the nation would deliberately continue to escalate in response to the opponent's escalatory moves.
26. For a discussion of the game of chicken and its relation to this kind of strategy, see Lawrence Freedman, *The Evolution of Nuclear Strategy* (New York: St. Martin's, 1981), pp. 186–89, 218–23. See also Robert Jervis, *The Illogic of American Nuclear Strategy* (Ithaca, NY: Cornell University Press, 1984), pp. 132, 152.
27. See Lawrence Freedman, "I Exist; Therefore I Deter," *International Security* 13, no. 1 (Summer, 1988), p. 185.
28. This idea of the deterrence dynamic is related to what has been called the rationality of irrationality, the notion that a nation, by irrationally running unacceptable risks, can limit a war and achieve advantage by inducing restraint in the opponent. Referring to Schelling's notion of a competition in risk taking, Lawrence Freedman remarks: "He was trying to develop rational tactics for irrational situations, and in doing so attempted to turn the elements for irrationality into coercive instruments." *The Evolution of Nuclear Strategy*, p. 223.
29. Jervis, *The Illogic of American Nuclear Strategy*, p. 149.
30. Jervis, *The Meaning of the Nuclear Revolution*, p. 98.
31. Thomas Schelling, "What Went Wrong with Arms Control," *Foreign Affairs* 64, no. 2 (Winter, 1985–86), p. 230.

32. Greg Herken claims that this phrase was coined by Kennedy in the 1960 presidential election. *Counsels of War* (New York: Alfred Knopf, 1985), p. 151.

33. Wolfgang Panofsky rejects the claim that under a MAD-based strategy "a counterattack must be a single massive strike." "The Mutual-Hostage Relationship Between America and Russia," *Foreign Affairs* 52, no. 1 (October, 1973), p. 115. Panofsky is responding to an article by Fred Ikle in which such a claim is made. "Can Nuclear Deterrence Last Out the Century?" *Foreign Affairs* 51, no. 2 (January, 1973). Jervis remarks: "The common claim that an American president might be left with only the choice between humiliation and holocaust is silly." *The Illogic of American Nuclear Strategy*, p. 167. Some madvocates charge that their counterforce critics know better than to make this claim, that they pretend for rhetorical purposes not to recognize the role of limited war in MAD-based strategies.

34. Schelling, *Arms and Influence*, p. 33. Schelling suggests that a nuclear war conceived as a competition in risk taking is more likely to be controllable than a nuclear war conceived as a competition for military advantage, claiming that in the latter case, "*uncontrolled* counterforce is probably what you would get." "What Went Wrong with Arms Control?" p. 230.

35. For criticism of the claim that countervalue attacks can serve as an effective intra-war deterrent, see David Lewis, "Finite Counterforce," in Shue, *Nuclear Deterrence and Moral Restraint*, pp. 80–82.

36. Thomas Schelling, "Comment," in Klaus Knorr and Thornton Read (eds.), *Limited Strategic War* (London: Pall Mall Press, 1962), p. 243. Other essays in this volume discuss the role of punitive strikes in limited nuclear war.

37. Jervis, *The Meaning of the Nuclear Revolution*, p. 79.

38. But a strategy of extended deterrence is not inconsistent with much smaller arsenals, though advocates of extended deterrence would generally oppose shrinking the arsenals to the size prescribed by the alternative MAD-based strategy, minimum deterrence. The fact that extended deterrence could leave everything as it was in terms of 1980s superpower deployments, but would prescribe a doctrinal shift from countervailing strategy, demonstrates the point made in Chapter 5 that countervalue strategies are not bothered, as counterforce strategies are, about the divergence of declaratory and operational policy. This is, of course, related to the different stands counterforce strategy and extended deterrence strategy take on the credibility problem.

39. Thomas Schelling, *The Strategy of Conflict*, new ed. (Cambridge: Harvard University Press, 1980), p. 188.

40. Something like this distinction is made by Jervis, *The Illogic of American*

Nuclear Strategy, pp. 148–50. This ambiguity in the notion of a threat is different from the one discussed in Chapter 5 between direct and indirect threats. The latter is an ambiguity in the object of the threat- ened action, whereas the former is an ambiguity in the mode of the threatened action, roughly – deliberate in contrast with accidental.

41. But a threat-2 is not a predication of one's own behavior alone, be- cause it concerns a runaway escalatory process involving both belligerents.

42. This discussion throws some light on the threat to act irrationally, discussed in Chapter 4. This threat is a kind of threat-2, but it can be effectively made or posed only when it is a threat to put oneself in a situation which would result in one's acting irrationally. In the absence of such a situation, it cannot be an effective threat.

43. For a discussion of the distinction between controlled and explosive escalation, see Jervis, *The Meaning of the Nuclear Revolution*, pp. 82–95.

44. One might think that threats-2 are dependent on threats-1 in the sense that the process leading to uncontrolled escalation would have to begin with the limited attacks that threats-1 threaten. But uncon- trolled escalation may begin not after the first limited nuclear attacks, but earlier in the developing crisis – for example, in the conventional war that may precede the nuclear war. Thus, nuclear war could occur without the nuclear threats-1 being executed, all of the exchanges in that war being part of an explosive escalatory process beginning at the subnuclear level.

45. Freedman, *The Evolution of Nuclear Strategy*, p. 223. Freedman is here reporting on the views of others, but this is likely his own view as well.

46. While threats-1 fail to achieve a high level of credibility because a limited nuclear war is not reasonably foreseeable, threats-2 fail to achieve a high level of credibility because an *un*limited nuclear war is not reasonably foreseeable.

47. Jervis, *The Illogic of American Nuclear Strategy*, p. 156.

48. McGeorge Bundy, *Danger and Survival* (New York: Random House, 1988), p. 544.

49. Jervis, *The Meaning of the Nuclear Revolution*, p. 38.

50. Kaiser, Leger, Mertes, and Schulze, "Nuclear Weapons and the Pres- ervation of Peace," pp. 1159–60.

51. See Herman Kahn, *On Thermonuclear War* (Princeton: Princeton Uni- versity Press, 1960), p. 145.

52. Barrie Paskins and Michael Dockrill, *The Ethics of War* (Minneapolis: University of Minnesota Press, 1979), p. 66.

53. Graham T. Allison, Albert Carnesale, and Joseph S. Nye, Jr., "Con- clusion," in Nye, Allison, and Carnesale (eds.), *Fateful Visions* (Cam- bridge, MA: Ballinger, 1988), p. 216. Another kind of virtual

doomsday machine is the potential for a nuclear winter. If the nuclear-winter hypothesis is correct, a moderate size nuclear attack might destroy the attacker's own society as a result of the global climatic effects resulting from the nuclear explosions on the opponent's territory. Such a natural doomsday machine has the "advantage" of requiring of the opponent no actions or apparatus at all.

54. Moreover, the virtual doomsday machine has the advantage of working for extended deterrence, an advantage that the full-fledged doomsday machine (envisioned as being triggered by a nuclear attack on the threatener's territory) does not have.

55. In Chapter 3, a presumption based on the perception that carrying out the threat would be prudentially rational was substituted for a demonstrated disposition to carry out the threat as the criterion for perceived willingness to carry out the threat, given that such a disposition could not be demonstrated short of nuclear war. This substitution is already a partial shift away from perceived will and toward perceived capability in determining credibility, because the rationality of attempting to carry out a threat is itself partly a function of what one is capable of doing.

56. Albert Wohlstetter, "Between an Unfree World and None: Increasing our Choices," *Foreign Affairs* 63, no. 5 (Summer, 1985), p. 970.

57. Lewis, "Finite Counterforce," p. 67. Lewis argues (p. 68) that existential deterrence is an empirical hypothesis based on "suppositions about the enemy's character (and ours)" which "stand to reason," meaning "that they cohere with our abundant but inchoate experience of human nature around us and of current events."

58. Bundy, *Danger and Survival*, p. 594.

59. McGeorge Bundy, "The Bishops and the Bomb," *The New York Review of Books* (June 16, 1983), p. 4.

60. Kahn, *On Thermonuclear War*, p. 8.

61. Bundy, "The Bishops and the Bomb," pp. 3, 4.

62. Bundy suggests that he regards existential deterrence as supporting MAD-based strategies rather than counterforce strategies when he speaks of existential deterrence as "independent of any particular theory of war-fighting." "The Bishops and the Bomb," p. 4. Elsewhere he asserts, apparently alluding to counterforce strategies, that "there is a certain unreality in debates among 'experts' about the precise weapons systems and doctrines that will deter." *Danger and Survival*, p. 593.

63. Jervis, *The Illogic of American Nuclear Strategy*, p. 155.

64. Lewis, "Finite Counterforce," p. 68. The analogy was originally suggested by Henry Shue in his contribution in the same volume.

65. Patrick Morgan, *Deterrence – A Conceptual Analysis*, 2nd ed. (Beverly Hills, CA: Sage, 1983), p. 16.

66. Freedman, "I Exist; Therefore I Deter," p. 184.
67. Bundy, "The Bishops and the Bomb," p. 3.
68. Lewis, "Finite Counterforce," p. 71.
69. Bundy, "The Bishops and the Bomb," p. 8. If one believed that existential deterrence could do everything, it would fall victim to a simple reductio argument, as Robert Foelber argues in "Deterrence and the Moral Use of Nuclear Weapons," p. 121.
70. One way to understand McNamara's position is not that he is advocating only a partial retreat from extended deterrence to basic deterrence, but that he understands the extended/basic deterrence distinction in a different way. The way of understanding the distinction put forth earlier is that basic deterrence concerns protecting the nation's homeland, whereas extended deterrence concerns protecting the nation's interests outside its borders. But if the distinction is drawn instead between protecting the nation's interests, whether at home or abroad, against nuclear attack and protecting those interests against conventional attack, then McNamara can be understood as recommending a complete retreat to basic deterrence. One confusing element in this issue is that as a result of fortunate geographical circumstances, the United States homeland was, in practice, immune from Soviet conventional attack. Thus the question whether or not it is the job of basic deterrence to protect the nation's homeland against conventional attack simply never arose in the Cold War debates over nuclear strategy.
71. Robert McNamara, *Blundering Into Disaster* (New York: Pantheon, 1987), p. 123.
72. One could refer to the strategy in question as finite deterrence in order to make the point either that what nuclear deterrence can do is limited or that only a limited number of weapons are needed to do what nuclear deterrence can do. In the latter sense, the idea is that there is only a limited number of targets that need to be covered with nuclear weapons for deterrence to be achieved, insofar as societal destruction can be threatened by nuclear weapons aimed at, say, the opponent's one hundred largest cities. In contrast, counterforce deterrence is "infinite" in the sense either that nuclear threats can be used to do virtually whatever a nation wants them to do or that, because there is a very much larger number of militarily relevant targets and this number can be multiplied indefinitely, a very large number of nuclear weapons are needed to make nuclear deterrence work.
73. Robert McNamara, "The Military Role of Nuclear Weapons: Perceptions and Misperceptions," *Foreign Affairs* 62, no. 1 (Fall, 1983), p. 68.
74. Jervis, *The Meaning of the Nuclear Revolution*, p. 76.
75. Both extended deterrence and minimum deterrence are versions of

the deterrence-only position, as explained earlier. But minimum deterrence is *nuclear* deterrence only, in the sense that, in regard to a nation's extra-territorial interests, only nuclear attacks can be deterred with nuclear weapons, whereas extended deterrence holds that nuclear weapons can deter both conventional and nuclear attacks abroad.

76. McNamara, "The Military Role of Nuclear Weapons," p. 61.
77. McNamara, "The Military Role of Nuclear Weapons," p. 73.
78. This argument suggests that minimum deterrence has something interesting in common with counterforce deterrence – namely, that both strategies, in contrast with extended deterrence, take seriously the credibility problem in determining what strategy a nation should adopt. This common feature will be discussed later.
79. McNamara, "The Military Role of Nuclear Weapons," p. 74.
80. McNamara, "The Military Role of Nuclear Weapons," p. 72.
81. Kaiser, Leger, Mertes, and Schulze, "Nuclear Weapons and the Preservation of Peace," p. 1161. The article to which they were responding is: McGeorge Bundy, George Kennan, Robert McNamara, Gerard Smith, "Nuclear Weapons and the Atlantic Alliance," *Foreign Affairs* 60, no. 4 (Spring, 1982).
82. More precisely, although advocates of minimum deterrence believe that the prospects for limitation of a nuclear war are poor, they do not necessarily believe that the prospects that a conventional war would stay conventional are poor. If the latter prospects were poor, the same reasoning that shows that nuclear threats of extended deterrence are ineffective would show that conventional threats by nuclear powers against other nuclear powers are ineffective as well. This would be an unwelcome conclusion for advocates of minimum deterrence, who count on conventional forces to deter conventional war between nuclear powers.
83. Jervis, *The Meaning of the Nuclear Revolution*, p. 80.
84. McNamara might respond that this criticism misses the mark because the factors making escalatory behavior in nuclear war likely do not necessarily make the decision to enter that war likely. The latter behavior, unlike the former, is unlikely to be made in an environment in which the decision makers have lost control and can no longer make voluntary and deliberate choices. The likelihood of escalation in nuclear war does not entail the likelihood of escalation to nuclear war. Critics might respond that the pressures making for loss of control would be as intense in the crisis immediately preceding the war as they are in the war itself. (See note 44.) If the critics are wrong, the uncertainty argument for the claim that nuclear threats can effectively deter conventional war – that is, the argument that nuclear

deterrence can be extended – may be weaker than advocates of extended deterrence believe it to be.

85. McNamara, "The Military Role of Nuclear Weapons," pp. 74–75, 75.
86. Morton Halperin, *Nuclear Fallacy* (Cambridge, MA: Ballinger, 1987),
p. 103.
87. See Jervis, *Meaning of the Nuclear Revolution*, p. 77, and also Donald
Hafner, Letter to the Editor, *Foreign Affairs* 60, no. 5 (Summer, 1982),
pp. 1177–78.
88. The problem for minimum deterrence may run deeper. Nearly
everyone, including advocates of minimum deterrence, assumes that
there is no credibility problem regarding the threat of nuclear retaliation in response to an all-out nuclear attack. But without something like existential deterrence, it is not clear how this would be
so. For, as some writers have pointed out, retaliation in such circumstances would gain nothing for the nation and, in fact, would
lose something important, the potential post-war assistance that the
attacker would be able to (and might well choose to) provide if it
remained intact. This implies that such retaliation would not be
prudentially rational, so that the threat to inflict it must depend
for its credibility on the belief that the threatened act of retaliation
would not be voluntary and deliberate, but would be the result of
things getting out of hand.
89. Harold Feiveson, "Finite Deterrence," in Shue, *Nuclear Deterrence and
Moral Restraint*, p. 283.
90. Halperin, *Nuclear Fallacy*, p. 107.
91. Halperin, *Nuclear Fallacy*, pp. 107, 85.
92. Bundy, "The Bishops and the Bomb," p. 4.
93. Two caveats are in order. First, a greater number of weapons by itself
does not create enhanced uncertainty. The enhanced uncertainty
comes only if the extra weapons are deployed in a way that would
increase the risk of escalation. But this is what advocates of extended
deterrence have often recommended – for example, in their support
for the stationing of American nuclear weapons abroad. Second, some
advocates of extended deterrence have argued for extra weapons on
a very different ground. They believe that a nation should have nuclear weapons comparable in number to those of its opponent, even
if the opponent has much larger forces than are needed to insure the
nation's vulnerability. The reason is the alleged negative political
effects of failure to achieve equality in numbers with one's opponent.
See Freedman, *The Evolution of Nuclear Strategy*, Chapter 24. But this
argument in favor of larger numbers is rejected by advocates of minimum deterrence. McNamara argues that "the 'width' of the 'band
of parity' is very, very great." *Blundering Into Disaster*, p. 45. Bundy

argues: "What we really need is only what *we need*, not what others may happen to have." "Existential Deterrence and Its Consequences," in Douglas MacLean (ed.), *The Security Gamble: Deterrence Dilemmas in the Nuclear Age* (Totowa, NJ: Rowman and Allanheld, 1984), p. 11.

94. A difference of opinion over how high the nuclear threshold should be may also be noted among advocates of different forms of counterforce deterrence. Albert Wohlstetter argues that given the increasing accuracy of missiles, conventional warheads can replace some nuclear warheads, which would "permit the raising of the threshold beyond which we might resort to nuclear weapons." "Morality and Deterrence: Albert Wohlstetter and Critics," *Commentary* 76, no. 6 (December, 1983), p. 18. He goes on to criticize those advocates of counterforce deterrence who would reject such a policy on the grounds that conventional war is almost as horrible as nuclear war. Presumably he is criticizing them because they prefer a lower nuclear threshold.

95. Advocates of extended deterrence also emphasize the value of nuclear powers' deploying conventional forces, but for a different reason. They believe that to use nuclear threats to deter conventional aggression against allies, a nation needs to deploy its conventional forces on the allies' territory (though likely at a lower level than that recommended by advocates of minimum deterrence), because the forces help to insure that the opponent believes that the nation is strongly enough committed to the allies that it would use nuclear weapons in their defense. Instead of being an effective fighting force that would keep the nuclear threshold high, the conventional forces are meant to be merely a "tripwire" or "plate-glass window." For a discussion of this, see Freedman, *The Evolution of Nuclear Strategy*, p. 290. This suggests that the extendibility of nuclear deterrence depends on how much of a stake the opponent perceives the nation as having in the region to which deterrence is to be extended. On the importance of the perceived stake in extending deterrence, see Freedman, "I Exist, Therefore I Deter."

96. One indication of the difference on this point is seen in how strategists interpret the Cuban missile crisis. Whereas advocates of extended deterrence tend to see the advantageous outcome achieved by the United States in that crisis as the result of nuclear threats, as Schelling does (*Arms and Influence*, p. 166), advocates of minimum deterrence tend to see this outcome as resulting from the great conventional superiority enjoyed by the United States in the Caribbean, as Bundy does ("The Bishops and the Bomb," p. 4). It should be noted that if the outcome of the Cuban missile crisis was the result of nuclear

threats, it would be a case of nuclear compellence rather than nuclear deterrence.

97. Tucker, *The Nuclear Debate,* p. 8.
98. Leon Wieseltier, "When Deterrence Fails," *Foreign Affairs* 63, no. 4 (Spring, 1985), p. 840.
99. Bundy, *Danger and Survival,* p. 604.
100. Schelling, *The Strategy of Conflict,* p. 193.
101. Tucker, *The Nuclear Debate,* p. 84. Wieseltier recognizes this objection, but chooses, in effect, to ignore it. He simply assumes "that the second use will occur" (though admitting that "an argument against it may be made"), that the nation will retaliate, asserting: "It is against third use, then, that I want us to plan." But if the purpose is to end the war as quickly as possible, why should the option of nonretaliation be placed out of consideration as a means to this goal? "When Deterrence Fails," p. 845.
102. Desmond Ball, *Can Nuclear War Be Controlled?* Adelphi Paper no. 169 (London: International Institute for Strategic Studies, 1981), p. 2. Advocates of minimum deterrence often recommend a retaliation that is smaller than the attack to which it is a response. For example, Bundy suggests that nuclear retaliation should occur at only one-half the level of the attack to which it is a response. *Danger and Survival,* p. 605. Schelling provides some support for this suggestion: "It is not necessarily a submissive response to destroy half as much in return rather than twice as much." The reason he offers might also support the nonretaliation position: "The cold-blooded *acceptance* of pain might be just as impressive as the cold-blooded infliction of it." *Controlled Response and Strategic Warfare,* Adelphi Paper no. 19 (London: Institute for Strategic Studies, 1965), p. 9.
103. Halperin, *Nuclear Fallacy,* p. 56. This idea of countervalue retaliatory attacks follows from the MAD-based notion that what deters is the threat of punishment. The difference between the MAD-based and counterforce paradigms of nuclear conflict can be seen in Wieseltier's remark: "There is a difference between a nuclear exchange and a nuclear war." "When Deterrence Fails," p. 846.
104. Assuming that nonretaliation is the preferable option, the reluctance of madvocates forthrightly to proclaim this truth is an example of how, for noncounterforce forms of deterrence, declaratory policy may diverge from operational policy.
105. It is important here that it is McNamara's second argument for minimum deterrence that works rather than his first, because the first argument denies that nuclear deterrence has an extended deterrent role, for example, in avoiding conventional war. As pointed out in Chapter 3, if nuclear weapons were not useful in deterring

conventional war, nuclear deterrence would not strictly be comparable with conventional deterrence. Nuclear deterrence would deter only nuclear war and conventional deterrence would deter conventional war, so that the sets of behaviors each sought to deter would not even overlap.

106. Wieseltier, "When Deterrence Fails," p. 829.
107. Jervis, *The Meaning of the Nuclear Revolution*, p. 121.
108. Michael Walzer, *Just and Unjust Wars* (New York: Basic Books, 1977), p. 282.
109. David Hollenbach claims that this is what Michael Walzer does. "Ethics in Distress: Can There Be Just Wars in the Nuclear Age?" in William O'Brien and John Langan (eds.), *The Nuclear Dilemma and the Just War Tradition* (Lexington, MA: Lexington Books, 1986), p. 16. But Walzer's discussion of supreme emergency could instead be understood as a suggestion that in the face of mutual vulnerability, just-war morality needs to be revised. Under this understanding, Walzer's position is not "so much the worse for morality" but "so much the worse for traditional morality." (Walzer's discussion of supreme emergency is in *Just and Unjust Wars*, pp. 251–68.)
110. Arthur Burns, *Ethics and Deterrence: A Nuclear Balance Without Hostage Cities?* Adelphi Paper no. 69 (London: Institute for Strategic Studies, 1970), p. 23.
111. Hans Morganthau, "Four Paradoxes of Nuclear Strategy," *American Political Science Review* 58, no. 1 (March, 1964), p. 35.
112. George Quester, "The Necessary Moral Hypocrisy of the Slide into Mutual Assured Destruction," in Shue, *Nuclear Deterrence and Moral Restraint*, p. 263.
113. Foelber, "Deterrence and the Moral Use of Nuclear Weapons," p. 142.
114. Bundy, Kennan, McNamara, and Smith, "Nuclear Weapons and the Atlantic Alliance," p. 766.
115. Jervis, *The Meaning of the Nuclear Revolution*, p. 125.
116. Quester, "The Necessary Moral Hypocrisy," p. 254.
117. Jervis, *The Meaning of the Nuclear Revolution*, pp. 116, 116–17.
118. Attacking civilians, as well as threatening to attack them, can serve this purpose because attacking them can serve as an intra-war deterrent, through bolstering the credibility of the threat to escalate further.
119. Ironically, as Jervis suggests, such an argument would show that in the case of strategic nuclear war, there is a rationale for a principle of combatant immunity.
120. Indeed, under this rationale as well, one should, in the case of strategic nuclear weapons, also recognize a principle of combatant

immunity, not as a replacement for the principle of civilian immunity, but as an addition to this principle. The point is that so few people are involved in the immediate harm caused the nation in a strategic nuclear war that virtually the whole of the opponent's population, military and nonmilitary, should be immune from attack.

121. In order to argue for the revision of the principles of everyday moral reasoning, one might appeal to a moral theory – for example, utilitarianism or social contract theory – to argue that in the light of mutual vulnerability, these principles ought to be revised so as to permit the large-scale hostage-holding characteristic of nuclear deterrence. But it is unclear whether moral theory could provide the critical leverage from which to justify a revision of the basic principles of everyday moral reasoning. If one views moral theory as an enterprise whose adequacy is judged in terms of how well it accords with the intuitions of everyday moral reasoning, it may be inappropriate to attempt to use a moral theory to revise everyday moral reasoning in a substantial way.

122. Bundy, "The Bishops and the Bomb," p. 3.

123. Foelber, "Deterrence and the Moral Use of Nuclear Weapons," p. 121.

124. Gregory Kavka, *Moral Paradoxes of Nuclear Deterrence* (Cambridge: Cambridge University Press, 1987), p. 48.

125. Lewis, "Finite Counterforce," p. 67.

126. Kavka, *Moral Paradoxes of Nuclear Deterrence*, p. 48.

127. One difference between scrupulous retaliation strategy, as Kavka understands it, and pure counterforce strategy is that the latter involves targeting only strictly military facilities, whereas the former includes economic assets as targets. But in contrast with Kavka's formulation, I will understand scrupulous retaliation strategy as not involving the targeting of economic assets. Kavka's concern is obviously that large numbers of civilians not be killed, but the principle of discrimination has historically shown a concern as well that the means of livelihood of civilians, such as crops, not be destroyed. This provides good moral ground for excluding the targeting of economic assets.

128. Lewis, "Finite Counterforce." Lewis notes that his finite counterforce is like Kavka's scrupulous retaliation, but he points out not only that his policy, unlike Kavka's, would eschew attacks on economic assets, but that because the purpose of the attacks would be damage limitation, his policy is not strictly a policy of retaliation. "Finite Counterforce," p. 110n33.

129. Lewis, "Finite Counterforce," p. 74.

130. Lewis, "Finite Counterforce," pp. 74–5, 109n30.
131. Anthony Kenny, *The Logic of Deterrence* (Chicago: University of Chicago Press, 1985), pp. 53, 84, 98–99.
132. James Sterba, "Between MAD and Counterforce," in Kenneth Kipnis and Diana T. Meyers, *Political Realism and International Morality: Ethics in the Nuclear Age* (Boulder, CO: Westview Press, 1987), p. 129. Sterba in this article presents a version of the no-intention strategy in which the other reason for the United States to have its nuclear weapons, should it adopt his policy, would be that it would then be in a position to threaten to use the weapons should the Soviet Union, through a change in leadership, adopt a policy of threatening a nuclear first-strike. But Sterba, unlike at least some other existential moralists, assumes that a no-intentions strategy would work only because the opponent (the Soviet Union) is relatively nonaggressive.
133. Douglas Lackey points out: "Since any missile that can hit a silo can also hit a city, it follows that counterforce ability implies countervalue ability (but not vice versa)." Douglas Lackey, *Moral Principles and Nuclear Weapons* (Totowa, NJ: Rowman and Allanheld, 1984), p. 112.
134. Paul Ramsey, *The Just War: Force and Political Responsibility* (1968, reprint ed., Lanham, MD: University Press of America, 1983), p. 253.
135. Kavka's moral criticism of scrupulous retaliation and no-intention strategies turns largely on the prudential and consequentialist issues – in particular, on the argument that existential deterrence is less robust than alternative strategies and so would make nuclear war more likely. *Moral Paradoxes of Nuclear Deterrence*, pp. 48–55. I consider the effectiveness of MAD-based strategies in general in the next section. For another argument that appeal to the notion of existential deterrence does not succeed in avoiding the deontological objection to nuclear deterrence, see C.A.J. Coady, "Escaping from the Bomb: Immoral Deterrence and the Problem of Extrication," in Shue, *Nuclear Deterrence and Moral Restraint*, pp. 182–83.
136. Walter Stein, "The Limits of Nuclear War: Is a Just Deterrence Strategy Possible?" in James Finn (ed.), *Peace, the Churches, and the Bomb* (New York: Council on Religion and International Affairs, 1965), pp. 80–81, emphasis omitted.
137. David Lewis might respond in this way. If a nation practicing scrupulous retaliation were attacked with nuclear weapons, the nation's nuclear attacks in the nuclear war would in fact be directed only at military targets and would have as their only purpose damage limitation. ("Finite Counterforce," p. 77.) As a result, though the nation seeks to achieve deterrence by posing a risk of massive civilian destruction in virtue of existential deterrence, in a nuclear war it would neither (1) cause massive civilian destruction nor (2) inten-

tionally harm civilians at all. Regarding (1), the assumption is that things would not in fact get out of hand, but, of course, they might, so the nation's threat that they might, through its practice of existential deterrence, cannot thus be morally absolved. Regarding (2), the argument falls victim to the objections discussed in Chapter 5 to a similar argument posed by Jeff McMahan. The point is that in a war the harm the nation's attacks caused civilians would be intended for the sake of intra-war deterrence. If a nation relies on the threat to civilians for pre-war deterrence, it would rely on it as well for intra-war deterrence. Thus Lewis's claim that the only purpose of nuclear attacks would be damage limitation is inconsistent with his claim (p. 98) that deterrence is more important than damage limitation. These claims are consistent only if one ignores intra-war deterrence. As noted earlier, Lewis raises doubts about the claim that countervalue attacks can serve as an effective intra-war deterrent (pp. 80–82). There are problems with his argument, but even if the conclusion is correct, it does not overcome the current objection. For rather than denying that countervalue damage can have some intra-war deterrent effect, he argues merely that counterforce retaliation would be more effective than countervalue retaliation. But counterforce attacks would do some countervalue damage, and as long as there is some reason to think that that damage would have some intra-war deterrent effect, even though the counterforce damage is believed to have more, the countervalue damage would be desired for that deterrent effect. So that the retaliatory attacks would not escape moral unacceptability.

138. Also necessary for the deontological unacceptability is that the nation practicing the form of pure counterforce strategy with these features desire the threat-2 it poses of societal destruction as a means to achieving deterrence. But because the nation does desire the deterrent effect, it follows that the threat-2 would be desired as a means to this end as soon as it was recognized that it is a means to that end.

139. Quester, "The Necessary Moral Hypocrisy," p. 261.

140. It is important to note, as should become clear later, that both "choice" and "aggression" are understood broadly here. The choices of concern may or may not be fully voluntary, and the aggression need not be military, but can include anything from a serious political challenge to a large-scale nuclear attack.

141. I seek a more general understanding of stability than that limited to crisis stability, as does John Mueller when he contrasts crisis stability with what he calls general stability. "The Essential Irrelevance of Nuclear Weapons," *International Security* 13, no. 2 (Fall, 1988), pp. 69–70. But Mueller is generalizing the notion of stability to in-

clude "non-military incentives and disincentives," which is further than I wish to go. Because my concern is the difference nuclear weapons make, I restrict my attention to military factors influencing stability.

142. Glenn Snyder, "The Balance of Power and the Balance of Terror," in Paul Seabury (ed.), *Balance of Power* (San Francisco: Chandler, 1965), pp. 196–97. The other aspect Snyder discusses is "the tendency or lack of tendency toward an arms race." This is the frequently discussed notion of arms-race (in)stability, the likelihood that a nuclear deterrence relationship will change in terms of there being a significant increase in the quantity and quality of the weapons deployed on each side. This is an important concern, because a significant increase in arms can lessen both crisis and noncrisis stability. But it is not a primary notion of stability, because its importance lies in its impact on crisis and noncrisis stability, so I will not be discussing it here.

143. Richard Garwin, "Reducing Dependence on Nuclear Weapons: A Second Nuclear Regime," in David Gompert, Michael Mandelbaum, Richard Garwin, and John Barton, *Nuclear Weapons and World Politics: Alternatives for the Future* (New York: Council on Foreign Relations, 1977), p. 146.

144. Gray, *Nuclear Strategy and National Style*, pp. 133, 135, 146.

145. Gray, *Nuclear Strategy and National Style*, pp. 149, 139.

146. Gray, *Nuclear Strategy and National Style*, pp. 159, 158.

147. A large part of Gray's argument for ambitious counterforce strategy and his preferred notion of stability is based on claims about the distinctive nature of Soviet "strategic culture" or "national style." I am not concerned here to address these claims and the extent to which they support his notion of stability, but rather to make clear that both notions of stability have relevance and that they are in inherent conflict with each other.

148. Gray, *Nuclear Strategy and National Style*, p. 146.

149. Richard Betts, "Surprise Attack and Preemption," in Graham Allison et al. (eds.), *Hawks, Doves, and Owls* (New York: Norton, 1985), p. 71.

150. Snyder, "The Balance of Power," pp. 198–99. Snyder here draws the line between the two forms of stability somewhat differently than I have. He sees what I have called noncrisis stability as the capacity to avoid even limited forms of nuclear aggression, and crisis stability as the ability to avoid a large-scale nuclear attack.

151. Jervis, *The Illogic of American Nuclear Strategy*, p. 31.

152. Jervis, *The Meaning of the Nuclear Revolution*, p. 20.

153. Gray seems to recognize that the ability of his ambitious counterforce strategy to achieve stability in a crisis is dependent on its removing

the nation's societal vulnerability. *Nuclear Strategy and National Style,* p. 158.

154. Herman Kahn, *Thinking About the Unthinkable in the 1980s* (New York: Simon and Schuster, 1984), pp. 33, 117–21.

155. Jervis, *The Meaning of the Nuclear Revolution,* p. 20.

156. Leon Sigal, *Nuclear Forces in Europe* (Washington: Brookings Institution, 1984), p. 10.

157. Earl C. Ravenal, Letter-to-the-Editor, *Foreign Affairs* 60, no. 5 (Summer, 1982), p. 1176.

158. For a discussion of the role that conventional forces played in deterring conventional war between the United States and the Soviet Union in Europe, see Michael Howard, "On Fighting a Nuclear War," in Bernard Brodie, Michael Intriligator, and Roman Kolkowicz (eds.), *National Security and International Stability* (Cambridge, MA: Oelgeschlager, Gunn, and Haim, 1983), pp. 34–35.

159. Jervis, *The Illogic of American Nuclear Strategy,* p. 33.

160. Jervis, *The Meaning of the Nuclear Revolution,* p. 21.

161. Snyder, "The Balance of Power," p. 199.

162. Lewis, "Finite Counterforce," pp. 72, 71.

163. In the next section, I will argue that extended deterrence is subject to a form of instability distinct from both crisis and noncrisis instability, such that there is little or no gap, in the case of extended deterrence, between the perception and the reality of that third form of instability.

164. This criticism would provide a way of responding to the argument that the empirical evidence of the history of the Cold War provides sufficient support for the claim that a strategy of extended deterrence avoids the paradox. See Jervis, *The Meaning of the Nuclear Revolution,* pp. 29–38.

165. Jervis, *The Illogic of American Nuclear Strategy,* p. 31.

166. Jervis, *The Illogic of American Nuclear Strategy,* p. 147.

167. Sigal, *Nuclear Forces in Europe,* p. 17.

168. Henry Shue, "Having it Both Ways," in Shue, *Nuclear Deterrence and Moral Restraint,* pp. 14–15.

169. The distinction between premeditated and preemptive war is discussed in Sigal, *Nuclear Forces in Europe,* pp. 8–9. Sigal and others have pointed out that an historical illustration of this kind of distinction is provided by the contrast between the causes of the First World War and the Second World War. The first began with a preemptive attack, and thus was a result of crisis instability, whereas the second began (in Europe) with a premeditated attack, and so resulted from noncrisis instability. (In further contrast, the Second World War began in the Pacific as a preventive war – that is, a war

seen by its initiator as inevitable though not imminent, but best waged now.) The point is, so far as nuclear weapons are concerned, the military posture that best avoids one kind of war will not do so well at avoiding the other kind. On a terminological note, Sigal does not regard preemptive war as a failure of deterrence. Referring to crisis instability, he says (p. 9): "War can result not only from a failure of deterrence but also from its instability." But it serves clarity to view all acts of aggression, and especially all wars, whether premeditated or preemptive, as failures of deterrence, and that is how I understand the matter.

170. See, for example, Richard Ned Lebow and Janice Gross Stein, "Rational Deterrence Theory: I Think, Therefore I Deter," *World Politics* 41, no. 2 (January, 1989), pp. 208–11.

171. Accidental-war instability is not as sharply distinct from crisis instability as is here suggested, because neither the small-strike/large-strike distinction nor the intentional/unintentional distinction marks sharp boundaries. In addition, each concerns a nuclear war's beginning in a crisis. Nevertheless, I believe that it is analytically useful to distinguish them.

172. The image is borrowed from J. Baird Callicott, who applies it to approaches to understanding our ethical relationship with animals. J. Baird Callicott, "Animal Liberation: A Triangular Affair," *Environmental Ethics* 2, no. 4 (Winter, 1980), pp. 311–338.

173. Some of the ways in which this happens were mentioned earlier. For example, if a nation adopts a first-use policy, this increases noncrisis stability, but lessens accidental-war stability, because the ways in which nuclear weapons would be deployed in support of the first-use policy make it more likely that they will be used under pressure for a quick decision or without the authorization of central authority. The debate between those advocates of first-use policy who recommend the threat of early use of nuclear weapons in a conventional war and those who recommend no-early-use is a debate over how much accidental-war stability is to be sacrificed for noncrisis stability. Advocates of minimum deterrence recommend against first-use policy precisely because they are more concerned with accidental-war stability than with noncrisis stability.

174. Brodie, *War and Politics*, pp. 430–31.

175. An enthusiastic madvocate might respond that because an accidental nuclear war would, in all likelihood, begin only in a crisis – indeed, only in a conventional war – the claim that nuclear weapons have ended great-power war stands. If a strategy of extended deterrence can avoid crises in virtue of the level of noncrisis stability it achieves, then an accidental nuclear war could never occur despite the risk. But this ignores the point, made in the last chapter in response to

a similar argument by counterforce strategists, that crises can arise in unforeseen ways.

8. CONFLICT RESOLUTION

1. The new understanding of morality referred to here is moral revisionism. The new understanding of prudence, prudential revisionism, is different, in that it does not require an alteration in the basic principles of prudence as moral revisionism requires an alteration in the basic principles of morality. Prudential revisionism requires only that we better understand the implications of the principles of prudence for our situation.
2. Although the success of the prima facie argument has no direct policy implications, its failure would. Its success does not, alone, imply nuclear disarmament, but its failure would imply that nuclear deterrence be maintained.
3. A point made in the early chapters is worth repeating. Although conventional deterrence is usually practiced along with nuclear deterrence, whenever I refer to conventional deterrence, I mean the deterrence a nation practices when it possesses only conventional weapons.
4. C.A.J. Coady distinguishes between "general unilateralism," the idea that all nations should individually abandon nuclear deterrence, and multilateralism, "the idea that you will give up your nuclear arsenal only if the other side(s) will reciprocate." He observes that the multilateralists "seem not to recognize the intrinsic immorality of deterrence." "Escaping from the Bomb: Immoral Deterrence and the Problem of Extrication," in Henry Shue (ed.), *Nuclear Deterrence and Moral Restraint* (Cambridge: Cambridge University Press, 1989), p. 200. In our terms, the point is that multilateralists ignore the deontological objection to nuclear deterrence.
5. As elsewhere in the discussion, the question of domestic political feasibility of a nation's adopting a policy of unilateral nuclear disarmament (or participating in an enterprise of mutual nuclear disarmament) is not considered.
6. Gregory Kavka, *Moral Paradoxes of Nuclear Deterrence* (Cambridge: Cambridge University Press, 1987), p. 124.
7. Russell Hardin, "Risking Armageddon," in Avner Cohen and Steven Lee (eds.), *Nuclear Weapons and the Future of Humanity* (Totowa, NJ: Rowman and Allanheld, 1986), pp. 206–07.
8. James Child, *Nuclear War: The Moral Dimension* (New Brunswick, NJ: Transaction Books, 1986), p. 111.
9. Jefferson McMahan, "Nuclear Deterrence and Future Generations," in Cohen and Lee, *Nuclear Weapons and the Future of Humanity*,

pp. 320–21. McMahan acknowledges that his argument shows only that unilateral nuclear disarmament is to be preferred to strongly counterforce policies of nuclear deterrence, not necessarily to a change to minimum deterrence (p. 321).

10. Douglas Lackey, *Moral Principles and Nuclear Weapons* (Totowa, NJ: Rowman and Allanheld, 1984), p. 84.

11. If this were the only kind of nuclear war that could occur subsequent to unilateral nuclear disarmament, it might be the case, Russell Hardin suggests, that such disarmament would be preferable to retaining nuclear weapons in consequentialist terms, but not in prudential terms. It might be better for the world as a whole though worse for the nation. "Risking Armageddon," p. 207. If so, this would show that the confluence of the prudential and consequentialist assessments of nuclear weapons policy postulated in Chapter 1 would not always hold. In the light of the argument in the next paragraph, however, it seems that the confluence holds here as well.

12. This point is discussed in Child, *Nuclear War*, p. 103.

13. Kavka, *Moral Paradoxes of Nuclear Deterrence*, p. 203.

14. George Quester, *The Future of Nuclear Deterrence* (Lexington, MA: Lexington Books, 1986), pp. 8, 9.

15. Kavka, *Moral Paradoxes of Nuclear Deterrence*, p. 205.

16. Kavka, *Moral Paradoxes of Nuclear Deterrence*, pp. 203, 204.

17. Robert McNamara, *Blundering Into Disaster* (New York: Pantheon, 1987), pp. 88–89.

18. McNamara points out that nuclear war subsequent to mutual nuclear disarmament would likely be on a smaller scale than the all-out nuclear war possible under nuclear deterrence. But given the possibility of nuclear rearmament, a major nuclear war would be a real possibility subsequent to mutual nuclear disarmament, as it would be subsequent to unilateral nuclear disarmament.

19. Jonathan Schell, *The Abolition* (New York: Avon Books, 1986).

20. Schell, *The Abolition*, pp. 125, 151.

21. For Schell, weaponless deterrence is not identical with the abolition of nuclear weapons. Rather it is a particular policy, one he describes in some detail, that nations may adopt along with their policies of abandoning nuclear weapons. (For example, at p. 202 in *The Abolition*, he speaks of "abolition backed up by weaponless deterrence.") The threat to rebuild would exist in any case, but weaponless deterrence is a way of structuring the capacity to rebuild on which that threat depends so as to maximize its effectiveness. Weaponless deterrence relies on international agreements and includes the deployment of defenses against nuclear attack to protect the rebuild capacity. But I will use the term "weaponless deterrence" in a broader way, to refer

to any policy of complete mutual nuclear disarmament between military adversaries.

22. Speaking of Schell's position, Harold Feiveson asserts: "The abolitionist position is, in effect, one of finite deterrence with the level of nuclear warheads set at zero." "Finite Deterrence," in Shue, *Nuclear Deterrence and Moral Restraint*, p. 286.

23. Schell, *The Abolition*, p. 153.

24. Schell, *The Abolition*, pp. 181–84.

25. Thomas Schelling and Morton Halperin, *Strategy and Arms Control* (1961, reprint ed., Washington: Pergamon-Brassey, 1986), p. 58.

26. In the history of attitudes toward nuclear weapons, the late 1950s and early 1960s marked a turning point where many who had been committed to the goal of nuclear disarmament came to recognize the importance of stability in the nuclear balance and shifted their allegiance to nuclear arms control. For a discussion of this, see Lawrence Freedman, *The Evolution of Nuclear Strategy* (New York: St. Martin's Press, 1981), Chapter 13.

27. This is the time interval that would be longer under weaponless deterrence. If instead the time interval in question were that between the beginning of the series of international events constituting the crisis that would lead to nuclear war and the commencement of the nuclear destruction, it is not clear that weaponless deterrence would provide any temporal advantage over weaponful deterrence, because rearmament may take no longer than the development of the crisis. To the extent that it is the latter interval rather than the former that is of greatest relevance, Schell's argument loses force. See Robert W. Tucker, *The Nuclear Debate* (New York: Holmes and Meier, 1985), pp. 35n15.

28. Schell, *The Abolition*, pp. 206, 207.

29. Schell, *The Abolition*, p. 195.

30. In the case of unilateral nuclear disarmament, noncrisis instability would result from the weakness of the nation's conventional threats in the light of the opponent's possession of nuclear weapons, which could lead to the opponent's aggression, which could lead to a major nuclear war through the nation's attempt to rearm itself with nuclear weapons. Crisis instability would result from the risk of the nation's nuclear rearmament, which would provide a greater temptation for a preemptive nuclear attack.

31. Schell, *The Abolition*, p. 169.

32. John Finnis, Joseph M. Boyle, Jr., and Germain Grisez, *Nuclear Deterrence, Morality and Realism* (Oxford: Clarendon Press, 1987), p. 105.

33. The other route to moral revisionism, discussed in Chapters 2 and 7, also makes use of the "ought implies can" principle, but in a different

way. There the question was not the inability of the nation to comply with the particular deontological requirements, but instead its inability to comply with the general requirement to behave in a morally acceptable way. But that argument and the one here are, in general, the same: Moral revisionism is necessitated because the "ought implies can" principle holds only if moral requirements are altered.

34. This is in contrast with the distinction between direct and indirect threatening discussed in Chapter 5, which is not morally relevant. In that case, the distinction is between different effects of the single action of nuclear retaliation, its effects on military forces, which are said to be directly threatened, and its effects on civilians, who are said to be indirectly threatened. In this case, the distinction is between different actions, the first being the rebuilding of the weapons and the second being the nuclear retaliation. Threatening the first is said to indirectly threaten civilians because the civilians could be directly threatened only after the first action had been accomplished. In the first case, to destroy the military forces is to destroy the civilians. In the second case, to rebuild the weapons is not to destroy civilians, but only to be in a position to then threaten to do so.

35. Because abandonment is itself a form of nuclear deterrence, and because it is acceptable from the deontological perspective, it is, in effect, a form of strategic revisionism. But it is different from the strategic revisionism considered in Chapter 5 in that its success would not show that retention of the weapons is acceptable from a deontological perspective. Indeed, at this point strategic revisionism and prudential revisionism converge, because a policy of abandonment avoids the conflicts only if it is acceptable from both deontological and consequentialist perspectives.

36. Coady, "Escaping from the Bomb," p. 197.

37. Barrie Paskins, "Deep Cuts are Morally Imperative," in Geoffrey Goodwin (ed.), *Ethics and Nuclear Deterrence* (New York: St. Martin's, 1982), pp. 99–100. Paskins is concerned in particular with unilateral disarmament, but his example applies as well to multilateral disarmament.

38. Finnis, Boyle, and Grisez, *Nuclear Deterrence, Morality and Realism*, p. 339.

39. Coady, "Escaping from the Bomb," pp. 204, 201. The analogy between slavery and nuclear deterrence is suggested by Gerald Dworkin, who uses it to make a point different from, and at least partly in conflict with, Coady's. The example is discussed by Marc Trachtenberg in a way supportive of Coady's use of it, but critical of Dworkin's. Marc Trachtenberg, "Strategists, Philosophers, and the Nuclear Question," in Russell Hardin et al. (eds.), *Nuclear Deterrence: Ethics and Strategy* (Chicago: University of Chicago Press, 1985), pp. 356–57.

40. Coady, "Escaping from the Bomb," p. 204.
41. Thomas Schelling, *The Strategy of Conflict*, new ed. (Cambridge: Harvard University Press, 1980), p. 260. The tradition of nonuse is also discussed in McGeorge Bundy, *Danger and Survival* (New York: Random House, 1988), pp. 586–88.
42. George Ball, "The Cosmic Bluff," *New York Review of Books* (July 21, 1983), p. 37. Ball speaks as if the nuclear taboo already exists, and Bundy's discussion of the tradition of nonuse suggests that he believes it already exists. *Danger and Survival*, pp. 586–88. But it is implausible to claim that the United States and the Soviet Union, in their relationship as it existed through the end of the Cold War, achieved the delegitimation of nuclear weapons. Though each nation learned a great deal about nuclear risks as the cold war progressed, and thus grew more cautious in its nuclear behavior, each still contemplated the use of nuclear weapons in certain situations, and so were not deeply committed to the belief that their use is illegitimate.
43. Morton Halperin, *Nuclear Fallacy* (Cambridge, MA: Ballinger, 1987), pp. 138, 49.
44. Robert Jervis, *The Meaning of the Nuclear Revolution* (Ithaca, NY: Cornell University Press, 1989), p. 111.
45. John Mueller, *Retreat from Doomsday: the Obsolescence of Major War* (New York: Basic Books, 1989), pp. 9–12, quotation from p. 11.
46. Dietrich Fischer, letter to the editor of *New York Times Sunday Magazine* (January 3, 1988), p. 5.
47. Earlier, the claim was made that the delegitimation of nuclear weapons, if it is to show that the abandonment of nuclear weapons is preferable, would have to ground an expectation that there would be no aggression between nuclear adversaries. The objective basis for such an expectation, it seems, would amount to the delegitimation of conventional weapons. But this would be a delegitimation of conventional weapons under conventional-2 deterrence. The present speculation that there may be something distinctive about nuclear weapons which makes possible their delegitimation, but not that of conventional weapons, concerns a revision of the prima facie argument, and thus assumes a situation of conventional-1 deterrence.
48. H.L.A. Hart, *The Concept of Law* (Oxford: Clarendon Press, 1961), pp. 55–56. Hart contrasts a rule with a mere habit, whereas I put habit on the side of rule, in contrast with a mere regularity – that is, with the mere fact that the parties in question are consistently behaving in a certain way. But we are talking about different kinds of habits, Hart about the habit simply of not doing the action in question and I about the habit of mind in virtue of which that action is unthinkable. Hart may not be crediting the normative element in habit. To paraphrase a point he makes about rules, one can distinguish between doing something

as a habit and doing something out of habit, where the former lacks the normative dimension implicit in the latter.

49. Michael Mandelbaum, *The Nuclear Revolution* (Cambridge: Cambridge University Press, 1981), p. 86. Mandelbaum compares the great-power peace brought about by nuclear weapons since 1945 to the long peace brought about in Europe by the Vienna System after the defeat of Napoleon, pointing out that the Vienna System eventually failed in a cataclysmic war.

50. There is an additional problem with the prospects for delegitimation, different in kind from those already discussed. Even if the habits of delegitimation could be created for a particular pair of nuclear adversaries, this does not insure that some other pair at that time will share these habits. The learning process involved in inculcating the habits may need to be gone through anew in each case. Nuclear proliferation makes delegitimation itself unstable.

51. As an example of this criticism, Henry Kissinger, on a panel discussion after the 1983 television showing of the movie *The Day After*, which portrayed life after a nuclear war, observed: "To engage in an orgy of demonstrating how terrible the casualties of a nuclear war are and translating into pictures the statistics that have been known for three decades . . . I would say, what are we to do about this? . . . Are we supposed to make policy by scaring ourselves to death?" *ABC News Viewpoint*, November 20, 1983, transcript from Journal Graphics, p. 5. The response to his rhetorical question is yes. Only when each side is convinced that the other side is scared to death of nuclear war can the habits of delegitimation be successfully fostered.

52. Halperin, *Nuclear Fallacy*, p. 150.

53. Consider again the motorist who switches from a large automobile to a small automobile. As mentioned, such a reduction in size does not necessarily indicate that the motorist will later abandon automobiling. Say, however, that the motorist thinks that private cars are illegitimate, given their environmental costs, but is prudentially unable to abandon hers because an adequate public transportation system does not yet exist. In that case, the switch from large to small car might have a hypothetical prudential justification, analogous to that of adopting minimum deterrence, if, for example, the motorist intends to donate the money saved from the switch to an organization promoting public transit, in the expectation that this would help to lessen the need for private automobiles to the point where her abandonment of the auto would be prudentially possible and autos might become "delegitimated."

54. Richard Ullman, "Denuclearizing International Politics," in Hardin, et al., *Nuclear Deterrence*, p. 191.

55. Halperin, *Nuclear Fallacy*, p. 148.

Index

Index

Index

intentions
  irrelevance of, in nuclear morality,
    266, 267, 269–71
  and just-war tradition, 42–3
  and nuclear threats, 176, 177–8, 180,
    223, 287
  see also threats
international conflict, in a nuclear age,
  233–4, 275, 294
irrationality
  and nuclear threats, 128–9, 132, 133

Jervis, Robert, 1, 245, 319, 344 n79
  on crisis stability, 277, 279, 281, 283
  on deterrence, 90, 250, 252
  on just wars, 263, 264
  on limited nuclear warfare, 17, 201,
    202, 235
  on military strategy, 27–8, 90
  moral views of, 22, 262
  on mutual vulnerability, 241, 248, 261
  on nuclear strategy, 179, 188, 193,
    195, 238, 284
Johnson, James Turner, 160
just-war tradition, 30, 42–43
  and moral reasoning, 34–6
  and nuclear deterrence, 32, 176, 261–
    2, 266
justifiability, 337 n11; see also moral ar-
    gument; prudential argument
just society, roughly, 74–6

Kahn, Herman, 246, 247, 279, 338 n20
Kant, Immanuel, 337 n12, 348 n21
Kavka, Gregory, 8, 37, 50, 297, 301,
  344 n81
  on counterforce strategy, 165, 166
  on nuclear deterrence, 43, 51, 52, 89,
    91, 350 n41, 357 n11
  on nuclear morality, 56–7, 60, 61, 62,
    66, 266
  on scrupulous retaliation, 397 n127,
    398 n135
Keeny, Spurgeon, 6
Kennedy, John F., 388 n32
Kenny, Anthony, 11, 19, 164, 267–8
Kissinger, Henry, 193, 408 n51

Lackey, Douglas, 42, 43–4, 62, 298, 347
  n20, 398 n133
  on Cold War, 53, 56
Lambeth, Benjamin, 156
legal deterrence, 95, 101

effectiveness of, 99–104, 106–7, 108,
  359 n33, 360 n35
fairness of, 107–8, 361 n42
and preventive detention, 361 n6
legal systems, 102, 104, 134
legal threats, 116, 118
Levine, Robert, 386 n17
Lewis, David, 247, 248, 249, 282, 398
  n137
  on counterforce strategy, 266–7, 268–
    9, 271–2
liability, legal, 115–16
limited nuclear warfare, 157–8, 162,
  187–92, 196–8
  in absolute sense, 13, 16–17
  aims of, 198–202, 257, 313
  and intra-war deterrence, 156–7,
    184–5
  likelihood of, 1–14, 15–17, 20
  middling credibility of, 235–6, 237
  and nuclear deterrence, 31, 123, 127–
    8, 145, 205, 206–8
  in relative sense, 13–14, 16–17

madvocacy, see countervalue strategy;
    deterrence, extended; deterrence,
    minimum
Mandelbaum, Michael, 12, 233, 325
massive retaliation, 244–7
MccGwire, Michael, 121
McMahan, Jefferson, 44, 298, 351 n54,
  367 n54
  on counterforce strategy, 166, 167–8,
    170, 178, 180
McNamara, Robert, 6, 192, 250–1
  on disarmament, 301–2, 305
  on minimum deterrence, 249–50,
    251–3
Mearshimer, John, 381 n71
military morality, 2, 262, 263
military strategy, 2, 152, 275, 341
  n53
military targets, 170–2, 241, 262
military threats
  execution of, 114–17, 124, 362 n11,
    364 n31
  and nuclear deterrence, 125–6
  see also nuclear threats
missile technology
  and counterforce strategy, 149, 150,
    185
  in defensive systems, 212–13, 369
    n8, 377 n12
moral antinomy, 65, 66, 68

413

Index

moral argument, ix–x, 79–80, 110
  against countervalue strategy, 160–1
  against nuclear deterrence, 18–20,
    25–6, 30–1, 46–9, 50–3
  for counterforce strategy, 148, 159–
    64, 175–81, 368 n2
  for minimum deterrence, 329–31
  for nuclear deterrence, 60, 61–2
  see also consequentialist moral argu-
    ment; deontological moral
    argument
moral conflict resolution, 62–4, 66, 78,
    260–1, 264–5
  approaches to, 78–80, 141, 142, 145–
    6, 354 n82
  and disarmament, 307–8, 311–12, 318
moral conflicts, 35, 72–3
  apparent, 62–3, 352 n65
  and everyday moral reasoning, 352
    n66
  real, 59, 62–3, 66, 73
moral dilemma
  definition of, 60–1, 64–5
  at institutional level, 65–6, 71–5
  nontragic, 65
  nuclear deterrence as, 59, 61, 69, 74
  tragic, 65, 66, 69
moral dissociation, principle of, 177–8,
    179, 270
moral Manichaeanism, 374 n60
moral paradox
  definition of, 61
  nuclear deterrence as, 60, 61, 62, 66
moral reasoning, everyday, 34, 36, 345
    n1, 352 n66
  and nuclear deterrence, 68, 76–7
  for disarmament, 308, 318
moral revisionism, see revisionism,
    moral
morality
  conflicting with prudence, 26, 31–2,
    34, 41–2, 76–7, 110
  political marginalization of, 32–3, 77
Morgan, Patrick, 90, 248, 362 n14
Morganthau, Hans, 12, 261
  military strategy by, 126, 145, 154
  nuclear strategy by, 221, 230
Mueller, John, 319, 380 n51, 399 n141
  on nuclear deterrence, 87, 355 n2,
    358 n26, 359 n28, 364 n21
mutual vulnerability, ix, xi–xii, 12, 14
  and aggression, 340 n48
  as viewed by counterforce strate-
    gists, 232

in crises, 220–1, 305, 306
  and crystal ball effect, 120–3, 144
  definition of, 5–6, 337 n13
  as viewed by madvocates, 231, 232,
    233–5, 241, 333
  as viewed by prevailing strategists,
    212, 213, 216
  and reassurance, 121–2, 144
  and stability, 123–4
  and threat of societal destruction,
    27–8, 245–7, 313
  versus one-sided vulnerability, 167,
    214, 216

national security, 1–3, 4
  and sovereignty, 2–3, 23, 31
  and war avoidance, 23–4, 31
NATO, 207, 251, 253
Nitze, Paul, 336 n5
Nobel, Alfred, 234
no-first-use policy, 252
no-intention policy, 266, 267–8, 271,
    323
nonconformity, 93, 138, 360 n37
  and legal deterrence, 95, 100–3, 108,
    134
noncrisis stability, 273, 274, 285
  and counterforce strategy, 274–5,
    278, 291
  with disarmament, 299, 300–2, 303–
    4, 305
  under extended deterrence, 281, 282,
    291, 298
Nozick, Robert, 80, 350 n47
nuclear adversaries, see Soviet Union;
    United States
nuclear arms controls, 304, 330, 332–3
nuclear blackmail, 297
nuclear deterrence, 41, 91–2, 119–20
  as central institution, 70, 73–4, 75–6,
    136
  as hostage holding, 46–9, 50, 67
  and morality, 59–63, 66, 69, 71–7 353
    n72
  see also deterrence
nuclear energy, 386 n13
nuclear firebreak, 197
nuclear parity, 206, 207, 225–6
nuclear proliferation, xii, 400 n142
nuclear realism, 27
nuclear strategies, 144, 145, 367 n55
  mixed, 147, 241, 268–9
  and impure counterforce strategy,
    151, 163, 177, 184

414

Index

quarantine rule, 57, 58, 59
Quester, George, 26, 29, 206
on disarmament, 300–301
on just wars, 263, 264
on nuclear morality, 32, 79, 261, 262, 272

Ramsey, Paul, 160, 169, 170, 171–2, 375 n74
on civilian damage, 177, 178–9
rationality paradox, 132–3, 237, 248–9 387 n28
Ravenal, Earl, 279–80
Rawls, John, 354 n79
Reagan, Ronald, 25, 26, 185, 342 n66
realism, 26–7
rearmament, nuclear, 299, 302–3
capacity for, 305, 311, 312
reassurance, 121–2, 123, 130, 132, 363 n18, 363 n19
in crises, 220–1, 229
in nuclear deterrence, 203–4, 216, 248
resolve, 125–6
restitution, legal, 372 n36
restraint, 188–92, 199, 237
and intra-war deterrence, 187–8
in limited nuclear warfare, 187–92
mutual, 15, 20
restraint limitations, 14–15
retaliation, 30, 167–68, 257–8
in counterforce strategy, 165, 167, 184–5
limited, in MAD-based strategy, 239, 244–5
prudential value of, 18
scrupulous, 266–7, 268, 271
revisionism, moral, 79–80, 260–1, 264–5, 405 n33
and disarmament, 312, 318, 327
and madvocacy, 232
see also moral conflict resolution
revisionism, prudential, 78, 80, 141–42, 145–6, 148, 293, 403 n1
and disarmament, 310, 311, 313, 317–18
failure of, in conflict resolution, 260, 293–4, 296
revisionism, strategic, 78–9, 80, 146, 406 n35
and counterforce strategy, 148, 164
and existential moralism, 265, 266, 272

risk taking, 236, 242
in limited nuclear warfare, 236–8, 240, 257
and mutual vulnerability, 195–6, 247–8
risk assessment
and morality, 351 n52
and statistical death, 347 n20
risks
of accidental nuclear warfare, 46, 49, 253–4, 256–7, 289–91, 323
of conventional warfare, 259, 276, 283, 301
creation of, 43–4
of crises, 227–8, 276–7
and hostage holding, 45, 48, 49
of nuclear escalation, 251–4, 276
of nuclear warfare, 228–9, 298, 299, 300, 302, 333–4
redistribution of, 56–7, 58
Russell, Bertrand, 87, 357 n10
Russett, Bruce, 170–2
Ryle, Gilbert, 355 n1

Sartre, Jean-Paul, 65
Schell, Jonathan, 32, 306, 311
on deterrence, 28, 137
on nuclear abandonment, 302–3, 304–5
Schelling, Thomas, 28, 49, 128, 220, 318, 361 n7, 395 n102
on military strategy, 22, 236, 240
on nuclear deterrence, 53, 89–90, 303–4
on nuclear strategy, 188, 218–19, 239, 257
on nuclear threats, 121, 125–6, 242
Schilling, Warner, 202–3
Schlesinger, James, 381 n60
Schonsheck, Jonathan, 350 n47, 359 n32, 367 n51
selective options strategy, 204–5
self-defense, 21, 52–3, 56–7
self-deterrence, 159, 211, 276, 332
see also reassurance
self-interest, 2, 264–5
and conventional deterrence, 115, 116, 117
and nuclear deterrence, 126, 128–9
Shaw, William, 47, 49
Shue, Henry, 285
Sigal, Leon, 279, 284, 338 n27, 401 n169
slavery, 70, 72, 315, 316, 319

416